Recentering Learning

Recentering Learning

Complexity, Resilience, and Adaptability in Higher Education

Edited by

Maggie Debelius, Joshua Kim, and Edward Maloney

JOHNS HOPKINS UNIVERSITY PRESS | *Baltimore*

Printed in the United States of America on acid-free paper
9 8 7 6 5 4 3 2 1

Johns Hopkins University Press
2715 North Charles Street
Baltimore, Maryland 21218
www.press.jhu.edu

Library of Congress Cataloging-in-Publication Data

Names: Debelius, Maggie, 1966– editor. | Kim, Joshua, 1969– editor. | Maloney, Edward, 1968– editor.
Title: Recentering learning : complexity, resilience, and adaptability in higher education / Edited by Maggie Debelius, Joshua Kim, and Edward J. Maloney.
Description: Baltimore : Johns Hopkins University Press, [2024] | Includes bibliographical references and index.
Identifiers: LCCN 2024013765 | ISBN 9781421450322 (paperback) | ISBN 9781421450339 (ebook)
Subjects: LCSH: Educational change. | COVID-19 Pandemic, 2020–| Education, Higher—Effect of technological innovations on. | Universities and colleges—Administration. | Education, Higher—Forecasting.
Classification: LCC LB2806 .R356 2024 | DDC 370—dc23/eng/20240520
LC record available at https://lccn.loc.gov/2024013765

Special discounts are available for bulk purchases of this book. For more information, please contact Special Sales at specialsales@jh.edu.

CONTENTS

Part IV. THE POST-PANDEMIC UNIVERSITY

Recentering Learning

Introduction

Maggie Debelius, Joshua Kim, and Edward Maloney

Historically, pandemics have forced humans to break with the past and imagine their world anew. This one is no different. It is a portal, a gateway between one world and the next. We can choose to walk through it, dragging the carcasses of our prejudice and hatred, our avarice, our data banks and dead ideas, our dead rivers and smoky skies behind us. Or we can walk through lightly, with little luggage, ready to imagine another world. And ready to fight for it.

—Arundhati Roy, "The Pandemic Is a Portal"[1]

As we begin to emerge from the public health crisis of the last few years, confront the social inequities of the last few hundred years, and recognize the challenges that artificial intelligence (AI) may bring to education, many faculty and staff have begun to ask what the "new normal" will look like. What would it mean for universities to accept the invitation to cross through the pandemic portal and see the world of teaching and learning anew? How should our collective and uneven response to racial injustice inform our understanding of the ideas that have long informed higher education? What have we in higher ed learned from the pandemic experience? What does it mean to create an inclusive environment that is both welcoming to our students and reflective of the principles of academic freedom and free speech that animate higher education? What are the dead ideas we can leave behind? How will new technologies change the landscape of student learning and faculty engagement. Can conflict, rigor, and ambiguity be embraced in an increasingly divisive world? And what vision are we ready to fight for moving forward?

We know there are no simple answers to these questions, but we believe that part of the path forward is greater attention to how we teach and how our students learn. The essays in this volume explore what this path forward might look like by considering where we have come from over the last few years and what the next period in higher education might look like. In this book, questions of design and engagement, of diversity and inclusion, and of pedagogy and practice, intersect with the aforementioned provocations.

The transition to virtual learning at the height of the pandemic for most students called into question much of what we thought we knew about the primacy of face-to-face learning, especially for undergraduates. The expectations of our students to feel a sense of belonging in a system that was arguably built on exclusion and differentiation challenged many of our core principles. The intersection of COVID-19 with a period of intense racial reckoning laid bare some of the contradictions of a higher education system that seeks to promote social mobility even as it exacerbates racial and economic exclusion. The structure of the US higher education system at best mirrors, and at worst amplifies, structural inequalities across the intersecting domains of race, class, gender, and immigration status. These structural inequalities, long imperfectly masked and obscured by the built university environment of classrooms, residence halls, and student centers, were exposed to anyone wishing to look during the depth of COVID-19 lockdowns.

Although the pandemic was isolating and stressful for every student regardless of family assets and social privilege, learners from minoritized groups and low-income households had a very different pandemic college experience than their peers did. Lacking a quiet and consistent place at home to study, or a reliable internet connection in which to participate in synchronous classes, many students struggled to keep mind and body together.

More recently, the introduction of generative artificial intelligence tools for public use has added a third point of tension for the present and future of higher education. Applications such as OpenAI, ChatGPT, or Anthropic's Claude have shown that computers are getting incredibly adept at capabilities such as writing, image creation, and creative thinking—capabilities that have long been considered fundamentally human. The impact of generative AI is only just starting, but its possibilities raise important questions about the role of human beings in the future of work. Perhaps most immediately, these questions will require us to think about questions of belonging, engagement, and presence from our students and our faculty that are not dissimilar to challenges of the COVID-19 pandemic and the social tensions of the last few years.

These tensions, then, among an emergency health crisis, our shared culture of inequity and injustice, and the role of technology in higher education form the foundation of this book. The essays in this book share a fundamental belief that care for our students, intentional investments in learning and teaching, and a reimagination of higher education can provide us with the tools we need to answer and address the challenges that we as a society face, whether those are driven by an emergency response to a virus, a growing climate disaster, or a social reckoning long in the making.

The COVID-19 public health crisis forced higher education to think differently, perhaps in ways that our response to racial injustice has not yet done. At many schools, the pandemic demonstrated the necessity of a dynamic and complex infrastructure to meet the demands the situation called for. During the depths of the COVID-19 public health emergency, the normally disconnected pieces within our universities came together to see, and then collectively try to support, the learners that our institutions are extensively designed to serve. For a short time, varying between perhaps 12 and 24 months, many of the activities of the multiversity (as coined by Clark Kerr) were put on pause. Depending on the institution, activities as varied as laboratory-based research and big-time sports were delayed.

At every institution, however, teaching and learning continued. Parts of the institution that seldom collaborated prior to March 2020, such as centers for teaching and learning (CTLs) and divisions of student life, accessibility, and counseling were attempting to work across academic organizational lines to support a remote student body. The pandemic centered teaching and learning as the overriding institutional priority across research-intensive universities and liberal arts colleges, regional publics, and community colleges alike.

As Randy Bass notes, the pandemic provided openings, including an "opening for listening to students in new ways," as well as "an opening for new connections across silos, loosening barriers between academic staff and student affairs, faculty and academic staff."[2] We hope this collection opens up new ways of engaging in scholarly conversations about centering learning. On many campuses, the urgency of the pandemic brought academic staff, student affairs professionals, graduate students, and contingent faculty into closer collaborations with administrators and tenure-line faculty. By bringing together these various perspectives, we hope that we can pull some voices traditionally on the edges of scholarly conversations closer to the center.

It's difficult not to wonder what it would mean for our institutions to come together with the same level of care, commitment, and collaboration around the issues of social inequity and racial injustice. During the writing of this book, the Supreme Court, in *Students for Fair Admissions v. President and Fellows of Harvard University* and *Students for Fair Admissions v. University of North Carolina*, reversed the long-standing precedent that gave colleges and universities tools to create greater diversity. What will the responses of our institutions be moving forward? Our belief is that greater attention to teaching and learning, cross-institutional collaboration, and care for our students even as we expect high levels of academic excellence will be necessary here too.

But we know these challenges are only the beginning. Artificial intelligence has reached milestones in language processing that may soon change how we think about the written word. Climate disruptions have the potential to affect everything from in-person instruction to the stability of endowments. Demographic shifts are affecting more and more schools in parts of the country that see their traditional population base moving elsewhere. And concerns about academic freedom and free speech are forcing us to ask important questions about the future of higher education.

All of these concerns will change how we in higher education think about teaching and learning. And yet we're concerned that many of the higher education lessons we learned while navigating the last few years are in danger of being lost even as we confront new challenges coming down the road. For the most part, teaching and learning at research-intensive universities have returned to their status of enjoying high levels of rhetorical support and low levels of institution-wide investments. Incentives for tenure-track faculty have bounced back to favor research productivity over pedagogical experimentation. Absent herculean efforts by leaders of academic departments, student-facing support organizations, administrative support units, and campus centers such as CTLs, our universities are undergoing a post-pandemic re-siloing. The communication and collaborative muscles across university organizational structures that were activated during the emergency pivot to remote learning have started to atrophy within the return to undergraduate residential instruction.

When AI came onto the public scene in late 2022, the response from colleges and universities varied. Policy statements went out that reinforced existing approaches to plagiarism and honor codes. Students were often characterized as suspect because they now had tools available to them that might allow them to do their work differently, if at all. Instead of recognizing the importance of embracing and integrating tools that are only going to become more and more sophisticated and prominent in our work, a common response was denial or defensiveness.[3] Instead of seeing this as an opportunity to embrace the lessons of the last few years, at least for a brief time, we instead found ourselves struggling to respond to what was treated as a new challenge.

For a brief time at the height of the worst moments of the pandemic, there was a (mostly) common feeling across (most) areas of the university enterprise that learning is a shared institutional responsibility, that learning needed to be at the center of effort and investment. It was understood that if a student is not thriving as a learner, the accountability rested beyond that individual student and the individual faculty member at the level of the institution. After all, individual instructors could not sustainably decide to deliver courses via Zoom on their own or unilaterally change grading policies. Most faculty needed help converting their face-to-face courses to remote. Faculty were certainly the tip of the spear in supporting their students through the pandemic, but across an astonishingly wide variety of institutions, our universities changed how things were done to support professors, educators, and students as learners.

During this time, the role of centers and educational developers took on greater centrality and significance. Suddenly, faculty developers and learning designers were called upon to do much more than offer syllabus workshops or help with a learning management system (LMS). The combined crises of the moment meant that some teaching centers that once may have stood on the periphery suddenly had a place at the table at universities and made decisions about remote learning and course modalities. Campus centers for teaching and learning, as well as centers for technology, innovation, writing, and other areas, played key roles in maintaining instructional continuity during the pandemic pivot.

The work of these centers of teaching excellence and their myriad colleagues in deans' and provosts' offices, student affairs, academic resource centers, libraries, and information technology (IT) departments, demonstrated that universities *can* rapidly pivot to devote additional resources to teaching and learning. Surely, one of the dead ideas we can leave behind as we pass through the pandemic portal is that universities are incapable of moving quickly and adapting. Or, as Catherine Ross and her coauthors argue in an essay that follows, "By now it is a time-worn trope that higher education is slow to change, but . . . the pandemic has upended the deeply entrenched status quo in ways that provide an opening."

Change is difficult in higher ed for a number of reasons. There's often a culture (or at least an aspiration) of shared governance, making it difficult for any single leader to push forward a quick change. We have multiple stakeholders with goals that may conflict, such as the mission to educate students, the need for greater efficiency, the push for more research, and the drive to expand enrollment, to name just a few. Despite these and other hurdles, universities across the globe were able to adapt very quickly and focus on teaching when forced to move online in March 2020. (Of course, many universities were already teaching partially or fully online before the pandemic; Amy M. Johnson, Jonathan Iuzzini, Peter Felten, and Tazin Daniels remind us in their essay that institutional humility in learning from other models should be another key lesson of this moment). Crisis and circumstances drove innovation. Faced with the possibility of having to shut down entirely if they didn't adapt, many universities devoted significant resources to teaching, upgrading not only technology (including but not limited to LMS and video conferencing software) but also professional development for faculty, some of which is described in the essays that follow.

The rapid shift to make teaching matter happened not only at the institutional level but also at the personal level. As Nancy Chick notes in her essay that follows, "the COVID-19 pandemic pushed nearly all faculty—even seasoned online teachers—into the students' seat, a change that promises to transform how we teach." Faculty who might have previously eschewed pedagogy workshops came to teaching centers to get the support they needed to begin teaching online. The resulting conversations were about so much more than Canvas and Zoom, enabling colleagues to have serious conversations about engagement, trauma-informed pedagogy, assessment, access, and more. Although it's too soon to say what the long-term impact on teaching may be, it's certain that many teaching centers saw a huge increase in the number of faculty who used their services and joined meaningful conversations about pedagogy. Many faculty who felt burned out from intense professional and affective demands of remote teaching received support and found community at teaching centers.

Given the intensity of this time, the desire to return to something approaching a higher education pre-pandemic and "business as usual" is understandable. There is something uniquely valuable about an in-person college experience. Too little space has been given for an in-depth and critical examination of what our institutions might retain and build on from the actions and activities we undertook to maintain instructional resilience. The struggles of so many of our students to balance competing demands of academic, family, and economic responsibilities were fully exposed by constraints imposed by remote learning. Yet those struggles don't go away once classes move from digital Zoom screens to physical classrooms. Learning, we are afraid, is moving once again to the margins.

We think one step in addressing these concerns is to *recenter learning*: to put teaching and learning back in focus across all institutions of higher education. The reader of this collection should come away with both inspiration that it can be done and some practical advice for how to lead (or at least catalyze) the organizational changes necessary for the task. A helpful framing as you read through the essays of this book is to always be asking yourself: what might my university look like if the institution was designed around learning and the learner? This framing for reading through this book, and our shared work to advance our institutions, can further be clarified by narrowing the goals of institutional change. We might ask, how might we design our universities to serve the learner with the least resources and the most barriers to learning? What if the responsibility for the success of *all learners* did not reside in discrete offices devoted to first-generation students and institutional diversity, equity, and inclusion (DEI) initiatives but instead the accountability of the entire university?

An institutional goal of recentering learning must exist in tension, or at least in conversation, with other institutional goals. Resources are both finite and declining, and institutional-level investments in student learning may seem to come at the expense of investments around other priorities, such as research productivity, student amenities, and campus physical infrastructure. An implicit argument that runs through the essays of this book is that the champions of recentering learning deserve a seat at the tables at which their institutional strategies are decided. If colleges and universities must increasingly make choices to trade off one set of strategic priorities for another, then those investments that support learners and learning deserve to be considered. What putting learners and learning at the center of institutional strategy looks like will differ across universities.

There is no single set of policies, structures, and incentives that will result in a university demonstratively and visibly standing with and for a vulnerable learner. The essays that make up this book originate from a variety of institutional contexts and will hopefully provide evidence that the project of recentering learning is not a luxury affordable by only the wealthiest of institutions but one that can be realized across the range of institutions that populate the higher education ecosystem. We are under no illusion that placing learning and the learner at the center of institutional strategy will be as simple as to push learning to the top rungs of institution-wide goals. This task is even more challenging at research-intensive institutions and at schools navigating permanent crises of budget shortfalls and demographic headwinds. Nor are we naïve enough to think that recentering teaching and learning is the only thing that needs to be done. This book is an argument and hopefully a map of how and why the work of recentering learning is worth the effort—and can even succeed—but it is not a guide to address all of higher education's challenges.

At stake in this book is a belief that our response to the pandemic, at least in pedagogical terms, was transformative. This transformative potential is as complex as the environment we find ourselves in currently. While we see the need for investment in teaching and learning, Stephen C. Ehrman and Jillian Kinzie argue in their book *Pursuing Quality, Access, and Affordability: A Field Guide to Improving Higher Education* that access, affordability, and quality are the "iron triangle" of challenges facing higher education. They focus on "3-fold gains," or the proposition that efforts to improve educational quality, access, and affordability are best pursued in tandem (in contrast to prevailing ideas that these problems either can't be solved or should be addressed separately).[4] In addition to Ehrman and Kinzie's three key challenges, there is also justified concern about learning loss, retention rates, mental health crises, racial inequity, climate change, polarization, AI, and more. In the end, we are at a point in which multiple challenges and opportunities—past, present, and future—intersect. The multiple crises of the early 2020s give us an opportunity—indeed have forced us—to work on all of these challenges in combination.

To work on these challenges all at once means perhaps first and foremost recognizing that, at their base, what colleges and universities are is a collection of humans coming together in community, an idea that should have, in retrospect, seemed obvious and irrefutable. Yet it took a global pandemic for those humans—and the relationships between and across them—to become fully centered in the operations of our institutions. Not before, and worryingly not since the COVID-19 emergency has calmed, have colleges and universities across the world matched behavior with rhetoric in care and concern for learners. Because much of this caring for learners was largely invisible, shouldered by faculty and non-faculty educators who were also navigating the best they could the family and professional disruptions of pandemic lockdowns, the potential gains for higher education as a system can easily be lost. In the relief and joy of returning to in-person classes and residential campus life, it can be forgotten how much beauty was co-created by learners and educators in the shared efforts to build educational resilience.

One reason that it is so easy to forget and learn from the positive lessons for higher education during the pandemic is the reality of how terrible that time was for everyone. Across college and university communities, we are still attempting to come to grips with the toll that COVID-19 placed on the mental health and overall well-being of our students. Among the most vulnerable of groups, those with the fewest resources and the longest histories of structural oppression, the impact of the pandemic in terms of academic success is likely the most acute.

At the time we are writing this introduction, the full costs to learners of the pandemic, as measured across outcomes as diverse as graduation rates and levels of depression and anxiety, are not known. It is still too early to count the full cost of COVID-19 on postsecondary learners, as the pandemic's long-term effects continue to play out. We do know that the pandemic both revealed and exacerbated many of the inequities that are reflected (and perhaps even fueled) by the structure of the US higher education system. We know even less about the impact the current cultural and social conditions are playing on our students. There is growing evidence that our students, especially our students of color and from underrepresented populations, are feeling disconnected and excluded from the systems that structure and define higher education.

Recentering learning, as we are defining it, is as much about creating an inclusive teaching and learning environment as it is about institutional strategy. It's increasingly clear that inclusive teaching and evidence-based teaching are the same thing. In a 2013 article in *CBE—Life Sciences Education*, Kimberly Tanner argued that in an inclusive classroom the instructor and students move away from assumptions that some students are lacking and move toward the idea that learning environments and course designs lacking structure are a problem.[5] The move to remote learning gave all faculty (as well as instructional designers, technology specialists, librarians, and more) the opportunity to pay close attention to the structure of their courses and class sessions. Squandering the opportunity to focus on the quality of teaching and learning as we also address equity and access gaps would be a generation-defining mistake. But how can we begin to tackle these seemingly insurmountable challenges? If this close attention to structure continues, we can envision a future where postsecondary education becomes more available to more students.

These are some of the questions the essays in this volume highlight (and why we brought these scholar-practitioners together) and the choices we now all have in front of us. Those choices involve either deciding to learn from all that was horrible about the pandemic and our current social environment—and all that was good in how educators and learners collaborated in response to the crisis—or forget these lessons and proceed along the path higher education was on prior to March of 2020. The essays herein make a strong case for continuing to see the last few years as a new starting point for rethinking the future of higher education.

Who This Book Is For

Readers of this book will no doubt occupy a broad variety of roles across the postsecondary ecosystem. Within universities, the traditional divides between faculty and staff are eroding. The growing presence and institutional centrality of non-faculty educators is reflected in the composition of the book's authors, and we suspect in its readers. In imagining who among our colleagues in higher education will spend time they don't have to read *Recentering Learning*, we again see consumers of this book as a mirror of its creators. Nowhere in the essays to follow will the reader find arguments in support of the status quo for teaching and learning. There is zero nostalgia for an imagined golden age of universities in the hazy past. Instead, what is reflected in diverse ways across the essays in *Recentering Learning* is an impatience for university structures, culture, operations, and practices that inhibit learning and student success.

If the essays included in *Recentering Learning* consisted mostly of a catalog of the shortcomings of colleges and universities to optimize student learning outcomes, then this book would be a failure. What the reader of *Recentering Learning* needs is assistance in connecting theory to practice, and scholarship to action, in advancing learning at their institutions. While covering a wide and diverse array of topics related to teaching and learning, the essays in this book share a common orientation around change. When read as a whole, the discrete case studies, frameworks, and research findings explored in the following essays allow the reader to understand the advancement, stagnation, or degradation of student learning through the lenses of institutional systems, structures, and culture. In this way of looking at how universities run, poor educational outcomes are less the result of individual failures among individual students or educators and more a result of suboptimal institutional structures, incentives, and investments.

The other side of this coin is that any successful effort to improve student learning, including measures of retention and time to graduation, must also take an institutional approach. Efforts to improve faculty teaching will fail to make sustainable, significant, and long-term improvements in student learning if the structures in which educators operate are not addressed. Investments in individual student learning support, although equally welcome as investments in faculty development, will ultimately be inadequate to the challenges that students face in their educational journeys.

The essays collected in this book, therefore, are a counterweight to a prevailing (if unspoken) narrative that student learning is solely an individual and individualized activity. Within this narrative, if a student fails to learn (or drops out of college), that failure is a function of actions or inactions on the students behalf. Perhaps that student lacked the preparation and skills necessary for academic success in college. Or maybe the academic failure was a byproduct of the growing mental health crisis that has been so well documented across the post-pandemic higher education landscape.[6] Although these stories to explain unwanted and harmful student learning outcomes may be partially true, they are also incomplete. College students learn within a structure in which the operations of teaching and learning are constructed and maintained. Those structures can serve to enhance and support student learning, or they can inhibit learning success.

It's perhaps most important then, that these observations and provocations be helpful to the students studying higher education. In graduate programs such as the Learning, Design, and Technology Program at Georgetown University, where we teach and serve as scholars in residence, students are learning about the complexities of higher education and the need for a strategic thinking that places teaching and learning at the core of an institution's mission and structural investments.

As such, much of the work that is done in the essays included in *Recentering Learning* is in the exploration of the university structures that undergird student learning. The actionable takeaways from the essays are in elucidating the structures, and offering ideas, theories, and models for how they can be improved. Through the essays, the authors do not shy away from the power imbalances, structural racism and sexism, class privilege, and persistent caste dynamics that are found across the higher education system. Although clear-eyed about the structural and cultural challenges of advancing student learning from the perspective of institutional and organizational change, the essays also represent a hopeful and positive vision of where universities might go. The following essays contain a fair number of stories of failed initiatives and intractable challenges in advancing student learning, but the overriding direction of the essays is one of positive institutional change.

While university-based educators will likely constitute the majority of readers of *Recentering Learning*, a significant proportion of those who find their way to this book will be non-university education professionals, including corporate and non-profit professionals. As higher education has evolved from an analog only to an analog+digital industry, the connections between non-profit institutions and for-profit companies have strengthened. Where universities have relied for decades on enabling technologies to run their business operations—think enterprise resource planning (ERP) and student information systems (SIS)—the fastest growing segment of non-profit university and for-profit company partnerships is today in the educational technology (edtech) space. What began with the universal adoption of LMS in the 1990s has expanded to schools and companies collaborating on core aspects of the universities' educational offerings, including student recruitment and online degree program development. Nowhere has the growth of university/company collaborations been more evident, or more controversial, than in the online education space. As enhanced regulatory scrutiny has made the financial model of for-profit universities increasingly not viable—the University of Phoenix went from 500,000 students to less than 85,000 in 2023—online program management (OPM) industry has grown rapidly.[7] The impact of AI is still an open question.

As noted above, the thinkers and educators represented in this volume primarily occupy non-traditional/non-tenure-track roles at their institutions (with some notable exceptions). Importantly, however, the essays' authors *are* situated within the non-profit postsecondary educational ecosystem. We point this out in recognition of the increasing entanglement between non-profit universities and for-profit companies in core academic areas such as teaching and learning. This connection between schools and companies in domains of degrees, courses, and instruction was catalyzed by the pandemic, with universities (and systems) reaching out to for-profit partners in order to fill instructional design gaps during the emergency pivot to remote learning (MJ Bishop, Nancy O'Neill, Briana Johnson, and Whitney Kilgore, "Converting Teaching from Solo Sport to Team-Based Activity: Lessons Learned from a Systemwide Instructional Design Support Initiative"). The school/company nexus has both deepened and broadened coming out of COVID-19 as institutions have turned to a variety of online program enablers to accelerate their presence in the distance education space.

About the Contributors

One of the goals of this volume is to provide a platform for educators whose practice and scholarship are infrequently expressed in a medium as durable (and valued) as an academic press monograph. While a handful of tenured (or tenure-track) academics contributed essays to this book, the plurality of authors are in academic roles outside a traditional faculty path. Because non-traditional academics occupy such a diversity of roles, the language we employ to describe this group is challenged, contested, and implicated in the academic caste system. Some of the authors represented in this volume have titles of "professor" to go along with other titles and roles at their university, but only a few are tenured. For almost no contributing authors of this volume will its publication be of substantial benefit for promotion. The writing, rewriting, and editing of the following essays had to be squeezed into the cracks of time available between the growing demands of programming, collaborating, managing, facilitating, and—well—everything that non-tenure-track educators do at colleges and universities. Scholarship is a core value across the range of non-traditional educator groups represented in this book, but seldom (if ever) is protected professional time afforded for its creation.

One way to understand the structural position in which the contributor authors for this volume occupy in academia is through job titles. Designations of "faculty" and "professor" are represented, but less frequently. More common titles include variations of director and learning designer. These non-faculty job titles for contributors illustrate the dramatic shift in the work that these authors, and all of those in similar roles across higher education, have experienced over the past few years. A theme across the diverse essays in this volume is the rapidity in which the work of the authors—and the units in which they are based—moved into positions of centrality in their institutions' operations. As the public health emergency of the COVID-19 pandemic forced colleges and universities to pivot from residential to remote (and then hybrid) instruction, the essential capabilities of non-faculty educators for institutional resilience became immediately apparent. Forced by the pandemic into prioritizing academic continuity ahead of all other institutional goals, campus organizations such as teaching and learning centers and academic innovation centers rapidly evolved into hubs of academic operations. As a result, a much wider array of teaching faculty—many of whom had not previously worked with faculty developers or instructional designers or other non-faculty educators—found it necessary to access services, training, collaboration, and consulting from their institutions' teaching and learning organizations.

The educators in this volume, many of whom work in CTLs, are actively engaged in diversity and inclusion efforts, encouraging faculty to consider the ways in which racism and oppression have shaped their own disciplines. Indeed there's growing consensus that equity work and engaged teaching are inextricably linked. The Professional and Organizational Development (POD) network, the scholarly organization for faculty developers, lists equity and evidence as two of its three core values (the third is collaboration). Similarly CTLs also list evidence-based practices and equity as being fundamental to their work. But what happens when equity and evidence exist in tension? In their 2022 article "A Call to Interrogate Educational Development for Racism and Colonization," Jamiella Brooks, Heather Dwyer, and Marisella Rodriguez point to educational developers' reliance on evidence-based practice as being one area in need of interrogation as we examine our own discipline and reflect on its role in perpetuating racism and oppression.[8] Evidence is often thought to be neutral, but this is hardly the case. Not all groups of students are equally represented in the context of most educational studies, meaning that the evidence collected can hardly be free from bias. This isn't to say that data have no place in this work but rather to suggest that there is room for multiple ways of knowing in our field.

As such, we have tried to make room for a diversity of voices and approaches in this collection. Some of the chapters included here approach the questions of recentering learning from the center, from the perspective of tenured faculty (such as Peter Felten, Nancy Chick, and Randy Bass) or center directors (like Mary Wright and Betsy Barre). But other voices come from different perspectives and bring with them different approaches. Kashema Hutchinson, Sujung Kim, Adashima Oyo, and Katina Rogers speak from the perspectives of graduate students and contingent educators inside and outside the academy, offering a narrative account of their experience of graduate teaching and learning during the pandemic. Because their chapter draws on experience rather than data, it tells a different story about the future of higher education. Others speak from the perspective of staff members, nonprofit leaders, independent scholars, and administrators. These are the voices of the collection. As much as possible, we have tried to leave these voices intact rather than trying to edit them into a uniform style.

The Essays

The essays in *Recentering Learning* are structured around the following themes: **New Systems and Structures**, **What We Have Learned about Teaching and Learning**, **Toward Greater Access, Equity, and Inclusion**, and **The Post-Pandemic University**. Individually, the essays included in this volume offer a diverse set of perspectives and provocations around the possible futures of postsecondary learning. Collectively, the essays can be read as arguments for institutional reprioritization of learning based on the knowledge gained through navigating the near existential crisis of the pandemic. Because the goal of *Recentering Learning* is to provide the reader with ideas, inspiration, and advice to assist their work in advocating for and leading institutional-level changes that advance individual student learning, we want to share a concise synthesis of each of the book's essays.

The essays in **New Systems and Structures** focus on the evolution of cross-university centers and organizations whose mission is to advance learning. As multiple authors point out, the role of these campus learning organizations gained new prominence and centrality as indispensable partners to faculty during the pivot to remote learning. In "Centering Resiliency: Principles for Academic Leaders and Teaching Center Directors," Matthew Kaplan, Mary C. Wright, and Derek Bruff argue that the time for universities to encourage collaborations between centers for teaching and learning and units is before a time of crisis. They write that "the range of staff skills and expertise, center connections across campus, and deep knowledge of the institution make our units much more like a multi-purpose Swiss army knife than a single-function Phillips head screwdriver."

As MJ Bishop, Nancy O'Neill, Briana Johnson, and Whitney Kilgore describe in their essay "Converting Teaching from Solo Sport to Team-Based Activity: Lessons Learned from a Systemwide Instructional Design Support Initiative," university organizations to advance student learning can also be developed at the system level. In that essay, the authors describe an initiative by the University System of Maryland's Kirwan Center for Academic Innovation to provide instructional design services during the pandemic across the system's 12 four-year public universities. The essay details the advantages and challenges of partnering with an outside entity to rapidly scale up an infrastructure to enable a wholesale systemwide transition from in-person to remote instruction. Among the lessons learned are that providing course-level development services must be accompanied by close attention to proactive empathetic relationship building between instructors and instructional designers.

In "Creating Transformational Change through Learning Innovation Departments," Sean Hobson and Natalie Landman argue for institutional investments in university organizations that are capable of expanding upon traditional faculty-facing teaching and learning-related services such as pedagogical expertise and educational technology support. They describe the development of EdPlus at Arizona State University (ASU) as a possible model for other institutions looking to develop new capabilities in areas such as business model design and creation, new product development, advanced operational support, partnership development, visual design, and communications. These new organizations, which Hobson and Landman call Learning Innovation Departments, or LIDs, are designed to "ensure an academic institution's viability and long-term sustainability in the constantly evolving environment."

In their essay titled "An Ecology of Change in Higher Education," Michael Goudzwaard and Cynthia A. Cogswell report on interviews conducted with educators and administrators at seven colleges and universities in the United States in order to develop an inclusive framework in which institutional learning innovations can be understood and evaluated. The authors propose adopting a framework that views university organizational change as following similar dynamics to complex ecological systems. For Goudzwaard and Cogswell, one of the lessons of universities' response to the pandemic is that sustained improvements in student learning outcomes require disciplined experimentation with "new modes of academic credit, teaching grants, and any ideas to meet students where they are." Adopting an ecological framework for developing and evaluating institution-wide learning initiatives may help avoid temptations to judge these interventions against binary (success/failure) metrics and instead view these experiments as contributing to somewhat more learning and learner-centric steady state.

The theme of what makes for effective university/non-university partnerships to advance learning is continued in the essay "Digital Education for Access and Equity" by Annie Sadler, Martin Kurzweil, and Matthew Rascoff. The focus of that essay shifts from institutional efforts to advance learning for existing university students to programs targeted at improving pre-college educational access, attainment, and success of high school students. The essay describes three programs, Davidson Next, OnRamps, and the National Education Equity Lab, as case studies in the role that universities can play to "engage faculty at highly selective institutions in offering online or hybrid format courses to secondary school students with the explicit goal of expanding equitable access to higher education." The lessons that the authors draw from these case studies of university/partner programs aimed at high school students have significant implications for all learning-centric institutional initiatives.

The role of data in developing, designing, and continuously improving institution-wide learning initiatives is explored in the final essay in the **New Systems and Structures** section "The Shifting Institutional Data Landscape and Why It Matters for Student Learning." Drew Allen asks how a shifting and increasingly complex institutional data landscape is impacting the core teaching and learning function of colleges and universities. The essay also explores the interaction between institution-wide initiatives to enhance individual learner outcomes and how data are collected, analyzed, and disseminated in support of those initiatives. Allen argues that in an environment of "overwhelming amounts of data and infinite data-related challenges," it is essential to have "individuals at the table who understand not only the role of data but also the fundamental connection to student learning."

The next part of the book, **What We Have Learned about Teaching and Learning**, narrows the focus of institutional changes to advance learning to attend more closely to the experiences of students and educators. These essays place the learner, and the learners' relationships with educators, at the core of the post-pandemic university narrative. In this section, the voices of students—as both the focus of the essays and as coauthors of some of the contributions—are front and center. Nancy Chick, in her essay "In the Role of Learners," ends this part with the observation that the pandemic made all faculty familiar with the challenges that our students face, something she sees as having the potential to transform how we teach. The direction and durability of this transition in teaching and learning remains an unknown, although one permanent shift may be a shared recognition of "the human connections at the core of teaching and learning." That focus on human connection is also explored in the essay "Recentering Relationships: What We Learned from Building Closeness at a Distance" by Molly Chehak and David Ebenbach. They argue that "the connections we focused on during remote teaching still matter now that we're face-to-face" and recommend strategies to strengthen learning relationships, such as designing more accessible office hours, creating opportunities for small group work, and by prioritizing presence and communications through available instructional platforms.

In the essay "The Work Goes On: Centering Relationships and Reimagining Practices That Support Learning," Catherine Ross, Amanda Irvin, and Suzanna Klaf explore some of the barriers to creating the institutional conditions for a relational-centered model of teaching and learning. For instance, the reversion back to standard grading policies across most universities occurred even with widespread recognition that grades motivate learning is a "dead idea." The authors build on the positive changes to course design and university-wide policies to support authentic learning during the pandemic to conclude that even the most "deeply entrenched status quo" can be upended but only with great difficulty and perhaps not sustainably. Betsy Barre explores the idea of disrupting the status quo in the area of faculty development in the essay "'Why Haven't We Always Done This?' The Future of Faculty Learning." She shares the story of the Center for the Advancement of Teaching at Wake Forest University's responses to the pandemic-necessitated emergency pivot to remote learning as a potential model for other CTLs. That Center was successful in moving away from deductive, short-form workshops on technology to a more inquiry-based model that "invited faculty to engage in extended periods of research, experimentation, collaboration, and critical reflection."

That critical stance around the challenges of structural organizational change to create more learning and learner-centric institutions is amplified in the essay "Everything Is Different but Nothing Is New: The Missed Opportunity for Reform in the Wake of COVID-19." In that essay, Kashema Hutchinson, Sujung Kim, Adashima Oyo, and Katina Rogers provide a series of first-person case studies to highlight the structural inequalities built into a range of university systems and operations. The authors argue that "[h]igher education doesn't have to be the way that it is. It doesn't have to be an environment with higher-than-average depression and anxiety. It doesn't have to be a workplace replete with labor inequity or racial and gender bias. Instead, it could be a space of mutual support and care."

The voice of students as co-creators of a more equitable, supportive, and humane learning environment is explored in the essay "Learning about Learning: Students' Insights from a Pandemic Year." Through a series of case studies written by students, Sophie Grabiec, Sherry Lee Linkon, Isabel McHenry, and Lillian Nagengast reflect on how pandemic-driven instructional changes impacted their learning. In synthesizing her students' experience, Linkon observes that "the context of the pandemic made students more aware of their conceptions of teaching and learning, more likely to pay attention to their perception of learning situations, and more intentional in their approaches." The part continues with an essay titled "Purpose, Learning, and Justice: Maintaining Hopeful Practices Past the Pivot" by Susannah McGowan and Isis Artze-Vega. In that essay, the authors introduce the concept of a "justice-centered" curricula. Among their hopes is that a post-pandemic university will find a way to "lean in to critical reflection on identity, positionality, privilege, and history" to "foster genuine partnership work with and among faculty, staff, and students" and that universities might approach justice efforts with "humility, curiosity, and time."

The essays in the section **Toward Greater Access, Equity, and Inclusion** expand on arguments about humility, structures, and social justice. In "Institutional and Instructional Humility for Equity-Forward Teaching and Learning," Amy M. Johnson, Jonathan Iuzzini, Peter Felten, and Tazin Daniels note the "persistent failure of many educators . . . at predominately white institutions—to take seriously the ways structural and individual inequities and traumas influence learning, teaching, and student success" and urge institutions to practice instructional humility as they attempt to advance student learning. Through a series of case studies, the authors demonstrate how institution-wide learning initiatives can be levers to drive critical self-reflection, challenge entrenched power imbalances, and work toward institutional and individual accountability.

Toward the goal of ameliorating structural inequalities endemic to higher education, Lorna S. Gonzalez, Megan Eberhardt-Alstot, and Jill Leafstedt examine the importance of the language employed around teaching and learning during the pandemic. In "Pandemic Fever Pitch Terms That Defined a Moment in Higher Education," the authors examine the ways that "rhetorical artifacts reify societal values and anxieties" and how artifacts such as the language of virtual learning and learning loss "might function as vehicles for innovation."

In "Beyond 'Zoom University': A Heuristic for Advancing Inclusive Digital and Online Pedagogy," Jenae Cohn develops a heuristic designed to aid decision makers in centering values at the core of an institution's online learning portfolio. Arguing that future instructional interactions and learning environments will need to "move fluidly between online and brick-and-mortar spaces," Cohn concludes that technology-centered strategies will be insufficient to meet institutional goals around access and inclusion.

Expanding on issues of access, Libbie Rifkin explores issues of barriers and enablers of learning in her essay "Ableism and Conflicts of Care in the Post-Pandemic University." She argues that an "accommodationist approach to access" will be self-defeating for building resilient institutions, concluding that "higher education investment in the broad infrastructure of care is a matter not just of ethics, but of economic exigency."

In the essay "Toxic to Transformational: Women and the Higher Ed Ecosystem Post-Pandemic," Patrice Torcivia Prusko refocuses the examination of institutional structures and student learning through the lens of gender. Observing that universities are built on power relationships that have historically disadvantaged women, Torcivia Prusko proposes that "future research around a theory of action that examines what kind of change occurs when university leaders practice critical self-reflection through a lens of feminist framework, and its effect on women's ability to persevere within the higher education ecosystem as students, staff, and faculty."

The part concludes with Rolin Moe's essay "Access ≠ Equity: A Primer on Reconsidering Edtech in Higher Education," in which the entire project of institution-wide learning initiatives to promote social justice aims is unpacked and scrutinized. Moe argues that "a focus on access not only misses the key obstacles of equity in higher education but perpetuates a solutionistic framework for recommendations and further exploration."

The essays in the concluding part of the volume, **The Post-Pandemic University**, provide a series of learning and learner-centric visions of institutional level experimentation and transformation. In the second essay of this section, Bryan Alexander draws connections between the opportunities that the pandemic opened up for rethinking core university educational systems and structures with the possibilities that a similar approach to addressing climate change might afford. In "From COVID-19 to Climate Change: Parallels, Parables, and Possibilities for the Future of Higher Education," Alexander argues that in crafting institutional-level strategies in response to the climate emergency, universities have the responsibility to rethink and redesign "everything from academic travel to assessment, campus energy to computation, [and] our roles as public intellectuals and community partners."

In their essay "The Post-Pandemic University: Critical Questions for Infrastructure, Practice, and Culture," Kathryn E. Linder, Constancio Nakuma, and Monique Snowden explore changes at the University of Colorado Denver in order to offer a generalized set of recommendations around institutional approaches to centering learning. The authors argue that strategic planning around evolving university infrastructure (inclusive of staffing, facilities, and technology) must explicitly align with the institution's values around access and inclusion. The essay proposes a series of questions that can guide strategic planning initiatives that connect the underlying structures of university operations in making a "cultural shift toward becoming an equity-serving institution."

In the penultimate essay in the section, "The New Experimental College," Elliott Visconsi takes the reader through an imagined institution designed around all that has been learned about learning. Providing a detailed schematic for the structure and operations of this proposed university, Visconsi explores the place that past efforts in creating experimental institutions have succeeded in catalyzing systemwide transformations.

The part concludes with "Architecture of the Unexpected: Beyond the Learning Paradigm," where Randy Bass invites the reader to look further into the "uncertain and perilous future" in shaping the post-pandemic structures of our universities. Bass traces the history of the shift from an instructional to a learning paradigm and argues that, in the next step, an institutional change must be built on "design principles that will allow for emergence and experimentation." Critiquing traditional methods of strategic planning that amount to searches for new business models within existing structures, Bass presents a vision for thinking about the learner-centric institution as one purpose built to accommodate change and uncertainty.

Conclusion

The most frequently used words in the essays that follow aren't "Zoom" or "virtual" or even "remote." Instead, a version of the word "collaborate" shows up in almost every essay, a testament to the way that the pandemic forced us out of our silos. We were asked to solve "wicked" teaching problems, which by definition require multiple perspectives. Teaching centers and other similar units are often hubs for community on campus, one of the few places that bring together staff, faculty, administrators, and students, as well as people from multiple disciplines. The most successful centers were those that had built strong relationships before the pandemic, allowing them to function when the crisis hit and provide a source of institutional resilience. Likewise, we believe that the most reasonable scholarly response to crisis is a collaborative one, which is why we are pleased to bring together the scholar practitioners in this volume to address the urgency of keeping learning at the center.

Another theme that appears frequently in these chapters is care. Facing a global pandemic gave students and faculty new insights into each other's lives, which included serious illness (or death), jobs lost, housing insecurity, mental health crises, increased caregiving responsibilities, hate crimes, and so much more. Whether in the form of empathy, equity, inclusion, or even adaptability, many of these chapters stress the importance of care and relationships in our teaching mission.

Yet another interesting thread that emerges across these essays is humility. We simply don't know what lies ahead and to suggest otherwise would be misleading. But there are steps we can take to prepare our institutions and our students for an uncertain future. Indeed, Bass argues that it was the "growth of the multi-layered practices related to good pedagogy and educational caretaking—that provided the essence of higher education's capacity to survive the pandemic." We firmly believe that institutional investments in recentering teaching and learning are the best way to prepare for the potentially disastrous educational interruptions that may come our way.

We are at a crossroads where we have the opportunity to make not only institutional but also systematic changes in the way higher ed supports and values teaching. Imagine a world in which the public saw colleges and universities ranked not only by *U.S. News and World Report* but also by measures of teaching effectiveness. It's not so far-fetched, given that *U.S. News* rankings are coming under increased scrutiny as we assemble this volume. In 2022, the Boyer 2030 Commission from the Association for Undergraduate Education at Research Universities released the *Equity-Excellence Imperative* report.[9] This report suggests that improving undergraduate teaching is an urgent and essential to achieving both equity and excellence. What if universities were classified as "T1" and "T2" as measures of teaching effectiveness to mirror the Carnegie Classifications (R1, R2, and so on) that have measured research activity? Scholars from the University of Portland and elsewhere have formed a working group that grew out of an National Science Foundation grant to pursue the idea of "T1" designation.[10] Now is the moment to advocate for change, as the Carnegie Foundation for the Advancement of Teaching and the American Council on Education are currently working together to reimagine the Carnegie Classifications that have been used since 1973.

It's too soon to tell whether those of us working at colleges, universities, and other educational ventures are ready to fight for a better world, or even better teaching and learning. A fervent hope that we don't squander this opportunity to re-envision higher ed systems and practices drives this collection. We are at an inflection point as we emerge from a period of collective trauma, with some communities suffering greater losses than others. As some of us return to in-person classrooms, we have the chance to rethink what teaching and learning looks like after this pandemic interruption. Despite the losses, we have the chance to write a new story about what we've learned about learning from the pandemic years. Taken together, the essays collected in this volume offer an alternative vision for the university. This is a university whose core structures and policies are explicitly designed to meet the needs of learners who have been marginalized by the current system.

Notes

1. Roy, "The Pandemic Is a Portal."
2. Higher Education's Big Rethink Project, *Openings.*
3. Maloney, "The 4 Stages of AI."
4. Ehrmann and Kinzie, *Pursuing Quality, Access, and Affordability.*
5. Tanner, "Structure Matters."
6. Abrams, "Student Mental Health Is in Crisis."
7. Swaak, "What a Possible U. of Phoenix Sale Says about the State of Higher Ed."
8. Brooks, Dwyer, and Rodriguez, "A Call to Interrogate Educational Development for Racism and Colonization."
9. *The Equity/Excellence Imperative: A 2030 Blueprint for Undergraduate Education at U.S. Research Universities.*
10. Prestholdt, Dillon, Anctil, McCaffery, Salomone, and Peterson, "Making Teaching Matter More–the Making of a T1 University."

Bibliography

Abrams, Zara. "Student Mental Health Is in Crisis; Campuses Are Rethinking Their Approach." *Monitor on Psychology* 53, no. 7 (October 1, 2022). https://www.apa.org/monitor/2022/10/mental-health-campus-care.

Brooks, Jamiella, Heather Dwyer, and Marisella Rodriguez. "A Call to Interrogate Educational Development for Racism and Colonization." *Faculty Focus,* April 25, 2022. https://www.facultyfocus.com/articles/equality-inclusion-and-diversity/a-call-to-interrogate-educational-development-for-racism-and-colonization/.

Ehrmann, Stephen C., and Jillian Kinzie. *Pursuing Quality, Access, and Affordability: A Field Guide to Improving Higher Education.* Sterling, VA: Stylus, 2021.

The Equity/Excellence Imperative: A 2030 Blueprint for Undergraduate Education at U.S. Research Universities. Fort Collins, CO: Association for Undergraduate Education at Research Universities, 2022.

Higher Education's Big Rethink Project. *Openings: Higher Education's Challenge to Change in the Face of the Pandemic, Inequity and Racism.* Georgetown Program in Learning, Design, and Technology, 2021.

Maloney, Edward. "The 4 Stages of AI." *Inside Higher Ed*, April 4, 2023. https://www.insidehighered.com/blogs/learning-innovation/4-stages-ai.

Prestholdt, Tara E., Heather Dillon, Eric Anctil, Carolyn McCaffery, Stephanie Salomone, and Valerie J. Peterson. "Making Teaching Matter More—the Making of a T1 University." Paper presented at 2021 ASEE Virtual Annual Conference Content Access, Virtual Conference, July, 2021. https://peer.asee.org/37476

Roy, Arundhati. "The Pandemic Is a Portal." *Financial Times*, April 3, 2020. https://www.ft.com/content/10d8f5e8-74eb-11ea-95fe-fcd274e920ca.

Swaak, Taylor. "What a Possible U. of Phoenix Sale Says about the State of Higher Ed." *Chronicle of Higher Education* 69, no. 12 (February 17, 2023). https://www.chronicle.com/article/what-a-possible-u-of-phoenix-sale-says-about-the-state-of-higher-ed.

Tanner, Kimberly D. "Structure Matters: Twenty-One Teaching Strategies to Promote Student Engagement and Cultivate Classroom Equity." *CBE—Life Sciences Education* 12, no. 3 (September 2013): 322–331. https://doi.org/10.1187/cbe.13-06-0115.

Part I

New Systems and Structures

chapter 1

Centering Resiliency

Principles for Academic Leaders and Teaching Center Directors

Matthew Kaplan, Mary C. Wright, and Derek Bruff

As higher education's mode of operation shifted from in-person to remote during the COVID-19 pandemic, the impact was felt by all sectors of US colleges and universities.[1] Students were attending class in their campus or family homes or from a McDonald's parking lot, struggling with sometimes suboptimal technology and what felt like increased course workloads,[2] and facing growing mental health challenges.[3] For most faculty, the shift to remote and, later, hybrid teaching entailed a crash course that ranged from the most basic, like learning video conference tools, to the more complex, like navigating remote exams and hybrid classrooms. While the pandemic was a very particular (and hopefully unique) event, higher education needs to draw lessons from the disruption caused by COVID-19, lessons for responding to similar or even very different types of crises in the future.

At many institutions of higher education, centers for teaching and learning (CTLs) played critical roles in helping faculty and other instructors respond to the challenges of pandemic teaching, often through rapid deployment of professional development for instructors and assessments of student learning needs. CTLs have been "coming in from the margins" of higher education to support organizational development and institutional change for more than a decade,[4] and 2020–2021 demonstrated that such work can happen very quickly when needed. As three directors of teaching centers (University of Michigan's Center for Research on Learning and Teaching, Brown University's Sheridan Center for Teaching and Learning, and Vanderbilt University's Center for Teaching), we saw firsthand the key role that CTLs played in this time of crisis. This led us to reflect on the aspects of our centers and our institutions that prepared us to take on that important role and to identify advice for higher education leaders for preparing for future disruptions.

Our contention is that volatility will be a constant feature of higher education in the future, whether from forces that can be predicted (e.g., continued pushes for online and hybrid education, the intervention of governing boards and legislatures around politically sensitive topics, changing population demographics) or those that will arise unexpectedly (pandemics, weather disasters, financial turmoil) and that CTLs are well positioned to help campuses navigate these disruptions, as they did during the COVID-19 pandemic. Indeed, a center for teaching and learning can be a kind of "center for resiliency," provided that academic leaders and center directors follow the three principles we suggest in this chapter. First, CTLs must practice a kind of improvisation when it comes to the complex challenge of resource allocation and responsiveness. Second, CTLs must acknowledge and build on the collaborative network for teaching support that has long characterized their work. And third, academic leaders need to understand the strengths that CTLs bring to their work and provide meaningful support to enhance the capacities of CTLs in advance of future disruptions. These principles build on the framework for center leaders by Mary C. Wright, Debra Rudder Lohe, Tershia Pinder-Grover, and Leslie Ortquist-Ahrens,[5] with a specific focus on center operations in a time of crisis.

Taken together, these three principles will allow centers to effectively bring to bear their resources and talents in times of crisis, while also offering a solid foundation for operations in "normal" times. They will also provide guidance to academic leaders about how best to leverage the talents and resources housed in CTLs.

Improvisation

The first principle that undergirds resilient centers for teaching and learning is improvisation. By this principle, we mean the ability for centers to creatively adjust programs and services they have developed in times of stability to be responsive in times of crisis. Although not explicitly named as improvisation, others have described how their educational development work during the COVID-19 pandemic leveraged this principle. For example, Patricia Dinneen writes about how the CTL at George Washington University adapted University of Virginia's course design institute model to their campus,[6] creating a virtual Forward Looking Explorations in Teaching Camp (FLEX Camp), which was very well-received by their faculty. Others have also described how they re-envisioned their long-running programs to meet the needs of remote teaching.[7]

Although these cases implicitly suggest that improvisation is valuable during a crisis, leadership literature suggests that this capacity holds value during times of stability as well, by helping to reflectively examine a center's programs and practices. In their discussion of a "jazz mindset" applied to leadership, Ethan S. Bernstein and Frank J. Barrett write, "Dynamic capabilities are not just a one-time response to an environmental jolt but represent persistent and structured efforts dedicated to improved performance."[8] Relatedly, the ability of an organization to recognize the value of new evidence and contextually apply the knowledge (elsewhere defined as "absorptive capacity") is crucial to improving practice.[9] Indeed, our teaching centers and others regularly use formative assessment about their programming from a variety of sources to improve those programs from year to year or even month to month.

At all three of our centers, we utilized the principle of improvisation to support academic continuity during the pandemic. For example, at Brown's Sheridan Center for Teaching and Learning, staff quickly developed the Anchor Course Design Institute,[10] which was drawn from our new faculty institute, Launch, which was itself adapted from an established model at the University of Virginia (UVA).[11] Similarly, Vanderbilt's Center for Teaching built its Online Course Design Institute in short order (also modeled after UVA's Center for Teaching Excellence course design institute) while suspending other programming not as immediately relevant to the crisis. As a third example, at the University of Michigan, Tazin Daniels, Elizabeth Bailey, and Anoff Nicholas Cobblah re-positioned the 20+-year-old Preparing Future Faculty Seminar to meet the learning goals of a remote audience of graduate students, writing that the pandemic was a valuable opportunity to "unfreeze" established practices.[12]

The principle of improvisation is similar to Etienne Wenger's conception of reflective practice, which closely joins engagement, or a close examination of work, with imagination, or a re-envisioned distancing from the original product.[13] Moments of crisis can help CTLs more clearly heed the call to engage in this process. However, as an ongoing principle in times of stability, improvisation can also be helpful to efficiently manage resources, highlighting when the best solution is not always to build something completely different and new.

Collaborative Networks

Disruption brings with it a high degree of uncertainty on multiple levels, from university policy, which often lags behind the precipitating events, to clarity about resources that can support both students and faculty. Teaching centers are well positioned to serve as an information hub in such situations because their work entails regular collaboration with a range of offices on campus, including central administration, deans of schools and colleges, instructional technology centers, and writing centers. As faculty development units, teaching centers typically have excellent collaborative relationships with individual faculty as well, and they actively build extensive networks of faculty collaborators across their own campuses. Andrea L. Beach, Mary D. Sorcinelli, Ann E. Austin, and Jaclyn K. Rivard note that "one of the hallmarks of a networked faculty development enterprise is collaboration across campus to reach a range of audiences."[14]

In times of disruption, academic leaders can leverage those connections to reach a wide audience for disseminating policies and information, and also expand connections and collaborations to avoid redundant programs and mixed messaging that can cause confusion and waste resources. All three of our campuses effectively leveraged pre-existing connections to respond to the needs arising from the COVID-19 pandemic. At the University of Michigan, the provost established a Response and Recovery group that included the Center for Research on Learning and Teaching and several other units on campus dedicated to teaching and technology support. The group was charged with developing plans for responding to instructional needs for the shift to emergency remote teaching. Pre-existing relationships among our offices—often across many years—facilitated the rapid deployment of this new working group and enabled us to leverage our offices' unique strengths.

At Vanderbilt, the Center for Teaching had to figure out how to support the new campus Zoom license with central IT very quickly, and was well positioned to do so thanks to previous collaborations around the learning management system (e.g., referring support tickets from one unit to the other). The Center for Teaching also leveraged its network of faculty "friends of the Center" to reach out to individual departments to identify and respond to pandemic teaching needs. A final example, at Brown University, involved the Sheridan Center's development of several campus-wide surveys, distributed by the Office of the Provost, that asked instructors about their need for support and served as a hub to coordinate requests to Center staff and campus partners (e.g., Library, Media Services, and Swearer Center for Public Service).

A rubric developed by the Network of STEM Education Centers[15] can be useful to both center and university leadership when considering collaborations. Overall, they suggest the following:

> Seeking and cultivating collaborations should reflect knowledge of both the vision and mission of the center as well as knowing the needs of the stakeholders and potential participants in the activities of the center. Stated differently, the mission should inform what organizations or which individuals you seek to collaborate with. Effective collaborations

support the center's mission and provide focus which can keep the center on track. One of the results of collaboration can be connections to other university activities that have overlap with the center's mission and can lead to constructive interactions that lead to future collaborations.

They suggest multiple steps to successful partnerships, including identifying potential partners, developing the collaboration, and maintaining those relationships. Newer centers will want to think carefully about the array of offices aligned with their mission and start building connections with them. And although more established teaching centers probably have robust collaborations already, it is worth revisiting this list as new issues arise and new offices are created.

Meaningful Support

Improvisational and collaborative centers for teaching and learning can be centers for resiliency in the face of disruption, but not without meaningful support from academic leaders. In this section, we provide explicit advice to academic leaders for equipping teaching centers so those centers can better support campus teaching missions, both during future disruptions and in more typical times.

Invest in the quantity and quality of a teaching center's staff. Although center funding directed to outside speakers or institutional consortia can be useful in a time of crisis, the teaching centers on our campuses each had ample staff at the start of the COVID-19 pandemic, which allowed us to quickly stand up the kind of programming that our teaching communities needed in 2020. Although it may not be feasible to have 10+ staff members as our centers do, it is important to consider a staff size, including support staff, sufficient to play a meaningful role on campus.

The other alternative is to scale back expectations for what a center can accomplish, at least in the short term. Stability counts here, because effective collaborative relationships (with faculty, with administrators, with other units) take time to build. For example, the model of a center with an individual faculty leader who turns over regularly does not allow for the kind of expertise that will promote improvisation and the longevity that will enable connections.

Experience counts, too, because the ability for a teaching center to improvise is enhanced when a center's staff has already developed high-quality programming. For example, the online course design institute at Vanderbilt, mentioned above, was developed by the six senior staff members of the Center for Teaching in about four weeks, building on existing resources from previous center offerings. The institute was offered every two weeks all summer long to about 500 faculty, while the staff continued to build just-in-time resources to meet emergent needs (e.g. hybrid teaching). This level of responsiveness is harder without a robust staff.

Encourage collaborations between teaching centers and other units, before a time of crisis. The kinds of collaborations described above are challenging to do well and quickly if initiated during a crisis. Leveraging existing relationships enables more agility. Academic leaders are in a position to endorse collaborations between units and to remove potential roadblocks to collaboration, especially when teaching centers are working with units that do not share reporting lines. When developing these collaborations, be clear about roles and play to each unit's strengths. For instance, campus units deliver varying amounts of faculty-facing programming. Because this is a regular practice for teaching centers, consider having them lead this component of a collaboration.

Provide teaching centers with access to information. As we saw during the COVID-19 pandemic, campus communication plays a key role in crisis response. Proactively include teaching centers in task forces, working groups, and response teams, so that they can learn about campus needs, and they can keep senior administrators informed about what they hear "on the ground" from faculty and other instructors. Although faculty-only committees have their place, consider the kinds of professional expertise teaching center staff members might provide and include them in key committees. One author found out about a committee on post-COVID teaching policies that didn't include anyone from the author's teaching center. That was a missed opportunity.

Recognize that teaching centers can play a variety of roles supporting an institution's teaching mission. Some centers are viewed as primarily useful for helping individual faculty craft better lectures or lead more engaging classroom discussions. Centers can indeed help in those areas, but they can also bring important resources to other areas, including course design, curriculum development and assessment, the intentional integration of technologies in teaching, community engagement, equity and inclusion efforts, and much more.[16]

At the Vanderbilt Center for Teaching, faculty support for the learning management system had been incorporated in the center's mission and resources for five years before the pandemic. This positioned the center to be a great source of help during the 2020 pivot to remote and online instruction. Consider also Brown's Sheridan Center for Teaching and Learning, which embedded assessment and student learning support into its pre-pandemic mission and was able to leverage both of those activities to gain a better picture of the university's teaching and learning support needs in 2020. And finally, the University of Michigan (UM)'s CRLT had been charged with university-wide support of inclusive teaching at the start of its Diversity, Equity, and Inclusion (DEI) initiative in 2016, and was therefore well positioned to offer revised, synchronous Zoom workshops on inclusive teaching in remote contexts when the pandemic shut down in-person teaching. Bear in mind that when asking centers to take on new tasks or missions, especially on short notice, they will have to either step away from existing work or be provided with new resources.

Conclusion

Although we are not suggesting that CTLs are the answer to all questions around the shifting landscape for teaching and learning, we do contend that the range of staff skills and expertise, center connections across campus, and deep knowledge of the institution make our units much more like a multi-purpose Swiss army knife than a single-function Phillips head screwdriver. The challenge centers will face moving forward is that specific needs will continue to shift, meaning that the tools in our collective portfolios will have to adapt accordingly. For center leadership, building in an understanding of the importance of flexibility and improvisation, and planning strategically for it, is a key component to succeeding in the coming years. It is also important to keep in mind the limits of flexibility. In our experience, center staff are quite adept and eager to explore new terrain—developing the necessary expertise and evidence-informed practices to support new directions—but there are start-up costs to such work, and an approach that includes a major pivot every year is not sustainable.

In addition, given capacity issues and the need for a defined mission, CTLs cannot by themselves carry all the tools needed for known and unknown eventualities. Thus, centers need to play a very conscious role as connectors, helping to leverage key collaborations and establish new ones as the need arises. Finally, for universities to fully leverage the potential of teaching centers to help fulfill the promise of a new and ever-changing educational landscape, they will need to retain and nurture center staff. Doing so requires strategies such as access to high quality professional development, creation of well-defined promotion pathways, and the budget flexibility to fund promotions. Making this vision a reality requires the support of academic leaders who recognize that robust investments in CTLs will have long-term payoffs for the institution.

Notes

1. Smalley, "Responses to Coronavirus (COVID-19)."
2. Barre, "The Workload Dilemma."
3. Gurung and Galardi, "Syllabus Tone."
4. Schroeder et al., *Role in Institutional Change*; Chism, "To the Front Office."
5. Wright et al., "The Four Rs."
6. Dineen, "How a Flexible Teaching."
7. Bulin et al., *Time of Crises*; Tassoni, "CTLs."
8. Bernstein and Barrett, "Strategic Change," 58.
9. Crain-Dorough and Elder, "Absorptive Capacity."
10. Kaldor et al., "Researching the Resilient CDI."
11. Palmer et al., "High-Impact Course Design Institute."
12. Daniels et al., "In Search of Silver Linings."
13. Wenger, *Communities of Practice.*

14. Beach et al., *Current Practices, Future Imperatives*, 37.
15. Network of STEM Education Centers, "Building Partnerships."
16. Kelley et al., "Moving toward the Center."

Bibliography

Barre, Betsy. "The Workload Dilemma." *Center for the Advancement of Teaching* (blog), January 22, 2021. https://cat.wfu.edu/2021/01/the-workload-dilemma.

Beach, Andrea L., Mary D. Sorcinelli, Ann E. Austin, and Jaclyn K. Rivard. *Faculty Development in the Age of Evidence: Current Practices, Future Imperatives*. Sterling, VA: Stylus, 2016.

Bernstein, Ethan S., and Frank J. Barrett. "Strategic Change and the Jazz Mindset: Exploring Practices That Enhance Dynamic Capabilities for Organizational Improvisation." In *Research in Organizational Change and Development*, edited by Abraham B. Shani, Richard W. Woodman, and William A. Pasmore, 55–90. Bingley, UK: Emerald, 2011.

Bulin, Aubra, D. Grant, M. Salazar, and M. Smutherman, eds. "Educational Development in the Time of Crises." Special issue of *To Improve the Academy* 39, no. 3 (Spring 2021).

Chism, Nancy V. "The Role of Educational Developers in Institutional Change: From the Basement Office to the Front Office." *To Improve the Academy* 17, no. 20210331 (January 1, 1998): 141–153.

Communication Strategies. "Increasing Visibility." Accessed May 7, 2023. https://serc.carleton.edu/StemEdCenters/toolkit/comm_strategies/visibility_impo.html.

Crain-Dorough, Mindy, and Adam C. Elder. "Absorptive Capacity as a Means of Understanding and Addressing the Disconnects Between Research and Practice." *Review of Research in Education* 45, no. 1 (March 2021): 67–100. https://doi.org/10.3102/0091732X21990614.

Daniels, Tazin, Elizabeth Bailey, and Anoff Nicholas Cobblah. "In Search of Silver Linings: Strategies for Preparing Future Faculty During the COVID-19 Pandemic." *To Improve the Academy* 39, no. 3 (March 25, 2021). https://doi.org/10.3998/tia.17063888.0039.306.

Dinneen, Patricia. "How a Flexible Teaching 'Camp' Answered Our Pandemic Teaching Emergency." *To Improve the Academy* 39, no. 3 (March 25, 2021). https://doi.org/10.3998/tia.17063888.0039.307.

Gurung, Regan A. R., and Noelle R. Galardi. "Syllabus Tone, More Than Mental Health Statements, Influence Intentions to Seek Help." *Teaching of Psychology* 49, no. 3 (July 2022): 218–223. https://doi.org/10.1177/0098628321994632.

Kaldor, Eric, Adriana Streifer, Kimberly Fournier, Maggie Vecchione, Melissa Kane, and Carl S. Moore. "Researching the Resilient CDI: Pandemic Lessons and Opportunities." Interactive on-demand session at Evolving beyond Crisis—Connecting to the Future, the 46th Annual POD Network Conference, virtual, October 25, 2021. https://podconference2021.sched.com/event/p8mj.

Kelley, Bruce, Laura Cruz, and Nancy Fire. "Moving toward the Center: The Integration of Educational Development in an Era of Historic Change in Higher Education." *To Improve the Academy* 36, no. 1 (January 2017): 1–8. https://doi.org/10.1002/tia2.20052.

Network of STEM Education Centers. "Building Partnerships." Accessed May 7, 2023. https://serc.carleton.edu/StemEdCenters/toolkit/partnerships/index.html.

Palmer, Michael S., Adriana C. Streifer, and Stacy Williams-Duncan. "Systematic Assessment of a High-Impact Course Design Institute." *To Improve the Academy* 35, no. 2 (June 2016): 339–361. https://doi.org/10.1002/tia2.20041.

Schroeder, Connie, Phyllis Blumberg, Nancy V. Chism, Catherine E. Frerichs, Susan Gano-Phillips, Devorah Lieberman, Diana G. Pace, and Tamara Rosier. *Coming in from the Margins: Faculty Development's Emerging Organizational Development Role in Institutional Change*. Sterling, VA: Stylus, 2010.

Smalley, Andrew. "Higher Education Responses to Coronavirus (COVID-19)." National Council of State Legislatures, last modified March 22, 2021, https://www.ncsl.org/research/education/higher-education-responses-to-coronavirus-covid-19.aspx.

Tassoni, John Paul. "CTLs in the Time of COVID." *Journal on Centers for Teaching and Learning* 12 (2020). https://openjournal.lib.miamioh.edu/index.php/jctl/article/view/215.

Wenger, Etienne. *Communities of Practice: Learning, Meaning, and Identity*. Cambridge: Cambridge University Press, 1999.

Wright, Mary C., Debra Rudder Lohe, Tershia Pinder-Grover, and Leslie Ortquist-Ahrens. "The Four Rs: Guiding CTLs with Responsiveness, Relationships, Resources, and Research." *To Improve the Academy* 37, no. 2 (June 2018): 271–286. https://doi.org/10.1002/tia2.20084.

chapter 2

Converting Teaching from Solo Sport to Team-Based Activity

Lessons Learned from a Systemwide Instructional Design Support Initiative

MJ Bishop, Nancy O'Neill, Briana Johnson, and Whitney Kilgore

Improvement in postsecondary education will require converting teaching from a solo sport to a community-based research activity.

—Herbert Simon (1996), Nobel laureate and professor at Carnegie Mellon University

Given the need to provide large-scale support to faculty making the move online during the onset of the COVID-19 pandemic, the University System of Maryland's Kirwan Center for Academic Innovation partnered with iDesign to create the Instructional Design Support Center (IDSC) as a robust and rapid response. Although this on-demand solution was well-equipped to meet the diverse needs of faculty—whose course loads, disciplines, and experience level with online teaching varied widely—we did not see as much uptake of these services as expected. This chapter discusses our lessons learned about passive versus proactive instructional design (ID) support and examine what it will take to convert postsecondary teaching "from a solo sport to a community-based research activity,"[1] helping universities create more learner-centric opportunities in the future.

Background

Like the rest of US higher education in March 2020, the institutions that compose the University System of Maryland (USM) closed their campuses and moved abruptly to emergency remote teaching for the remainder of the spring semester. This was, of course, in the early days of the COVID-19 pandemic, and the USM's William E. Kirwan Center for Academic Innovation was pressed to find ways to support the institutions in their efforts to scale high-quality online learning experiences as quickly as possible.

Although most of the USM's 12 four-year public universities have teaching and learning centers that provide instructional design support, these units did not have the capacity to address the horizontal scale necessary to meet the immediate need of moving online en masse.[2] In response, the Kirwan Center launched USM *OnTrack*, a partnership with the system's primarily online institution, University of Maryland Global Campus. The partnership included $2.6 million in funding passing to the Kirwan Center to support the system institutions in moving toward high-quality online instruction and course development at scale. Through USM *OnTrack*, the Kirwan Center coordinated 57 faculty development workshops, systemwide access to online virtual reality laboratory simulations, and access to adaptive learning technologies. But the primary focus of USM *OnTrack* was our effort to provide instructional design at scale, both to ensure that all faculty had the support they needed to pivot to online education and to re-examine our beliefs about what truly effective teaching would require from now on.[3]

A "Solo Sport"

In 1967, Herb Simon noted that whereas other professions ensure that practitioners have the training and experience needed to produce optimally effective and efficient outcomes, at colleges and universities, few faculty possess "professional knowledge in the laws of learning, or the techniques for applying them."[4] Simon knew it would mean a major change in how instruction of complex subjects happens, moving the creation of learning environments from the "solo sport" of individual faculty working in isolation to a "community-based research activity." In this vision, teams of subject matter experts, instructional designers, assessment experts, and learning engineers develop instructional materials and experiences based on learning science—and continually refine them based on data.

In fact, findings from the pre-COVID *Changing Landscape of Online Education* (*CHLOE*) surveys of chief online officers suggest a strong association between institutions that had adopted "a systematic and multi-actor approach to online course design" and those that were employing a "greater variety of techniques and activities" known to improve student engagement, such as digital simulations and gamification.[5] Moreover, survey responses from both 2019 and 2020 suggest that although staffing issues left many institutions facing "severe challenges in providing ID support across their online curriculum," fully online students at institutions that required instructional designer involvement in the development of online courses were performing comparably or better than face-to-face students.[6]

But Simon was also right when he noted that there would be resistance from those faculty convinced they already know perfectly well how to teach.[7] When the 2019 *CHLOE* report asked why some institutions were not requiring instructional design support, chief online officers primarily cited faculty autonomy/academic freedom, equal to or in some cases even rated higher than insufficient resources or contractual restrictions in union agreements.[8] Anticipating this pushback more than 50 years ago, Simon opined, "Surely, however, academic freedom does not include the freedom to approach a professional task—the principal task to which the faculty member's career is devoted—as an amateur."[9]

Continuing Our Story . . .

As part of USM *OnTrack*, the Kirwan Center partnered with iDesign to develop an instructional design support service that made concierge-level help available to faculty transitioning to online teaching. The Kirwan Center prepurchased 4,500 hours of instructional designer's time from iDesign—500 hours for each of the nine institutions that opted in—that the teaching and learning centers and instructional design units could use as needed. In addition, iDesign worked directly with the institutions to create customized online Instructional Design Support Center (IDSC) hubs as a just-in-time solution for faculty seeking support for online course development. The hubs provided the portal through which faculty could access the institution's instructional design hours, and they also housed resources on best practices for online pedagogy and student orientation materials for online learning. For institutions that didn't already have an online course template in place, iDesign developed an easy-to-use framework to help faculty quickly structure their content, with an emphasis on usability for students.

Anticipating a huge demand for the instructional design services starting in summer 2020, the Kirwan Center budgeted an additional 250 hours for each campus and established reporting "safeguards" to ensure that if any one campus started using too many hours, Kirwan Center staff would be alerted immediately in order to reallocate hours to manage demand. But even though this on-demand solution met the diverse needs of faculty—whose course loads, disciplines, and experience with online teaching varied widely—we did not see as much uptake by faculty as we had expected. As illustrated in figure 2.1, usage experienced a bit of a surge in July, but by the start of the fall semester, faculty had used only a little over 700 of the 4,500 hours the Kirwan Center had retained. This occurred despite the fact that USM decided early to continue fully online instruction in fall 2020, and we knew from colleagues across the system that a majority of faculty were actively engaged over the summer in moving their courses online.

We began to explore the reasons behind the lack of uptake so that we could understand any hesitation and ensure that the purchased ID hours were well used by the end of the funded project in May 2021. Several hypotheses emerged, including one that explored the perspectives of the institutional teaching and learning center and instructional design staff: did they view these ID hours as extending their own capacity

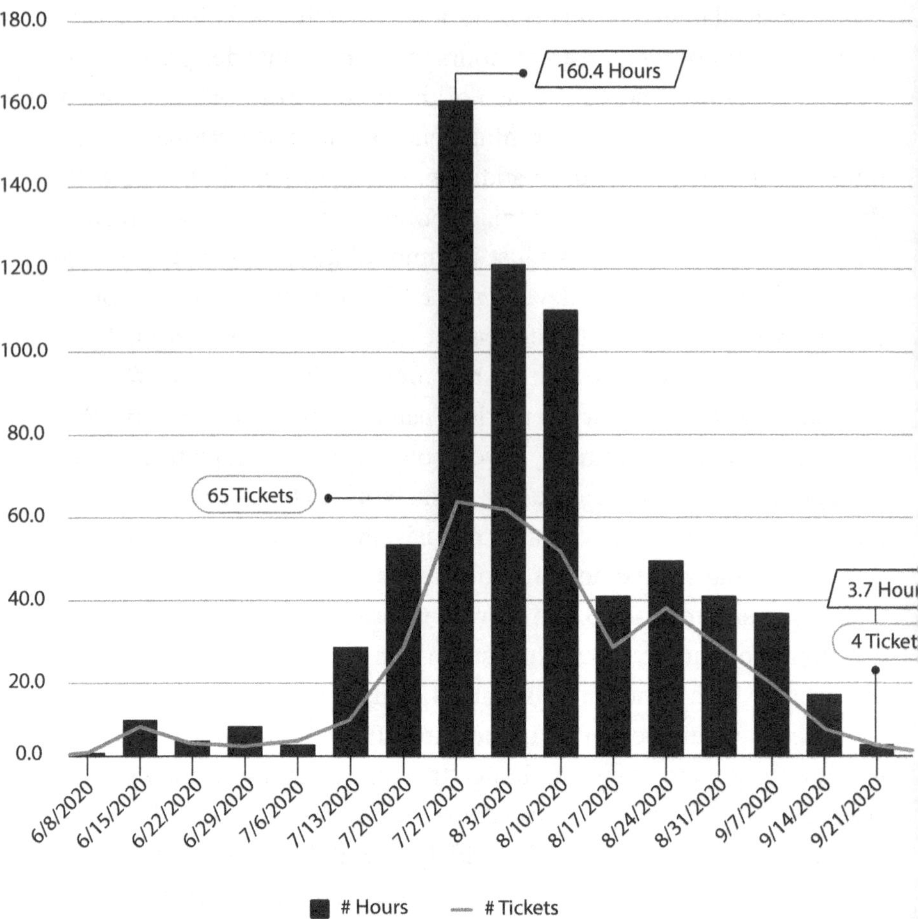

Figure 2.1. Usage of instructional design hours by week and number of support tickets posted from June 1, 2020, through September 21, 2020.

to support faculty or as something that would supplant their roles in faculty support? An even more fundamental hypothesis related to our sense that faculty themselves simply didn't understand what instructional designers do or how instructional designers could help them.

Current State of Instructional Design

Prior to COVID-19, instructional designers at many USM institutions worked primarily with faculty teaching online or with a significant level of educational technology in their courses, often only when faculty sought out their support. It wouldn't be surprising, then, if faculty lacked awareness about the role of instructional designers when the instructional design support hours rolled out in summer 2020. Indeed, Inside Higher Ed's annual *Survey of Faculty Attitudes on Technology* found that in the years leading up to the pandemic, although a large majority of those faculty who had worked with instructional designers had positive experiences, only a small minority had actually used an instructional designer to help create their online, blended, or face-to-face course.[10]

Moreover, instructional design and instructional technology are distinct areas of practice but have some overlap, which could introduce additional confusion to faculty. Instructional design is also not well understood as a distinct field with its own sets of competencies. Although there are a growing number of formal degree and training programs for instructional designers, a growing body of research in the field, and theories and methods associated with it, individuals can still break into instructional design from other sectors without this formal training or expertise. As noted by Rhiannon Pollard and Swapna Kumar in a 20-year review of the research on instructional design as a field (emphasis in original):

> Several studies pointed out the variety of backgrounds and career paths that lead to becoming an instructional designer in higher education. In general, these instructional designers are highly and diversely qualified, often possess backgrounds in teaching, and frequently consider their professions *found* as opposed to *sought*; rather than taking a path through a degree or other training in order to become an instructional designer, they find their way into those roles as a result of their experiences and skill sets.[11]

Parallel to these entry paths into the career of instructional design, the job titles, roles, and functions of instructional designers in higher education are similarly variable.[12] As a result, faculty may encounter great variation in terms of the levels and kinds of expertise that instructional designers bring to the course development enterprise.

In 2016, Intentional Futures surveyed instructional designers working in higher education to learn more about their roles and how institutions and faculty utilized their expertise. Respondents reported a wide range of activity making up their roles at their institutions, with many different titles and reporting up through many different units on campus. At the same time, some reported that they are often viewed as "glorified IT personnel who simply move courses online,"[13] suggesting a need to better communicate to faculty about the diversity of expertise that can be found within this group. Julie Rubley also observed that about 62% of instructional designers believed their role and expertise is not well understood by others at their institutions, which means that their help is often not sought.[14] Furthermore, when their assistance is sought or required, conflict can erupt between faculty and instructional designers over role confusion and questions as to who "owns" the course design and development process.[15] Finally, as Pollard and Kumar note, "because the practice of instructional design cannot be separated from the environment in which it takes place, the culture of the institution is a strong influence as to how and what instructional designers do and therefore how they are perceived by faculty."[16]

Back to Our Story . . .

Concerned with how to make optimal use of the resources that the Kirwan Center had received from the University of Maryland Global Campus to support the other USM institutions, we met in late summer 2020 to brainstorm ways to encourage faculty to make better use of the help. We quickly realized that one potential issue lay in the relatively passive approach we were taking, by essentially building a help desk and hoping that faculty would come. So, starting in fall 2020, we began an outreach campaign aimed at more actively bringing just-in-time support to faculty.

To start, we offered 24 "ask-and-answer" sessions between mid-November and mid-December 2020 that were open to faculty from across the USM. We focused on specific topics that the team identified were of particular concern from our earlier workshops, such as balancing synchronous and asynchronous learning, writing meaningful learning objectives, crafting and using rubrics, and rethinking video and its uses. These 20-minute, one-on-one sessions gave 19 faculty an opportunity to get initial answers to their questions and to set up time with a designated instructional designer to continue the conversation, if needed.

We also developed a series of synchronous faculty development workshops tailored to institution-specific requests. These workshops functioned as mini-communications campaigns to help faculty better understand instructional designers' capabilities and what was possible with their support. More than 120 faculty and staff attended sessions running from late fall 2020 through mid-March 2021. Topics focused on active engagement in online courses, inclusive pedagogy, and leveraging the institution's technology ecosystem to create interactive experiences.

This more proactive approach of providing topically focused instructional design support yielded more uptake in the IDSC hours; we observed spikes in usage every time that we offered workshops and one-on-one sessions. As shown in figure 2.2, which provides data through the end of the project, the number of tickets posted began climbing in November and, other than dipping over holiday breaks, remained high well into the start of the spring semester. Weekly usage stayed above 20 hours during this period, as well. Figure 2.3 illustrates the increased slope in cumulative usage between mid-November and mid-March.

Moving to a Team-Based Activity

We learned important lessons from this experience that can help inform how higher education might move closer to Simon's vision, in which the creation of postsecondary learning environments becomes a collaboration among educational professionals, working as a team to support student success.

Lead with the Problem You're Trying to Solve. Our communication about the support we were providing needed to do more than

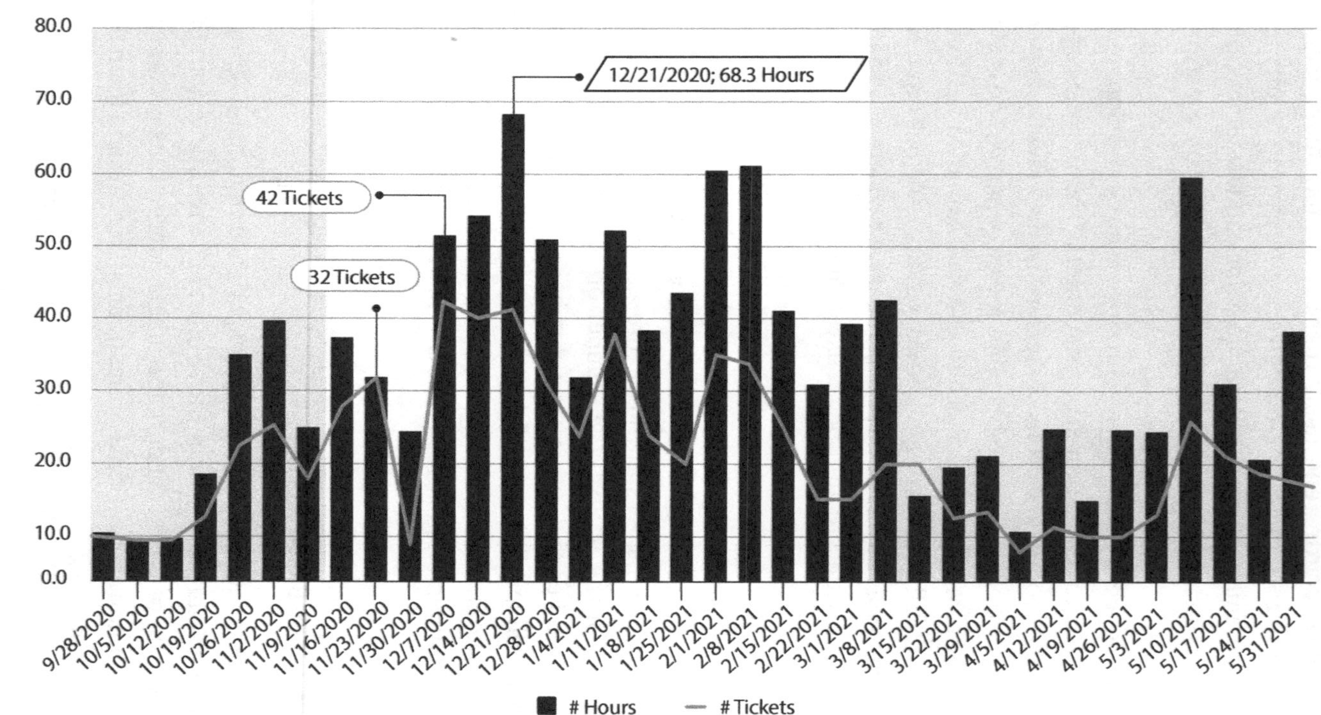

Figure 2.2. Usage of instructional design hours by week from September 28, 2020, through May 31, 2021. There was greater uptake in use of hours during workshops and "ask-and-answer" sessions between mid-November and mid-March.

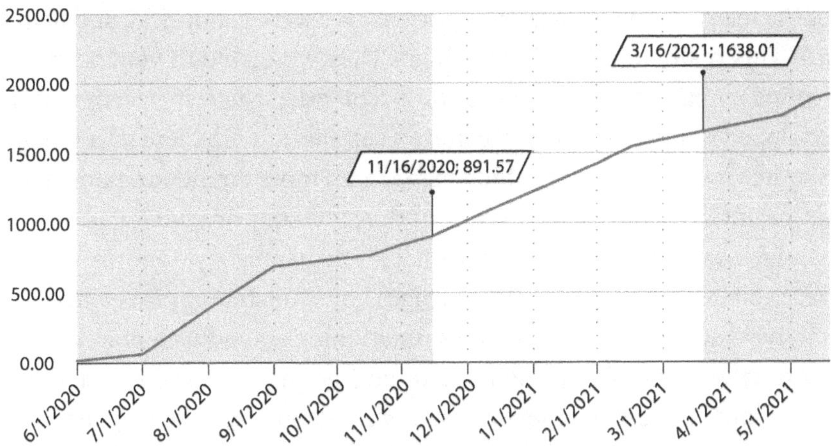

Figure 2.3. Cumulative hours used, from June 1, 2020, through May 30, 2021, show an upward slope between mid-November and mid-March.

simply say, "I'm an instructional designer. How can I help?" Overwhelmed by the enormity of moving their fall semester courses online, faculty needed *us* to tell *them* about the problems instructional designers could help them solve.

When we took a more proactive approach by providing just-in-time support along with concrete examples of how instructional designers could help, we began to see more faculty availing themselves of the IDSC hours. During these one-on-one and workshop sessions, the instructional designers focused on sharing information and resources while being open-minded collaborators and problem-solvers. They offered their expertise, identified how their skills could align with faculty needs, and connected faculty to relevant resources. As faculty became better acquainted with what the instructional designers knew and could do, they signed up for follow-on support and began establishing working relationships with their designated instructional designer.

Build Empathic Relationships. Once faculty had connected with an instructional designer, it quickly became clear how important relationship-building was in the collaboration. Through those exchanges with faculty, we discovered they were experiencing stress and anxiety that they were reluctant to share with campus colleagues. One of the instructional designers reported: "We were calm, kind, and helpful. This really resonated with them. They were able to vent without feeling embarrassed—then they took a breath—then they were better equipped to meet with their teams on campus or help themselves. Faculty needed reassurance, which made them more confident. Some faculty wanted to meet every day until they felt comfortable."

Much like trauma-informed medicine and heutagogy—a form of self-determined learning that acknowledges how threatening circumstances can have adverse effects on one's functioning and adjusts practice accordingly—we realized the need to engage in "trauma-informed instructional design" by meeting faculty needs in a safe, reassuring, and empathetic manner.[17] As one faculty member shared, "Thank you for your nice words about my ability to survive the internet challenges in a very difficult time. I was able to make it through because you were a great mentor to me, and I was lucky I was assigned to you."

We also discovered that it was useful for faculty to work with designers who had skill sets that matched their specific disciplinary needs. In one instance, the faculty member matched with someone in their field, which cemented the ID-as-mentor relationship even further: "Her background in law, technology, and education has provided me with the help I need now. She is also patient and kind. She is flexible with her schedule. And she is extremely resourceful whenever I encounter problems with my course. Her support has encouraged me to keep going on the days I have felt like giving up." Having an empathetic and knowledgeable collaborator not only reassured faculty, but began to open their minds to how instructional designers could help advance their pedagogy, as well.

Be a Thought Partner. Early uncertainty about the long-term ramifications of COVID-19 left many in higher education believing that a temporary shift to remote teaching over video conferencing tools would get us through. As the reality set in that campus closures would continue through Fall 2020 and Spring 2021, the instructional designers' role as a thought partner became increasingly important. As "Zoom fatigue" set in for both faculty and students, instructional designers made gentle suggestions and asked probing questions about the best use of synchronous time and what could be moved to asynchronous learning; this helped instructors realize they needed to make more systemic changes to their courses.

The instructional designers helped faculty think about how to make the most of their institution's instructional technology ecosystem. They were ready with suggestions that helped faculty realize that synchronous time could be more than just having students sit through a live lecture. Instructional designers posed alternatives, such as using discussion boards and live chat to facilitate conversations. This helped faculty break free from the assumption that many of the things they did in face-to-face classes could be simply transferred online. As one faculty member shared, "Why hasn't someone told me this before now? I wish I had been advised better about how you can't cover as much material remotely. I should have been warned against so many video lectures. I specifically asked this question [of] others, but never had someone help me apply the concepts. I had to adjust when students revolted, and I'm glad I had this help."

The IDSC support gave faculty an unbiased thought partner in facilitating online collaboration, class discussions, and even group projects by providing tangible examples and supporting them through the technological barriers they encountered. As faculty became increasingly aware of how these collaborations were helping them, they also began sharing with colleagues the ways in which instructional designers could support the move to online.

In the chaos that ensued during the early days of the pandemic, we adopted an "if we build it, they will come" mentality to creating a systemwide instructional design support solution. We believed there was pent-up demand for instructional design support and faculty would be clamoring for it. However, our expectations did not match reality. There was clearly a need to evolve from emergency remote teaching to higher-quality online learning offerings, but faculty did not reach out for support. Despite the narrative that was playing out in the media at the time about instructional designers as the "sherpas of online learning teams,"[18] we observed that faculty were likely to continue preparing their courses in isolation until they better understood the role these education professionals play as problem-solvers and thought partners. Working together, we were able to reframe our approach to providing instructional design support; along the way, we learned important lessons about what it will likely take in the future to move postsecondary teaching from a "solo sport to a community-based research activity."[19]

Conclusion

Today, most higher education courses are developed by faculty working in isolation and lacking the training and experience needed to produce optimally effective and efficient outcomes. As we turn our attention toward diversifying and expanding our academic portfolios by creating more student-centered, inclusive, and lifelong learning, we must also diversify and expand the teams we form to design those learning opportunities—bringing together faculty, students, assessment and evaluation experts, data analysts, and instructional design professionals through a collaborative design process.

Unfortunately, instructional design is not a core competency at many higher education institutions. Even for those with some instructional design capacity, scaling up quickly to respond to an emergency or even a large curricular project is not something most institutions can do well. Leaning on a partner to get over some of these hurdles can allow institutions to be more agile, flexible, and responsive.

But until faculty better understand the role these education professionals play as problem-solvers and thought partners, they are likely to continue preparing their courses in isolation. Until instructional designers get better at leading with the problem they're trying to solve, building empathetic relationships, and being a thought partner, they are likely to continue to be left off the team. Much institutional culture must still change before we can optimize instructional design expertise to create truly learner-centric environments. In some cases, moving teaching and learning from a solo activity to a team sport will need support from senior leadership to reinforce that cultural change.

Notes

1. Simon, "Loner's Sport?"
2. Bishop et al., "Time of Crisis."
3. Feldstein, "Learning Engineering Is Learning."
4. Simon, "College President," 73.
5. Garrett et al., *CHLOE* 3, 21.
6. Garrett et al., *CHLOE* 3, 23; see also Garrett et al., *CHLOE* 4.
7. Simon, "College President," 77.
8. Garrett et al., *CHLOE* 3.
9. Simon, "College President," 77.
10. Jaschik and Lederman, *Survey of Faculty Attitudes*, 2018, 2019.
11. Pollard and Kumar, "Roles, Challenges, and Supports," 4.
12. Anderson et al., "Looking Beyond Physician Educator"; Morgan, "Intentional and Operational Agency"; Moskal, "Instructional Designers in Higher Education"; Schwier and Wilson, "Unconventional Roles and Activities."
13. Intentional Futures, *Experience of Instructional Designers*, 3.
14. Rubley, "Course of Next-Generation Learning."
15. Tate, "Easing Instructional Designer–Faculty Conflicts."
16. Pollard and Kumar, "Roles, Challenges, and Supports," 4; see also Pan et al., "Pulling Tigers' Teeth"; Schwier et al., "Practice and Change Agency"; Sims and Koszalka, "New-Age Instructional Designer."
17. Roberts, "Trauma-Informed Teaching"; Substance Abuse and Mental Health Services Administration, *Trauma-Informed Care.*
18. Decherney and Levander, "Instructional Designer," para. 5.
19. Simon, "Loner's Sport?"

Bibliography

Anderson, Max C., Linda M. Love, and Faye L. Haggar. "Looking Beyond the Physician Educator: The Evolving Roles of Instructional Designers in Medical Education." *Medical Science Educator* 29, no. 2 (2019): 507–513. https://doi.org/10.1007/s40670-019-00720-6.

Bishop, M. J., Nancy O'Neill, and Paul Walsh. "Fostering a Culture of Academic Innovation in a Time of Crisis." In *Moving Horizontally: The New Dimensions of At-Scale Learning at the Time of COVID-19*, edited by Yakut Gazi and Nelson Baker, 101–114. Atlanta: Georgia Institute of Technology, 2020.

Decherney, Peter, and Caroline Levander. "The Hottest Job in Higher Education: Instructional Designer." *Inside Higher Ed*, April 24, 2020. https://www.insidehighered.com/digital-learning/blogs/education-time-corona/hottest-job-higher-education-instructional-designer.

Feldstein, Michael. "Learning Engineering Is Learning about Learning. We Need That Now More Than Ever." *EdSurge*, April 16, 2020. https://www.edsurge.com

/news/2020-04-16-learning-engineering-is-learning-about-learning-we-need-that-now-more-than-ever.

Garrett, Richard, Ron Legon, and Eric E. Fredericksen. *CHLOE 3: Behind the Numbers.* Annapolis, MD: Quality Matters, 2019. https://www.qualitymatters.org/qa-resources/resource-center/articles-resources/CHLOE-project.

———. *CHLOE 4: Navigating the Mainstream.* Annapolis, MD: Quality Matters, 2020. https://www.qualitymatters.org/qa-resources/resource-center/articles-resources/CHLOE-project.

Intentional Futures. *Instructional Design in Higher Education: A Report on the Role, Workflow, and Experience of Instructional Designers.* Seattle, WA: Intentional Futures, April, 2016. https://uploads-ssl.webflow.com/61bb092a5c21437cb3a10798/624241a510e63d6f7eee6cd0_Instructional-Design-in-Higher-Education-Report.pdf.

Jaschik, Scott, and Doug Lederman, eds. *Survey of Faculty Attitudes on Technology: A Study by Inside Higher Ed and Gallup.* Washington, DC: Inside Higher Ed, 2018. https://www.insidehighered.com/booklet/2018-survey-faculty-attitudes-technology.

———. *Survey of Faculty Attitudes on Technology: A Study by Inside Higher Ed and Gallup.* Washington, DC: Inside Higher Ed, 2019. https://www.insidehighered.com/booklet/2019-survey-faculty-attitudes-technology.

Morgan, Tannis. "Instructional Designers and Open Education Practices: Negotiating the Gap Between Intentional and Operational Agency." *Open Praxis* 11, no. 4 (December 31, 2019): 369–380. https://doi.org/10.5944/openpraxis.11.4.1011.

Moskal, Tami M. "Instructional Designers in Higher Education." Ph.D. dissertation, University of Nebraska, Lincoln, 2012. https://digitalcommons.unl.edu/cehsedaddiss/121/.

Pan, Cheng-Chang, Jennifer Deets, William Phillips, and Richard Cornell. "Pulling Tigers' Teeth Without Getting Bitten: Instructional Designers and Faculty." *Quarterly Review of Distance Education* 4, no. 3 (2003): 289–302.

Pollard, Rhiannon, and Swapna Kumar. "Instructional Designers in Higher Education: Roles, Challenges, and Supports." *Journal of Applied Instructional Design* 11, no. 1
(February, 2022): 1–13. https://edtechbooks.org/jaid_11_1/instructional_design.

Roberts, Leah M. "Trauma-Informed Teaching During COVID-19." Nashville, TN: Vanderbilt Center for Teaching, July 28, 2020. https://cft.vanderbilt.edu/2020/07/trauma-informed-teaching-during-covid-19.

Rubley, Julie, N. "Instructional Designers in Higher Ed: Changing the Course of Next-Generation Learning." *Chronicle of Higher Education*, 2016. https://interactive.holoniq.com/reports/2016_Instructional%20Designers_v9_Pearson_Interactive%20Final.pdf.

Schwier, Richard A., Katy Campbell, and Richard Kenny. "Instructional Designers' Observations about Identity, Communities of Practice and Change Agency."

Australasian Journal of Educational Technology 20, no. 1 (2004): 69–100. https://doi.org/10.14742/ajet.1368.
Schwier, Richard A., and Jay R. Wilson. "Unconventional Roles and Activities Identified by Instructional Designers." *Contemporary Educational Technology* 1, no. 2 (2010): 134–147. https://doi.org/10.30935/cedtech/5970.
Simon, Herbert A. "The Job of a College President." *Educational Record* 48, Winter (1967): 68–78. https://digitalcollections.library.cmu.edu/node/35317?search_api_fulltext=The%20job%20of%20a%20college%20president.%20.
———. "Need Teaching Be a Loner's Sport?" Lecture presented at the Center for Innovation in Learning, Carnegie Mellon University, Pittsburgh, PA, April 2, 1996. https://digitalcollections.library.cmu.edu/node/53830.
Sims, Roderick C., and Tiffany A. Koszalka."Competencies for the New-Age Instructional Designer." In *Handbook of Research on Educational Communications and Technology*, 3rd ed., edited by J. Michael Spector, M. David Merrill, Jeroen van Merriënboer, and Marcy P. Driscoll, 569–575. New York: Lawrence Erlbaum Associates, 2008.
Substance Abuse and Mental Health Services Administration. *Trauma-Informed Care in Behavioral Health Services.* Treatment Improvement Protocol (TIP) Series, No. 57. Rockville, MD: Substance Abuse and Mental Health Services Administration, 2014. https://www.ncbi.nlm.nih.gov/books/NBK207201.
Tate, Emily. "Easing Instructional Designer–Faculty Conflicts." *Inside Higher Ed*, May 2, 2017. https://www.insidehighered.com/digital-learning/article/2017/05/03/easing-conflicts-between-instructional-designers-and-faculty.

chapter 3

Creating Transformational Change through Learning Innovation Departments

Sean Hobson and Natalie Landman

In early 2020, COVID-19, a worldwide pandemic, forced every college and university worldwide to pivot to a remote-first model (online and digital teaching)—a model that was still a fringe activity for most institutions, and often viewed as a lesser option to traditional in-person learning. Data from the National Student Clearinghouse Research Center show that the COVID-19 outbreak precipitated a 6.6% decline in undergraduate Fall enrollment between 2019 and 2021.[1]

Many universities have announced integrations, hiring freezes, furloughs, and faculty cuts. Disruptions to college athletics, student housing, and international student enrollment have massive impacts on university budgets and operating priorities, and the long-term impacts won't be fully understood for years to come.

Although the pandemic is unquestionably a significant environmental event, the authors believe that it largely highlights a pre-existing problem best summarized by education writer and theorist Clay Shirkey, who stated, "The biggest threat to those of us working in colleges and universities is not video lectures or online tests. **It is the fact that we live in institutions perfectly adapted to an environment that no longer exists.**"[2]

In fact, higher education in the United States has been experiencing a massive environmental shift over the last two decades. This shift has been driven by technological advancements, changing demographics, international competition, and wavering confidence in outcomes against the rising cost and return on investment of the degree. And the pandemic has greatly accelerated the pace of these changes.

As the environment surrounding higher education institutions continues its rapid pace of change, do those in academia have strategies to help navigate the changing tides? **Does higher education's approach to change leave it more vulnerable to disruptive forces, or is higher education already a resilient and ever-changing industry?** Although many institutions have a change "management" strategy in place, very few have developed and implemented a change "design" strategy.

The stakes are high. Many universities are contemplating reinvention in the face of these changes,[3] yet the majority of change in universities to date has been incremental in scale and scope and faculty or institution-centric over student-centric.[4]

What we need is deliberate and designed "transformational change," which "involves the radical pursuit of design-specific aspirations that redefine the why, what, and how of a university's operations."[5] We believe that one way that institutions can position themselves for success is to establish units, departments, or centers dedicated to leading transformational change—what we call here "Learning Innovation Departments," or LIDs.

Joshua Kim and Edward Maloney define learning innovation as follows:

> The interplay between the complex set of practices, methods, and designs that are part of the attempts by higher education to improve teaching and student learning. The practices not only bring together learning science, applied educational technologies, and learning analytics, but they do so within the framework of the institutional structures, policies, investments, and strategic leadership that enable this work.

> In this respect, learning innovation is as much about innovations in teaching and learning (in the classroom, course, or curriculum) as it is about sustainable innovations at the institutional level.[6]

Although we agree with this definition of Learning Innovation, we also argue that some of these complex practices, methods, and designs may necessitate or lead to new frameworks and institutional structures, policies, and investments to be adopted outside the institution's traditional operating model(s). In this chapter, using Arizona State University (and one of its LIDs, EdPlus) as a case study, we argue that having a well-designed LID best positions the organization for continuous innovation and truly transformational change. Moreover, our argument contends this organizational development is key to successfully navigating the changing environment in and around higher education institutions.

Institutional transformation is not innovation, adaptation, or strategic change, as generally demonstrated within higher education.[7] Instead, transformation is more radical. It "(1) alters the culture of the institution by changing underlying assumptions and overt institutional behaviors, processes, and structures; (2) is deep and pervasive, affecting the whole institution; (3) is intentional; and (4) occurs over time."[8]

Michael Crow and Derrick Anderson likened routine and transformational change to organic and designed change, respectively: "Through organic [routine] change, a university's structure and practices adapt in response to external pressure or environmental stimulus. Organic change tends to be incremental in scale and scope and the general direction of a university's existing operational momentum."[9]

In turn, the goal of designed [transformational] change is to "devise a course of action aimed at changing existing situations to preferred ones."[10] If organic or routine change occurs naturally, designed or transformational change is intentional or *artificial*.[11] Adrianna Kezar discussed designed change as second-order change, "where the change process described is so substantial that it alters the operating system, underlying values, and culture of an organization or system."[12]

Although design and design thinking is most often considered in the context of specific products, services, or technologies, Richard Buchanan has pointed to an emerging design movement "that brings innovations . . . to organizations that have to adapt to new circumstances . . ." and where the focus of the design process is "not an artifact or a customer service, but the organization itself."[13] At its core, design thinking is a process, a series of steps to solve a problem.[14] By taking an imagine-the-possible approach, "Designers take on problems, model them, frame them, and create responses," thus bringing new things into the world.[15] The design process is iterative and exploratory, beginning with an idea, a brief, and finalizing with a product through experimentation and simulation.[16]

Organizations are increasingly drawn to the potential of design thinking in promoting transformation and innovation,[17] better decision-making,[18] and the creation of competitive advantages,[19] and so on. This new approach "is in large part a response to the increasing complexity of modern technology and modern business" and the recognition that the design of an organization has a significant impact on its performance.[20] Many corporations have established design programs and processes, and many universities have created curriculum and executive education programs teaching the design thinking process. Arizona State University (ASU) is no exception. In fact, in an internal email, ASU President Michael Crow characterized ASU as "a large, design-thinking organization." Moreover, by creating a dedicated learning innovation department (EdPlus), underpinned by instructional designers and design principles, technologists, and operators, the university has uniquely positioned itself for continuous transformational change, which is seeded not only within EdPlus but also by individual designers, departments, and organizations that are connected to and in some cases have spun off from the EdPlus model. We believe that the existence and work of this LID have allowed ASU to not only successfully navigate the challenges of environmental disruptions like the pandemic, but thrive despite them.

So what is a LID? Rooted in a services model culture of continuing and professional development centers, central information technology

(IT) offices, centers for teaching and learning, libraries, and technology transfer offices, LIDs (and the change agents working within them) are a new and necessary addition to the traditional university organizational structure. Although LIDs still offer traditional faculty services, such as pedagogical expertise and educational technology support, it is their new capabilities, such as business model design and creation, new product development, advanced operational support, partnership development, visual design, and communications in support of new revenue streams for the university that are unique to the modern LID (figure 3.1). We acknowledge and understand that for some universities, and the faculty and staff working within them, words like business model design and product development may be seen as counter to their academic mission or downright objectionable. However, we believe that units pushing the status quo are critical to the evolution of universities and that some organizational components of the university very much need to operate as a business to ensure organizational viability and long-term adaptation.

At its core, the LID has two primary assignments. First, and of most significance, is its role as a service unit that helps advance and propel the university forward in new and complex ways. Most often this is achieved through the design, delivery, support, and scaling of digital teaching and learning products such as online courses and degrees. In this role, the LID is at the service of students, faculty, university administration, and the partners it works with.

The second assignment, which works in balance with the first, is that of an innovation unit or Skunkworks.[21] Developed by Lockheed Aerospace Corporation during World War II, Skunkworks is a place and/or set of individuals handpicked to work on innovative, cross-functional projects without the constraints of standard administrative processes, routines, and speed of the organization.[22] These Skunkworks activities are meant to support both the service objective of the unit, as well as the overall mission of the institution. We highlight a few examples in the case study below.

To date, there is no blueprint in the literature for how to best design a LID. Much has been written on change in higher education, but

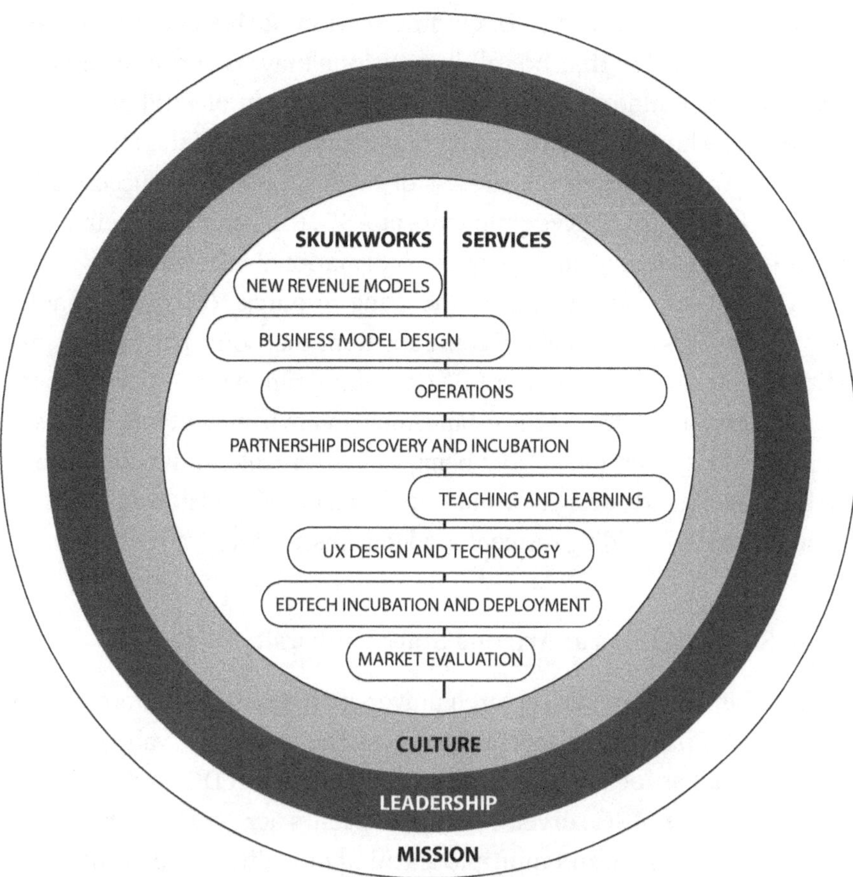

Figure 3.1. Characteristics of a Learning Innovation Department. UX = user experience.

few studies have investigated how to design the organizations necessary to keep higher education institutions viable and evolving in transformational ways. As a result, each new "college or university that is working on these transformations is doing so—de novo."[23]

The authors of this chapter acknowledge that what works for one university may be difficult to generalize across other academic institutions. However, we do believe some key characteristics and insights can be applied and adapted across the academic environment to reduce redundancy and enhance the probability of long-term success.

We highlight those in the concluding section of this chapter. Moreover, we recognize that not all institutions may have the necessary resources to build out their own full-scale version of EdPlus nor require one. Thus, we wanted to highlight that many of the structural elements that underpin the success of EdPlus, have been successfully adapted by individual academic units at ASU, thus creating their own, mini-LID sustainable engines of transformational innovation.

In addition, by examining your existing resources (people, technology) and processes, it might become apparent that some parts of the institution already function as a LID or require minimal additional input to take it to scale. The key is establishing an environment where these innovative activities move from being ad hoc, organic, and incremental, to being deliberate, designed, and transformational, which we believe is fundamental to building resilient academic institutions for the future.

Case Study: EdPlus at Arizona State University

ASU is the largest public research university in the United States, with four residential campuses spread across the so-called "valley of the Sun," as well as locations in California, Washington DC, and London, UK. In FY2022, ASU served 140,000 students across more than 500 academic programs and multiple learning modalities, including full-immersion, hybrid, and online. It wasn't always this way. In 2002, under the leadership of Michael M. Crow, ASU embarked on a major organizational transformation with goals to (1) significantly improve student success, (2) increase access for a broader base of students, and (3) dramatically grow its research expenditures. Twenty years later, those overarching goals remain, with constant and frequent evolutions in the tactics and strategies used to achieve and continuously improve on them.

The two major indicators of transformational change are attitudinal and structural evidence, and both must be present. Attitudinal evidence can be seen in how groups or individuals interact, how university officials refer to the campus and institution, the types of conversations, and new stakeholder relationships.[24] In turn, structural elements could include "substantial changes to the curriculum, new pedagogies, changes in student learning and assessment practices, new policies, the reallocation of funds, the creation of new department or institutional structures, and new processes or structures for decision-making."[25]

During President Crow's tenure, ASU has achieved both of these indicators. ASU's transformation has been supported by a lean, centralized management team whose members think entrepreneurially and make decisions quickly in pursuit of the above goals. Although ASU is a multi-campus university, it maintains integration as one entity to ensure consistent quality and strong governance, with clear and consistent communication.

Moreover, the evolution of university culture to one committed to a joint mission of academic excellence and access for all has resulted in remarkable outcomes. Since 2002, the population of first-generation students has tripled, accounting for over a third of the overall student population at the time of writing. In 2020, 50% of ASU's first-year students from Arizona identified as students of color, and 42% of all undergraduates were eligible for a Pell Grant. The US Department of Education also recently designated ASU as a Hispanic Serving Institution, a major recognition of the university's commitment to diversity and inclusion, and its efforts to serve the growing Hispanic community nationwide.

At the same time, ASU invested significant resources into evolving the institution toward a student-centric model that supports innovation, agility, change, and collaboration to deliver excellent education at scale. To that end, ASU established a dedicated learning innovation unit—**EdPlus**—which (1) builds and operates ASU Online that serves around 62,000 students enrolled in about 300 fully online degrees and certificates, and (2) advances a portfolio of transformational projects and partnerships. The impact of this structural change is reflected not only in the number and types of learners served, but also in freshman persistence and all measures of quality in ASU graduates. Parallel growth in research infrastructure and expenditures has made ASU the fastest-growing research university in the country, while largely maintaining the same faculty body.[26]

The origins of EdPlus can be traced back to ASU Online, a unit responsible for designing and managing fully online degree programs for ASU students. The early work at ASU Online was highly customized. A small team of instructional designers, media production experts, operators, and technologists offered training and learning design services to build online offerings for primarily in-person students.

A significant shift in strategy and structure came about when Philip Regier, who currently leads EdPlus, was appointed dean of ASU Online in 2009. Major transformations included (1) the development of incentive models for academic units and faculty, (2) reducing the course length from 16 to 7.5 weeks to allow for more frequent start periods, and (3) most notably, the establishment of a partnership with Pearson Education to help ASU promote its offering nationally, serving as one of the very first Online Program Management (OPM) partnerships.

In 2014, due to the growth of ASU Online and the role it was playing as the primary academic innovation department at the university, it became necessary to create EdPlus at ASU, which to this day serves as the umbrella organization for ASU Online and many of the other academic innovation activities necessary to help the university reach its objectives. In his introduction of this reorganization, ASU President Michael Crow described EdPlus at ASU as, "the enabler for the projection of our teaching, learning and discovery environment for the broadest audience possible using the most sophisticated learning tools and technologies that human beings can build."[27]

EdPlus has several components. Foundationally, it builds and operates ASU Online (the LID service function) in partnership with the ASU academic enterprise. The program catalog has evolved significantly in number and subject matter offerings over the years, with more than 300 fully online degrees and certificates focused primarily on the undergraduate learner.

In addition to ASU Online, EdPlus also advances a portfolio of transformational projects and partnerships (the LID Skunkworks/R&D function), including the Starbucks College Achievement Plan and PLuS Alliance, educational technology partnerships with Salesforce, Google, and YouTube, and the ASU/Global Silicon Valley (GSV) summit partnership and annual Educational Technology Conference to name a few.

Through its relationships with the ASU faculty and external partners, EdPlus has helped generate significant new tuition and grant revenues that support many parts of the institution beyond its online offerings. The innovative concept and development of EdPlus have also been instrumental in recognition of ASU as the "Most Innovative University in the Country" for eight consecutive years, from 2014 to 2021.[28]

The efforts that went into establishing EdPlus were also key to the seamless and successful transition to a remote-first teaching model when ASU came face to face with the realities of the pandemic in March 2020. During the transition from what was ASU Online into EdPlus, the university went through a significant instructional design process with thousands of faculty, built support systems to support learners remotely, and developed the working network and relationships between the enterprise technology office and critical operational units to deploy the necessary support infrastructure to faculty and students. The ongoing extension and evolution of these early investments in digital teaching and learning allowed the institution to pivot quickly and naturally to maintain its operations and deploy essential services to faculty and students.

To achieve and maintain this level of success, the LID's service function and the R&D or Skunkworks function must remain in balance. For example, some Skunkworks projects will require significant resources and may not lead to innovations. At the same time, these projects, although critical for the evolution and growth of the organization, should not distract from the unit's core service and revenue-generating functions. Conversely, if the unit is not consistently experimenting with new models and ideas, the core product will remain stagnant and fall at risk to the changes surrounding the institution.

To better demonstrate some of these phenomena, and rapid adaptation to a changing environment we explore one public/private Skunkworks project between the National World War II Museum in New Orleans and ASU's School of Historical, Philosophical, and Religious Studies (SHIPRS), supported by EdPlus.

In 2015, fresh off starting a capital fundraising campaign for its physical infrastructure, the National World War II Museum in New Orleans was forced to deal with its own environmental change circumstances. Widely regarded as one of the best museums in the country, the Museum suddenly found itself shut off from the world for nearly a year after Hurricane Katrina ravaged the city and cut off the museum from its constituents. During this time, the leadership of the museum decided to consider a foundational question, "How can we evolve to be a museum without walls?" Through a series of conversations, they ended up on the other side of the country, working with Arizona State University to develop a fully online master's degree in World War II History.

EdPlus helped design the vision, the mechanics of the partnership, and the business model, i.e., the Skunkworks activity, while also providing more traditional services in the form of instructional design and educational technology support. EdPlus also served as the conduit between the faculty in ASU's School of Historical and Philosophical Sciences, and the historians and unparalleled content curated by the museum. Both the museum and the university shared in recruitment and enrollment costs and risks, and the resulting tuition revenues from the success of the program.

The result of the partnership is a first-of-its-kind degree in World War II studies, which combines the research and teaching prowess of the university with unique narrative-based content and assets of the museum, including their historians. In addition to the degree, the two teams built a series of non-credit courses that align to the degree, but also build off the narrative and topics that visitors would experience in the museum. This provides a new model for ASU to expand its access and impact through public/private partnerships while generating the new resources required to support the initiative.

Conclusion

To be clear, the authors acknowledge the success of EdPlus is highly dependent on its context within ASU, and the environmental circumstances surrounding the creation of EdPlus are unique to that point in time. A few critical events worth noting that created a unique environment for the establishment of EdPlus included:

- A dramatic reduction in per-student funding from the state due to the 2008–2009 recession.
- Political and consumer backlash to for-profit online education in the form of regulations and reduction in for-profit enrollment.
- ASU Online was an early market entrant offering fully online undergraduate programs in the western United States.
- Unique alignment among mission, president, provost, and unit leadership.

However, we can't help but wonder if the pandemic, combined with the other environmental conditions discussed at the start of this chapter is creating another moment of opportunity.

Although EdPlus itself has gone through a major transformation—from a unit of fewer than 20 staff with a singular objective (to build and grow new online programs), to an organization of more than 600 employees involved in a broad range of activities and initiatives, the authors think there are several foundational recommendations for any institution, consortia, or higher education organization that is looking to seed Learning Innovation from the inside out.

First, it is critical to establish or have plans to establish **alignment** across the LID's governance, leadership, culture, organizational design, objectives, and resources. While this may seem obvious, we find it rarely the case that full alignment occurs, and the result is a state of misfit between the context, people, and productivity of the unit.[29] Each of these themes should also be adapted to the mission of the LID, and not transferred over from any other service model within the existing institution. The concept of alignment is also a grounding theoretical model in the instructional design literature, which is increasingly a core and leading function of LIDs.[30]

We also believe the LID must remain **adaptive** to the changing environment within and outside of the parent institution. The LID should serve as the beachhead for new ideas to incubate and new revenue opportunities to be explored, and it should also serve as the interpretation layer between the comfortable and the unknown. Much of the staff in a LID should be able to thrive in ambiguity and help imagine and execute new models for the institution.

The last critical and non-negotiable item when standing up or converting an existing unit to an LID is selecting the right leadership. The right LID leader(s) should understand and have support from the academic organization. The right LID should understand the business of and around higher education. It should also understand the role of pedagogy, and how technology and design can be thoughtfully deployed in the advancement of the university's learning innovation objectives.

We believe that several critical questions and considerations should be addressed by an academic institution or administrator contemplating building an LID in support of transformational change efforts:

1. **What are the environmental factors** necessitating transformational change?
2. **Is there clear alignment around the need for transformational change** among the faculty, administrative staff, and its oversight stakeholders?
3. **How will you measure success?** What outcomes are driving your educational technology strategy and deployment?
4. **What is the institutional appetite** and process for building and supporting public/private partnerships?
5. **How will the LID be governed?**
6. **What are the attributes of the leader(s) of your LID?** What is their relationship with the academic core and acumen for the business of higher education?
7. **How should the LID fit into the overarching organizational structure** of the academic unit or institution?
8. **How will the LID be funded?** Will it be centrally funded or be able to run its operations from the revenue it generates?
9. **What are the job functions and competencies for the LID team?** What makes them unique, and how will you recruit them?

To ensure an academic institution's viability and long-term sustainability in the constantly evolving environment, we believe continuous innovations must permeate all aspects of the organization. One way that can be accomplished is by establishing and nurturing the LID organizations or activities within your institutions. We are optimistic about the recognition and growth of these organizations for the future vitality of the academic community and its mission for public support. The LID work is happening across higher education in many organizational design manifestations. From the entrepreneurial activities of a single instructional designer to organizations as big as EdPlus, both LIDs and their stakeholders are present in some form in almost every higher education organization. We hope this chapter provides this community of professionals with a framework to organize their efforts and highlight their role and contribution to the mission and objectives of their parent institutions.

Notes

1. Conley and Massa, "The Great Interruption."
2. Clay, "Higher Education's Golden Age."
3. Kezar, *How Colleges Change.*
4. Crow and Anderson, "Design-Build: Making Sense."
5. Crow and Anderson, "Design-Build: Making Sense," 2.
6. Maloney and Kim, *Learning Innovation*, 6.
7. Eckel and Kezar, *Taking the Reins.*
8. Eckel and Kezar, *Taking the Reins*, 17.
9. Crow and Anderson, "Design-Build: Making Sense," 2.
10. Simon (1998), p. 67, as quoted by Crow and Anderson, "Design-Build: Making Sense," 2.
11. Simon (1998), as quoted by Crow and Anderson, "Design-Build: Making Sense."
12. Kezar, *How Colleges Change*, 85.
13. Buchanan, "Worlds in the Making."
14. Brown, *Inspires Innovation.*
15. Pendleton and Brown, *White Water World.*
16. Razzouk and Shute, "What Is Design Thinking"; Van De Ven et al., "Returning to the Frontier."
17. Brown, *Inspires Innovation.*
18. Liedtka, "Perspective: Linking Design Thinking."
19. Martin, *Design of Business.*
20. Kolko, "Design Thinking"; Doty et al., "Two Configurational Theories"; Burton, "Fit, Misfit, and Design."
21. Selingo, "Chief Innovation Officer."

22. Oliver and Cole, "Inductive Model."
23. Maloney and Kim, *Learning Innovation*, 15.
24. Kezar, *How Colleges Change*, 86.
25. Kezar, *How Colleges Change*, 86.
26. Crow, "National Service Universities."
27. Arizona State University, *ASU EdPlus*.
28. Greguska, "ASU Ranked No. 1."
29. Donaldson and Joffe, "Fit."
30. Biggs, "Constructive Alignment."

Bibliography

Arizona State University. *ASU EdPlus: Arizona State University*, 2014. https://vimeo.com/111799827.

Biggs, John. "Enhancing Teaching through Constructive Alignment." *Higher Education* 32, no. 3 (October 1996): 347–364. https://doi.org/10.1007/BF00138871.

Brown, Tim. *Change by Design: How Design Thinking Transforms Organizations and Inspires Innovation*. New York: Harper Business, 2009.

Buchanan, Richard. "Worlds in the Making: Design, Management, and the Reform of Organizational Culture." *She Ji: The Journal of Design, Economics, and Innovation* 1, no. 1 (2015): 5–21. https://doi.org/10.1016/j.sheji.2015.09.003.

Burton, Richard M. "Fit, Misfit, and Design: JOD Studies That Touch Reality." *Journal of Organization Design* 9, no. 1 (December 2020): 5. https://doi.org/10.1186/s41469-020-00081-0.

Conley, Bill and Richard Massa. "The Great Interruption." *Inside Higher Ed*, February 27, 2022. https://www.insidehighered.com/admissions/views/2022/02/28/enrollment-changes-colleges-are-feeling-are-much-more-covid-19.

Crow, Michael. *National Service Universities: Arizona State University and The Fifth Wave of American Higher Education*, version 2.5. Tempe, AZ: Arizona State University Office of the President, 2017. https://president.asu.edu/sites/default/files/national_service_universities_2018.pdf.

Crow, Michael. *The Fifth Wave*. Baltimore, MD: Johns Hopkins University Press, 2020. https://doi.org/10.1353/book.73164.

Crow, Michael M., and Derrick M. Anderson. "Design-Build: Making Sense of Routine and Transformational Change in Higher Education." In *Taking the Lead: A Guide for Emerging Leaders in Academic Medical Centers*, edited by A. M. Cauce, J. S Antony, T. P. Nicola, and L. M. Gangone. Cham, Switzerland: Springer International, 2022. https://doi.org/10.1007/978-3-031-16711-9.

Donaldson, Lex, and Greg Joffe. "Fit—the Key to Organizational Design." SSRN Scholarly Paper. Rochester, NY, December 30, 2014. https://papers.ssrn.com/abstract=2549607.

Doty, D. H., W. H. Glick, and G. P. Huber. "Fit, Equifinality, and Organizational Effectiveness: A Test of Two Configurational Theories." *Academy of Manage-*

ment Journal 36, no. 6 (December 1, 1993): 1196–1250. https://doi.org/10.2307/256810.

Eckel, Peter D., and Adrianna J. Kezar. *Taking the Reins: Institutional Transformation in Higher Education.* ACE/Praeger Series on Higher Education. Westport, CT: Praeger, 2003.

Greguska, Emma. "ASU Ranked No. 1 in Innovation for 6th Year by US News and World Report." *ASU News*, September 13, 2020. https://news.asu.edu/20200913-asu-news-us-news-world-report-no-1-innovation-sixth-year.

Kezar, Adrianna J. *How Colleges Change: Understanding, Leading, and Enacting Change.* 2nd ed. New York: Routledge, 2018.

Kezar, Adrianna, and Peter Eckel. "Examining the Institutional Transformation Process: The Importance of Sensemaking, Interrelated Strategies, and Balance." *Research in Higher Education* 43, no. 3 (2002): 295–328. https://www.jstor.org/stable/40196456.

Kim, Joshua, and Edward Maloney. *Learning Innovation and the Future of Higher Education.* Tech.Edu: A Hopkins Series on Education and Technology. Baltimore: Johns Hopkins University Press, 2020.

Kolko, Jon. "Design Thinking Comes of Age." *Harvard Business Review*, September 1, 2015. https://hbr.org/2015/09/design-thinking-comes-of-age.

Liedtka, Jeanne. "Perspective: Linking Design Thinking with Innovation Outcomes through Cognitive Bias Reduction: Design Thinking." *Journal of Product Innovation Management* 32, no. 6 (November 2015): 925–938. https://doi.org/10.1111/jpim.12163.

Martin, Roger L. *The Design of Business: Why Design Thinking Is the Next Competitive Advantage.* Boston: Harvard Business Press, 2009.

Meyer, Kyle P., and Rob Kramer. *Taking the Lead: A Guide for Emerging Leaders in Academic Medical Centers.* Cham, Switzerland: Springer International, 2022. https://doi.org/10.1007/978-3-031-16711-9.

Oliver, David, and Benjamin M. Cole. "The Interplay of Product and Process in Skunkworks Identity Work: An Inductive Model." *Strategic Management Journal* 40, no. 9 (September 2019): 1491–1514. https://doi.org/10.1002/smj.3034.

Pendleton-Jullian, Ann M., and John Seely Brown. *Design Unbound: Designing for Emergence in a White Water World.* Infrastructures. Cambridge, MA: MIT Press, 2018.

Razzouk, Rim, and Valerie Shute. "What Is Design Thinking and Why Is It Important?" *Review of Educational Research* 82, no. 3 (September 2012): 330–348. https://doi.org/10.3102/0034654312457429.

Selingo, Jeffrey J. "The Rise of the Chief Innovation Officer in Higher Education." *Entangled Solutions*, January 2018: 8. https://ai.umich.edu/wp-content/uploads/The-Rise-of-the-Chief-Innovation-Officer-in-HigherEd.pdf.

Shirky, Clay. "The End of Higher Education's Golden Age." *Shirky.com* (blog). January 29, 2014. http://shirky.com/weblog/2014/01/there-isnt-enough-money-to-keep-educating-adults-the-way-were-doing-it.

Smalley, Andrew. *Higher Education Responses to Coronavirus (COVID-19)*. National Council of State Legislatures, last modified March 22, 2021, https://www.ncsl.org/research/education/higher-education-responses-to-coronavirus-covid-19.aspx.

Simon, Herbert A. *The Sciences of the Artificial*. 3rd ed. Cambridge, MA: MIT Press, 1996.

Van De Ven, Andrew H., Martin Ganco, and C. R. (Bob) Hinings. "Returning to the Frontier of Contingency Theory of Organizational and Institutional Designs." *Academy of Management Annals* 7, no. 1 (June 2013): 393–440. https://doi.org/10.5465/19416520.2013.774981.

"What We Do | EdPlus at ASU." Arizona State University. Accessed May 7, 2023. https://edplus.asu.edu/what-we-do.

chapter 4

An Ecology of Change in Higher Education

Michael Goudzwaard and Cynthia A. Cogswell

In the spring of 2020, colleges and universities underwent radical changes, shifting in-person instruction to emergency remote teaching in response to the COVID-19 pandemic. Higher education institutions are historically slow to change, but experience "ecosystemwide adaptation"[1] when external forces are great enough, providing the possibility of a revolutionized system.[2] This comparison of universities to ecological systems provides the opportunity to examine the behaviors and organizational principles of universities during the early parts of the pandemic.

Cynthia (Cindy) A. Cogswell is currently the Director of Data Strategy for Student Affairs, Global Programs and Student Life at New York University and previously worked for Ohio University as the Director of Strategic Planning and Assessment. Michael (Mike) Goudzwaard is the Associate Director of Learning Innovation in the Dartmouth Center for the Advancement of Learning at Dartmouth College. Mike was introduced to the principles of ecological systems in graduate school by his professor and author of *Myth of Progress*,[3] Tom Wessels. During the last decade of teaching and working in higher education, an ecological framework seemed to lend some understanding to the complex systems of universities. The rapid changes of the COVID-19 pandemic provided a new opportunity to apply ecological principles to a rapid-change event.

After the first sprint of emergency remote teaching to address the COVID-19 pandemic, we took a collective moment to talk to some colleagues about their experiences of those and subsequent months. This resulting chapter brings new understanding of our own work during and post pandemic through talking with colleagues at other institutions about their work and impacts and applying a lens of ecological systems, and it provides practical guidance to readers based on these cases.

In 2021, we interviewed educators and administrators at seven higher education institutions in the United States to better understand how they managed early pandemic changes to their educational operations. Taking the principles of complex natural systems, we asked how they might apply to the systems of colleges and universities during the pandemic, and if they might apply to long-term changes in higher education. We found that ecological systems provided a useful framework to understand the rapid change during the pandemic. Institutions adapted to the environmental changes and some of those adaptations permanently changed how individuals and the system operate. Finally, we provide some practical advice for educational practitioners about adapting during change, suggestions to get started, and how to be more ready for the next rapid change in higher education.

Guiding Ecological Frameworks

Ecology is a branch of biology that focuses on how organisms relate to one another as well as their surroundings. Using an ecological framework to understand higher education is not new. Samuel Fugazzotto examined the logic of ecology and evolution to unpack why research-oriented higher education has shifted to be more entrepreneurial and suggested that institutions need not move in this way. Fugazzotto was examining from a place of financial restraint that institutions were evolving in search of more funding—and used an ecological approach to suggest other ways of evolving.[4]

Ronald Barnett looked more widely at the evolutionary patterns of universities proposing three kinds of universities: the metaphysical university, "university-in-itself," and the research university.[5] These universities strive to increase academic impact and thus measure outcomes to maximize economic prosperity. Further, universities can take on forms, and he conceptualized the ecology university concepts. The ecological concept "comprises two dimensions, authenticity and responsibility, satisfying both inward quality and outward advancement."[6] This is suggesting that the metaphysical, the "university-in-itself," and the research universities could move toward an ecological university, therefore evolving to be more sensitive and responsive to their environments.

Further structuring an ecological approach, Félix Guattari identified three dimensions within ecology worth examining—the environment, social relations, and human subjectivity.[7] As summarized by Chia-Ling Wang, "Guattari proposed that people experience a singular event that changes their lives . . . this chance event is a singular point that can lead people in a new direction and enable alternative movement in life."[8] In this study, we consider a single event that changed campus lives.

In his book, *The Myth of Progress: Toward a Sustainable Future*,[9] Tom Wessels establishes two types of ecological systems, linear and complex. Linear forces might be applied to colleges and universities such as governmental mandates or public health guidance; however, the universities themselves are complex systems because they have embedded feedback that interact with each other. To Wessels, the attributes of a complex system include

- emergent properties: the properties of a system develop through interactions, rather than by design or mandate;
- self-organization: there is increasing complexity in a complex system over time;
- nestedness: complex systems are embedded within larger complex systems; and
- bifurcation: complex systems remain more or less status quo until there is a big shift.

With this theory, our research question is this: does an ecological framework apply to higher education institutional adaptations to COVID-19?

Method

We conducted interviews to explore this question. With institutional review board approval, virtual video interviews were held using a semi-structured guide, designed to facilitate a one-hour discussion.[10] The purposeful sample ($n = 7$) was selected to maximize variation by institution type, individual role, and gender. Institutions ranged from community college to research comprehensive, public to private, small to large. Individuals' roles varied from instructor to director, administrator, and vice president. We included institutions regardless of level of remote learning.

We leveraged a two-cycle coding technique.[11] First, we met to review recordings and facilitator notes, synthesizing interview responses using a table to organize themes by question. Next, we worked separately to re-review transcripts to integrate the findings for reliability. Through discussion, working case by case, we arrived at case descriptions and findings, presented below.

Seven Cases

LaGuardia Community College. LaGuardia Community College, a public two-year institution in Long Island, New York, enrolled approximately 17,000 undergraduate students in 2020.[12] We spoke with the First Year Institute Program (FYIP), which provides a variety of programs and support services for new and first-year continuing students. Pre-pandemic, FYIP offered 40 sections of math and English every three weeks. All courses, instructional materials, and services are provided to eligible students at no cost.

FYIP traditionally relied on students coming to the physical campus for advising, mentoring, technology use, scheduling, and other academic support. In a rapid shift to remote operations, they adapted to provide technology at pick-up points to students who needed it. Lacking even an office phone that could be accessed remotely, they quickly established new phone supports using freely available tools. What had been previously run out of a single physical location spanned time and space to meet student needs.

The First Year Institute Program provides an example of self-organization. FYIP traditionally relies on students' ability to access the campus to receive support, technology access, and mentoring. With the access to campus gone, each of those functions needed to be addressed by a more complex sub-systems, providing loaner technology and internet access. A practical take away from this institution is offering core functions in a variety of modalities to meet differing student needs.

University of Texas at Austin. The University of Texas at Austin (UT Austin), a public research university in Austin, Texas, enrolls approximately 50,000 students. We spoke with the First-Year Experience Office (FYE), whose work focuses on coordinating signature courses and first-year learning communities. Signature courses are credit-bearing courses taught by faculty with approximately 220 available options. All first year and transfer students are required to enroll. First year learning communities organize students into clustered courses. Additionally they meet weekly in a non-credit seminar with their academic advisor and a peer mentor.

Pre-COVID, the FYE met with faculty to prepare, but in light of pandemic adaptations, they added optional training on how to teach online and engage and connect with students. The FYE worked with their center for teaching and learning to create additional tools for faculty.

Faculty were coached intentionally on how to create connections with students in these gateway courses. Center for teaching and learning staff discussed how to model their humanness, recognizing that these faculty might be the only point of connection to campus that these students have. Other campuses could consider coaching on these same topics in mentorship models, in large entry-level courses, and with new faculty to set the campus precedent for empathy with students at all times, pandemic or not.

Princeton University. Princeton University, a private non-profit research university located in Princeton, New Jersey, enrolls around

7,800 students. We spoke with the Emma Bloomberg Center for Access and Opportunity to learn about the Freshman Scholars Institute (FSI) and the Freshmen Scholars Connect (FSC). FSI is a seven-week residential summer program for "first-generation college students and/or from lower socio-economic backgrounds." This is also an opportunity for incoming students to "experience the intellectual, co-curricular, and social life at Princeton."[13] FSC is an online alternative to FSI; however, its courses were non-credit-bearing prior to the pandemic.

In the summer of 2020, FSI and FSC were merged into a single online summer pre-enrollment experience. For the first time, credit could be earned for the one or two online courses participants took during the summer program. Prior to 2020, FSI provided participants receiving any amount of aid with room and board and all tuition/fees covered for participation; in 2020, FSI participants were offered a stipend to take the place of room and board. Additionally, technology gaps were addressed by providing Wi-Fi hotspots and laptops to students who needed them.

The online version of FSI lacked the social and informal connections; sharing meals together and walking around campus were an important part of building community. FSI introduced an online discussion platform, which allowed students some of the connections that were lost to the pivot online.

Princeton's first year program, like many of the programs we examined, faced a lack of social connection that had previously been met by program students being physically on campus together during the summer program. Princeton introduced a new online discussion board (Discord) where students could interact outside of the academic portions of the program providing an example of self-organization. That online discussion space continues today for students to continue to connect even as they are located back on campus, adding a beneficial, but more complex layer to social connection of program participants.

We appreciated how the COVID-19 adaptation of FSI created digital communities, using chatting platforms like Discord and digital events. And, unlike prior to the pandemic, these continued beyond 2021. Even though the formal FSI program ends at the start of fall term, the students from the program continued to use Discord to connect with the community. Readers could consider this when fusing communities in their campuses. Although funneling all course-related communication through a learning management system is organized, it is also likely to cease to be used at the end of term. Could you suggest to student groups that they use chatting platforms (such as Slack or Discord) to connect with each other? Or the same to a faculty or staff book club?

Dartmouth College. Dartmouth College, a private non-profit research university in Hanover, New Hampshire, enrolls approximately 6,000 students. We spoke with the First-Year Student Enrichment Program (FYSEP), which is a pre-matriculation residential summer program for first generation, low-income students. FYSEP provides a "rigorous, dynamic and transformative experience that puts participants in a position to thrive at Dartmouth both academically and socially."[14]

In the summer of 2020, FYSEP's academic courses were offered remotely on Zoom. One challenge was addressing the social components of the typical on-campus experience. Shared experiences are difficult to replicate remotely. To address this challenge, faculty made "virtual floors," grouping students together as if they were living on campus. They also introduced games, such as Assassin, to provide social engagement outside of the curriculum.

The summer courses are traditionally project-based, including one project involving growing plants and measuring growth. FYSEP attempted to mail students the seeds and supplies, but quickly realized that seeds are not easily shipped internationally due to customs restrictions. Additionally, students were globally located with little overlapping daytime hours, making group work nearly impossible. An additional pressure was that students were sharing their space with their families, with responsibilities to contribute and engage with their families.

As examples of nestedness, UT Austin and Dartmouth both saw collaboration across departments and units to rapidly develop training and resources for faculty and students shifting to a remote teaching and learning environment. In these trainings, the concept of care for students was emphasized as faculty became the front line of their institutions' many functions. The functions of student affairs and academic affairs were blurred in emergency remote teaching. However, as various units continue to self-organize, complexity increased, establishing and reestablishing boundaries.

Dartmouth's case illustrates that to some extent, the COVID-19 adaptations had limits. All things cannot be replicated online, even with hard work and thoughtfulness.

Vanderbilt University. Vanderbilt University, a private non-profit research university in Nashville, Tennessee, enrolls around 13,500 students. We spoke with the Center for Teaching (CFT). During the summer of 2020, the CFT staff began preparing Vanderbilt's approximately 500 faculty, many who had never taught online before, to teach remotely for Fall 2020. Each staff member developed at least one workshop that could be flexibly deployed and repeated. The demand for workshops quickly outpaced available staff time to mentor faculty cohorts. With support from university leadership, the CFT appointed faculty who had completed the institute as peer mentors for additional institute cohorts. The faculty mentors were paid a stipend in exchange for their service during the summer, although many mentors embraced the opportunity to "do something" to prepare for an unknown fall semester.

The CFT established a $500 grant fund with simple award criteria. If $500 could enable you to continue or pilot some engagement with your students in a course, that fully met the expectations of the grant. Faculty were grateful for this show and offer of support to allow flexible innovation within their courses.

An example of bifurcation, Vanderbilt's teaching and learning center experienced a rapid increase in the number of faculty who engaged with their center in preparing to teach remotely. The success of the first cohorts provided positive feedback, increasing participation and causing the bifurcation event of trainers and mentors being recruited from the faculty, a function that was traditionally only served with center staff. The incentive of paying faculty mentors was further positive feedback, allowing the change to persist for the summer and to scale to nearly half the teaching faculty.

Vanderbilt's approach to training faculty to become cohort leaders to new institute participants complexified their educational development model. This example of self-organization provided new "energy" to course delivery by providing micro grants ($500), resulting in an increase of complexity of courses because faculty can experiment in their teaching practice. Imagine how different post-secondary learning would be if modest funding (even $100) was available to instructors to enhance their courses?

Emergent properties are the properties of a system that develop through interactions, rather than by design or mandate (self-organized task forces and informational sharing). At Vanderbilt, the interaction between the Center for Teaching and faculty in the early cohorts of the summer institute led to increasing demand, need for more mentors, and ultimately the train-the-trainer model of faculty development. This was held up as one of the most successful partnerships between CFT and the Vanderbilt faculty to date.

Ohio University. Ohio University, a public research university in Athens, Ohio, enrolls 25,000 students. We spoke with a senior student affairs leader. With a rural campus and staff living in remote locations, they were challenged to create access in a distanced campus. First, many staff worked on campus and exclusively had technology on campus, so an immediate barrier was to identify portable technology for staff to work remotely. Secondly, some staff could not afford internet at home. Third, some employees shared that their home dynamic was not conducive to working from home.

Student Affairs was invited to meetings and conversations with many new partners and at senior levels. One leader attributed this rapid change and staffs' willingness to join efforts outside their stated responsibilities as a response to the "senses of the enormity of the work." Due to these new collaborations, the Division of Student Affairs' reputation grew within the broader Ohio community.

Although the levels and rate of information sharing proliferated, this did not always lead to faster decisions. "Conversations overlapped and intertwined," noted our interviewee. "Sometimes you had the right technical people in the room, but not the right political people in the room to say, 'this is what we should be doing.'"

An example of nestedness, the Division of Student Affairs held online town halls to share information about the rapidly changing divisional-, institutional-, and state-level plans for the upcoming semester. These meetings were often held when there were more questions than answers, but many staff outside of the division attended just to bring whatever information was shared back to their own work units, fuzzing those previous boundaries of information.

Transferring learnings from Ohio University, how can departments and divisions be brought into conversations beyond their silos? In addition, how can we foster communication that is transparent and accessible to all, untethered from communication hierarchies, especially in tense times?

New York University. New York University (NYU), a private, non-profit research university in New York City, New York, enrolls approximately 60,000 students. The city and campus were hit hard early in the pandemic, experiencing loss of faculty, staff, and students. An early campus adjustment was to ask the campus leader of the health center to be a part of how the university would structure its response to the pandemic. The campus COVID-19 response team was established to bring together staff, medical experts, and a few administrators to design the process and protocol for quarantine and isolation. Further, if any other group, task force, or committee needed to consult on COVID-19-related protocols, they were provided with a university-appointed medical expert. These consulting medical experts became de facto members of these smaller groups, sharing medical and operational information at many levels of the organization.

With new committees and task forces on campus, NYU tried to identify a response that kept pace with the rate of change. Key groups met every day to keep moving forward. NYU's practice of providing medical experts to any administrative group making decisions on strategy and operations stands out as emergent practice. As the experts interacted with the groups to which they were appointed, they became embedded in those groups, contributing beyond their initial consultations. When we spoke, 18 months into the pandemic, our interviewee shared that many of these groups still meet although the pace has slowed to either a couple of days a week or once a week.

Recentering

Our guiding research question was, does an ecological framework apply to higher education's response in COVID-19? We found that it does in most cases. We were encouraged by the many instances where the pandemic aided in removing barriers and made work more equitable and accessible to underrepresented populations and implore readers to do the same as we look to the future. The comparison of linear and complex systems provided lenses to analyze iterative and rapid change. The ecological framework of complex systems lends analyses to what we now see as partial pendulum swing returning to previous operational conditions at many institutions. However, other ecological frameworks might have provided more structure for the cases.[15] Further, our framework failed to adapt as the stories unfolded with time in the cases. Ecological systems are inherently impacted by external forces and respond accordingly.

There were some instances where the change was, perhaps, not disruptive enough. After the early months of the pandemic, the temporary credit granting of online courses at the Ivy League institutions waned. The requirement and option for almost all work to be performed remotely also faded.

Having examined these seven institutions' navigation of rapid change, we hope some adaptations will persist, such as increased support for students, increasing faculty engagement with teaching and learning development, working across silos, and making resources more available to those with diverse needs. Practically, this could look like the following:

- Increased flexibility in use of technology for administrative functions and services to students, staff, and faculty.
- Lowered thresholds and access to funding (such as $500 or $100) to improve classroom instruction available to faculty.
- Doing something, anything to increase support for students.
- Coaching faculty on how to empathize and show their humanness to their students.
- Continuing to offer at distance resources.

- Offering technology and internet connectivity to those need it.
- More specifically than just a general increase of empathy, continuing to accommodate students with temporary needs (such as when they are sick, injured, or have travel difficulties)—keeping the guidance of how faculty and staff can support this within a residential higher education context.

As leaders and innovators, we might clutch to bifurcation magnitudes of change as the only force great enough to make swift and large-scale changes. We know from complex ecological systems that after such disruption, the system again seeks a steady state. We would do well to understand these natural cycles and welcome the new steady state, realizing it will never be the old state (or the previous normal). When the next bifurcation occurs, be it through political, climate change, or social movements, you should experiment with new modes of academic credit, teaching grants, and any ideas to meet students where they are. Don't worry if an idea is not sustainable over time. Not all these ideas will last, but when the new steady state arrives, the system will have settled somewhere quite different, somewhere more centered on learning.

Notes

1. Maloney and Kim, "Learning from COVID-19."
2. Boyd et al., "Flexible Course Design."
3. Wessels, *The Myth of Progress.*
4. Fugazzotto, "On the Evolution of Colleges and Universities."
5. Barnett, "Response to Pavel Zgaga's."
6. Wang, "Curricula without Boundaries," 1404.
7. Guattari, *The Three Ecologies.*
8. Wang, "Curricula without Boundaries," 1406.
9. Wessels, *The Myth of Progress.*
10. Patton, *Qualitative Research and Evaluation Methods.*
11. Saldaña, *Coding Manual for Qualitative Researchers.*
12. LaGuardia Community College reported in their *Institutional Profile* an all-students total of 16,952 for 2020. That is the timeframe of when the interview was conducted. Enrollment has declined since 2020. La Guardia Community College Office of Institutional Research and Assessment, *Institutional Profile*, 7.
13. Princeton University, "Freshman Scholars Institute."

14. Dartmouth College, "About FYSEP."
15. Bronfenbrenner, *Ecology of Human Development.*

Bibliography

Barnett, Ronald. "Response to Pavel Zgaga's Review of Being a University." *Studies in Philosophy and Education* 31, no. 4 (2012): 427–429. https://doi.org/10.1007/s11217-012-9305-8.

Boyd, Diane E., Kent Andersen, Lew Ludwig, and Amy E. Jasperson. "'Designing into the Unknown': Harnessing the Promise of Flexible Course Design." *Change (New Rochelle, N.Y.)* 53, no. 5 (2021): 33–40. https://doi.org/10.1080/00091383.2021.1963153.

Bronfenbrenner, Urie. *The Ecology of Human Development Experiments by Nature and Design*. Cambridge, MA: Harvard University Press, 1996.

Dartmouth College. "About FYSEP | First Generation Office." Accessed February 22, 2022. https://students.dartmouth.edu/fgo/about/about-fysep.

Fugazzotto, Sam J. "On the Evolution of Colleges and Universities." *Tertiary Education and Management* 16, no. 4 (December 1, 2010): 303–312. https://doi.org/10.1080/13583883.2010.532564.

Guattari, Félix. *The Three Ecologies*. English ed. London: Athlone Press, 2000.

LaGuardia Community College, Office of Institutional Research and Assessment. *Institutional Profile*. New York: LaGuardia Community College. https://www.laguardia.edu/uploadedfiles/main_site/content/ir/docs/institutional-profile-2022.pdf.

Maloney, Edward, and Josh Kim. "Learning from COVID-19." *Inside Higher Ed.* Accessed November 18, 2022. https://www.insidehighered.com/blogs/learning-innovation/learning-covid-19.

Patton, Michael Quinn. *Qualitative Research and Evaluation Methods*. 3rd ed. Thousand Oaks, CA: Sage, 2002.

Princeton University. "Frequently Asked Questions | Freshman Scholars Institute." Accessed February 22, 2022. https://fsi.princeton.edu/faq.

Saldaña, Johnny. *The Coding Manual for Qualitative Researchers*. 3rd ed. Los Angeles: Sage, 2016.

Wang, Chia-Ling. "Curricula without Boundaries: Developing an Ecological Connection for Higher Education Curricula." *Educational Philosophy and Theory* 46, no. 13 (2014): 1402–1411. https://doi.org/10.1080/00131857.2014.964162.

Wessels, Tom. *The Myth of Progress: Toward a Sustainable Future*. Rev. and expanded ed. Book Collections on Project MUSE. Baltimore: Project Muse, 2013.

chapter 5

Digital Education for Access and Equity

Annie Sadler, Martin Kurzweil, and Matthew Rascoff

There is substantial evidence that high school students who take college-level courses realize substantial benefits in terms of their college access and attainment.[1] However, differential access to these programs, in general, and to programs with different characteristics, appear to reinforce systemic socioeconomic and racial inequities.[2] Black, Latinx, and Indigenous students, and lower-income students in general, are most likely to have access to Advanced Placement (AP) courses or dual-enrollment courses taught by high school teachers with minimal training and support. With some important exceptions, highly trained faculty at selective, well-resourced colleges have offered courses to high school students through expensive summer schools accessible only to the wealthy, or through fully online, asynchronous massive open online courses (MOOCs) with limited instructor interaction and very low completion rates.

This chapter focuses on an emerging category of advanced coursework intended to break this mold. We offer case studies of three programs that engage faculty at highly selective institutions in offering online or hybrid format courses to secondary school students with the explicit goal of expanding equitable access to higher education.

Davidson Next, which was in existence from 2014 to 2022, engaged Davidson College faculty to design supplementary, online modules that can be used to support the teaching of AP courses and for individual self-guided instruction. *OnRamps* is a dual enrollment and professional development program created by the University of Texas at Austin (UT Austin) that offers college-level courses to Texas high school students in a hybrid format co-taught by UT Austin (and, more recently, other college) faculty and local high school teachers. The *National Education Equity Lab* is a not-for-profit that partners with selective universities to offer hybrid college credit–bearing courses to students at Title 1 high schools across the country.

We selected these three examples because they illustrate variations on the theme. Each has a different type of "host" organization—a private liberal arts college, a public research university, and a not-for-profit organization. Each takes a different curricular approach—a modular supplement to AP courses, a small set of core introductory courses, and a growing set of popular courses that stoke intellectual curiosity. The projects are also at different stages of development, with Davidson Next sunsetting in 2022, OnRamps running at full maturity, and the National Ed Equity Lab still starting up and expanding.

Comparing these cases elucidates the varying motivations of the providing institutions and their leaders. These ranged from searching for a meaningful societal problem to address with a technology (Davidson Next) to responding to a larger state wide requirement in dual enrollment (OnRamps), to building equitable pathways for admission to selective colleges (the Lab). The case studies draw out the features and strategies that drive or constrain success, such as the finances, institutional capacity, technology, student mindset, and networks. Although each case played out differently, they are alike in centering learning in their efforts to improve college access for historically underserved high school students. This model of outreach and access, scaled through technology and grounded in learning and equity, is particularly important in the current moment given recent litigation in the Supreme Court around the prevailing system of affirmative action.[3]

Davidson Next

Davidson Next was a Davidson College initiative that aimed to supplement AP instruction with online modules designed for in-class hybrid instruction and for individual self-guided instruction.[4] Starting in 2014, Davidson Next offered six courses that covered the most challenging concepts in AP Physics, AP Calculus, and AP Macroeconomics on edX. Students could take the courses on their own through edX or their teacher could use a private version of the course as materials for their local class via school district partnerships.[5] Due to partnership challenges, funding concerns, and shifts in strategy, Davidson Next was sunsetted in 2022, although all videos remain available on YouTube.[6]

Davidson Next began when Davidson joined the edX consortium and sought to make a unique educational contribution to that platform.[7] Davidson focused on AP students and teachers as its primary audience because four faculty members had leadership roles with College Board's AP program and understood where students need additional support.[8] The Arnold Foundation (now known as Arnold Ventures) provided grant funding of $2 million to support the initiative,[9] most of which was spent on "hacking edX" to make the platform work for Davidson's use case.[10]

Davidson Next was in many ways a technology-driven project—a platform in search of a problem to be solved. And the problem had to fit within Davidson's mission. As Carol Quillen, Davidson college president, explains:

> Davidson, for all of its exclusionary history, has had since its founding, this idea that a free and democratic society needs educated citizens. . . . Even the largest of colleges still only serve a limited number of students. So we need to think beyond the students we directly serve and think about what else [we can] do to build the postsecondary landscape that serves all. For Davidson, it is about building stronger pipelines to higher ed. . . . We can reach teachers and honor the work that they do. We are a tiny institution and Davidson Next does not replace teachers but it helps teachers with a dramatic expansion of access for students.[11]

With Davidson Next, Davidson entered into the digital learning space with exploratory goals. There wasn't a larger strategy around digital access.[12] The question being asked in 2014 was "can we do this? And can we do this well?"[13] Between 2017 and 2021, Davidson Next attracted 104,366 edX enrollments and 481 classrooms with private MOOC instances run by teachers.[14] But the impact went beyond strictly numerical terms: Davidson President Carol Quillen says it demonstrated what can happen when an institution with a particular expertise looks around and says, "what can we do with this to share it as broadly as possible?"

The project struggled with financial sustainability. There was a desire to move beyond the grant-funded pilot, but contradictory concerns about charging for access. On the basis of this experience, Julie Goff, former director of Davidson Next, reflects that philanthropy may not be best suited to funding pilot projects because this reduces the obligation to plan for sustainable operations using institutional resources.[15]

Davidson Next differs from the other initiatives examined in this chapter in its dependence on external partnerships. These presented the greatest challenges for the project team of three staff members. Davidson approached the College Board about collaborating, and although College Board agreed to list the program on their website, they did not partner on content development or marketing.[16]

Another sticking point was Davidson's decision to focus on challenging concepts versus the Arnold Foundation's desire for more comprehensive content coverage.[17] Davidson faculty were concerned about diminishing the role of teachers by providing all of the content in a standalone course.[18] As a compromise, Davidson Next used Open edX, the open-source version of the edX platform, to allow high school teachers to access the Davidson content and adapt it for their students, while retaining local control of grading.[19] Goff explained that "we were hacking a MOOC platform for blended learning which it was not designed to do—especially in 2015."[20] The content was lauded by teachers and students, but there was frustration with the technology and how to make it work in the context of a classroom.

Although the program did not survive at Davidson as the college's digital strategy shifted away from kindergarten to grade 12 (K–12) pathways, its influence extended beyond the campus:[21] College Board and edX have both launched AP-related courses and preparatory materials in recent years.[22] In the end, Davidson Next piloted a new concept in digital learning and served as an experiment in how a liberal arts college can scale its reach to achieve access goals.

OnRamps

OnRamps is a dual-enrollment and professional development program offered by the University of Texas at Austin, providing 16 courses to 154,491[23] students and professional development to 1,200 teachers across Texas as of 2022.[24] The program was created in 2011, following a legislative requirement that every Texas high school student be offered the opportunity to take at least 12 hours of college credit.[25] In anticipation of a significant increase in demand for dual-credit options, the founders of OnRamps sought to provide consistent course quality and impactful teacher training that could scale to meet the demand.[26]

More fundamentally, OnRamps aimed to increase the number and diversity of students who engage authentically with the academic expectations of leading research universities.[27] This differentiated the program from other dual-credit opportunities in Texas, which were offered mostly by community colleges.[28] As Jennifer Porter, managing director of OnRamps, describes, "OnRamps's goals are to close the gap of understanding between colleges' expectations and student's ability to meet them at an individual and systems level before students' first semester of college."[29]

OnRamps is structured as a hybrid program where students are enrolled in a course taught by their high school teachers for high school credit as well as a remote course taught by a University Instructor of Record.[30] Students work between two Canvas courses, one managed by their high school teacher and another managed by the University. Content is woven between the two instances, with students studying college-level content in one instance and completing a high school–

level comprehension check in another.[31] In this way, college-level expectations are clear, and students have guided high school–level support on how to reach them. Students watch pre-recorded lectures from Instructors of Record, participate in discussions facilitated by their local teachers, and complete college-level assignments.[32] They receive two grades for the two classes. This design is intended to maintain academic rigor while reducing the risk that a student who struggles in the university-level portion of the course puts their high school success at risk.[33] Overall, 92% of eligible students who enrolled in OnRamps in the 2020–2021 academic year earned college credit.[34]

A distinctive feature of OnRamps is extensive teacher professional development. First-year OnRamps teachers must apply to participate and are required to attend a two-week summer teaching institute; returning teachers attend a truncated summer institute.[35] New OnRamps teachers receive a minimum of 80 hours of professional development and coaching, and returning teachers receive a minimum of 35 hours per year.[36] Teachers receive coaching support throughout the year and are recognized as teacher affiliates of UT Austin. The goal is to help teachers build a culture that brings together pedagogical understanding, technology skills and tools, and college expectations.[37]

OnRamps has achieved significant scale within Texas, offering 16 unique courses[38] to 154,491 students in 196 districts.[39] All courses offered correlate to core credit and transferability within the Texas Common Core Numbering system.[40] Course design starts with determining the assessment methodology and making sure it can scale. (That requirement means there are no seminar-style writing intensive courses offered.)[41] Each class is designed so it can scale up to 6,000–8,000 students. Funded through state appropriations, OnRamps has approximately 70 full time staff as well as part-time staff who help with grading.[42]

In terms of impact, a 2018 white paper reported, "OnRamps participants were . . . nearly twice as likely to attend a four-year college compared to non-OnRamps students (52.3% vs. 29.9%), and roughly two-thirds of OnRamps credit eligible students attended a four-year college (66.9%)."[43] With this level of success, the plan is to continue to grow the program within Texas through partnerships with such regional institutions as Tarleton State, and possibly later to grow to other states.[44]

OnRamps's theory of change is that educators are the most critical contributors; content and technology are enablers, but not the drivers.[45] According to Harrison Keller, one of the founders of OnRamps, "OnRamps' secret sauce is building a facilitated network of educators as committed professionals grounded in mutual respect. In many ways, it's not about the credit or about acceleration, it's about increasing the likelihood that students are ready for the next thing."

OnRamps is a successful example of a statewide investment in dual enrollment with the aim of increasing universal college readiness. With a design built for scale and an investment in teacher professional development, OnRamps aims to serve the college preparatory needs of all students.

The National Education Equity Lab

The National Education Equity Lab (the Lab) partners with selective universities to provide hybrid college credit–bearing courses to Title 1 high schools. Its goal is to reduce "undermatching" by helping students build knowledge and skills and prove to themselves and colleges that they are college ready.[46] Classes are taught within schools, during the school day, by a hybrid teaching team consisting of a local high school teacher, a remote Teaching Fellow from the university, and a faculty member who creates content and assessments and serves as Instructor of Record. The Lab currently works with 12 universities to offer 23 discrete courses, ranging from poetry to computer science, to over 298 Title 1 high schools from 112 districts.[47]

High schools select the students who participate based on the Lab's criteria, including prior coursework, grades, or teacher recommendations. The Lab also works with each student to provide a laptop and Wi-Fi access if needed, and through partners, helps them navigate college and financial aid applications.[48]

The Lab requires a commitment to equity from the leadership of all of its university and district partners.[49] It has some requirements that maintain a similar structure across the courses but leaves the level of commitment up to the university partner. This can range from a team of 10 staff supporting courses (Stanford) to smaller teams supporting faculty and Teaching Fellows.

The Lab seeks to reach the highest performing students from low-income and underrepresented minority backgrounds, at the lowest performing schools.[50] Classes are free for students but cost school districts approximately $250 per student per course, which most districts cover using state or philanthropic funds.[51] This fee is split between the Lab and the providing college or university. (The Lab is funded through a combination of district fees and philanthropic support).[52]

In selecting college and university partners, the Lab seeks institutions whose course credits will transfer widely. To the Lab, this means selective colleges.[53] This criterion also helps with the Lab's larger goal around changing mindsets, according to Alexandra Slack, chief operating officer, "selective colleges are important in confidence building for students to know that they are capable of college level work with known institutions."[54] High schools partner with the Lab because the courses are designed be embedded in school day; expose their students to advanced education; and, there are typically multiple assessments, which is closer to the college model than AP, in which credits are based on performance on a single end-of-course exam.[55]

Beyond the academics, the Lab also strives to support a college-going mindset among students. The Lab celebrates students' achievements with ceremonies at the start, midpoint, and end of each course and inculcates the idea that the course, for students, is part of something larger. Staff reach out to struggling students with coaching to help them get back on track.[56] The model can be described as college-level learning with high school–level support.

To date, the Lab has enrolled 11,000 students in 29 states,[57] with the goal being to scale as large as there is a need.[58] Across the Lab's courses, on average 15% of students drop soon after enrollment; an additional 10–15% of students drop during the course; and among the students who remain, approximately 85% of students who complete the course earn college credit with passing grades.[59] Reasons for students' dropping range from the challenging nature of the material to external pressures from work.[60]

The Lab's theory of change is to "connect the dots" between high achieving students and colleges.[61] The founder and CEO, Leslie Cornfeld, describes the courses as a "Trojan horse" to build a college-going mindset and help students get the support they need to apply and succeed in college.[62]

The Lab's approach relies on partnerships with recognized institutions, Title 1 high schools and districts, and philanthropic and university resources to support students. Still in its early stages, the Lab is working on finding a sustainable financial model that relies less on philanthropic grants. And by relying on asynchronous delivery, courses can scale at the relatively modest marginal costs of additional Teaching Fellows, who are typically staffed at a 1:15 ratio to students.

Conclusion

Higher education access is in flux. Many colleges have institutionalized test-optional admissions policies adopted during the COVID-19 pandemic. Affirmative action admissions policies are being challenged at the highest levels of the judicial system. To build diverse, talented student bodies in the future, colleges must innovate.

The programs profiled in this chapter offer three models to consider. But in their commonalities, they collectively represent a shift in approach. Davidson Next, OnRamps, and the Lab each use digital learning to engage students and build more equitable pathways to college. This has three benefits that cut across all these programs: enhancing the students' college readiness, equipping students with a signal of their college readiness, and bolstering their confidence. This approach represents an important change from "discovering" prospective students through their accumulation of traditional markers of accomplishment to intentionally offering college-level learning experiences to broaden opportunity and mobility.

These case studies offer lessons for equity-driven, learning-centered access programs. First, it is critical to have a sustainable financial model.

While all three programs rely on external funding, establishing sources of recurring revenue—from organizations, not directly from students—has been essential to both OnRamps' and the Lab's success. By contrast, Davidson Next was unable to overcome its perception as a source of free content.

Second, there must be a clear connection between the program and the strategy of its providers. In the case of both OnRamps and the Lab, institutions are offering their own courses to a broader population of students, training K–12 partner teachers, and validating their quality, in support of public interest missions as well as their own enrollment goals. Although Davidson Next shared some of these features, supporting AP courses was not seen as core by Davidson.

Third, networks are necessary to expand impact beyond just content delivery. Davidson Next relied heavily on local teachers to meld the AP content into their classrooms to support their students. OnRamps has invested in teacher professional development to enhance teachers' ability to build college readiness skills that go beyond content absorption. OnRamps has also built a network of partnerships within Texas. The National Education Equity Lab has used a network of partnerships with colleges and universities to scale quickly. Each college is able to reach a maximum number of students with their course while being a part of a larger consortial effort.

Network-building also mitigates a tension at the core of this work: the institutions offering these programs are not currently positioned to enroll all the students who participate in them on their own. Engaging multiple institutions with a shared confidence in the meaningfulness of the students' success expands their enrollment options. To fully realize this potential, participating institutions' admissions offices likely need to be more involved in these programs than they are today.

The United States' diverse K–12 population needs more equitable pathways to college, and higher education must reimagine how it uses its human capital, technology, trust, and networks to blaze them. These case studies demonstrate the possibilities, as well as some of the risks associated with those new pathways. To build the classes of the future, colleges and universities should continue to innovate in access and reach “upstream” into the K–12 system to prepare students for success.

Notes

1. US Department of Education, “Dual Enrollment Programs.”

2. Taylor, “Accelerating Pathways to College”; Chatterji et al., “Closing Advanced Coursework Equity.”

3. When this chapter was drafted in Fall of 2021, the Supreme Court had not yet decided to hear *Students For Fair Admissions, Inc. v. President and Fellows of Harvard College*, also known as the Affirmative Action Case. This chapter speculated on what a post-affirmative action landscape looks like and the role of selective institutions. Although the case has since been deliberated, we believe that the case studies in this chapter still provide value. The case studies illustrate three models for Higher Ed Institutions on how to move from “discovering” prospective students through their accumulation of traditional markers of accomplishment to intentionally offering college-level learning experiences to broaden opportunity and mobility.

4. EdX, “Davidson Next.”

5. EdX, “Davidson Next.”

6. Sundi Richard (assistant director of digital learning at Davidson College), in discussion with the authors and Kristen Eshleman, November 3, 2021.

7. Carol Quillen (president of Davidson College), in discussion with the authors, December 6, 2021.

8. Julie Goff (Davidson Next project manager, 2014–2016), in discussion with the authors, November 11, 2021.

9. Kristen Eshleman (director of digital learning and innovation at Davidson College, 2015–2019), in discussion with the authors and Sundi Richard, November 3, 2021.

10. Goff, discussion.

11. Quillen, discussion.

12. Eshleman, discussion.

13. Quillen, discussion.

14. Richard, discussion.

15. Goff, discussion.

16. Goff, discussion.

17. Goff, discussion.

18. Goff, discussion.

19. Goff, discussion.

20. Goff, discussion.

21. Richard, discussion.

22. Welcome to the AP and Pre-AP Community, “AP Teacher Community”; edX, “Get College Ready.”

23. OnRamps, "OnRamps Implementation Summary." This is the sum of each academic year's unique enrollment from the 2011–2012 to 2021–2022 academic school year. This is not the number of unique students.

24. OnRamps, "OnRamps."

25. Harrison Keller (commissioner, Texas Higher Education Coordinating Board, 2020–present; vice provost for higher education policy and research, 2009–2015; deputy to the president for strategy and policy, 2015–2019, University of Texas at Austin), in discussion with the authors, November 12, 2021. This legislation accelerated a preexisting trend: dual credit participation by Texas high school students increased by approximately 650% between 2000 and 2018; Giani et al., "OnRamps to College."

26. Keller, discussion.

27. Katie Brock (senior director to the president for strategy and policy at University of Texas at Austin), in discussion with the authors and Jennifer Porter, December 8, 2021.

28. Keller, discussion.

29. Porter, discussion.

30. "What Is UT OnRamps?"

31. Brock, discussion.

32. "What Is UT OnRamps?"

33. Keller, discussion.

34. OnRamps, "Our Impact."

35. Jennifer Porter (managing director of OnRamps), in discussion with the authors and Katie Brock, December 8, 2021.

36. Porter, discussion.

37. Porter, discussion.

38. The 16 course offerings include college Chemistry I and II; Biology I; Geoscience; Physics I and II; Algebra; Precalculus; Statistics; Computer Science; United States History; Writing; and Art.

39. "OnRamps Implementation Summary."

40. Core credit and transferability—in Texas, this is related to the Texas Common Core Numbering (TCCN) system.

41. Porter, discussion.

42. Brock, discussion.

43. Giani, et al., "OnRamps to College," 3.

44. Porter, discussion.

45. Keller, discussion.

46. National Education Equity Lab, "Equity Lab | Home."

47. Alexandra Slack, email message to author, October 4, 2022.

48. Leslie Cornfield (founder and CEO, National Education Equity Lab), in discussion with the authors, November 22, 2021.

49. Cornfield, discussion.

50. Cornfield, discussion.

51. Green, "Shake Up Elite Admissions."

52. Matthiessen, "Small Nonprofit's Equity Work"; Smalley, "Bridging the Gap."

53. Partner institutions include Arizona State University, Barnard College of Columbia University, Brown University, Cornell University, Georgetown University, Howard University, Princeton University, Spelman College, Stanford University, University of Pennsylvania, Wesleyan University, and the Wharton School of the University of Pennsylvania.

54. Alexandra Slack (chief operating officer at the National Education Equity Lab), in discussion with the authors, November 23, 2021.

55. Slack, discussion.

56. Slack, discussion.

57. Slack, October 4, 2022.

58. Slack, discussion.

59. Across all of our courses, we count a student as having "completed" a course when they completed at least two assignments and at least one of the finals (e.g., exam, project, paper, etc.) Cornfield, discussion.

60. Cornfield, discussion.

61. Cornfield, discussion.

62. Cornfield, discussion.

Bibliography

Chatterji, Roby, Abby Quirk, and Neil Campbell. "Closing Advanced Coursework Equity Gaps for All Students." Center for American Progress, June 30, 2021, https://www.americanprogress.org/article/closing-advanced-coursework-equity-gaps-students.

EdX. "Free Online Courses from Davidson Next." Davidson Next. Accessed May 8, 2023. https://www.edx.org/school/davidson-next.

———. "Get College Ready. Get Ahead. Get Learning!" Accessed May 8, 2023. https://www.edx.org/high-school.

Giani, Matt S., Julie Schell, Emily Wade, and Harrison Keller. "OnRamps to College: Examining the Impact of OnRamps Participation on College Enrollment." Education Research Center, University of Texas at Austin (July 2018): 5. https://files.eric.ed.gov/fulltext/ED612288.pdf.

Green, Erica L. "A College Program for Disadvantaged Teens Could Shake Up Elite Admissions." *New York Times*, February 18, 2021. https://www.nytimes.com/2021/02/18/us/politics/college-admissions-poor-students.html.

Matthiessen, Connie. "Education Funders are Throwing Weight Behind this Small Nonprofit's Equity Work. Here's Why." *Inside Philanthropy*, June 24, 2021. https://www.insidephilanthropy.com/home/2021/6/24/education-funders-are-throwing-weight-behind-this-small-nonprofits-equity-work-heres-why.

National Education Equity Lab. "National Education Equity Lab | Home." National Education Equity Lab. Accessed May 8, 2023. https://edequitylab.org.

OnRamps. "OnRamps." University of Texas at Austin. Accessed May 8, 2023. https://onramps.utexas.edu.
———. "Implementation Summary." University of Texas at Austin, March 2022. https://onramps.utexas.edu/about.
———. "Our Impact | High-Quality Educational Opportunities." University of Texas at Austin. Accessed May 8, 2023. https://onramps.utexas.edu/impact.
Smalley, Suzanne. "Bridging the Gap between Low-Income Students and Top Colleges." *Inside Higher Ed*, November 2, 2021. https://www.insidehighered.com/news/2021/11/02/ed-equity-lab-bridges-gap-low-income-students-colleges.
Taylor, Jason L. "Accelerating Pathways to College: The (In)Equitable Effects of Community College Dual Credit." *Community College Review* 43, no. 4 (October 2015). https://journals.sagepub.com/doi/abs/10.1177/0091552115594880.
US Department of Education. "Dual Enrollment Programs: Transition to College." What Works Clearinghouse, Institute of Education Sciences, February 2017. https://ies.ed.gov/ncee/wwc/Docs/InterventionReports/wwc_dual_enrollment_022817.
Welcome to the AP and Pre-AP Community. "AP Teacher Community." College Board. Accessed May 8, 2023. https://apcommunity.collegeboard.org.
"What Is UT OnRamps? Dual Enrollment vs. Dual Credit." Hays Consolidated Independent School District, January 21, 2020. https://www.hayscisd.net/cms/lib/TX02204837/Centricity/Domain/65/UT_OnRamps_Program_Information_2020–21.pdf.

chapter 6

The Shifting Institutional Data Landscape and Why It Matters for Student Learning

Drew Allen

Data are increasingly playing a more active role in higher education. The real and perceived value of data and evidence in supporting institutional decision-making has increased dramatically over the last decade. For example, enrollment management teams increasingly rely on market research and predictive models to guide admission and finance aid decisions. Library staff are using data to identify future investment needs and collections usage. Alumni offices track recent graduates' engagement and interactions to guide fundraising strategies. Student affairs programs collect and analyze program participation and satisfaction data to evaluate progress toward goals and outcomes. Moreover, the COVID-19 crisis only ramped up the near-constant need to answer questions quickly based on whatever data could be collected.

Coupled with this trend, however, has been the dramatic growth in the complexity of the systems used to collect and store data and the types of challenging questions around who owns data and who can access data. Although the pandemic significantly sped up the pace of change, the increasingly complex data landscape was well underway before 2020. More data have been collected and produced by colleges and universities. However, an associated increase in transparency or the capacity to manage such data in meaningful ways has not kept pace. More data have not necessarily equated to better data-informed decision-making. As new data collection methods through surveys, polls, and digital capture become more accessible, institutions struggle with an overwhelming amount of new data being generated.

So what does this mean for student learning? How are this shifting data landscape and increasing complexity impacting the academic enterprise at the core of our colleges and universities? How might teaching and learning influence the future directions of an institution's data strategy? Having spent much of my professional career working in institutional research, evaluation, and assessment at various institutions, I have witnessed these trends and effects first-hand. It is from this perspective that I outline how I see the data ecosystem changing, how colleges and universities have tended to respond, and why it matters for reaching and learning.

I write this chapter having just recently stepped into a new role leading institutional research and analytics for Harvard University. Over the last several months, I have had many conversations with Harvard staff, faculty, and students about the changing nature of data and its implications on all facets of university life. "Too much data" and "we need access to more data" have often been uttered in the same conversation. Students have expressed concerns over data privacy and discussed fatigue with repeated requests to fill out institutional surveys. Faculty members inquired about data availability for purposes of course assessment planning. And staff expressed excitement about the benefits of using institutional data to advance conversations about equity and inclusion, for instance, but also found it challenging to navigate university structures and policies to access the correct information.

Harvard is certainly not representative of higher education institutions across the United States. But even with its significant resources and elite reputation, it too is dealing with many of the same types of challenges my colleagues in community colleges, four-year regional institutions, liberal arts colleges, and flagship public institutions face:

institutions have an increasing abundance of data and information but struggle to manage and use these assets effectively.

These are the critical data challenges ahead for colleges and universities. How, then, can we harness the value of a vast amount of new and existing data in meaningful ways to support institutional goals, strategies, and decisions? And how can this all be accomplished while keeping sight of institutions' core teaching and learning mission?

In this chapter, I first highlight the increasingly complex data ecosystems that have developed at institutions and how these relate to the parallel shifting landscape of student learning. Next, I discuss critical lessons learned over the last several years as the data evolution has sped up. Then, I present key themes that characterize how institutions will likely tackle future data challenges and their implications for student learning. Finally, I recommend how student learning might be integrated more fully into the shifting data landscape in the future.

The Parallel Shifting Landscapes for Data and Learning

As data have become increasingly valuable for institutions, the types of data collected and the systems needed to manage those data have become increasingly complex. At the same time, teaching and learning have become more complex as new approaches and innovative practices have introduced new types and venues of learning on college campuses. These developments have happened in parallel and often intersected.

Institutions are awash with data, and for a good reason. Data have played a valuable role in decision-making in areas ranging from financial aid allocation to alumni engagement to facilities planning. Institutions—particularly public institutions and those relying on external funding to support their mission—also use data to track progress toward goals and to demonstrate effectiveness. Institutions are required to college and report key metrics to the federal government, rating agencies, and accreditors. Core operations, such as admissions, rely on applicant data to decide admission and placement into courses and programs.

Institutional research offices have also changed over the last few decades—shifting from primarily serving as a reporting function (e.g., providing descriptive information and critical university metrics, such as student demographics, retention and graduation rates, and faculty counts) to an office that integrates data from various sources to answer critical strategic questions, assess program or policy effectiveness, and support decision-making. Even at Harvard, the Office of Institutional Research has recently changed its name to the Office of Institutional Research and Analytics, reflecting the demand for more advanced types of analyses and the expanded role these offices are taking on. Other university areas have responded to the increasing data-focused environment by hiring staff whose job is solely or partly responsible for collecting and analyzing data for operational and decision support.

The COVID-19 pandemic only ramped up data collection efforts further. Many institutions launched data collection efforts to track testing, infection, and vaccination information to guide public health decisions and feed COVID-19 dashboards. Students were surveyed repeatedly about academic and social engagement during this unprecedented time. Information was collected on where students lived, including their time zones, to better plan for online learning opportunities. Underlying transaction and login data from course management systems and video conferencing platforms were compiled to understand the fundamental shifts in teaching learning due to the pandemic.

This deluge of new data provided valuable information in some areas but highlighted that merely collecting large amounts of data did not lead to meaningful decision-making. These data must be analyzed in meaningful ways. Data often exist in silos and must be integrated, which requires significant collaboration. Adequacy staffing and analytical infrastructure are also often lacking, which limits the amount of analysis that can take place. Institutional research offices, like others university offices, are experiencing staffing challenges.

In parallel with data landscape changes, higher education's teaching and learning enterprise has undergone a fundamental shift over the years. New programs of study are being created and expanded, new learning experiences are being offered, and institutions are connecting classroom and cocurricular learning experiences. In addition, the pandemic reinforced the need for instructors to create effective learning environments. These changes have made collecting and using data to improve teaching and learning even more critical. Evidence that students have acquired specific skills and competencies, particularly in the face of this change, has become crucial. As such, assessment plans have tended to become more complex and have required new types of data—thus adding to the pressure on institutions to expand the collection.

What Colleges and Universities Have Learned

The increasing complexity of the data landscape and teaching and learning has led to some important lessons learned by institutional leaders. First, the deluge of data available to institutions has meant that editing and focused storytelling have become critical. A long list of charts, tables, and dashboards without appropriate context and focus almost always falls flat. Increasingly, higher education administrators and faculty must shape data into narratives humans can understand and remember. A compelling story cannot involve large volumes of tables of descriptive statistics and countless pie charts. The most effective data stories communicate data from multiple perspectives and sources and focus the reader on what is essential for the specific moment. They connect the dots in a way that strings findings into a narrative or provides data in the context of more encompassing university questions or challenges. Institutions have learned that effective use of data has meant focusing on what was most important: it meant communicating key metrics and information in a way that connected to the intended audiences in a coherent narrative. They have learned to understand where an audience is coming from and how different individuals will react to certain types of data.

In the spring of 2020, Georgetown University conducted a campus-wide student climate survey to understand better a range of issues related to students' sense of belonging, experiences involving bias, prejudice, and discrimination, campus accessibility, and the classroom environment.[1] The survey, which employed a complex instrument with over 100 questions, ultimately produced vast data. The University's internal Office of Assessment and Decision Support analyzed the response data, and results were initially communicated in two reports totaling almost 400 pages. Although these reports contained a significant amount of valuable information, leaders at Georgetown quickly learned that highlighting critical findings in digestible, focused reports around a single issue became a more effective tool for communication. The University needed to tell a data story, not simply release data tables. As a result, Office of Assessment and Decision Support (OADS) ultimately created brief "Spotlight Reports" that presented critical themes with the content edited based on the most salient findings.[2]

Georgetown's Center for New Designs in Learning and Scholarship (CNDLS) also used basic editing and storytelling concepts to frame the Student Cultural Climate Survey results to answer critical questions about student learning. In their analysis of survey data, CNDLS linked student survey responses to essential themes of inclusive pedagogy, classroom climate, and mentoring practices that enabled leaders to communicate a coherent data narrative to faculty.[3] In their approach to this report, its authors tried to anticipate faculty members' questions about the data and their diverse perspectives and entry points into future data conversation. Empathy is an implicit motivation behind good data storytelling and was a crucial ingredient in the creation of the report.

A second critical lesson learned over the last few years of the data transformation has been that more advanced data systems have not necessarily meant that critical questions are more easily answerable. In fact, as institutional operations, organizational structures, data systems, and educational offerings have become more complex, historically easy-to-answer questions that inform teaching and learning have sometimes become more difficult or even impossible to answer. For instance, the COVID-19 crisis caused many institutions to ask: where are students living while taking courses? Unfortunately, this question is answerable only if institutions collect up-to-date information on students' physical locations. Although institutions often collect permanent or mailing addresses, actual addresses or locales indicating where students live and participate in remote instruction are often not collected systematically. Furthermore, if an institution wanted to begin collecting additional location information, it would usually require a complex set of changes to existing structures, systems, and data models to allow the information to be analyzed correctly. This left many institutions scrambling, ultimately leading to only rough estimations in many cases.

Another important question that often arose during the height of the pandemic was related to who was actually in the classroom at a given point in time. How do we know which students attended which classes? How do we track which teaching assistants or other teaching support might be in the classroom along with a lead instructor or instructors? Institutions almost always maintain data on lead instructors and enrolled students in courses. Still, the COVID-19 crisis highlighted the importance of understanding a more accurate picture of who is in the classroom for contact tracing or simply understanding the impacts of COVID-19 on the classroom environment status quo. Unfortunately, colleges and universities found that the types of data they collected were either (1) insufficient to answer basic questions, or (2) not the correct data to begin with. With all the attention focused on advanced analytics and "big data," often fundamental data elements have yet to be integrated into universities' data collection efforts.

One question directly related to teaching and learning that many institutions' advanced data systems often still do not allow us to answer the question: what is a faculty member's teaching commitment? With advances and innovations in pedagogical approaches, new models of instruction, the proliferation of service-learning and workplace-based curricula, fieldwork, dual enrollment, and alternative methods of student advisement, what counts in an accurate "teaching load" metric has become increasingly complex.

For instance, bedside teaching in hospitals is increasingly becoming a common practice in clinical clerkships as an effective way to develop students' clinical competencies. Even during the height of the pandemic, virtual teaching was carried out using iPads strapped to computers on wheels in hospital patient rooms.[4] For a university to fully report on the teaching commitments of faculty, it must develop ways to accurately capture data on instructional activities like bedside teaching. Otherwise, any analyses of data based only on traditional classroom credit hours may not capture the total teaching commitment of faculty.

Key Themes Guiding Institutions' Approaches to Data Challenges

While institutions have tried to grapple with the shifting data landscape, integrate lessons learned into their solutions, and get ahead of the curve in terms of meeting institutional needs with data systems, policies, and strategies, significant challenges remain. A few institutions, however, have made notable progress in certain areas. They have been early adopters of new ways of thinking about managing data challenges, and their approaches give us hints of what may come. I have seen three common themes that characterize institutions' approaches to data: (1) the development of a coherent data strategy and governance program, (2) an appreciation for various types of data, and (3) an investment in collective data literacy. I believe each of these will undergird the continuing evolution of the data ecosystem in many higher education institutions in the years ahead. In the following sections, I describe each of these and what they might mean for student learning.

Theme I: Development of Coherent Data Strategy and Governance

When institutional research offices at colleges and universities were first created, approaches to data primarily focused on the complication of descriptive statistics to satisfy reporting and compliance requirements. Today, however, institutions are looking to data to help answer strategic questions, solve urgent problems, better engage with funders or stakeholders, and generally support decision-making across multiple levels of an organization. This new way of using data has required merging data from various sources, collecting new data from the entire campus community, and sharing data in unprecedented ways with levels of detail never seen before. For all of these activities to take place effectively and responsibly, however, a systematic method for institutions to govern those activities must be developed (i.e., "data strategy" or "data governance"). Institutions leading the charge on building innovative, responsible data ecosystems are developing institutional data strategies and governance programs that help facilitate reliable, efficient data integration and access.

Institutions increasingly discuss data governance, but what does effective data governance mean? As a general principle, data governance encompasses practices, processes, and analytics projects that help to ensure the formal and sustainable management of an institution's data assets. It includes ensuring that data are defined and documented, access to those data is given to individuals who need access, and incentives are in place for individuals and offices to maintain data in a way that respects the individuals within the data. Without a transparent governance system, there is a lack of clarity about informed consent, data releases, data definitions, and data integrity, which can often prevent meaningful data analyses from taking place—and thus prevent institutions from making progress on tackling challenges around student success. Employing a strategy to govern a university's data resources using transparent approaches that engage the entire university community is another way that institutions advance equity and inclusion goals.[5]

An institution's approach to data governance has clear implications for student learning in various ways. First, colleges and universities need to understand overall institutional effectiveness. One way to do this is the merge academic outcomes data with information on expenditures to analyze the costs and benefits of various educational programs or interventions.[6] Other types of institutions are keenly interested in linking data on students' preparation in high school with performance in introductory college courses to understand the college preparedness of its students better. These two examples both rely on the integration of data from various sources. A key barrier to the effective merging of data often is not technical; instead, it often lies in the fact that no formalized process governs who can merge data and for what purposes.

Transparent data governance strategies that include clear pathways for sharing institutional data with faculty (and, for that matter, straightforward processes whereby faculty can request data) also have direct implications for student learning. Providing faculty data and information about their students' progress is critical to improving student success. Steven Mintz argues for improved faculty and department-level access to course withdrawal and failure rates, grade distributions, course demand, and other information traditionally only available to select institutional decision-makers.[7]

For instance, researchers at the City University of New York (CUNY) recently conducted a large-scale survey of the institution's faculty about their knowledge of student transfer. They found significant gaps in what faculty knew about course and program transfer and that these gaps may have significant negative impacts on student progress and learning: "Given that we know that faculty members make many or even most of the decisions about credit transfer—by evaluating individual transcripts or courses, setting transfer credit policies, approving articulation agreements and/or advising students, we can reasonably infer that what they know and think about transfer have implications for transfer student progress and success."[8]

How might a university ensure that faculty have access to coherent transfer data? Creating a data governance structure that facilitates equitable access to student academic data for faculty as part of a data governance strategy is one effective approach.

Data governance also provides a framework whereby data sharing can be safeguarded and limited to protect the teaching and learning activities within a physical or virtual classroom. For example, COVID-19 raised questions about accessing data generated within the classroom, such as transcriptions and digital records. Faculty and other stakeholders expressed valid concerns about how these data were being used and questions about monitoring and surveillance.[9] Comprehensive data governance strategies provide guardrails in data usage that consider these concerns.

In the years ahead, more institutions will pursue the development of data governance programs and hire leaders to oversee data strategy. It is imperative that student learning be a focus of these conversations.

Theme II: An Appreciation for Various Types of Data

As data become more integral to decision-making processes, assessment efforts, and overall operations, colleges and universities are beginning to understand the value of different data types. As a result, much attention has been paid to "big data" and massive data sets containing millions of records of quantitative information. New digital technologies and large-scale administrative data collection efforts during the initial COVID-19 epidemic have only heightened this focus.[10] Indeed, massive administrative data sets certainly have value and enable statistical analyses where sufficient statistical power is needed to make findings meaningful. However, universities are also beginning to see limitations in focusing too much on large-scale institution-wide data and predive analytics systems that mask substantial variation, nuance, and context.

An individual student's text response to a question on a course evaluation also represents valuable data, as does the text in faculty members' syllabi. Beginning and end-of-class surveys administered by an instructor often contain as much helpful information as large-scale institution-wide surveys about students' experiences in the classroom. Notes from peer classroom observations might constitute critical data that can help facilitate ongoing discussions about effective teaching and learning. Curriculum mapping—a method of graphically illustrating and documenting the relationship between a curriculum and student learning outcomes—results in meaningful data that can and should be archived in a way that could facilitate analyses.[11]

Institutions ahead of the curve in their data ecosystem development are beginning to appreciate the need to consider non-traditional types of data in their policies and infrastructure-building to support a data-informed organization. Institutions are starting to value all types of data generated within an institution—not just the information housed in a big data warehouse only accessible to a few data analysts. In the coming years, institutions will not only expand their use of large "big data" sets, but they will also start to harness "small data" or more qualitative data from non-enterprise-level sources.

Of course, the prospect of harnessing more information from various nontraditional sources raises important questions about data privacy and governance. Suppose institutional leadership now find more significant and increasing value in text responses to pre-course surveys administered as part of a department's assessment plan, for instance. What systems and policies are in place to govern the access and use of these data? Again, there is an opportunity for educators who have engaged with all types of data within the context of teaching and learning to play an active role in the next stage of an institution's data strategy.

Many issues and questions around using multiple sources and data types have been front and center for faculty and departments conducting assessments for years. This theme is directly related to teaching and learning because it reflects an idea in learning assessment that many faculty and departments have pursued for years: obtaining the most complete understanding possible of student learning, experiences, and outcomes depends upon multiple measures and perspectives. Both indirect and direct evidence of learning has been vital to the assessment enterprise. In this way, lessons learned through assessment can help inform institution-wide approaches to data strategy and governance. This also means that faculty and student voices will become increasingly crucial in institution-wide conversations about what types of data can be used and for what reasons.

Theme III: Investment in Collective Data Literacy

In a 2020 study by Harvard University's Strategic Data Project, results from interviews of higher education leaders and analysts pointed to the notion that technical infrastructure alone was not good enough to support strategic data use. Instead, it was developing staff capacity to ensure that the appropriate skills and understanding of data and their role in making decisions were essential, mainly related to student success.[12] Although technical skills and communication are essential components of building capacity, the institutions successfully developing their data ecosystem realized that data literacy among all levels of staff and faculty is essential.

Amelia Parnell defines data literacy as "the extent to which one can understand and describe quantitative or qualitative information to address a challenge, monitor progress, understand a scenario, plan for the future, or another business-related activity."[13] Data literacy means that individuals in colleges and universities can consume and communicate data in meaningful contexts but also understand the constructs, methodologies, and analytical methods used to produce data and appreciate the potential value of such data.

Individual data literacy might look differently for different individuals, depending on their role in college or university. It involves understanding how data connect to one's specific organizational role. For educators, data literacy may center on individuals' abilities to effectively access, interpret, act on, and communicate data with the explicit goal of improving student outcomes.[14]

However, data literacy is not just an individual concept. An approach taken by some institutions embraces more of a *collective data literacy* approach, one that values both individual data literacy development but also an institution's set of policies and investments that signal that data literacy is valued. For example, Human Resources departments may proactively review job descriptions to ensure new job postings include requirements or competencies related to data literacy. Other institutions may embed data literacy to develop culturally responsive approaches to campus climate. Finally—and this is where the explicit connection to student learning can be made—institutions often make a case for data literacy as integral in course and program assessment. In order to develop effective assessment plans, a fundamental understanding of what data are available and their limitations and meaning is necessary.

A tool that some institutions are beginning to use to develop collective data is the "Data Walk." During a typical Data Walk, information and research findings are shared with stakeholders in a structured way that resembles a museum exhibit. Administrators, faculty, students, and other stakeholders are invited to a physical or virtual space to review data presentations, visuals, and interactive exhibits. Often organized into small groups, Data Walk participants move to various data "stations" or "exhibits" and discuss their reactions among themselves, often responding to prompts or driving questions posed by the organizers.[15] The practice originates in a pedagogical technique, a Gallery Walk, that involves small groups of students interacting with information posted on classroom walls.[16]

Looking Ahead: Student Learning at the Center of a Data Strategy

The previous sections have highlighted key developments in the higher education data landscape and themes that characterize many institutions' responses—many of which have real connections and implications for student learning. As we look ahead to the future of data, are there ways to situate student learning into the foundation of institutions' evolving data strategies? Can considerations of instructor and student needs be integrated more fully into conversations regarding institution research, assessment, and the role of data in decision-making? I conclude by offering a recommendation based on my own experience.

As mentioned at the beginning of the chapter, I have recently joined Harvard University as Associate Provost for Institutional Research and Analytics. I oversee the University's internal and external reporting, lead projects to support decision-making through data integration, and I will be helping to craft the institution's future data strategy and governance program. The job is unique among similar leadership positions across US institutions. It is structured to include a 50% teaching responsibility as a joint faculty appointment with the Harvard Graduate School of Education. Not only am I responsible for thinking about the role of data for Harvard as an institution, but I am expected to teach courses on the use of data and evidence in organizational decision-making. This approach—a deliberate decision by Harvard when hiring for the position to combine this administrative leadership role with instructional responsibilities reflects a growing acknowledgment—allows for new ways of connecting institutions' teaching and learning activities with institutional decision-making. Moreover, for me, taking this role provides an opportunity to take my experience in the classroom and as a faculty member and let it directly influence my decisions and advocacy as an administrator.

Only after a few months in this role, I already see the benefits of having this key administrative position be part of a faculty. Attending faculty meetings, for example, has given me a front-row seat to some meaningful discussions that have potential implications for an institutional data investment. How do faculty better understand trends relating to academic integrity? How do we measure the short- and long-term effects of a curriculum redesign? Are students taking advantage of academic accommodations, and are faculty understanding their role in this process? All these questions are essential to consider, and their answers require data.

However, even an institution as resourced as Harvard may not have the systems and processes set up in a way that allows for the sustained collection and analysis of data to answer these questions. However, I can now report to institutional research staff, information technology offices, assessment teams, and other individuals I work with about the need to consider these questions as the institution develops the next generation of data systems, analyses, and strategies. We need to be able to track academic accommodations in a secure, confidential system that does not rely on a shared color-coded spreadsheet! My mere presence in conversations among faculty, instructional technology teams, and students gives me a window and context into potential data needs I never had before.

This intersection has also highlighted areas where institutions should be cautious about how data are used in inappropriate ways or how assumptions might be built into data analyses that are incorrect or inherently biased. I see the limitations in only using a letter grade that I report to the registrar as an indicator of academic progress, for instance. I also am in a position to advocate for data privacy and security in areas where disclosure or sharing of data about students' experiences, identities, and opinions expressed inside and outside the classroom may be problematic. I can make the case, with evidence to support it, for a faculty member's voice in data governance conversations.

Not all institutions have the resources or organizational structures that allow for a joint institutional researcher/faculty role like what Harvard created. However, we can consider other ways to proactively connect the "data people" on campus with those involved in teaching and learning. Making these connections helps institutions develop collective data literacy and support compelling data storytelling because they allow for sharing of context and nuance. Having multiple perspectives around the table ensure that data are not interpreted by campus leaders as simply "facts" but are instead the results of complex systems, decision, assumptions, and biases. As Amelia Parnell highlighted in *You Are a Data Person*, successful institutions consider and support all individuals on campus as valuable participants in the data-informed decision-making process.

Data's growing complexity and availability mean that institutions must make tough decisions about allocating recourses and prioritizing what matters in their data. Having individuals at the table who understand not only the role of data but also the fundamental connection to student learning can ensure that institutions can sort through the overwhelming amounts of data and infinite data-related challenges to focus on what is most important to the success of its students.

Notes

1. Georgetown University, *Student Cultural Climate Survey*.
2. Office of Assessment and Decision Support, "Cultural Climate Survey."
3. Center for New Designs in Learning and Scholarship, *Cultural Climate Survey*.
4. Hofmann et al., "Virtual Bedside Teaching."
5. Borgman and Brand, "Capturing and Exploiting Data."
6. Project, "Improve Postsecondary Success."
7. Mintz, "The F Word."
8. Rabinowitz et al., "What Faculty Know."
9. Borgman and Brand, "Capturing and Exploiting Data."
10. Williamson et al., "Datafication of Teaching."
11. National Institute for Learning Outcomes Assessment, *Mapping Learning*.

12. Project, "Improve Postsecondary Success."
13. Parnell, *You Are a Data Person*, 6.
14. Arnold and Crane, "Making Decisions."
15. Murray et al., "Data Walks."
16. Francek, "Using Gallery Walks."

Bibliography

Arnold, Jessica, and Eric W. Crane. "Making Decisions: Using Assessment Data in the Time of COVID-19 and Beyond." WestEd, 2021. https://files.eric.ed.gov/fulltext/ED614173.pdf.

Borgman, Christine L., and Amy Brand. "Data Blind: Universities Lag in Capturing and Exploiting Data." *Science* 378, no. 6626 (December 23, 2022): 1278–1281. https://doi.org/10.1126/science.add2734.

Center for New Designs in Learning and Scholarship. *Cultural Climate Survey: CNDLS Pedagogy Report for Faculty: Inclusive Pedagogy, Classroom Climate, and Mentoring Practices at Georgetown and their Correlation with Student Belonging and Academic Dispositions.* Washington, DC: Georgetown University, 2021.

Francek, Mark. "Promoting Discussion in the Science Classroom Using Gallery Walks." *Journal of College Science Teaching* 36, no. 1 (2006): 27–31. https://doi.org/10.2505/4/jcst06_036_01_27.

Georgetown University. 2021. *Student Cultural Climate Survey*. Washington, DC: Georgetown University.

Hofmann, Heather, Cameron Harding, Julie Youm, and Warren Wiechmann. "Virtual Bedside Teaching Rounds with Patients with COVID-19." *Medical Education* 54, no. 10 (2020): 959–960. https://doi.org/10.1111/medu.14223.

Mintz, Steven. "The F Word: Faculty Is the Key to Student Success." *Inside Higher Ed* (blog), December 6, 2022. https://www.insidehighered.com/blogs/higher-ed-gamma/f-word.

Murray, Brittany, Elsa Falkenburger, and Priya Saxena. "Data Walks: An Innovative Way to Share Data with Communities." Research Report. Washington, DC: Urban Institute, November 2015. https://www.urban.org/sites/default/files/2022-03/2000510-data-walks-an-innovative-way-to-share-data-with-communities.pdf.

National Institute for Learning Outcomes Assessment. *Mapping Learning: A Toolkit of Resources.* Urbana, IL: University of Illinois at Urbana-Champaign, National Institute for Learning Outcomes Assessment (NILOA), 2018. https://www.learningoutcomesassessment.org/ourwork/curriculum-mapping/.

Office of Assessment and Decision Support. "Cultural Climate Survey Spotlight Reports." Washington, DC: Georgetown University, 2021. https://oads.georgetown.edu/surveys/cultural-climate-survey-spotlight-reports/.

Parnell, Amelia R. *You Are a Data Person: Strategies for Using Analytics on Campus.* Sterling, VA: Stylus Publishing, 2021.

Project, Strategic Data. "Strategic Data Use in Higher Education: Using Data to Improve Postsecondary Success." Cambridge, MA: Harvard University Center for Education Policy Research, 2020.

Rabinowitz, Vita, Yoshiko Oka, and Alexandra W. Logue. "What Faculty Know (and Don't Know) About Transfer—and Why It Matters." *Inside Higher Ed* (blog), September 8, 2022. https://www.insidehighered.com/blogs/beyond-transfer/what-faculty-know-and-don%E2%80%99t-know-about-transfer%E2%80%94and-why-it-matters.

Williamson, Ben, Sian Bayne, and Suellen Shay. "The Datafication of Teaching in Higher Education: Critical Issues and Perspectives." *Teaching in Higher Education* 25, no. 4 (2020): 351–365. https://doi.org/10.1080/13562517.2020.1748811.

Part II

What We Have Learned about Teaching and Learning

chapter 7

Learning about Learning

Students' Insights from a Pandemic Year

Sophie Grabiec, Sherry Lee Linkon, Isabel McHenry, and Lillian Nagengast

Sherry

The shift to online and hybrid instruction during the COVID-19 pandemic required many faculty to change or at least adapt their teaching practices. The shift certainly disrupted long-standing habits and assumptions, but it also made us more aware of them and even invited rethinking. Dozens of articles have documented, reflected on, and evaluated pandemic teaching practices.[1] In my own research, colleagues have reported that they cut back on readings or reframed assignments during the initial pivot to online teaching in the spring of 2020, and some have indicated that this led them to rethink their teaching habits and turn some pandemic adjustments into long-term pedagogical changes.[2] Books like this one capture the new ways of thinking and the potential for deeper transformation in higher education emerging from what faculty, administrators, and faculty developers learned during the mass adventure in online education.

Scholars have also evaluated students' learning and experiences during the pandemic, often highlighting students' sense of how well online courses worked or on what they needed from faculty in order to succeed in online or hybrid instruction. Some studies have tracked students' learning in specific courses or programs. But my conversations with colleagues about how moving their teaching online made them think in new ways about how learning works led me to wonder if something similar had happened for students. What did they learn *about learning* from their pandemic experience? And what difference might that make as they return to in-person classrooms?

As Susan Ambrose argues in *How Learning Works: Seven Research-Based Principles for Smart Teaching*, metacognition plays a central role in students' ability to manage their own learning.[3] Although we often try to measure metacognition by analyzing students' awareness of their processes and performance in a particular moment or project, it also involves awareness of learning more generally. Michael Prosser and Keith Trigwell argue that understanding how students see learning can help faculty design experiences that support students and enable them to be self-directed and social learners.[4] As faculty and faculty developers imagine possible new directions for college teaching after the pandemic, this suggests we would do well to take note of how an extended period of online learning influenced how students see themselves as learners and learning as a process.

Prosser and Trigwell identify four elements that come into play as faculty and students think about learning. First, they emphasize context, which includes the broader historical moment as well as the institutional setting and the particular course. Second, they point to conception, mental models based on prior experiences of how learning works, as a generic process but also individually. This ties directly to perception, what an individual observes in a particular context and how they interpret what they see. Finally, Prosser and Trigwell make clear that these first three elements generate approaches—strategies and attitudes that students bring to a learning situation. These four elements shape how people think about and navigate learning situations. They come together in the hypothesis that led to this article: the **context** of the pandemic made students more aware of their **conceptions** of teaching and learning, more likely to pay attention to their **perception** of learning situations, and more intentional in their **approaches.**[5]

To test this hypothesis, I invited three students from my fall 2020 courses to reflect on their experiences during a year of online learning and as they returned to classrooms a year later. Isabel, Lillian, and Sophie all started at Georgetown in August 2020 and spent their entire first year in online courses. They all also have a particular interest in learning. Two work at the Center for New Designs in Learning and Scholarship (CNDLS), which supports and evaluates teaching practices and innovations at Georgetown, and the other served as a teaching assistant in a summer bridge program, working with first-year first-generation students. Two took my graduate course on the teaching of writing in fall 2020; the other was in a one-credit fully asynchronous course I taught that term called Race and Class in Detroit. In those courses and others, they encountered faculty whose pedagogies emphasized reflection on learning. That combined with their campus jobs and interests probably makes them more attuned to learning as a practice, experience, and process than the average college student. However, their reflections suggest some important metacognitive insights that students are taking from the pandemic experience.

Isabel

Beginning my undergraduate career in the midst of online learning meant that I had to learn what higher education and remote learning should look like at the same time. Unlike Lillian and Sophie, I did not have the reference of complete undergraduate study under my belt, or any real experience of what "normal" college looked and felt like. Some structured learning methods felt the same: lectures were still lectures, and they still served the same function. However, I found myself missing the kind of accidental, organic learning that happens almost naturally and relies on a physical classroom environment. On top of a new academic landscape, I encountered my college community for the first time, all of them through the distance of an internet connection and a screen. Transitioning directly from a classroom where I had known most of my peers for four years to a Zoom screen full of unfamiliar faces only exacerbated the loss of casual group learning.

All of my learning started to feel very independent, whether that was the intention of an assignment or not. Friends had warned me that

I would have to rely on my own learning outside of class more in college than I did in high school, but the pandemic made what might have been an ordinary transition harder because remote learning left me feeling isolated. Although starting the independence of college is always exciting and disruptive, independent learning in the context of moving from home to campus and beginning a new chapter of life is a necessary development. I felt even more unmoored without the anchoring space of the classroom and the campus as a whole. The natural scaffolding of the physical classroom and in-person contact with peers and professors required students to build new systems for themselves.

Online engagement necessitates an intentionality that can sometimes serve as a roadblock; incidental interactions like running into classmates in the hallway generally disappear from our daily lives. There is no hallway on a Canvas course page, and although that type of interaction may feel inconsequential and supplemental, it often provides important opportunities to debrief and affirm learning. Zoom learning removed some of the humanity from the classroom; my peers and professors were mostly disembodied voices, not people I could ask for a pencil or share a joke about the weekend with. These small interactions often help create organic communities in classes, which in the past I had generally considered a social asset of the classroom.

However, after a year spent fully remote, I now appreciate the intellectual safety that community can add to the learning experience. Professors can foster this intellectual safety through a number of interpersonal methods in the classroom, but its most organic form is student-driven and informal. However, online learning spaces also felt more formal than physical classroom spaces, which took a level of necessary psychological safety out of the classroom. Especially in classes where professors did not facilitate generative discussions for the bulk of our meeting times, the act of brainstorming and building on peer thinking felt limited.

Along with eliminating most informal interactions, Zoom makes in-class interactions more formal, which made me less comfortable speaking up in discussions or making points that I wasn't yet sure about.

Because Zoom learning required such intentional action, students lost the opportunity to functionally think out loud. If I was going to unmute myself in the Zoom classroom or raise my digital hand, I needed to make sure my thought was fully formulated before I took action. Some professors made spaces comfortable by encouraging genuine student bonding. They encouraged thinking out loud with participatory activities like group projects and icebreakers, and they modeled ways to use the Zoom whiteboard and eraser function. However, many classrooms transitioned from spaces that encouraged trial and growth to spaces that required clear statements and certain, stand-alone thoughts.

Accidental social interactions facilitate learning, but they are harder to achieve in online courses. As a student, this phenomenon most affected how much meaning I was able to make out of the content I learned in my classes. Ideas often become stickiest when I can share them in a group, thinking out loud, informally tossing together phrases and ideas until an entire concept takes shape. Unfortunately, Zoom made all of that clumsy. Signing in to Zoom, the awkwardness of overlapping Zoom mics, and the sense of formality made it less comfortable to share my independently formed ideas in this setting than it was in person.

Yet good facilitation matters in all classrooms, virtual or in-person. Professors can remove logistical barriers to encourage students to participate and draw out a wide range of student opinions. I benefit from peer interaction in the lecture hall the same way I did from my bedroom at home. I found that de-formalizing my learning made it effective in the long run and engaging in the short run. Especially with large, abstract ideas, I can best deliver a formal academic analysis after understanding the concept in simpler terms and talking it through in conversation with peers or less formal writings.

Now that we're back on campus, I find myself keeping my eyes peeled for opportunities to connect informally with my peers, and raising my hand with a simple question or the beginning of a thought feels less daunting than it was online. Although I can't definitively attribute this difference to the transition back to online learning rather than maturing as a student, in-person learning certainly feels "more like college" than Zoom did. Having begun my higher education virtually, I am glad we can revise and build on the precedent that remote learning set.

Lillian

In my intersecting roles as a graduate student and a teaching assistant to a first-year bridge writing class at Georgetown in the fall of 2020, I considered myself attuned to thinking about learning. As both a student and instructor, I knew what I liked and disliked, my strengths and weaknesses, and was familiar with different pedagogical practices. However, the COVID-19 pandemic forced me to reconsider what I *thought* I knew about myself as a learner.

When Professor Linkon posed this chapter's guiding question to me, I immediately thought of the ways in which I had become more **intentional in my approaches to learning.** By this I mean I became more conscious of my learning processes. Much of the conversation about education in the pandemic warned of "learning loss," sounding alarm bells about what students would miss out on by not being in a face-to-face classroom. With this in mind, I entered the academic year expecting that remote learning would differ from face-to-face learning, and I was wary of being "left behind." I began to constantly check in with myself during and after class, asking myself content-based questions—*what does Peter Elbow argue about voice?*—and conceptual ones—*what is the difference between space and place?* I also frequently checked in with my peers, asking them for help to clarify confusing concepts or speaking with them casually about their experiences in the class or with remote learning more generally. Keeping tabs on my learning and my peers' learning made me feel responsible for my—and their—learning. Furthermore, as a graduate student in a master's program, I felt it was up to me to get the most out of my experience, especially while learning remotely. I took initiative to make virtual office hour appointments, attend university guest lectures, and set up informal study groups.

I continued to develop a more intentional approach to learning by **consciously engaging in metacognitive strategies.** In Approaches to

Teaching Writing, I learned about the role of metacognition in learning and the ways in which teaching practices such as scaffolded assignments, reflections, and portfolios foster metacognition. Thus, when my classes incorporated these types of assignments, I consciously engaged in metacognition. For instance, in Race, Place, and Representation with Professor Amani Morrison, I turned in a final portfolio that consisted of a draft conference-length essay and a response to peer feedback, noting how I would revise and expand the essay. In drafting my portfolio, I not only reflected on my choices but also on the strengths of the essay and challenges I encountered while writing it. I found this portfolio assignment more challenging than having to turn in a final essay or simply incorporate my peers' feedback. Instead, I had to recognize gaps in my writing and think about how I would integrate my peers' feedback into my essay.

Furthermore, my conscious engagement in metacognitive strategies while learning during the pandemic made me more **aware of my conceptions of teaching and learning** than during in-person learning. Because metacognition encourages students to activate their prior knowledge and learning experiences, I intentionally drew upon my prior learning experiences and knowledge and shared them with others. While some of my instructors directly inquired about our past learning experiences—for instance, asking if we had ever taken a class online—my drawing upon these experiences was largely on my own accord. For the first time, I felt comfortable sharing and reflecting on my past learning experiences, especially those as a rural student. My newfound comfort in the classroom encouraged me to take risks with my learning during the pandemic. I felt braver and bolder as I produced work in new genres. For instance, I created a PechaKucha—a presentation with 20 slides shown with 20 seconds of commentary each—published an op-ed, and created a website. Because of my increased comfort with risk, I also incorporated media into nearly all of my final projects—a practice that I have typically avoided in face-to-face learning.

As I noticed my conceptions of learning, I also became more aware of the choices faculty made about assessment and the structure of classes. I noticed which classes felt never-ending and how that seemed to correlate with rigid, non-negotiable syllabi. However, for the most part, teaching during the pandemic felt transparently student-driven for the first time. Although nearly all graduate-level English courses are seminars, in most of my classes, it felt like students had a voice in the classroom, and faculty were more willing to listen. In my experience, students had a say in when the class met and for how long, how grading should work, and how to incorporate asynchronous assignments like discussion boards. Helping shape these once seemingly "set in stone" aspects of teaching made me feel more comfortable and empowered as a learner. I felt confident enough to propose discussion topics, suggest passages for close reading, and negotiate the syllabus with instructors.

My new confidence in the classroom in concert with remote learning software such as Zoom demystified higher education. I watched as instructors of all ages and statuses forgot to unmute themselves on Zoom, were interrupted by children or pets, or lost internet connection. Although seemingly inconsequential, having a literal window into people's lives humanized instructors who perhaps once seemed inaccessible or distant. Reflecting on all of my new insights about learning gleaned during the pandemic, I realize that much of what I witnessed in the classroom over the past year is what I *wish* learning always looked like: transparent, student-driven, and rooted in metacognitive strategies.

Sophie

My experience as a graduate associate at the Center for New Designs in Learning and Scholarship has informed my perceptions as a graduate student in the English master's program. In 2020, I noticed assessments began to slow down. By this, I mean I noticed much more reflection and intention being built into the fabric of assessment details. To echo Lillian, the reflective portion of the final portfolio in Professor Morrison's class offers a model for positioning thinking processes as central to summative assessment. After receiving feedback from our peers on our drafts, we used that feedback to develop a meta-plan, outlining how and why we would expand arguments *here*, cut tangents *there*, better frame a point *here*. The conscious deliberation necessary for that assignment prioritized metacognitive, reflective, and intentional learning. As a student, to be given the space and time to refine and even change ideas felt, to me, more productive than supporting a thesis in one round and potentially never thinking about it again. As a required part of the class, this encouraged us to slow down and take time thinking about what we were trying to accomplish in the space we had.

Although the COVID-19 pandemic likely inspired this final assignment's parameters because it may seem "less demanding," the portfolio model's success begs the question: How can we maintain this level of reflective learning moving forward while prioritizing academic growth? As a student, to slow down and be given the time, space, and structure to *think* about what we create/write/build offers us room to more deeply engage with those ideas. Building opportunities for reflection into an assignment—or into a course as a whole—forefronts the thoughtful labor required to produce good work in the first place. This example highlights how assessments communicate priorities and goals to students. I'm now keenly aware of how integrating reflective steps in the writing process provides students with the structure upon which they can explore ideas, think them through, and revise as an argument or context changes. This small shift—incorporating reflective writing—isn't "easier"; it grants more thoughtful and intentional approaches to learning content.

I have developed an appreciation for the slowed-down assessment style that emerged with greater velocity in the last two years, which guides students to think about the impact of any given choice in their work. I have carried this concept with me beyond any one course and now set aside time to articulate why I make certain argumentative, design, and intellectual choices in projects, essays, and even my work outside of the English department. Slowing down just enough to name an intention gives me space to think about what learning work I am doing.

Online learning also offered some useful affordances for intentional collaboration *before* classes. In face-to-face classrooms, I always relied on seminar discussion for explanation and guidance about a piece of difficult theory or literature that I only *kind of* understood but wasn't entirely sure about. Discussions helped me make my strongest connections to prior knowledge and brought out new ideas. Typically, I would not develop my most meaningful questions about texts until the class was nearly over or until I stewed over ideas from the discussion on my walk home from class. Last year's online courses changed that. They gave me the opportunity to read collaboratively (using tools like Perussall or Hypothes.is) and make some sense of a text alongside peers *prior* to meeting together. The discussion in class was *so* much richer when I had a designed, defined space to ask questions beforehand.

Informal conversation about texts prior to class moves some of those beginning-of-class cobwebs (what's the scholar's definition of *X* again?) into a space outside the primary class discussion. Even if they take informal shape—like talking about readings with peers just before class to acknowledge confusion, disagreement with authors, or even confidence in understanding—the social space becomes available to discuss and learn from each other's perspectives. Seeing these conversations be explicitly structured in the asynchronous, online environment helped me see how important they really are, and I wonder how grasping this concept can enrich future course design. I can read something by myself three-times over, but until a peer mentions an idea or aspect that I didn't consider or asks a clarifying question, my comprehension and contextual knowledge can only grow so much. As such, I thoroughly enjoyed being primed for discussion by thinking through guided questions before meeting as a class. If the pandemic hadn't led some professors to deploy online tools to implement pre-class "asynchronous" engagement, I don't think I would have realized this distinction so quickly or strongly. I learned that flipping the classroom to initiate some true collaboration prior to the class meeting strengthens what happens once everyone comes together.

Sherry

As these reflections suggest, spending a year in fully online courses led these students to notice some otherwise largely invisible elements of learning as well as some of their own habits, both because of experiences they missed and because of new practices that compensated for things that students or faculty could not do virtually. Isabel and Sophie both note shifts in social aspects of learning—the loss of informal interactions for Isabel and the effects of pedagogical interventions that offered new ways of interacting for Sophie. Lillian and Sophie gained new appreciation for reflection not only as part of a process of learning but also as a way of defining what they had learned. Intentionality emerged as an important element, as well. They recognized the decisions faculty made and communicated, but they also embraced the importance of their own intentionality. Although Isabel, Lillian, and Sophie are more attuned to teaching and learning than most students, their experiences suggest that the disruptions of pandemic learning prompted new awareness of teaching and learning, at least for some.

The pandemic changed the **context** of learning and led many faculty to try new **approaches,** while discourse about pandemic education encouraged all of us, students and academics, as well as commentators and observers, to reconsider our **conceptions** of education and our **perceptions** of specific settings and practices. Some of this was prompted by the strangeness of pandemic learning, but media reports, social media interactions, and campus communications also encouraged this kind of thinking. Much of the public discourse expressed anxieties, including concerns about students' engagement. The *Chronicle of Higher Education* warned that many students seemed disengaged—more so than before the pandemic. As Beth McMurtrie reported, faculty saw declines in preparation, attendance, and participation. Possible causes include the multiple social traumas of recent years and the new strangeness of the in-person masked classroom. Online learning seems to have led some students to think of education as a process of observation rather than interaction.[6]

How do we re-engage students—especially those who are not already as curious about learning as Isabel, Lillian, and Sophie? I believe that their stories and my own experiences point to a good starting place: overtly invite students to notice and reflect on how learning works for them. My argument for this is based largely on my experience as a professor. Unlike so many colleagues, I would describe my recent students as *more* engaged than before the pandemic, and that has paralleled two changes in my own pedagogy. One was asking students to document and analyze their learning, an ungrading strategy that gives students responsibility for their learning but also for articulating what learning looks like.

To facilitate this, I also incorporated class discussions and resources that offered frameworks for thinking about knowledge and learning. In one of the courses I teach, a graduate course on teaching writing, that is built in to the subject matter, but in my first-year seminars on race, class, and cities, it is both a means of helping students think about how disciplinary and interdisciplinary analyses work and a strategy for helping them transition to college learning. I did not incorporate these strategies in order to generate engagement, nor have I done any research to test or validate the correlation. I can only report that attendance, preparation, participation, and interest in course concepts and materials, as well as students' interactions and collaborations with each other, were among the strongest I have seen in 40 years of teaching.

That's my story, and of course, these strategies might not work for everyone. My classes are small, which enables me to read and respond to every student's reflections. They are also not required, although some fulfill requirements, and this predisposes students to respond openly to assignments like this. Building in time and attention to this kind of metacognition and reflection might not fit with every course, and most of us are constantly worried about fitting in everything we want to cover. But short reflections like minute papers or informal tools like online surveys can invite students to consider their conceptions of education, the context of a course, their perceptions of pedagogy, and their own approaches. Better yet, hearing what students think can help us understand their behavior, communicate our own conceptions and perceptions, and connect with them. And all of that can improve our teaching and their learning.

Notes

1. A Google Scholar search for "pandemic teaching" on September 14, 2021, yielded nearly 350,000 hits. A search of the *Chronicle of Higher Education* website on the same date yields more than 39,000 articles. Although not all represent examples of faculty rethinking pedagogy, and many fewer point to changes in classroom practices after the pandemic, it's clear that the pandemic generated significant new attention to teaching.

2. During the summer of 2020, together with staff from Georgetown's Center for New Designs in Learning and Scholarship, I interviewed colleagues from across campus about their experiences with the quick pivot to online teaching earlier that year.

3. Ambrose, *How Learning Works.*

4. Prosser and Trigwell, "Experience of Teaching."

5. Prosser and Trigwell, "Experience of Teaching," 6.

6. The *Chronicle of Higher Education* published a series of articles in spring 2022 about students' disengagement, starting with Beth McMurtrie's April 5 piece, "A 'Stunning' Level of Student Disconnection," a follow-up piece sharing thoughts from several faculty on April 11, and a collection of commentaries by six faculty about "How to Solve the Student-Disengagement Crisis" (May 11, 2022). McMurtrie, "Energy Into a Void"; Glazier et al., "How to Solve."

Bibliography

Ambrose, Susan A. *How Learning Works: Seven Research-Based Principles for Smart Teaching.* San Francisco: Jossey-Bass, 2010: 191.

Glazier, Rebecca A., Tobias Wilson-Bates, Kristin Croyle, Emily Isaacs, Elaine M. Hernandez, and Nicole Green. "How to Solve the Student-Disengagement Crisis." *Chronicle of Higher Education* 68, no. 19 (May 11, 2022). https://www.chronicle.com/article/how-to-solve-the-student-disengagement-crisis.

McMurtrie, Beth. "A 'Stunning' Level of Student Disconnection." *Chronicle of Higher Education* 68, no. 17 (April 5, 2022). https://www.chronicle.com/article/a-stunning-level-of-student-disconnection.

——— "'It Feels Like I'm Pouring Energy Into a Void.'" *Chronicle of Higher Education,* April 11, 2022. https://www.chronicle.com/article/it-feels-like-im-pouring-energy-into-a-void.

Prosser, Michael, and Keith Trigwell. "Student learning and the experience of teaching." *HERDSA Review of Higher Education,* Vol. 4, 2017. https://www.herdsa.org.au/system/files/HERDSARHE2017v04p05_0.pdf.

chapter 8

Recentering Relationships

What We Learned from Building Closeness at a Distance

Molly Chehak and David Ebenbach

What might seem like irony really wasn't: as remote work and learning became the norm in 2020, the importance of relationships came into focus. Administrators and employers worried that the online format would make it all too easy to "tune in and drop out" by turning off one's camera, multi-tasking through class sessions, and backchanneling during lectures. It seemed possible that education, now delivered via laptops, would necessarily become flat and impersonal.

This was an important concern. Research on the value of relationships in educational environments is abundant, and it predates the pandemic. A sense of connectedness has been shown to promote motivation to learn, as well as actual learning, academic achievement, satisfaction, and even more general benefits that extend beyond the classroom, including a sense of belonging and personal well-being.[1] In short, we've known for some time how crucial relationships are to learning. And of course, much of this "invisible work" has been a long-standing labor of love for faculty and staff, as our Georgetown colleague Randy Bass has noted.[2]

But crisis mode (a.k.a. 2020) brought with it powerful new motivation to nurture relationships even while we were employing "social distancing"—and that motivation challenged us to figure out new ways to make it happen. We were so panicked about losing touch that, in fact, many new forms of outreach emerged. Both authors of this chapter work at the Georgetown University group that was responsible for training faculty to move online in March 2020, the Center for New Designs in Learning and Scholarship (CNDLS), where we urged faculty to try a variety of things to help build relationships. Faculty wrote notes to their students and sent them via email or the announcement feature in their learning management system (LMS). They used icebreakers to warm up their classes, made frequent use of breakout rooms to get students into small groups, and developed comfort with conducting office hours as phone calls or Zoom sessions. Students, for their part, reported feeling more engaged as a result of these forms of connection and hoped they would continue.[3]

For the most part, we're no longer teaching from a distance—but the connections we focused on during remote teaching still matter now that we're face to face. If we're going to foster successful in-person (and sometimes de facto hybrid) learning in the wake of these experiences, we need to give relationships the same level of attention we did in 2020 and 2021. And, far from expecting a return to some past version of our classes, we need to carry what we learned in that period with us, not the least because studies show that the stronger connections students feel to their instructor and classmates, the more permanent or "sticky" that learning is.[4]

In other words, recent experience has taught us a lot about our need to be connected to each other. More specifically, over two years of slowly evolving relationship norms, we've observed that (1) relationships are not only important but essential to learning, (2) we can adopt strategies to center relationships in our teaching practice, and (3) we shouldn't think about this issue only when we're in crisis mode. In this chapter, we'll draw on the experience of faculty and students gleaned through surveys, consultations, and workshops, as well as interviews from a podcast we produce, and examine how they may indicate widespread changes to teaching and learning post-pandemic.

Case Study

To illustrate these points, we look at the first two years of the COVID-19 pandemic from our vantage point at the Center for New Designs in Learning and Scholarship at Georgetown University. During those two years, we worked with hundreds of faculty trying to create vibrant learning experiences under unfamiliar constraints. In case after case, we saw faculty centering relationship-building in their approach to teaching, using a range of techniques to foster community—at a distance.

Below, we explore some approaches, mastered by many during the pandemic, that have great potential to continue serving us and our students well, now and going forward. These approaches include making good use of office hours and small group work, active use of the learning management system for communication, making space for students' lives outside the classroom, identifying potential areas for adaptable course policies, and seeking feedback from students. We found that these connections were made stronger by the techniques we share here.

Accessible Office Hours

One-on-one time is an important way to build and maintain instructor–student relationships. Faculty achieve this in various ways: a questionnaire via Google docs or a Canvas quiz prior to the semester's start, or an in-person "access needs check-in" with each student. But office hours are a tried-and-true technique to get that one-on-one time. Especially for first-year students, office hours have proved crucial to building relationships.

According to a spring 2020 survey of Georgetown students, many students reported that they became frustrated at the reduced accessibility of their professors after the loss of onsite office hours.[5] Faculty responded to this need by extending virtual office hours and, in some cases, instituting mandatory office hours. Thomas Kerch, a professor in Georgetown's Department of Government and in the Graduate

Liberal Studies Program and the associate director of the Tocqueville Forum for Political Understanding, is a prime example: "The first couple of weeks, I insisted upon individual meetings with each student. Fifteen minutes is sufficient time for doing this. And, much to my delight and surprise, all fifty-six of them made appointments to come and see me, just so I could get to know them, they could get to know me a little better. And it worked very well. It was a very nice icebreaker, in other words."[6]

On the Georgetown campus, students have responded positively to this outreach on the part of faculty. Gwyneth Murphy, a junior in the School of Foreign Service, shared that her Islam professor set up a 20-minute meeting with every single one of his students—not to talk about the course, but just to talk. The gesture itself went a long way to engaging Gwyneth and making her feel included. In her words, it was "amazing" because when "I go to class, I feel like I know them in a way that I didn't feel like I knew them" before.[7] As we seek new ways to build an overall sense of belonging for all our students, this more assertive approach to establishing a connection with one's students is widely successful as well as widely doable.

Whether students are required to attend or just show up, techniques for building relationships through in-person office hours include starting with non-class-related questions: "How's your semester going?" or "What are you looking forward to this week?" This approach can build rapport that transfers when faculty shift to discussing the class and the student's efforts and progress. Similarly, conducting these hours online can help build rapport by keeping a modicum of the personal. Some faculty hypothesized that the informality of the virtual office hours environment (compared with traditional in-person office hours) led students to be more willing to attend because the process of just getting into office hours—complicated in the past by barriers like distance, weather, or scheduling—has become easier because those barriers are eliminated by Zoom.[8] It's so easy, in fact, to conduct virtual office hours that making them mandatory has proved not only uncontroversial but popular among students.[9]

Small Group Work

We can add to one-on-one relationships by building community in the classroom. Small group work is one tool that can promote community and foster a powerful learning environment for students. Many faculty rediscovered this potential during online teaching, when the use of breakout rooms surged in an effort to keep students actively engaged. Of course, the same effect obtains in person. In a sufficiently small group, every student is called to an active experience of learning; each is asked to contribute effort and expertise, creating a dynamic where all are involved, and all get the chance to recognize the value of their own and others' work. This approach also helps to decentralize the classroom, such that students discover that they can learn not only from the instructor but from their peers and themselves.

Providing student choice or agency around their roles in the group also creates engagement, whether the group work is in person or using a discussion board. Justin Goldstein, who was a first-year Georgetown student in 2020–2021, shared this experience with us: "One of my favorite assignments [involved appointing a] group leader."[10] Throughout the semester, students met in the same small groups, and each student would sign up for the group discussion leader role once per semester. Goldstein felt that was effective to "have that community of people you're more familiar with so you know the dynamic going into it."[11] He added that the relationships created in the small groups helped him not only engage with the material, but better understand the implications of what he learned.

In addition, many faculty, equipped with new technology tools, have become conversant with a wider range of ways to make small group work happen. That range remains available. Synchronous collaboration, for example, doesn't have to consist solely of oral discussion and/or physical whiteboards in classrooms; students can work together in Google Docs, Jamboards, or Slides—and video-conferencing tools make live work easier when class isn't in session. In other cases, when student schedules are complicated to coordinate or when the task lends itself to asynchronous progress, those same Google suite apps can come in handy, and so can social annotation tools like Hypothes.is—and discussions in the LMS are always an option.

LMS Communication

The pandemic era of teaching saw a widespread increase in the robust use of a campus learning management system or LMS like Canvas, Blackboard, and Moodle.[12] Faculty used learning management systems for a variety of reasons, all of which helped enormously during remote learning and which still make sense now. Even as LMS use has been reasonably critiqued (see below), we find the benefits have outweighed the costs in terms of transparency, community, and clarity.

First, rather than just being a repository of readings, the LMS became a more welcoming space in many courses. Faculty used home pages and/or orientation modules to communicate the purposes and goals for the semester and to provide crucial information, all of which students began to access before the course even started. Many also used the quiz function of their LMS to create (ungraded) pre-semester surveys, asking students about their learning situations and needs, in order to shape their teaching accordingly. Others asked students to participate in discussions that invited them to post introduction videos. And many faculty have continued using these tools to get to know their students and set themselves up to teach successfully.

Faculty also leaned on their LMS to establish a clear presence in the virtual "classroom." In the absence of a physical gathering space, the use of announcements and other communications helped everyone stay on track while also creating connections. This tactic has the same benefits when the class is meeting in person because typically course meetings are separated by several days.

Of course, LMS use varies widely based on the user; similar to the way in which an in-class discussion, colored by spontaneous commentary and reaction, can lead a path down a path of collective discovery, the LMS needs to be harnessed to foster more serendipitous interaction that leads to informal learning.[13] In this way, learning is a deeply social experience that can be more effective and "sticky" when student driven. Therefore, it is wise to heed the observation that the success or failure of any LMS depends on the connectedness of student-driven features with faculty-driven features; or rather, we should aim to decrease the divide between chat rooms, discussion forums, and Zoom, on the one hand, and quizzes, assignments, and grading, on the other.[14] The study further "argues for the inclusion of students' personal features (values, self-direction, and love/passion, identities) in order to blend all respective LMS features for effective learning" in higher education.[15] Indeed, Green and Chewing have found such "integrative use of the LMS highly beneficial in facilitating individualized, formative feedback, and maintaining engagement in larger introductory courses."[16] If LMS feature integration discussed above occurs at a wider scale, digital tools can and will more effectively provide a springboard for relationship-building and participation.

Designing for Students' Lives Outside the Classroom

Meanwhile, the remote video-based interface had some advantages over the in-person classroom, which can create a false sense of sameness within the learning community; in person, we're all in the same physical space, and typically that environment hosts a very narrow range of activities, all focused on the academic goals at hand. Unless students make their outside-the-classroom lives visible (e.g., by talking about it), we might never know much more about them than how they perform on our assessments. Even larger world events might seem to stop at the classroom door unless we let them in. Virtual learning, on the other hand, made students' lives more visible. During the quarantine, teachers saw into the many different living spaces of students. Some learners were Zooming in from large private rooms in their parents' vacation homes, whereas others were in living rooms that also served as dining rooms and kitchens, with people bustling all around them. Laptop cameras made it hard to ignore cultural and familial and economic differences.

Because these differences were so vivid, the faculty we worked with made adjustments: accommodating people who couldn't attend synchronous class sessions for one reason or another via asynchronous activities like discussion boards, annotation software, and online quizzes; considering issues of privacy and sensitivity and offering alternative ways to engage (e.g., via the chat, Google docs, or discussion boards); or recording class sessions and sharing the recordings, or dividing their classes into sections that met at different times.

We saw many teachers take student well-being into account by introducing brief mindfulness exercises to class sessions, reducing demands in terms of reading loads and assignments, and allowing room for deadlines to shift, where possible and appropriate, when students faced significant challenges. And some addressed societal events directly in the classroom, whether using course-related tools for analysis or making space for students to express themselves.

Some of these issues fade away in an in-person classroom, where we don't have to worry about differences in time zones, learning environments, or internet access. But our students remain wonderfully diverse and continue to be affected by events outside the classroom. Teachers can reduce less visible but important economic disparities by assigning students free or low-cost texts. Giving students multiple synchronous and asynchronous ways to engage with course material can help accommodate the complexity of student lives. Addressing or incorporating world events allows students to bring their whole selves to the learning and deepen the learning experience. And, as we explore in the next section, it's possible to adapt more deeply and individually to events in students' lives.

Adaptation

Whole-student education, a core element of the Georgetown University campus culture known as *cura personalis*, means responding to individual student needs. This kind of responsiveness might take the form of working with students, in advance and during the semester, to make the experience as accessible as possible and remove barriers that might get in the way of learning. Faculty may also give students latitude about the focus of their assignments, explicitly allowing them to focus on aspects of their own lives where relevant or offering choice in assignment topics. Barriers to learning may include mandatory attendance policies that penalize students even in the face of a crisis, or health differences, both physical and mental, as well as life circumstances. Immovable deadlines can be similarly unresponsive to individual situations. Grades and competition, which have been shown to reduce intrinsic motivation and creativity, constitute additional possible barriers to learning and an authentic teacher–student relationship.[17] In other words, responding to student needs with all the tools at our disposal increases academic engagement and inspires student academic excellence.

While the degree of adaptation necessarily depends on the size of the class, flexible deadlines and assignments may lead to individual responses to individual situations, which yields information that builds relationships. The pandemic surfaced many personal situations that were intimately connected with our ability to learn and work; those factors haven't always receded as the pandemic has. Thus, "instructors may want to stretch out those deadlines to avoid some of the challenges we will undoubtedly face as a result of illness or unpredictable connectivity. Increasing peer review groups (from 2 to 3, for example) will reduce the complications if one student cannot complete their review on time."[18] This strategy encourages student–student relationships as well as encouraging students to be open and vulnerable with faculty as to how they are balancing their time and needs.

We would be remiss if we didn't acknowledge that adapting a course or assignment can be a double-edged sword in that it can create more work for a faculty member. At the same time, some of these adaptations actually makes these easier; for example, spread-out assignment submissions even out the grading crunch. Finding low-impact-for-faculty ways to meet students where they are can create high-impact results in terms of engagement and academic success.

Soliciting Feedback to Create and Maintain a Feedback Loop

Faced with a new, online format, many faculty were concerned that they were also facing steep learning curves for their own teaching and found that they had less of an easy read on how things were going for students who were confined to Zoom windows. So many took the time to ask students about their experience—not just at the end of the semester but throughout. In fact, as we noted above, one common practice was to solicit student input in pre-course surveys—on their learning circumstances, on their goals for the course, and on course topics and materials.

Once the semester was underway, quite a few faculty checked in with their students one or more times to see how they were feeling about in-class and asynchronous activities, readings, assignments, and so on. After all, for instructors who had spent their entire careers designing courses around the assumption of in-person experiences, much of their virtual course design was inherently somewhat experimental. And so they surveyed their students via the LMS or other apps, asked students to take online polls or leave their "muddiest point" comments in chat, and/or invited colleagues or staff from CNDLS to observe their classes or talk with their students.

Gathering this feedback meant that plans had to change mid-semester in some cases, but the benefits to the students were significant. Professors were able to make adjustments that helped students learn—and, as we already know, the process of incorporating feedback boosts student morale and engagement.[19] Even as we return to the relative comfort of in-person learning, mid-semester feedback has the potential to make a course more responsive to student needs and experience, and therefore to be more effective.

Conclusion

The strategies we discuss above have helped faculty connect with students and make learning happen at a distance—but we don't want to overstate the case. Everyone was concerned that remote learning would lead to decreased student engagement, and indeed at our own school, we found, through surveys of our students, that engagement was lower than we would have wanted during the early pandemic period, and that it continued to decrease as public health restrictions continued to affect teaching and learning modalities.[20] Most of us were very relieved when we were able to come back together in person. So we're not making the case that these strategies made remote learning better than in-person learning. But, from all that we observed and heard from our faculty, we do feel that the approaches outlined above not only made the best of a very challenging situation, but that several of the lessons learned made and will continue to make learning more student- and relationship-centered.

We have the opportunity to bring the best of what we had to embrace when physical class meetings were impossible. Learning names quickly thanks to the Zoom labels and easily connecting with students in virtual office hours were wins, and so were new discoveries about our student lives and the power of the LMS. We learned that being adaptable and maintaining rigor can and do coexist. Certainly, we learned that students responded positively to these techniques which indicated the need to continue to prioritize relationships in our classes going forward, especially given the emotional and cognitive aftermath of a global pandemic in addition to social and political conflict, not to mention a deepening mental health crisis among youth.[21]

Where Do We Go from Here? Why Does It Matter?

Of course, we can't underestimate the larger context in which the changes we are proposing need to take root. As Peter Felten and Leo Lambert have noted, "Institutional culture regulates relationship building, for good or ill."[22] As we write this chapter, learning environments are still in flux. Widespread online school at the K-12 level showed the cracks in the system: learning became transactional for a generation of students at a critical point in their social and intellectual development; many lost motivation.[23] Meanwhile, threats old and new to the status quo of higher education continue to evolve. Existing challenges like declining enrollments and financial inaccessibility have been joined by new ones such as climate change, economic instability, and faculty/staff shortages, not to mention existential crises about the role of a liberal arts education in workforce preparation.[24] At their very core, our institutions are having to adapt and become nimbler, which requires both human ingenuity and human connection.

All in all, it feels like some of our recent discoveries are here to stay. It's hard to imagine that students will give ground on what they have gained during years of disruption and trauma during the pandemic. They have been able to find success even while—or perhaps because of—the ability to Zoom into class when in quarantine or confronting other personal issues. They have connected with faculty on a human level that has not heretofore been widespread. They are able to integrate a bit more their whole selves while studying, working, and responding to the world around them.

Faculty, too, are unlikely to walk these gains back. The deepened relationships have formed an anchor during uncertain times and given many of us a renewed appreciation for the power of intentional, connected teaching. As Georgetown University Philosophy professor Huaping Lu-Adler said in an interview for our podcast, "We do better work because we brought ourselves to the classroom, because we felt that we were being noticed as whole human beings, the professors and students alike."[25] We, as faculty and staff, have the opportunity to continue our core teaching practices to buoy ourselves and our students and reassert the primacy of relationships to the learning process, thereby acting as the center that can hold.

For all these reasons, we must build techniques for relationship-building into our planning regardless of what circumstances we meet . . . both because circumstances are bound to change and quickly and because the one thing that won't change is the importance of human connection. Ironically, the challenges of distance learning have taught us more than we ever anticipated about how to encourage and nurture the all-important learning community.

Notes

1. Bovill, "Co-creation in Learning"; Felten and Lambert, *Relationship-Rich Education*; Frisby et al., "Participation Apprehensive Students"; Frisby and Martin, "Instructor–Student and Student–Student Rapport"; Hirsch and Clark, "Multiple

Paths to Belonging"; MacLeod et al., "Student-to-Student Connectedness"; Stanton et al., "Well-Being in Learning Environments."

2. Felten and Lambert, *Relationship-Rich Education.*

3. Instructional Continuity, "Student Feedback."

4. Zhou, "Student Learning Outcomes"; McGrath and Bergen, "Who, When, Why."

5. Instructional Continuity, "Student Feedback."

6. Kerch, discussion panel.

7. Murphy, "What We Are Learning."

8. Instructional Continuity, "Faculty Feedback,"

9. Instructional Continuity, "Student Feedback."

10. Center for New Designs in Learning and Scholarship, "Student Perspectives."

11. Goldstein, "What We Are Learning."

12. Hill, "Massive Increase in LMS."

13. Costley et al., "How Use of Learning."

14. Mpungose and Khoza, "Canvas Learning Management System."

15. Mpungose and Khoza, "Canvas Learning Management System."

16. Green and Chewning, "Fault in Our Systems."

17. Amabile, "Labor of Love."

18. Reynolds et al., "Engagement, Flexibility, and Workload."

19. Payette and Brown, "Variations to Improve Instruction."

20. Office of Assessment and Data Services, "Academic Engagement Pulse Survey."

21. "US Surgeon General Issues Advisory on Youth Mental Health Crisis Further Exposed by COVID-19."

22. Felten and Lambert, *Relationship-Rich Education.*

23. McMurtrie, "Student Disconnection."

24. Alexander, *Universities on Fire*; Fisher, "Shrinking of Higher Ed"; Nugent, "Shaping Higher Education."

25. Ebenbach, "Supporting Student Well-Being."

Bibliography

Alexander, Bryan. *Universities on Fire: Higher Education in the Climate Crisis.* Baltimore: Johns Hopkins University Press, 2023.

Amabile, Teresa. "Creativity and the Labor of Love." *The Nature of Human Creativity*, edited by Robert J. Sternberg and James C Kaufman, 1–15. Cambridge, UK: Cambridge University Press, 2018. https://doi.org/10.1017/9781108185936.

Bovill, Catherine. "Co-Creation in Learning and Teaching: The Case for a Whole-Class Approach in Higher Education." *Higher Education* 79, no. 6 (June 2020): 1023–1037. https://doi.org/10.1007/s10734-019-00453-w.

Center for New Designs in Learning and Scholarship. "Create Opportunities for Students to Build Rapport with Each Other and with You at the Beginning of and throughout the Semester." *Inclusive Pedagogy Toolkit*, accessed December 13, 2021. https://cndls.georgetown.edu/inclusive-pedagogy/ip-toolkit/climate/#create.

Center for New Designs in Learning and Scholarship. "Student Perspectives on Pandemic Learning." December 9, 2020, in *What We're Learning about Learning*. Podcast produced by Georgetown University, 40:35. https://spotifyanchor-web.app.link/e/wJCMlT8wPtb.

Costley, Jamie, Ashleigh Southam, Daniel Bailey, and Shaibou Abbdoulai Haji. "How Use of Learning Management System Mediates the Relationships between Learner Interactions and Learner Outcomes." *Interactive Technology and Smart Education* 19, no. 2 (May 11, 2022): 184–201. https://doi.org/10.1108/ITSE-12-2020-0236.

Ebenbach, D. "Supporting Student Well-Being and Learning." *What We're Learning about Learning* (podcast) episode 6, May 2022. CNDLS. https://cndls.georgetown.edu/podcast/season2/episode6.

Felten, Peter, and Leo M. Lambert. *Relationship-Rich Education: How Human Connections Drive Success in College*. Baltimore: Johns Hopkins University Press, 2020.

Fisher, Karin. "The Shrinking of Higher Ed." *Chronicle of Higher Education*, August 12, 2022. https://www.chronicle.com/article/the-shrinking-of-higher-ed.

Frisby, Brandi N., Erin Berger, Molly Burchett, Emina Herovic, and Michael G. Strawser. "Participation Apprehensive Students: The Influence of Face Support and Instructor-Student Rapport on Classroom Participation." *Communication Education* 63, no. 2 (2014): 105–123. https://doi.org/10.1080/03634523.2014.881516.

Frisby, Brandi N., and Matthew M. Martin. "Instructor–Student and Student–Student Rapport in the Classroom." *Communication Education* 59, no. 2 (2010): 146–164. https://doi.org/10.1080/03634520903564362.

Godlewska, Anne, Wanda Beyer, Scott Whetstone, Laura Schaefli, John Rose, Breah Talan, Sean Kamin-Patterson, Christopher Lamb, and Melissa Forcione. "Converting a Large Lecture Class to an Active Blended Learning Class: Why, How, and What We Learned." *Journal of Geography in Higher Education* 43, no. 1 (2019): 96–115. https://doi.org/10.1080/03098265.2019.1570090.

Goldstein, Justin. "What We Are Learning about Learning." Interview by Molly Chehak and Kim Huisman-Lubreski. Episode 1. CNDLS, Georgetown University. December 2020. https://cndls.georgetown.edu/documents/43/What-We-Are-Learning-About-Learning-Ep-1-Transcript-1.pdf.

Green, Kathryn R., and Haynes L. Chewning. "The Fault in Our Systems: LMS as a Vehicle for Critical Pedagogy." *TechTrends* 64, no. 3 (May 2020): 423–431. https://doi.org/10.1007/s11528-020-00480-w.

Hedtrich, Sebastian, and Nicole Graulich. "Using Software Tools To Provide Students in Large Classes with Individualized Formative Feedback." *Journal of Chemical Education* 95, no. 12 (2018): 2263–2267. https://doi.org/10.1021/acs.jchemed.8b00173.

Hill, Phil. "Massive Increase in LMS and Synchronous Video Usage Due to COVID-19." *Phil Hill & Associates* (blog), April 3, 2020. https://philhillaa.com/onedtech/massive-increase-in-lms-and-synchronous-video-usage-due-to-covid-19/.

Hirsch, Jennifer L., and Margaret S. Clark. "Multiple Paths to Belonging That We Should Study Together." *Perspectives on Psychological Science* 14, no. 2 (2019): 238–255. https://doi.org/10.1177/1745691618803629.

Instructional Continuity. "Community in the Remote Classroom," Georgetown University, 2020. https://instructionalcontinuity.georgetown.edu/pedagogies-and-strategies/community-in-the-remote-classroom/.

———. "Faculty Feedback," Georgetown University, 2020. https://instructionalcontinuity.georgetown.edu/faculty-feedback/.

———. "Peer Learning," Georgetown University. https://instructionalcontinuity.georgetown.edu/pedagogies-and-strategies/peer-learning/.

———. "Student Feedback." Georgetown University. https://instructionalcontinuity.georgetown.edu/student-feedback.

Kerch, Thomas. Discussion panel at Digital Learning Days. Hosted by Center for New Designs in Learning and Scholarship, Georgetown University. December 8, 2020.

MacLeod, Jason, Harrison Hao Yang, and Yinghui Shi. "Student-to-Student Connectedness in Higher Education: a Systematic Literature Review." *Journal of Computing in Higher Education* 31, no. 2 (2019): 426–448. https://doi.org/10.1007/s12528-019-09214-1.

McGrath, Kevin F., and Penny Van Bergen. "Who, When, Why and to What End? Students at Risk of Negative Student–Teacher Relationships and Their Outcomes." *Educational Research Review* 14 (February 2015): 1–17. https://doi.org/10.1016/j.edurev.2014.12.001.

McMurtrie, Beth. "A 'Stunning' Level of Student Disconnection." *Chronicle of Higher Education* 68, no. 17 (April 5, 2022). https://www.chronicle.com/article/a-stunning-level-of-student-disconnection.

Mpungose, Cedric Bheki, and Simon Bheki Khoza. "Postgraduate Students' Experiences on the Use of Moodle and Canvas Learning Management System." *Technology, Knowledge and Learning* 27, no. 1 (March 2022): 1–16. https://doi.org/10.1007/s10758-020-09475-1.

Murphy, Gwyneth. "What We Are Learning about Learning." Interview by Molly Chehak and Kim Huisman-Lubreski. Episode 1. CNDLS, Georgetown University. December 2020. PDF transcript. https://cndls.georgetown.edu/documents/43/What-We-Are-Learning-About-Learning-Ep-1-Transcript-1.pdf.

Nugent, Ciara. "The Unexpected Ways in Which Climate Change Is Shaping Higher Education." *Time*, April 16, 2021. https://time.com/5953399/college-education-climate-change/.

Office of Assessment and Data Services. "Academic Engagement Pulse Survey Results." https://oads.georgetown.edu/surveys/academic-engagement-pulse-survey-results.

Payette, Patricia R., and Marie Kendall Brown. "Gathering Mid-semester Feedback: Three Variations to Improve Instruction." *IDEA Paper* 16 (2018): 1–8.

Reynolds, Julie A., Victor Cai, Julia Choi, Sarah Faller, Meghan Hu, Arthi Kozhumam, Jonathan Schwartzman, and Ananya Vohra. "Teaching during a Pandemic: Using High-impact Writing Assignments to Balance Rigor, Engagement, Flexibility, and Workload." *Ecology and Evolution* 10, no. 22 (November 2020): 12573–12580. https://doi.org/10.1002/ece3.6776.

Stanton, Alisa, David Zandvliet, Rosie Dhaliwal, and Tara Black. "Understanding Students' Experiences of Well-Being in Learning Environments." *Higher Education Studies* 6, no. 3 (2016): 90–99. https://files.eric.ed.gov/fulltext/EJ1109954.pdf.

"US Surgeon General Issues Advisory on Youth Mental Health Crisis Further Exposed by COVID-19," US Department of Health and Human Services. https://www.hhs.gov/about/news/2021/12/07/us-surgeon-general-issues-advisory-on-youth-mental-health-crisis-further-exposed-by-covid-19-pandemic.html.

Zhou, Jiangyuan. "The Effects of Reciprocal Imitation on Teacher-Student Relationships and Student Learning Outcomes." *Mind, Brain & Education* 6, no. 2 (2012): 66–73.

chapter 9

The Work Goes On

Centering Relationships and Reimagining Practices That Support Learning

Catherine Ross, Amanda Irvin, and Suzanna Klaf

Reflecting on 2020, it is clear that pandemic teaching brought learning into new focus for faculty, staff, and students as they responded to the demands on higher education to shift, adapt, and seek creative solutions. At the Columbia University Center for Teaching and Learning (CTL), the pandemic centered our work in supporting teaching and learning by making the CTL visible across the University as the go-to resource for all instructors as they navigated a variety of teaching modalities—from in-person to remote, to online, to hybrid. For our Center, the pandemic shifted our relationship with instructors. Instructors sought us out as they attempted to provide learning continuity while humanizing their courses and empathizing with their learners. They exhibited a new willingness to learn from colleagues who had transformed their teaching practices prior to the pandemic, those who had already abandoned conventional teaching practices in favor of methods that demonstrably improved learning outcomes. Despite this openness, the challenge of sustaining these efforts remains, and so the work goes on to disrupt the practices and policies around teaching and learning that do not serve university teaching communities or collegiate learners.

In this chapter, we draw on the voices of students, instructors, and experts, noting the important messages they conveyed through their interviews for the CTL *Dead Ideas in Teaching and Learning* podcast series that launched in spring 2020.[1] Like our listeners, we found what podcast guests shared both inspiring and a good reminder of what it takes to make teaching and learning happen. From these interviews, we note the areas that higher education must continue to work on if the focus is to remain on learning: the role of relationships in promoting/fostering learning, and re-examining systemic policies and practices that serve neither instructors nor students, such as those related to assessment, grading, and evaluation of teaching.

CTLs play a pivotal role in these efforts by educating faculty, departments, and schools; bringing instructor and student voices to the conversations; sharing the literature on evidence-based practices; and contributing when invited to the table to inform decision-making. Even through the extraordinary change wrought by the pandemic and the resulting faculty innovation, there is still resistance to change at the individual level and barriers at the institutional levels. And so we conclude this chapter with hope for the future and a call to action. University leaders at every level can navigate institutional constraints and seize opportunities to bring the advancement of student learning to the core of university operations and culture.

Case Study: Relationships Matter to Learning

As educational developers at the Columbia CTL who worked with instructors to pivot their courses online, we placed a lot of emphasis on the importance of building community, recognizing that the connections between the instructor and students and between students and students make such a difference in learning. Reflecting back on the spring 2020 semester, Mae Butler, a Columbia sophomore majoring in comparative literature and society, notes the importance of relationships to her learning and the challenge of replicating them in a virtual setting: "anthropologist Jean Lave said that learning is becoming a member of a sustained community of practice. And I think something that I've really faced this semester is having to renegotiate what community looks like. Because for me, that social bond and the community-based experience of learning is such a motivator."[2] The foray into remote teaching and learning that began in 2020 was distancing for some, for others it seemed to break down the barriers that distance students from faculty. While on Zoom, students and instructors got a glimpse into each other's lives, they spoke openly with one another of the challenges of teaching and learning during times of stress, uncertainty, and challenge, and recognized the role they each play in maintaining educational continuity.

In her discussion of instructor-student relationships, Dr. Laura Rendón, professor emerita at the University of Texas, San Antonio, and author of *Sentipensante (Sensing/Thinking) Pedagogy: Educating for Wholeness, Social Justice, and Liberation*, focuses on authenticity and care saying, "If there's one thing that we've learned from the pandemic, it's the importance of relationships and how we meet each other. When the world shut down and we were by ourselves, we realized how much we needed each other. We need to have a model where faculty establish authentic, caring relationships, validating relationships as I would call them, with students."[3] In order to build these relationships trust must be established. Both students and instructors are responsible for this work. In a May 2020 podcast conversation, Columbia undergraduate student majoring in Civil Engineering, Haya Ghandour told listeners "Trust your students. It's a partnership at the end of the day, and we're all here wanting to learn, otherwise we would not be in these spaces."[4] Indeed, in her season 3 conversation, Dr. Denise Cruz also leaned into the importance of trusting the student experience, saying, "There is tremendous value in remembering what it was like to be a student."[5] The take-away message: trust that your students want to learn.[6]

So although many instructors instinctively moved toward building trust[7] and relationships with their students during pandemic teaching and learning, certain institutional practices and policies, such as those around grading and assessing learning, remain challenging for many. Institutions recognized the need to adjust certain practices like grading and course evaluations in the spring 2020 semester. Many if not most universities changed to pass/fail grading and suspended the use of course evaluations. Dr. Jesse Stommel notes this tension in his *Dead Ideas* podcast interview in season 2, episode 2, saying, "And so trust is hard to develop, but I think it's made harder and more difficult by bureaucratic systems that are institutional, that get in the way and frustrate that work."[8] If higher education is to sustain relationship-based trust, then it requires an exploration of how instructors, experts, and students envision the changes needed to assessment and grading practices.

Barriers Remain: Reimagined Assessment and Grading Practices

As noted above, given the suddenness and chaos surrounding the movement of students off campus and of face-to-face courses to online, many institutions temporarily opted for a pass/fail model in order to reduce the pressure on students and instructors. With the traditional assessment pressures on pause, the focus for instructors and students alike could be on learning. For a brief moment, students were not consumed by competing for grades and cramming for high-stakes exams. Instead, they were able to focus on their learning, explore intellectual curiosity, and take risks. These changes to assessment and grading practices disrupted the relationship that students had to grades and created the kind of learning environments for which CTLs advocate.

In a discussion with the Columbia CTL, Stommel spoke directly to the challenge that grading poses to establishing positive relationships saying, "More than anything, I think the grades do harm to the relationships. The sort of very important relationships that we're trying to develop between students-teachers, but also between students. So students with one another, with their colleagues and peers, turn learning environments into competitive environments."[9] A practitioner and advocate of ungrading, Stommel shares how being a learner in an ungraded class was a transformational experience as he developed supportive relationships with his fellow students and his instructor. For instructors looking to intentionally change their grading practices, Stommel recommends "open conversations with students about grading, about how they're doing it, their feelings about it," and he highlights the importance of including student voices in the grading process by asking students to self-reflect and self-evaluate.

Like Stommel, Dr. Jenny Davidson, professor of English and Comparative Literature at Columbia and longtime resistor of conventional grading practices, recognizes the anxiety that students have and the pressure they place on themselves to get good grades. In season 1, episode 5 of the *Dead Ideas in Teaching and Learning* podcast,[10] she shared her approach to foster a supportive learning environment, one in which assessment and grading policies did not add to or cause needless stress. Davidson explicitly communicates her approach to grading to her students. She assigns short creative assignments that get students thinking and writing often about the texts explored in class, and that are evaluated using a check, check plus, check minus approach, instead of "triggering letters or numbers."

Similarly, Dr. Denise Cruz, associate professor of English and comparative literature at Columbia, shares how she moved away from using an in-class midterm and a final exam that required some memorization to using more frequent lower stakes assignments throughout the course. In season 3, episode 6 of the podcast, she shared that these gave her a better sense of "how they [students] were learning or how their learning was developing over the course of the term."[11] Additionally, Cruz recognized that arbitrary assessment policies and practices that counter pedagogies of care can hinder students' abilities to do their best work: "I've learned to reframe how I work with students by thinking about what do we ask for ourselves, and what kinds of generosity do we seek? . . . I started to think about the number of times that I personally have needed an extension in order to produce better work. Or even approaching an [in-class] exam, . . . when my best writing occurs when I have my notes scattered everywhere across the table in front of me."[12]

Davidson and Cruz both highlight here the importance of reexamining our assessment and grading practices to focus on learner-centered practices that privilege development and growth that contribute to an equitable learning experience for all students. And they're not alone: many instructors reimagined assessment practices, moving away from high-stakes assessments and giving their students alternative ways to demonstrate their learning.

For the student consultants who are part of the Columbia CTL's Students as Pedagogical Partners program, the change to pass/fail gave them a glimpse at what was possible. While grades were on pause, they confronted Pike's "dead idea" that grades motivate learning. Michelle Yao, an undergraduate student majoring in biological sciences, thought a lot about what she was learning. In her words, going from in-person to remote "made me realize that I need to start taking a step back in my learning and really reevaluating what exactly it is that I'm chasing. Is it the grade or is it the subject itself?"[13]

Similarly, undergraduate Engineering student Sajan Barr recognized the need to refocus on learning. As Barr reflected back on traditional high stakes exams, he told us: "You study really hard to get the good grade on the exam, but you spend so much time doing that—you forget why you're there and what you're learning. I'm just working to memorize it or working to get something done as opposed to actually learning what this material is and what it means."[14] Barr was driven by his professional goal to become an engineer and yet the traditional grading system imposed a lot of pressure and allowed little room for him to take risks and learn from failure. Barr noted that with the pressure of grades on pause, he came to the realization that it was okay to fail, it was not the end of the world but an opportunity for learning—"if you're not failing it's really hard to learn and grow from that experience."[15]

However, as Dr. Kevin Gannon, director of the Center for Excellence in Teaching and Learning and Professor of History at Grand View University, notes in season 3, episode 3 of the podcast, "we tell them [students], we want them to learn from failure, to learn from adversity, but everything they've been told up to this point has been that failure is that door closing, that that's the end of the story."[16] For a real turn to learning through failure to become normalized, instructors need to create learning spaces in their courses where risk taking is encouraged and failure is not penalized.

As Stommel and the Columbia faculty and student voices highlight, it is the relationships that matter: student–instructor relationships, student–student relationships, and the relationship that students have with themselves as learners. When it comes to assessment and grading, there is much room for improvement if we can imagine changing our pedagogical and institutional practices and policies to remove the causes of undue stress that are known barriers to learning. This is exactly where CTLs can help instructors and their institutions.

Changes to Teaching and Learning Can Happen and CTLs Can Help

In season 3, episode 3 of the *Dead Ideas in Teaching and Learning* podcast, Gannon provides hope to listeners saying, "we know what higher education can do and potentially do." In the interview, he notes that institutions made changes during the pandemic such as not using student ratings of instruction and that "the world didn't end, higher education did not collapse, our institutions soldier on as we did before. And so I think what we've learned is that these seemingly permanent ways that we've always approached things aren't really permanent, they're actually fairly arbitrary and we could get along just fine without them."[17]

At the outset of the pandemic, institutions removed many of the barriers to access and innovation, primarily as a way to clear the path to fully remote online learning in the middle of a public health emergency—freeing faculty from the institutional pressures to cover specific content, replicate traditional course grade distributions, and produce positive course evaluations. Trusting students and faculty to engage in the learning process—to show up every day, in the middle of a global health crisis—speaks to the potential higher education has to transform from within when faculty, students, and institutions truly partner to co-create meaningful, innovative and equitable learning experiences.

Although 2020 saw great trust between students and faculty when policies and practices were temporarily paused, longer, systemic changes must take place in order for institutions to truly center their missions on student learning and address the challenges to equity that are encoded in the systems. CTLs are positioned to navigate the landscape of this change. As Dr. Joshua Kim notes in a podcast conversation with the Columbia CTL: "At no time have centers for teaching and learning been more central to the resilience and ongoing operations of our colleges and universities. . . . So much of what's happened at universities has had to run through university CTLs."[18] Throughout the disruption of the pandemic, as professional staff from the Columbia CTL worked on the frontlines to support faculty through teaching pivots, we witnessed the learner-centered, evidence-based, and inclusive practices that we had been promoting for years become more pervasive in college classrooms.

Conclusion

By now, it is a time-worn trope that higher education is slow to change, but as noted above, the pandemic has upended the deeply entrenched status quo in ways that provide an opening. In order to sustain these valuable pandemic-driven teaching practices, how can CTLs address the barriers once the grades and teaching evaluations return to "normal?" Systemic change entails working along the entire continuum of change spaces, from individual instructors and students, to schools and departments, senate committees, education deans, and provost and diversity office allies. But what does this look like in practice? Serving on committees or offering to chair or co-chair subcommittees dedicated to specific topics like evaluation of teaching; sharing research and resources to help universities make informed decisions and policies based on the best and latest research to support teaching and learning; amplifying the voices of instructors who are advocating for change through their course design choices and sharing their lived experiences; or identifying instructor and faculty change-makers and supporting them as they serve on committees. CTLs can offer their work and expertise on topics like teaching evaluation, classroom design, diversity and inclusion, and thereby share in the labor that supports the social justice missions of our institutions while improving the conditions for continued creativity, adaptability, and student-centeredness to promote deeper levels of trust between students and instructors, as well as between instructors and the CTL. In this way—by offering support at all levels—can CTLs encourage institutions of higher education to address policies, procedures, and practices that can disrupt the trust needed by both instructors and students to do their best teaching and learning.[19]

Another avenue to create change is to leverage the placement of CTLs in the academic landscape. Because many teaching centers report through the provost's office, they have access to support, resources, and validation from high-level administrators. For instance, with the backing of the Office of the Provost, the Columbia CTL was able to collect faculty narratives on the lessons learned and the teaching innovations developed during the pandemic. The culminating project, *Teaching Transformations: Faculty Reflections and Insights on Pandemic Practices*,[20] documents the work of Columbia faculty and their pedagogical innovations, in hopes of inspiring other instructors and furthering broader changes to teaching across the community.

Students have changed, instructors have changed, and we (those of us who work in CTLs) have changed; there is no returning to "normal," only to better. The relationships and trust that have been forged are the foundation for this new way of approaching teaching and learning, both for individuals and for institutions. CTLs can support efforts in the work of change and of centering equity in our higher education landscape through the focus on relationships, the ones we build with others and the ones we help others build. The trust that CTLs have earned supports the work ahead of reimagining practices and policies that focus on learning and the relationships that make it possible. Building and sustaining these important relationships is ongoing work and all constituents in higher education—instructors, future instructors, students, administrators, staff—have a role to play.

Notes

1. *Dead Ideas in Teaching and Learning* is a podcast hosted by Columbia CTL Executive Director, Catherine Ross. It is inspired by Diane Pike's article "The Tyranny of Dead Ideas in Teaching and Learning" (2011). In each episode, guests are invited to share their discoveries of "dead ideas"—ideas that are not true but that are often

widely believed and embedded in the pedagogical practices in higher education. Listeners are encouraged to reflect on what they believe about teaching and learning.

2. Rendón, "Why Educating for Wholeness, Social Justice, and Liberation Is the Future of Higher Education."

3. Rendón, "Why Educating for Wholeness, Social Justice, and Liberation Is the Future of Higher Education."

4. Butler et al., "Columbia Undergraduates on Dead Ideas in Learning."

5. Cruz, "Power of Blended Classroom."

6. We acknowledge the fraught nature of trust during pandemic teaching and learning, primarily around issues of proctoring software, which seemed to peak during pandemic online teaching; automated proctoring platforms became red flags that highlighted the divide between trusting our students and not trusting them. Taking into account the pushback for being discriminatory, the invasion of privacy, the added stress and hindrance to academic performance (Young, 2020), there have been calls to check our assumptions about cheating and to refocus on student learning and rethink assessment and grading practices.

7. Building trust with students is about the relationship between students and instructors. Bain (2004) reminds us of how the best college instructors treat their students with "fairness, compassion, and concern" (Bain 2004, 145). Instructors who trust their students are open with them. They believe that their students want to learn and that they can learn. They share power with their students, co-create a constructive classroom environment and community in which all students feel a sense of belonging, and redefine the teacher-student relationship (Weimer 2013; Bain 2004). They recognize that "education is a shared endeavor and that learning and teaching are done *with* students not *to* them" (Cook-Sather et al. 2014; Bovill 2019). These instructors engage in pedagogical caring–they care about their students as learners and as human beings (Eyler 2018) and this matters to student learning (Cavanaugh 2020; O'Brien 2010; Meyers 2009; Thayer-Bacon and Bacon 1996).

8. Stommel, "Ungrading."

9. Stommel, "Ungrading."

10. Davidson, "Dead Ideas in Grading."

11. Cruz, "Power of Blended Classrooms."

12. Cruz, "Power of Blended Classrooms."

13. Barr and Yao, "One Year Later."

14. Barr and Yao, "One Year Later."

15. Barr and Yao, "One Year Later."

16. Gannon, "Dead Ideas in Faculty Evaluation."

17. Gannon, "Dead Ideas in Faculty Evaluation."

18. Kim and Maloney, "Learning Innovation."

19. See Schinske and Tanner, "Teaching More"; Linse, "On Evaluation Committees"; Kreitzer and Sweet-Cushman, "Recommendations for Ethical Reform"; American Sociological Association, "Statement on Student Evaluations."

20. "Teaching Transformations."

Bibliography

American Sociological Association. "Statement on Student Evaluations of Teaching." September 2019. https://www.asanet.org/sites/default/files/asa_statement_on_student_evaluations_of_teaching_feb132020.pdf.

Bain, Ken. *What the Best College Teachers Do*. Cambridge, MA: Harvard University Press, 2004. https://doi.org/10.2307/j.ctvjnrvvb.

Barr, Sajan, and Michelle Yao. "One Year Later: Learning in a Pandemic with Two Columbia Undergraduate Students." April 22, 2021, Season 2, Episode 2 in *Dead Ideas in Teaching and Learning*. Podcast produced by Catherine Ross, Stephanie Ogden, Laura Nicholas, Abie Sidell, and John Hanford, Columbia Center for Teaching and Learning, 36:59. https://ctl.columbia.edu/resources-and-technology/resources/podcast.

Bovill, Catherine. "Co-Creation in Learning and Teaching: The Case for a Whole-Class Approach in Higher Education." *Higher Education* 79, no. 6 (June 2020): 1023–1037. https://doi.org/10.1007/s10734-019-00453-w.

Butler, Mae, Haya Ghandour, Jennifer Lee, and Kalisa Ndamage. "Columbia Undergraduates on Dead Ideas in Learning," November 25, 2020, Season 1, Episode 4, in *Dead Ideas in Teaching and Learning*. Podcast produced by Catherine Ross, Stephanie Ogden, Laura Nicholas, Abie Sidell and John Hanford, Columbia Center for Teaching and Learning, 24:20. https://ctl.columbia.edu/resources-and-technology/resources/podcast.

Cavanaugh, Sarah Rose. "How I'm Spending My Pandemic Summer Vacation." *Chronicle of Higher Education*, June 9, 2020. https://www.chronicle.com/article/how-im-spending-my-pandemic-summer-vacation.

Cook-Sather, Alison, Catherine Bovill, Peter Felten, and Michael Cook. *Engaging Students as Partners in Learning and Teaching: A Guide for Faculty*. San Francisco: Jossey-Bass, 2014.

Cruz, Denise. "The Power of Blended Classrooms." December 2, 2021, Season 3, Episode 6, in *Dead Ideas in Teaching and Learning*. Podcast produced by Catherine Ross, Stephanie Ogden, Laura Nicholas, Abie Sidell and John Hanford, Columbia Center for Teaching and Learning, 36:13. https://ctl.columbia.edu/resources-and-technology/resources/podcast.

Eyler, Joshua R. *How Humans Learn: The Science and Stories behind Effective College Teaching*. Morgantown, WV: West Virginia University Press, 2018.

Ezarik, Melissa. "COVID-Era College: Are Students Satisfied?" *Inside Higher Ed*, March 24, 2021. https://www.insidehighered.com/news/2021/03/24/student-experiences-during-covid-and-campus-reopening-concerns.

Davidson, Jenny. "Dead Ideas in Grading." December 10, 2020, Season 1, Episode 5, in *Dead Ideas in Teaching and Learning*. Podcast produced by Catherine Ross, Stephanie Ogden, Laura Nicholas, Abie Sidell and John Hanford, Columbia Center for Teaching and Learning, 31:01. https://ctl.columbia.edu/resources-and-technology/resources/podcast.

Gannon, Kevin. "Dead Ideas in Faculty Evaluation." October 21, 2021, Season 3, Episode 3, in *Dead Ideas in Teaching and Learning*. Podcast produced by Catherine Ross, Stephanie Ogden, Laura Nicholas, Abie Sidell and John Hanford, Columbia Center for Teaching and Learning, 31:45. https://ctl.columbia.edu/resources-and-technology/resources/podcast.

Kim, Joshua, and Edward Maloney. "Learning Innovation and the Future of Higher Education." November 18, 2021, Season 3, Episode 5, in *Dead Ideas in Teaching and Learning*. Podcast produced by Catherine Ross, Stephanie Ogden, Laura Nicholas, Abie Sidell and John Hanford, Columbia Center for Teaching and Learning, 39:25. https://ctl.columbia.edu/resources-and-technology/resources/podcast.

Kreitzer, Rebecca J., and Jennie Sweet-Cushman. "Evaluating Student Evaluations of Teaching: A Review of Measurement and Equity Bias in SETs and Recommendations for Ethical Reform." *Journal of Academic Ethics* 20, no. 1 (March 2022): 73–84. https://doi.org/10.1007/s10805-021-09400-w.

Linse, Angela R. "Interpreting and Using Student Ratings Data: Guidance for Faculty Serving as Administrators and on Evaluation Committees." *Studies in Educational Evaluation* 54, (September 2017): 94–106. https://doi.org/10.1016/j.stueduc.2016.12.004.

Meinking, K. A. and E. E. Hall. "Co-Creating in the Classroom: Challenge, Community, and Collaboration." *College Teaching* 68, no. 4 (October 1, 2020): 189–198. https://doi.org/10.1080/87567555.2020.1786349.

Meyers, Steven A. "Do Your Students Care Whether You Care about Them?" *College Teaching* 57, no. 4 (2009): 205–210. http://www.jstor.org/stable/25763396.

Pike, Diane L. "The Tyranny of Dead Ideas in Teaching and Learning: Midwest Sociological Society Presidential Address 2010." *Sociological Quarterly* 52, no. 1 (February 2011): 1–12. https://doi.org/10.1111/j.1533-8525.2010.01195.x.

Rendón, Laura I. "Why Educating for Wholeness, Social Justice, and Liberation Is the Future of Higher Education." October 7, 2021, Season 3, Episode 2, in *Dead Ideas in Teaching and Learning*. Podcast produced by Catherine Ross, Stephanie Ogden, Laura Nicholas, Abie Sidell and John Hanford, Columbia Center for Teaching and Learning, 42:20. https://ctl.columbia.edu/resources-and-technology/resources/podcast.

Rendón, Laura I. *Sentipensante (Sensing/Thinking) Pedagogy: Educating for Wholeness, Social Justice and Liberation.* Sterling, VA: Stylus Publications, 2009.

Schinske, Jeffrey, and Kimberly Tanner. "Teaching More by Grading Less (or Differently)." *CBE Life Science Education* 13, no. 2 (Summer 2014): 159–166.

Stommel, Jesse. "Ungrading." February 4, 2021, Season 2, Episode 2, in *Dead Ideas in Teaching and Learning*. Produced by Catherine Ross, Stephanie Ogden, Laura Nicholas, Abie Sidell and John Hanford, Columbia Center for Teaching and Learning, 33:28. https://ctl.columbia.edu/resources-and-technology/resources/podcast.

Thayer-Bacon, B. J., and C. S. Bacon. "Caring Professors: A Model." *Journal of General Education* 45, no. 4 (1996): 2555–2569.

"Teaching Transformations: Faculty Reflections and Insights on Pandemic Practices." Columbia University, 2022. https://ctl.columbia.edu/transformations.
Weimer, Maryellen. *Learner-Centered Teaching: Five Key Changes to Practice*. 2nd ed. San Francisco: Jossey-Bass, 2013.
Young, Jeffrey R. "Pushback Is Growing against Automated Proctoring Services. But so Is Their Use - EdSurge News." *EdSurge*, November 13, 2020. https://www.edsurge.com/news/2020-11-13-pushback-is-growing-against-automated-proctoring-services-but-so-is-their-use.

chapter 10

"Why Haven't We Always Done This?"

The Future of Faculty Learning

Betsy Barre

In a quest to improve student learning, higher education has long devoted considerable resources to the professional development of faculty.[1] For almost as long, educational developers have been exploring the conditions under which these programs are most likely to succeed. Like the research on student learning, research on faculty learning has investigated both pedagogical strategies and barriers to learner participation and change.[2] Yet scholars disagree about which barriers are most salient and whether the most effective strategies will remain effective at scale.

This chapter will argue that our experience working with instructors throughout the COVID-19 pandemic has the potential to reshape our understanding of this literature and our overall approach to faculty learning. In March 2020, many barriers to participation evaporated overnight, and we could finally see how previously unreached faculty responded to strategies we had honed with their peers. By putting the results of this natural experiment in conversation with the extant literature, we can refine our theories of change and develop new strategies to support a significantly changed professoriate.[3]

What We Knew

Before the pandemic, scholars of educational development were in general agreement about the ideal conditions for faculty learning. We knew, for example, that short-form "training" designed to disseminate knowledge was less likely to be effective than inductive, inquiry-based programs that encourage faculty to approach their teaching as they approach their scholarship.[4] As Randy Bass and others have noted, there is a severe mismatch between deductive, top-down training models and how faculty acquire new knowledge in their areas of expertise.[5] In the former, new knowledge is acquired to remediate; in the latter, it becomes part of an ongoing, scholarly investigation.

Consistent with this insight, we knew that programs were most likely to succeed if they encouraged faculty to engage with the research on teaching and learning, experiment in their classrooms, reflect on their experiments, and do each in collaboration with their peers.[6] There is an extensive literature on each of these practices, and one is rarely discussed without reference to the others.[7] Stephen Brookfield's work on critically reflective teaching, Kathleen McKinney's work on scholarly teaching, and those writing about the merits of peer collaboration paint a common picture of the ideal conditions for faculty learning.[8]

Given this agreement, teaching centers have long prioritized collaborative, inquiry-based programming. Nevertheless, there has been a large and well-known gap between the availability of these programs and the widespread adoption of evidence-informed teaching practices across our institutions.[9] We know these programs worked well with the "usual suspects" eager to engage, but they have proved difficult to scale.[10] As a result, an equally important line of research has investigated barriers to faculty participation and change.[11]

Many have argued that time is the most significant structural barrier.[12] When asked, faculty regularly share that the increasing demands of their job (to teach more students, produce more research, and serve on more committees) make it hard to set aside time to engage in extended periods of pedagogical reflection.[13] Other scholars contend that institutional policies are the primary structural driver. By setting up reward systems that prioritize research, institutions may be undermining pedagogical reflection.[14] Yet recent research has also found that policy change may do little to shift faculty behavior without also shifting the messages sent by institutional cultures.[15] If one's peers do not value and support this inquiry, university policies may be ignored or even resented.[16]

Another line of research has explored the cognitive, emotional, and motivational dimensions of faculty engagement.[17] Applying self-determination theory to educational development, Gary Smith has recently argued that faculty may fail to participate if doing so threatens their basic psychological needs to direct their own learning, establish bonds with their peers, and display competence.[18] This framework echoes the critical work of Linda Hodges on the motivational role of faculty fear—fear of being controlled, fear of being judged by their peers, and, most importantly, fear of looking incompetent if they take pedagogical risks and fail.[19]

Others have emphasized the importance of individual beliefs and values. Most obviously, faculty must value teaching to dedicate time to its development.[20] But they must also value the inquiry itself, and certain beliefs about teaching can undermine its significance. For example, some believe teaching is a natural gift rather than a skill that can be learned.[21] Still others, particularly those with many years of experience, think they've already learned everything they need to know.[22] In either case, faculty might value their teaching but see little value in faculty learning initiatives.[23]

Given this research, we entered the pandemic with a meaningful yet opaque understanding of faculty learning. We knew inductive, inquiry-based programs had been effective with a subset of our faculty, but we couldn't be confident they would scale to those we had not yet reached. We knew a great deal about potential barriers to participation and change but didn't know which would prove most significant. Three years later, we still have many questions. But the scale of faculty learning throughout the pandemic allowed us to test our theories and deepen our understanding of previously hidden mechanisms.

What We Saw

If there was ever any doubt about the importance of faculty learning initiatives, that all changed in March of 2020. In the space of a week, over 1 million faculty were asked to pivot their in-person courses to an entirely new instructional modality. That spring, educational developers offered pedagogical "lifeboats" to help faculty and students weather the storm.[24] And as it became clear the storm would not lift anytime soon, we began thinking about how we might use the summer months to launch more substantive learning initiatives.[25]

Like many other institutions, Wake Forest developed structured learning opportunities that were informed by the research on faculty learning. Instead of deductive, short-form workshops on technology, we opted for an inquiry-based model that invited faculty to engage in extended periods of research, experimentation, collaboration, and critical reflection. Our Peer Learning Initiative brought together 70 faculty leaders from across the institution to participate in one of four learning communities that spent four weeks preparing to design and facilitate their own two-week learning communities with colleagues in their departments.[26] This program introduced all faculty to the literature on teaching and learning, encouraged them to reflect on their spring experience, and helped them build communities that would support one another into the fall.

Most notably for our purposes, these communities were well received by a wide range of previously unreached faculty. When 97% of WFU faculty opted to participate in this initiative, our teaching center experienced 15 years' worth of "high-engagement" participation in the space of three months.[27] Moreover, we received consistently positive feedback from those who participated in the program. They appreciated that the initiative was faculty-centered, discipline-specific, and an opportunity to engage in sustained conversations about pedagogy with their colleagues. We heard from many who planned to make permanent changes to their teaching and others who were eager to continue their collaboration with peers. Some wondered why they hadn't always used specific teaching strategies, and others wondered why their departments hadn't always made time for such rich conversations about teaching.

Two years later, long after our students and faculty have returned to the in-person classroom, Wake Forest continues to see the impact of our pandemic learning communities. Prior to the pandemic, we engaged close to 40% of our full-time faculty each year. In 2020, that number was close to 100%. Although we knew we could not sustain those levels of engagement in 2021, we were not sure what to expect. Would faculty exhaustion suppress engagement below our pre-pandemic baseline? Or would their near-universal participation in learning communities increase engagement beyond our usual suspects? One year later, we had an answer. Despite their very real exhaustion, over 66% of our full-time faculty continued to engage with our center during the 2021–2022 academic year—a 25% increase beyond our baseline.[28] We have also seen a marked increase in institutional teaching initiatives, and numerous departments have continued to hold regular meetings dedicated to the discussion of pedagogy.

Wake Forest is a well-resourced teaching-oriented institution with committed faculty and a supportive administration. Yet, this volume makes clear that the experience of our faculty was not unique. Teaching centers across the country launched similar programs with similar reach, and those at institutions without formal support managed to find their way to similar learning experiences. Faculty across the country formed discipline-based pedagogical communities on social media, created and shared scholarship on teaching and learning, attended conferences, experimented with new strategies, and reflected on their experiences in informal digital essays. It may be too soon to know whether these experiences will have transformative effects on higher education, but they have given us new insight into how faculty learn.

What We Learned

Unsurprisingly, faculty learning throughout the pandemic affirmed the importance of inquiry-based programs that prioritize scholarship, experimentation, reflection, and collaboration with peers. Whether they were engaging with teaching centers for the first time or building their own curriculum without formal support, previously unreached faculty were drawn to programs and approaches that mirrored the scholarly process.

The unprecedented level of faculty participation also gave us new insight into the structural and motivational variables shaping faculty engagement. Although it would not be unreasonable to argue that *everything* changed during the pandemic, the context shifted some barriers more than others. By reflecting on these shifts, we can better understand what drove participation and improve our theories of faculty change.

Time had been the most cited barrier to engagement in the past, but its relationship to pandemic participation was complex. On the one hand, time did seem to free up when it was impossible to pursue research, travel, or participate in public activities and events. But that time was also filled with a set of new demands. Primary caregivers were suddenly asked to do multiple jobs, and all of us had to attend to the psychological demands of living through a pandemic. At best, we can say that the affordances of additional time were not equitably distributed across all faculty participating in our programs.

Shifts in policies were also complex but relatively stable during the first few months of the pandemic. At most, expectations for research were put on hold. There was, however, no sense that policies would shift to place greater emphasis on teaching in promotion and tenure decisions. In fact, the few policy changes we did see were designed to *discount* the impact of pandemic teaching in such decisions.[29]

In terms of individual beliefs and values, we can reasonably assume that teachers did not suddenly change the extent to which they valued teaching as part of their professional identity. And it is hard to imagine major shifts in beliefs about whether teaching was a natural talent or a skill to be learned. Nevertheless, it was clear that many more faculty saw the immediate value of participation in pedagogical inquiry. Those who thought they had nothing more to learn were suddenly confronted with a pedagogical situation for which they felt unprepared.[30] Change suddenly became less risky than sticking with the comfortable status quo.[31]

More substantially, we witnessed massive shifts in cultural expectations. It is too early to know whether the culture of higher education has changed in lasting ways. But there was at least a temporary period when our institutions and professional networks were speaking with one voice. University presidents, disciplinary associations, and departmental colleagues made it clear that teaching was a priority and that we should be using the summer to prepare for the fall.

Because everyone was working on their teaching, and there was an awareness that such work was needed, there was also an understanding that failure was to be expected. If even the best teachers faced challenges, teaching problems were not a reflection of teaching skills. They were, instead, interesting phenomena to be investigated and explored with peers. Moreover, the experimentation at the heart of inquiry was less risky. A failed experiment was no longer an embarrassment but a contribution to an ongoing intellectual project.

Finally, many faculty took more responsibility for the well-being of their students than they had in the past. Because we were all quite literally struggling to survive, it was difficult to ignore the extent to which students' lives shaped their ability to learn. And as the summer prompted a further reckoning with racial injustice, many grew more sensitive to the differential impact of their teaching on their students. In both cases, faculty were further motivated to rethink their teaching assumptions and experiment with new approaches.

Taken together, these insights can help us paint a more nuanced picture of what does and does not motivate faculty to participate in faculty learning initiatives. Put simply, faculty may be most likely to engage when they (1) believe they have something to learn; (2) anticipate that what they learn will have practical value; (3) feel safe to experiment and fail; and (4) understand they are not the only ones in their professional networks who value this work. Although policies and structural change are undoubtedly important, they may only be important as means to these other ends.

Where We're Headed

As educational developers have begun to reflect on the last three years, we have been especially attentive to the effect of the pandemic on faculty well-being. Numerous sessions and multiple keynotes at the 2022 Professional and Organizational Development (POD) Network in Higher Education Conference focused on re-engaging faculty who were exhausted, burnt out, or demoralized.[32] As those sessions and this volume make clear, the last few years have taken their toll. Instructors worked extraordinarily hard under exceedingly challenging conditions, and too many have felt abandoned or undervalued by their institutions. Given this climate, it is understandable that our eyes are currently fixed on repair. Yet this need not be, and should not be, the only legacy of the pandemic.

We have already seen that our experiences, as trying as they were, have helped us confirm and refine our understanding of how faculty learn. But I would also argue they have changed our faculty, and the landscape of educational development, in lasting ways. Those who participated in our programs increased their knowledge, improved their skills, and developed a deeper appreciation for pedagogical inquiry and growth. And when they asked, "why haven't we always done this?" they revealed a metacognitive awareness that what they learned has been, and will continue to be, widely applicable. This suggests that if they can overcome burnout, faculty may be better prepared and more motivated to engage in faculty learning initiatives moving forward.

Our experience at Wake Forest seems to confirm this shift. As previously noted, significantly more faculty engaged with our center in the past year than was typical in previous, pre-pandemic years. After more than a year of remote work, many were eager to come together to talk about teaching with their peers. In April, classes were cancelled to host a day-long event on inclusive teaching, and 60% of our full-time faculty voluntarily participated. Even more promising, we found that the conference had a greater impact on those who had high levels of previous engagement with collaborative learning initiatives. This suggests that participation in our pandemic learning communities may have created something of a virtuous cycle whereby engagement and growth led to further engagement and growth.

Beyond this individual engagement, we have also seen a greater interest in departmental and institutional teaching initiatives. Departments have been meeting more regularly to discuss teaching, and we regularly hear colleagues propose "something like the peer learning communities" when thinking about how to scale faculty learning in a variety of domains. Most significantly, our Undergraduate College has recently embarked on an initiative to revise their processes for assessing teaching. They have also expressed an explicit interest in developing a system that rewards pedagogical experimentation, failure, and iterative growth—three essential elements of the inquiry-based approach we encouraged throughout the pandemic.

It is difficult to know whether the shifts we have seen will be sustained, or whether they are generalizable to other institutions. Even so, this chapter suggests several important lessons for educational developers and administrators as they look to the future.

First, teaching centers would do well to engage faculty in metacognitive reflection about their learning experiences throughout the pandemic. Although many of us have invited faculty to reflect on the *substance* of their learning, reflection on *how* they learned could be just as important. As we saw, their beliefs about their own learning—whether it was needed, valued, or risky—were a primary driver of near-universal engagement in 2020. If faculty reflect on these connections, they may rethink their pre-pandemic assumptions and increase their appreciation for sustained pedagogical inquiry.

Second, senior-level administrators can pull several levers to sustain the engagement we saw in 2020. Even though institutional policies and procedures were not the most critical variables at the time, they could be used to recreate conditions that arose naturally that summer. They might, for example, formalize some of the grace we extended to faculty during the pandemic, creating policies that allow faculty to experiment and fail on a path toward growth. They could also rethink faculty workload to make space for the time it takes to sustain this kind of inquiry.[33] But most importantly, senior leaders must continue to communicate that teaching, and the pedagogical inquiry that sustains its development, are institutional priorities.

Finally, the design of new programs should be informed by what we've learned about faculty over the last three years. We confirmed that faculty prefer to engage through inquiry and that collaboration deepens their learning and appreciation for pedagogy. But we also saw that engagement increases when programs address pragmatic challenges faculty are motivated to solve. To maintain high levels of meaningful engagement, educational developers should resist calls for deductive, top-down training and lean into programming that supports extended inquiry driven by faculty concerns.

Three years after the seismic disruptions of March 2020, the future of faculty learning remains uncertain. In one scenario, our institutions will move on, and faculty will file their experience away as a *sui generis* response to an emergency. But another, more promising, future is one where faculty will transfer what they have learned to their in-person courses and embrace the enduring value of pedagogical inquiry. If we hope to see the latter, institutional leaders and educational developers must take concrete steps to support its realization.

We have learned a great deal over the last three years, and our faculty have surely changed in meaningful ways. Yet it would be easy for our institutions and teaching centers to return to the status quo. To realize the potential before us, we must have intentional conversations about what has been gained. And we must work together to build a better future—a future where we are no longer burdened by emergency remote teaching, but where we continue to support one another as if we were.

Notes

1. Beach et al., *Future Imperatives*, 5; Condon, *Assessing the Connections*; Schroeder et al., *Role in Institutional Change*; Wright et al., "De-Centered Educational World."

2. Some scholars worry that the language of "development" can reinforce a deductive, deficit-based model of faculty learning. Following their lead, I try to use "faculty learning initiatives" as an alternative to "faculty development." Yet in cases like this, when I am referring to our professional field or the professionals within it, I opt for the language of the field. Stabile and Ritchie, "Clarifying the Differences."

3. In doing so, we will be participating in what Randy Bass calls "design for emergence"-the creation of new structures that value experimentation, adaptability, and a "heightened capacity for organizational learning." Bass, "What's the Problem."

4. Bass, "What's the Problem"; McKinney, *Joys of Juggling*; Qualters, "Creating a Pathway"; Hutchings et al., *Institutional Integration and Impact*; Stabile and Ritchie, "Clarifying the Differences"; Corbo et al., "Support Educational Innovation"; Brookfield, *Critically Reflective Teacher*; Froyd et al., "From Dissemination to Propagation"; Dancy et al., "Sustained Teaching Transformation." For a great example of what an ideal inquiry-based initiative looks like, see Tovar et al., "Discipline-Specific Faculty Learning Communities."

5. Bass, "What's the Problem"; Qualters, "Creating a Pathway for Teacher Change," 5; Stabile and Ritchie, "Clarifying the Differences," 74; Smith, "Motivated Reasoning."

6. Johnson et al., "Metacognition by Design"; Smith and Bradbury, "Wiser Together."

7. For more on the importance of engaging with scholarship, see Richlin, "Scholarly Teaching"; McMurtrie, "Often Ignored"; Brookfield, *Critically Reflective Teacher*, 73; Shulman, "End to Pedagogical Solitude."

For more on the importance of experimentation, see Brookfield, *Critically Reflective Teacher*, 229; Smith and Schwartz, "Improving Teaching by Reflecting."

For more on the power of collaboration with peers, see Menges, "Colleagues as Catalysts"; Shulman, "Those Who Understand"; Cox, "Faculty Learning Communities"; Cox et al., "Practice in Higher Education"; Denecker, "Conversation, Collaboration, and Change"; Saroyan and Trigwell, "Process and Outcome"; Waes et al., "Uncovering Changes"; Carney et al., "Teaching-Intensive Universities," 29; Corbo et al., "Support Educational Innovation"; Benbow and Lee, "Development of Social Capital"; Himelein and Anderson, "Developing Community Among Faculty"; Smith, "Motivated Reasoning," 106–108.

And for more on the importance of reflection, see Johnson et al., "Metacognition by Design"; Dancy et al., "Sustained Teaching Transformation," 14; Nguyen et al., "Five-Component Model"; Benbow and Lee, "Development of Social Capital," 70; Schön, *Reflective Practitioner*; Dewey, *Experience and Education*; Hurney et al., "Pedagogy Scale."

8. Brookfield, *Critically Reflective Teacher*; McKinney, *Joys of Juggling*; Benbow and Lee, "Development of Social Capital," 70. In some ways, this should be unsurprising because versions of these practices create the conditions for *all* learning. As Lisa Bosman and Philip Voglewede remind us, the National Research Council argues that people learn best when learning experiences are "learner-centered, knowledge-centered, assessment-centered, and community-centered." "Change Classroom Practices."

9. Quan et al., "Department-Level Interventions"; Gibbs and Coffey, "Learning of Their Students"; Cox et al., "Practice in Higher Education," 809; Smith, "Motivated Reasoning," 96.

10. Smith, 97–98; Skogsberg et al., "#iteachmsu," 186.

11. Saroyan and Trigwell, "Process and Outcome," 98. For an interesting typology of various theories of faculty motivation and change, see Kezar, *How Colleges Change*. See also Sturtevant and Wheeler, "STEM Faculty," 35.

12. Himelein and Anderson, "Developing Community Among Faculty," 26.

13. Schalkwyk et al., "Reflections on Professional Learning," 4; Benbow and Lee, "Development of Social Capital," 83.

14. Dennin et al., "Teaching at Research Universities."

15. Cox et al., "Practice in Higher Education."

16. Cox et al., "Practice in Higher Education"; Corbo et al., "Support Educational Innovation," 4.

17. Hurney et al., "Pedagogy Scale"

18. Smith, "Motivated Reasoning," 115–116.

19. Hodges, "Deal With Fear"; Smith, "Motivated Reasoning," 110; Dancy et al., "Sustained Teaching Transformation," 6.

20. Although some would have us believe that faculty do not value their teaching, nearly all faculty see teaching as a core part of their professional identity. For example, 98% of full-time faculty at four-year institutions noted that teaching was *personally* "essential" or "very important" in the 2017 HERI Faculty Survey. Stolzenberg et al., "Faculty Survey 2016–2017."

21. McMurtrie, "Often Ignored"; Hutchings et al., *Institutional Integration and Impact*, 24–25; Benbow and Lee, "Development of Social Capital," 82.

22. Note that this does not necessarily mean an instructor believes they are an exceptional teacher, or that there is nothing more they *could* learn. It simply means they have learned enough to meet the expectations they and others have placed on their teaching. See Qualters, "Creating a Pathway," 5–6; Brookfield, *Critically Reflective Teacher*, 79; Smith, "Motivated Reasoning," 109.

23. In a study of teaching-focused social networks, Benbow and Lee interviewed faculty who share that their experience makes "[teaching] conversations of little practical value." "Development of Social Capital," 81.

24. Hart-Davidson, "Imagining a Resilient Pedagogy."

25. As Patricia Dinneen notes in her excellent account of that summer, "Faculty who had cobbled together a virtual end to their spring semester wanted to feel more in control of their courses." "How a Flexible."

26. Walker, "Power of Professors."

27. Credit for this calculation goes to Derek Bruff, who argues that teaching centers should compare the number of faculty who participated to the number of faculty who participate in our "high-engagement" activities in a typical year. Although most Wake Forest faculty participate in workshops each year, only 40–45 participate in intensive programs that require 30–40 hours of dedicated work. In 2020, 750 faculty participated in these programs. For more of Derek Bruff's thinking about these comparisons, see Baecher and Doukopoulos, "Thoughts from Derek Bruff."

28. See more details inCenter for the Advancement of Teaching, "Year in Review."

29. Many institutions implemented policies that required promotion and tenure (P&T) committees to make decisions without data from Spring 2020. Yet, most of these policies were not finalized until Fall of 2020.

30. Korsnack and Ortquist-Ahrens, "Holding Tight," 135; Skogsberg et al., "#iteachmsu," 184.

31. Qualters, "Creating a Pathway," 6; Dinneen, "How a Flexible," 100.

32. See the conference schedule at POD 2022 Seattle, "POD 2022 Seattle Schedule."

33. Calkins and Harris, "Promoting Critical Reflection," 36.

Bibliography

Baecher, Laura, and Lindsay Doukopoulos. "Some Thoughts from Derek Bruff." June 18, 2021, in *Centering Centers*. Podcast produced by POD Network, 55:02. https://anchor.fm/podnetwork-podcast/episodes/Some-Thoughts-from-Derek-Bruff-e1318kt.

Bass, Randall. "The Scholarship of Teaching: What's the Problem?" *Inventio: Creative Thinking about Learning and Teaching* 1, no. 1 (1999).

———. "What's the Problem Now?" *To Improve the Academy* 39, no. 1 (January 14, 2020). https://doi.org/10.3998/tia.17063888.0039.102.

Beach, Andrea L., Mary Deane Sorcinelli, Anne E Austin, and Jaclyn K Rivard. *Faculty Development in the Age of Evidence: Current Practices, Future Imperatives*. Sterling, VA: Stylus Publishing, 2016.

Benbow, Ross J., and Changhee Lee. "Teaching-Focused Social Networks among College Faculty: Exploring Conditions for the Development of Social Capital." *Higher Education* 78, no. 1 (July 1, 2019): 67–89. https://doi.org/10.1007/s10734-018-0331-5.

Bosman, Lisa, and Philip Voglewede. "How Can a Faculty Community of Practice Change Classroom Practices?" *College Teaching* 67, no. 3 (July 3, 2019): 177–187. https://doi.org/10.1080/87567555.2019.1594149.

Brookfield, Stephen. *Becoming a Critically Reflective Teacher*. 2nd ed. San Francisco: Jossey-Bass, 2017.

Calkins, Susanna, and Muveddet Harris. "Promoting Critical Reflection: An Evaluation of the Longer-Term Impact of a Substantial Faculty Development Program." *Journal of Faculty Development* 31, no. 2 (2017): 29–36.

Carney, Mary A., Laura E. Ng, and Tom Cooper. "Professional Development Amid Change: Fostering Academic Excellence and Faculty Productivity at Teaching-Intensive Universities." *Journal of Faculty Development* 30, no. 2 (2016): 27–35.

Center for the Advancement of Teaching. "Year in Review." 2022. https://2022.annualreport.cat.wfu.edu/review.html.

Condon, William, Ellen R. Iverson, Cathryn A. Manduca, Carol Rutz, and Gudrun Willett. *Faculty Development and Student Learning: Assessing the Connections*. Bloomington, IN: Indiana University Press, 2016.

Corbo, Joel C., Daniel L. Reinholz, Melissa H. Dancy, Stanley Deetz, and Noah Finkelstein. "Framework for Transforming Departmental Culture to Support Educational Innovation." *Physical Review Physics Education Research* 12, no. 1 (2016): 1–15. https://doi.org/10.1103/physrevphyseducres.12.010113.

Cox, Bradley E., Kadian L. McIntosh, Robert D. Reason, and Patrick T. Terenzini. "A Culture of Teaching: Policy, Perception, and Practice in Higher Education." *Research in Higher Education* 52, no. 8 (December 1, 2011): 808–829. https://doi.org/10.1007/s11162-011-9223-6.

Cox, Milton D. "Introduction to Faculty Learning Communities." *New Directions for Teaching and Learning* 97 (2004): 5–23.

Dancy, Melissa, Alexandra C. Lau, Andy Rundquist, and Charles Henderson. "Faculty Online Learning Communities: A Model for Sustained Teaching Transformation." *Physical Review Physics Education Research* 15, no. 2 (2019): 020147. https://doi.org/10.1103/physrevphyseducres.15.020147.

Denecker, Christine. "The Teaching Partners Program: A Place for Conversation, Collaboration, and Change." *Journal of Faculty Development* 28, no. 1 (2014): 59–65.

Dennin, Michael, Zachary D. Schultz, Andrew Feig, Noah Finkelstein, Andrea Follmer Greenhoot, Michael Hildreth, Adam K. Leibovich, et al. "Aligning Practice to Policies: Changing the Culture to Recognize and Reward Teaching at Research Universities." *CBE-Life Sciences Education* 16, no. 4 (2017): es5. https://doi.org/10.1187/cbe.17-02-0032.

Dewey, John. *Experience and Education.* New York: Simon & Schuster, 1938.

Dinneen, Patricia. "How a Flexible Teaching 'Camp' Answered Our Pandemic Teaching Emergency." *To Improve the Academy* 39, no. 3 (2021): 99–113. https://doi.org/10.3998/tia.17063888.0039.307.

Froyd, Jeffrey E., Charles Henderson, Renée S. Cole, Debra Friedrichsen, Raina Khatri, and Courtney Stanford. "From Dissemination to Propagation: A New Paradigm for Education Developers." *Change: The Magazine of Higher Learning* 49, no. 4 (2017): 35–42. https://doi.org/10.1080/00091383.2017.1357098.

Gibbs, Graham, and Martin Coffey. "The Impact of Training of University Teachers on Their Teaching Skills, Their Approach to Teaching and the Approach to Learning of Their Students." *Active Learning in Higher Education* 5, no. 1 (March 1, 2004): 87–100. https://doi.org/10.1177/1469787404040463.

Hart-Davidson, Bill. "Imagining a Resilient Pedagogy." *Medium* (blog), April 5, 2020. https://billhd.medium.com/imagining-a-resilient-pedagogy-40a9622d5678.

Himelein, Melissa J., and Hannah L. Anderson. "Developing Community Among Faculty: Can Learning Circles Provide Psychosocial Benefits?" *Journal of Faculty Development* 34, no. 1 (2020).

Hodges, Linda C. "Preparing Faculty for Pedagogical Change: Helping Faculty Deal With Fear." *To Improve the Academy* 24 (2006). https://doi.org/http://dx.doi.org/10.3998/tia.17063888.0024.012.

Hurney, Carol A., Jordan D. Troisi, and Lori H. Leaman. "Development of a Faculty Appreciation of Pedagogy Scale." *To Improve the Academy* 39, no. 2 (2020): 27–50. http://dx.doi.org/10.3998/tia.17063888.0039.202.

Hutchings, Pat, Mary Taylor Huber, and Anthony Ciccone. *The Scholarship of Teaching and Learning Reconsidered: Institutional Integration and Impact*. San Francisco: Jossey-Bass, 2011.
Johnson, Teresa A., Sarah A Holt, Margaret Sanders, Lindsay Bernhagen, Kathryn Plank, Stephanie V Rohdieck, and Alan Kalish. "Metacognition by Design: How a Course Design Experience Can Increase Metacognition in Faculty." *To Improve the Academy* 36, no. 2 (2017). https://doi.org/10.3998/tia.17063888.0036.201.
Kezar, Adrianna. *How Colleges Change: Understanding, Leading, and Enacting Change*. New York: Routledge, 2018.
Korsnack, Kylie, and Leslie Ortquist-Ahrens. "Holding Tight to Our Convictions and Lightly to Our Ways: Inviting Shared Expertise as a Strategy for Expanding Inclusion, Reach, and Impact." *To Improve the Academy* 39, no. 3 (2021): 133–50. https://doi.org/10.3998/tia.17063888.0039.309.
McKinney, Kathleen. *Enhancing Learning Through the Scholarship of Teaching and Learning: The Challenges and Joys of Juggling*. Bolton, MA: Anker Publishing, 2007.
McMurtrie, Beth. "The Damaging Myth of the Natural Teacher." *Chronicle of Higher Education*, October 29, 2021.
———. "Why the Science of Teaching Is Often Ignored." *Chronicle of Higher Education*, January 3, 2022. https://www.chronicle.com/article/why-the-science-of-teaching-is-often-ignored.
Menges, Robert J. "Colleagues as Catalysts for Change in Teaching." *To Improve the Academy* 6, no. 1 (1987): 83–93. https://doi.org/10.1002/j.2334-4822.1987.tb00109.x.
Nguyen, Quoc Dinh, Nicolas Fernandez, Thierry Karsenti, and Bernard Charlin. "What Is Reflection? A Conceptual Analysis of Major Definitions and a Proposal of a Five-Component Model." *Medical Education* 48, no. 12 (2014): 1176–1189. https://doi.org/10.1111/medu.12583.
POD (Professional and Organizational Development Network in Higher Education). "POD 2022 Seattle Schedule." Accessed May 10, 2023. https://pod2022seattle.sched.com.
Qualters, Donna M. "Creating a Pathway for Teacher Change." *Journal of Faculty Development* 23, no. 1 (2009): 5–13.
Quan, Gina M., Joel C. Corbo, Noah D. Finkelstein, Alanna Pawlak, Karen Falkenberg, Christopher Geanious, Courtney Ngai, et al. "Designing for Institutional Transformation: Six Principles for Department-Level Interventions." *Physical Review Physics Education Research* 15, no. 1 (2019): 010141. https://doi.org/10.1103/physrevphyseducres.15.010141.
Richlin, Laurie. "Scholarly Teaching and the Scholarship of Teaching." *New Directions for Teaching and Learning* 2001, no. 86 (June 1, 2001): 57–68. https://doi.org/10.1002/tl.16.
Saroyan, Alenoush, and Keith Trigwell. "Higher Education Teachers' Professional Learning: Process and Outcome." *Studies in Educational Evaluation* 46 (September 1, 2015): 92–101. https://doi.org/10.1016/j.stueduc.2015.03.008.
Schalkwyk, Susan Van, Brenda Leibowitz, Nicoline Herman, and Jean Farmer. "Reflections on Professional Learning: Choices, Context and Culture." *Studies in*

Educational Evaluation 46 (2015): 4–10. https://doi.org/10.1016/j.stueduc.2015.03.002.

Schön, Donald A. *The Reflective Practitioner: How Professionals Think in Action*. New York: Basic Books, 1984.

Schroeder, Connie, Phyllis Blumberg, Nancy Van Note Chism, Catherine E. Frerichs, Susan Gano-Phillips, Devorah Liberman, Diana G. Pace, and Tamara Rosier. *Coming in From the Margins: Faculty Development's Emerging Organizational Development Role in Institutional Change*. Sterling, VA: Stylus, 2010.

Shulman, Lee S. "Teaching as Community Property: Putting an End to Pedagogical Solitude." *Change: The Magazine of Higher Learning* 25, no. 6 (1993): 6–7. https://doi.org/https://doi.org/10.1080/00091383.1993.9938465.

———. "Those Who Understand: Knowledge Growth in Teaching." *Educational Researcher* 15, no. 2 (1986): 4–14. https://doi.org/10.3102/0013189x015002004.

Skogsberg, Erik, Melissa McDaniels, Madeline Shellgren, Patricia Stewart, and Makena Neal. "#iteachmsu Centering an Educator Learning Community (ELC)." *To Improve the Academy* 40, no. 1 (2021): 183–208. https://doi.org/10.3998/tia.161.

Smith, Gary A. "Motivated Reasoning and Persuading Faculty Change in Teaching." *To Improve the Academy* 39, no. 1 (2020): 95–135. https://doi.org/10.3998/tia.17063888.0039.105.

Smith, Ronald, and Fred Schwartz. "Improving Teaching by Reflecting on Practice." *To Improve the Academy* 7, no. 1 (1988): 63–84. https://doi.org/10.1002/j.2334-4822.1988.tb00129.x.

Smith, Tracy W., and Leslie U. Bradbury. "Wiser Together: Sustaining Teaching Excellence With a Self-Study/Critical Friend." *To Improve the Academy* 38, no. 1 (2019). https://doi.org/10.3998/tia.17063888.0038.106.

Stabile, Christopher, and William F. Ritchie. "Clarifying the Differences between Training, Development, and Enrichment: The Role of Institutional Belief Constructs in Creating the Purpose of Faculty Learning Initiatives." *New Directions for Teaching & Learning* 2013, no. 133 (January 1, 2013): 71–84. https://doi.org/10.1002/tl.20047.

Stolzenberg, Ellen Bara, Kevin Eagan, Hilary B. Zimmerman, Jennifer Berdan Lozano, Natacha M. Cesar-Davis, Melissa C. Aragon, and Cecilia Rios-Aguilar. "Undergraduate Teaching Faculty: The HERI Faculty Survey 2016–2017." Los Angeles: Higher Education Research Institute, University of California, Los Angeles, 2019.

Sturtevant, Hannah, and Lindsay Wheeler. "The STEM Faculty Instructional Barriers and Identity Survey (FIBIS): Development and Exploratory Results." *International Journal of STEM Education* 6, no. 1 (2019): 35. https://doi.org/10.1186/s40594-019-0185-0.

Tovar, Mariela, Rosalie Jukier, Jennie Ferris, and Kristen Cardoso. "Overcoming Pedagogical Solitude: The Transformative Power of Discipline-Specific Faculty Learning Communities." *To Improve the Academy* 34, no. 1–2 (2015). https://doi.org/10.3998/tia.17063888.0034.110.

Waes, Sara Van, Piet Van den Bossche, Nienke M. Moolenaar, Ann Stes, and Peter Van Petegem. "Uncovering Changes in University Teachers' Professional Networks during an Instructional Development Program." *Studies in Educational Evaluation* 46 (September 1, 2015): 11–28. https://doi.org/10.1016/j.stueduc.2015.02.003.

Walker, Cheryl. "The Power of Professors: Peer Learning Communities Advance the Art of Teaching During a Pandemic." *Wake Forest News*, August 4, 2020. https://news.wfu.edu/2020/08/04/the-power-of-professors-peer-learning-communities-advance-the-art-of-teaching-during-a-pandemic/.

Wright, Mary C., Debra Rudder Lohe, and Deandra Little. "The Role of a Center for Teaching and Learning in a De-Centered Educational World." *Change: The Magazine of Higher Learning* 50, no. 6 (2018): 38–44. https://doi.org/10.1080/00091383.2018.1540826.

chapter 11

Purpose, Learning, and Justice

Maintaining Hopeful Practices Past the Pivot

Susannah McGowan and Isis Artze-Vega

What does *justice* look like in a curriculum? What does it mean for learning and teaching when our curriculum provides space for sensemaking, dialogue, and responding to geopolitical, racial, and societal challenges? We set out to understand more about how we are using and enacting the construct of justice in learning and teaching and curriculum. This chapter explores the ways in which college and university practices recenter learning about and through concepts such as critical hope and justice-oriented learning. Educational development processes support colleagues to learn about these concepts in order to enact them in their own work. Many universities have increased their emphasis on both racial justice and learning in the last three years through an increase in initiatives, committees, and think tanks. We examine what a renewed focus on justice affords in terms of the future of learning, and we outline the possibilities of including justice as central to the cognitive and emotional learning we desire for students. In order to recenter our efforts on justice, we attempt to establish a throughline from what we learned in our respective institutions during the past four years, from the values of abolitionist educational thinking to the possibilities for recentering learning on justice within higher education. The current liminal space we occupy—neither at the beginning nor the end of the COVID-19 pandemic—is, as Gloria Anzaldúa has written,[1] one of hybridity, transformation and hope.

What We've Learned in the Past Two Years

We are a small part of continuing efforts to transform the curriculum toward the compassion, imagination, and critical thinking of justice-oriented education. In the last three to four years, the inextricable connectedness of equity, justice, and care surfaced as important touchstones in how we worked with faculty, staff, and students. The collective trauma of an emerging, unpredictable pandemic brought into bold relief our shared humanity. In colleges and universities around the world, our varied missions and hierarchies faded into the background while commitments to teaching and learning took center stage. We learned the value of a narrow, intentional set of goals. The online pivot forced us to choose what was of absolute importance to teach in an online environment. It forced us to determine how students should understand and determine their own progress in a setting requiring independence and uncertainty. And as we focused on teaching, we had no choice but to approach our work with humility. How could we possibly have known how to teach online or during a pandemic?

It was likewise impossible to ignore the complexity of students' lives or the multifaceted challenges occupying their mental bandwidth. We felt it too, and faculty responded with unprecedented levels of care and compassion—from flexible deadlines and new grading schemes, to fewer assignments and more authentic assessments.[2] We also disrupted many traditional practices, such as lengthy lectures and high-stakes testing, in order to focus on supporting and engaging students using practices grounded in connection.

Only a few months into our pandemic mode of teaching and living, racial injustice captured our attention, and as with pandemic pedagogies, we disrupted many traditional practices and sought to teach in more inclusive and justice-oriented ways. For both of us, we also experienced the administrative labor of large-scale efforts to form new committees and centralize efforts among colleagues engaged in siloed initiatives. There is no formula for this work, yet for many faculty, this moment represented a threshold. For the first time, many educators noticed their complicity in perpetuating inequity and in turn, renewed commitments to equity-mindedness. Here, too, humility was essential, and our best efforts came from learning with and from students. We were involved in multiple initiatives addressing racial justice where there is no roadmap for this work nor guidance when the urgency subsides. It is a journey of learning requiring persistence and vulnerability, if we, as administrators and educational developers, invest in the development of justice-oriented mindsets.

We learned the value of collaboration and learning from one another. Valuing this journey leads to questions moving forward: How might we normalize not knowing how to be equity-minded practitioners? How might we assume postures of humility and create spaces for learning how to do this work together, while also recognizing and appreciating expertise? Through dialogue, vulnerability, and humility, we have recentered the conversations on learning around the idea of presence in the classroom to help "make visible the intersections of justice/injustice in the present while orienting towards new social futures."[3] It is this idea of iterating on these conversations as central to establishing throughlines to what we imagine can be the role of justice-oriented learning.

What We Value about Learning: Reframing and Recognizing Justice

What we have learned in the past three to four years of working, teaching, and collaborating during a pandemic tells us we must revisit and reevaluate what is vital at the core of learning, particularly the questions exploring the relationship between seeking justice and learning. Vital to this exploration is the idea that this is not new nor does it deviate from what many educators might call traditional learning outcomes such as critical thinking, collaboration, and independence and agency in the learning process. Incidentally, these learning outcomes do not differ from what many employers identify as essential to future workforces.[4]

Justice-learning is about "making visible the contingency of our present situations; that we are always-in-the-making of our beliefs, practices, and structures."[5] One could not define better what it has meant to maintain and sustain learning in a pandemic, where the contingency of ongoing situations demanded a restructuring of what we taught and how we taught, questioning the very structures and systems in which we were teaching and learning. In conversations about bringing racial justice into the curriculum, faculty often discuss strategies to help students understand structures and systems in addition to goals around critical thinking, positionality, and power. "Always-in-the making" as an approach to justice-oriented learning and teaching grounds students in understanding forces at play in order to outline their positionality, articulate their stance, make connections, and recognize patterns. This exemplifies a metacognitive approach to learning with important developmental and cognitive implications for students.

Justice-oriented learning, of course, requires that educators notice and acknowledge injustice, both historical and present, and with specificity. To do this effectively, we must do our homework. As faculty, this means, at minimum, that we consider educational history and the varied ways education, at all levels, has maintained inequity. Engaging with vivid accounts of racial and economic discrepancies in our nation's schooling such as Jonathan Kozol's *Savage Inequalities* helps each of us see how our students' experiences are shaped by powerful forces outside of their control.[6]

Increasingly, understanding injustices often leads educators to uncover the history of injustice within our own institutions. Such efforts at Georgetown University emerged within the last decade on its complicit connections to slaveholding by Jesuit priests in mid-nineteenth century.[7] More recent conversations on understanding this history through the lens of justice within curricula emerged, particularly voiced by Georgetown students as being essential and necessary to know before one graduates. Current student-led efforts look to various touchpoints to engage with this history from the moment they step on campus to the moment they enter a classroom.

What We Value about Learning: Reorient toward Liberatory Spaces

We wish to define what we mean by justice while also situating where learning happens and why. Although institutional efforts to advance learning and those to advance equity have existed in parallel, or perhaps in competition to one another (as in so-called "curricular fatigue"), we have learned during the last several years that they are inextricable. This was understood by the original equity practitioners: fugitive and abolitionist educators and the essence of Carter G. Woodson's observation in *The Negro in Our History*: "Knowing the value of *learning as a means of escape* and having longing for it, too, because it was forbidden, many slaves continued their education under adverse circumstances."[8] Learning spaces embodied sacred, liberatory places with multiple possibilities and pathways towards justice mindsets.

Today, learning spaces comprise physical classrooms and institutional buildings as well as virtual spaces, and reflecting on their potential as places of liberation would serve us well. Trabian Shorters recently reflected on his experience as a programmer and its connection to transformational change: "A really good technologist understands that in order to hack something well, you have to understand a system well enough to get it to do something it wasn't designed to do."[9] It is fair to say our university systems were never designed for a massive online shift, yet this shift plus the tumultuous events since 2020 have opened up productive avenues for conversations about learning, engagement, and connection. What are students learning, and how might we recenter our teaching and learning towards a justice orientation that will affect change in student mindsets? What structures can we put in place to enable this learning and mindset development?

Building on the idea of why it matters to know and understand how a student is situated within the spaces of an institution (its history, its buildings, its classrooms) invites us to question the constructs of inclusivity and belonging when centering justice in our curricula. Barton and Tan explore the idea of "rightful presence" in a classroom as a counterpoint to inclusivity and belonging.[10] They call for educators to reimagine shared learning spaces as speaking to the "embodied and epistemological consequences" of moving toward justice-oriented learning. If we adhere to a justice-oriented learning approach that advocates for students' presence or agency in their own learning, Barton and Tan view this shift as contributing to larger intellectual and social possibilities: "The shared commitment to collective disruption focuses on how individual outcomes are an extension of social transformation, reconfiguring the discourses and practices of who, and what, legitimately belong in the disciplines and society."[11] To support the development of this shared commitment, we require curriculum design to encompass a direct focus on critical thinking, questioning positionality, recognizing privilege, and examining power in order to make sense of societal forces.

To legitimate what it means to belong to a discipline, our society, or in the world, future curricula need to attend to what it means to develop a sense of belonging through our curricula and in our learning spaces. Generating a sense of belonging as an aspect of inclusion is well known to contribute to retention, performance, and well-being for all students, particularly for first-generation and historically underrepresented minorities.[12] Recently, Heidi Weston, Peter Felten, and Alison Cook-Sather, at a 2021 virtual conference,[13] discussed their latest thinking on the role of "mattering" for students in higher education as an evolution from the construct of belonging. They based their definition of *mattering* not only on maintaining presence or having invested relationships but also on "the perception that, to some degree and in any of a variety of ways, we are a significant part of the world around us."[14] Belonging takes on a new, expanded meaning when we think about the possibilities for our students learning within justice-oriented curricula. This work has the potential to provide a sense of belonging not simply to our disciplines or institutions, but also to the past, in the present, and the future of society. Situating students within an environment that communicates significance, rightful presence, and belonging signals possibilities for how we might define what justice looks like in our teaching and learning processes.

What Gives Us Hope: The Possibilities and Partnerships within Justice-Learning

On January 6, 2021, one of the authors entered a conversation with faculty members in the business school to discuss curricular transformation and racial justice. The meeting started two hours after the storming of the Capitol Building in the United States by insurrectionists seeking to overturn presidential election results. The questions posed to faculty members at the opening of the meeting were "*What are we going to do in our curriculum to help our students make sense of what led to this attack? How will our curricular changes make an impact on understanding what is just or unjust?*" The moment was a familiar moment during the pandemic: the relentless slog of moving from Zoom meeting to Zoom meeting while the world and our system of government crumbled. On that day, we found ourselves in a situation where it was imperative to recenter the upcoming conversation on curriculum changes to really matter for the learning development of students to deal with ambiguity, uncertainty, and an inclination to act.[15]

Grounding justice-oriented curricular efforts in such moments of history-in-the-making ensures that our thoughtful yet overscheduled students are motivated to see the relevance and connections in their academic journey. In partnership with faculty, we discussed what it meant to steer curriculum changes toward what mattered most for students. In a sense, we were discussing how to develop justice-oriented learning. Engaging in the work at the level of curricula instead of individual courses, course readings, or assignments represented an important step in advancing and deepening our commitments to justice to endure.

How else might we empower our colleagues to reclaim the *liberatory* aims of this coursework? And how might we help our colleagues see the value of justice-learning to their teaching, disciplines, and corresponding professions? We learned that we will be met with varying types of resistance, ones that test our conviction as practitioners, and others that test our own hope and resolve. Working collectively serves to mitigate against resistance—when our own hope "tank" is running low, we can tap into our colleagues' hope and agency. When structuring justice-learning efforts in our colleges and universities, it will be crucial for us to infuse this work into the core of our institutional initiatives and classrooms, such that justice does not become yet another "initiative" competing for time and resources. We are aiming for developing multiple sites of justice throughout our respective institutions from the course level to the numerous committees on which we serve.

We return to the guidance of practitioners like Howard J. Ross, author of *Reinventing Diversity*, on how to frame our efforts.[16] Ross argues that one of the main reasons so-called diversity efforts have failed is that organizations approached the work from a corrective stance—assuming or implying willful intent among those who do not yet have a justice orientation or know how to enact justice-oriented practices. This, of course, results in defensiveness and other forms of self-protection that prevent the vulnerability and openness the work necessitates. Ross challenges us to leverage the power of hope and optimism, showing our colleagues a "bigger vision of how the work will serve the organization they are part of."[17]

Kyoko Kishimoto echoes Ross' conviction that reframing our efforts toward justice involve not just the objectives of our efforts, but also the *ways* we work with each other to make this happen: "Anti-racist organizing involves sharing, helping, and collaborating rather than competing and taking from others. It follows an open, transparent, and democratic decision-making process, rather than secretive, exclusionary, and manipulative procedures. . . . [w]e need to have the humility to listen and learn from others and to constantly self-reflect on our white privilege or internalized racism."[18] Our experience in working together as partners in equity course design efforts found that agency and persistence existed when meaningful changes for student learning occurred generating hope for further transformation at scale.[19] We witnessed collective levels of reflection and organizational change occur during the pandemic, and we wish to sustain the momentum towards justice-oriented learning.

Our final hope for making justice transparent in our curricular efforts is through student partnerships. In the summer of 2020, amidst the ongoing uncertainty of the pandemic pivot, we turned towards a "partnership mindset"[20] to make the virtual experience effective for all involved while employing students reliant on the Federal Work Study program. The Center for Teaching and Learning partnered with multiple campus units to establish a system to match undergraduate students needing jobs to support faculty in managing their virtual environments.[21] We learned these "instructional technology aides" (ITAs) supported courses by monitoring Zoom sessions, organizing materials in the LMS, monitoring student engagement, and collecting feedback from students about their wellbeing and experiences in their courses.

One faculty member noted, "Just a quick note of thanks for offering the ITA program. [The student] was a huge help to me and the class . . . [freeing] me up to do my primary duty - teaching and interacting with the students." Another faculty member noted, "she was able to show us [all 49 students] how to keep everything that we need to know going in a way that I could not have done without her." Across the faculty feedback received, there were descriptions of true partnerships in making the courses engaging, relevant, and spaces in which to connect to students. The improvised, innovative nature of this program to meet basic technological needs formed previously unimaginable possibilities for students, staff, and faculty alike. Focusing on working in partnership contributes to the open, transparent organizational curricular change we seek to forge justice-oriented ways of knowing and learning.

Conclusion

Returning to our opening question of what justice looks like in the curriculum, we witnessed multiple moves during the pandemic that will help us collectively move curricular efforts toward embodying Daniel Butin's idea of an "always-in-the making" approach where any given university community works together to understand systemic forces at play in order to outline their positionality, develop a voice, make connections, and analyze patterns. Not only do we want to maintain hopeful practices past the pandemic pivot, we wish to fuse justice-oriented practices and mindsets into the very bones of university architecture to realize educational transformation.

Reflecting on what we have learned, reminding ourselves of what we value, and what gives us hope provides a useful heuristic for creating "always-in-the-making" learning environments. Creating a sense of belonging for our students to creating a sense of justice in partnership with them provides the equity we envision for all of our students. In 2021, Isis Artze-Vega delivered a provocative keynote in which she outlined her five hopes for equity.[22]. They are framed within the language of hope; yet, for the purposes of this chapter, we see these as actionable steps to recenter our curricula for a future of justice-oriented learning:

- **Hope 1:** Bring the same spirit of urgency, of possibility, and of care to your equity and justice work with which you responded to the pandemic.
- **Hope 2:** Aim for transparency, depth, and tangibility in centering justice within curricula.
- **Hope 3:** Lean in to critical reflection on identity, positionality, privilege, and history to do your homework.
- **Hope 4:** Foster genuine partnership work with and among faculty, staff, and students.
- **Hope 5:** Approach your justice efforts with humility, curiosity, and time.

Maintaining an emphasis on transparency, reflection, partnership, and humility can support the continued urgency to redesign curricula toward justice-oriented learning. We believe these five actions are necessary to maintain what Bryan Alexander[23] sees in universities' purpose to serve as "precious nodes for humanity's intelligence and imagination." What we learned in the pandemic past—adaptation, invention, and intention—hurtles us toward the possibilities for justice mindsets in the future.

Notes

1. Anzaldúa, *Borderlands/La Frontera*.
2. McGowan, "Managing Pace."
3. Calabrese Barton and Tan, "Beyond Equity as Inclusion," 436.

4. Finley, "What Matters Most."

5. Butin, "Justice-Oriented Education," 181.

6. Here, we reference Kozol's original text as an excellent account of racialized realities in education. We also wish to point readers to a newer text not available at time of writing this article. Based on advanced reading, this newer response to Kozol to promote asset-based, justice-oriented educational approaches should be considered. Patton, *Reauthoring Savage Inequalities.*

7. Georgetown University, "Georgetown Reflects on Slavery."

8. Woodson, *Negro in Our History*.

9. Tippett, "Trabian Shorters."

10. Calabrese Barton and Tan, "Beyond Equity as Inclusion," 434.

11. Calabrese Barton and Tan, "Beyond Equity as Inclusion," 437

12. Eddy and Hogan, "Getting Under the Hood"; Meehan and Howells, "In Search."

13. International Society for the Scholarship of Teaching and Learning, "ISSOTL 21 Program," 45.

14. Elliott et al., "Mattering."

15. Finley, "What Matters Most."

16. Ross, *People, Purpose, and Performance.*

17. Ross, *People, Purpose, and Performance*, 34.

18. Kishimoto, "Anti-Racist Pedagogy," 551

19. McGowan et al., "Fostering Evidence Informed Teaching."

20. Peseta et al., "The Partnership Mindset," 115.

21. Debelius et al., "Course Design Institute Collaboration."

22. Artze-Vega, "Design for Justice."

23. Murphy, "Academic Gives Me Hope."

Bibliography

Anzaldúa, Gloria. *Borderlands/La Frontera*. San Francisco: Aunt Lute Publishers, 2012.

Artze-Vega, Isis. *Design for Justice: Connecting Equity and Innovation. Virtual Summer Institute for Equity in the Academic Experience.* Virtual conference hosted by Georgetown University (June 21, 2021). https://youtu.be/DdYFn9ECSQM?si=7lDETRwoC536BQqj.

Butin, Dan W. "Justice-Learning: Service-Learning as Justice-Oriented Education." *Equity & Excellence in Education* 40, no. 2 (2007): 177–183. https://doi.org/10.1080/10665680701246492.

Calabrese Barton, Angela, and Edna Tan. "Beyond Equity as Inclusion: A Framework of 'Rightful Presence' for Guiding Justice-Oriented Studies in Teaching and Learning." *Educational Researcher* 49, no. 6 (2020): 433–440. https://doi.org/10.3102/0013189X20927363.

Debelius, Maggie, Susannah McGowan, Aiyanna Maciel, Clare Reid, and Alexa Eason. "'Things Are Different Now' A Student, Staff, and Faculty Course Design Institute

Collaboration." In *Resilient Pedagogy*. Denver, CO: Utah State University Press, 2021. https://uen.pressbooks.pub/resilientpedagogy/chapter/things-are-different-now-a-student-staff-and-faculty-course-design-institute-collaboration/.

Eddy, Sarah L., and Kelly A. Hogan. "Getting Under the Hood: How and for Whom Does Increasing Course Structure Work?" *CBE—Life Sciences Education* 13, no. 3 (2014): 453–468. https://doi.org/10.1187/cbe.14-03-0050.

Elliott, Gregory, Suzanne Kao, and Ann-Marie Grant. "Mattering: Empirical Validation of a Social-Psychological Concept." *Self and Identity* 3, no. 4 (2004): 339–354. https://doi.org/10.1080/13576500444000119.

Finley, Ashley. "How College Contributes to Workforce Success: Employer Views on What Matters Most." Association of American Colleges and Universities, 2021. https://www.aacu.org/research/on-the-same-page.

Georgetown University. "Georgetown Reflects on Slavery, Memory, and Reconciliation." Accessed May 10, 2023. https://www.georgetown.edu/slavery/.

International Society for the Scholarship of Teaching and Learning. "ISSOTL 21 Program." International Society for the Scholarship of Teaching and Learning, 2021. https://issotl.com/2022/01/ISSOTL-21-Program.

Kishimoto, Kyoko. "Anti-Racist Pedagogy: From Faculty's Self-Reflection to Organizing within and Beyond the Classroom." *Race Ethnicity and Education* 21, no. 4 (2018): 540–554. https://doi.org/10.1080/13613324.2016.1248824.

Kozol, Jonathan. *Savage Inequalities: Children in America's Schools*. New York: Crown, 2012.

McGowan, Susannah. "Managing pace and workload in online courses." In *Creating Inclusive and Engaging Online Courses*, 71–87. Cheltenham, UK: Edward Elgar, 2022.

McGowan, Susannah, and Peter Felten. "On the Necessity of Hope in Academic Development." *International Journal for Academic Development* 26, no. 4 (2021): 473–476. https://doi.org/10.1080/1360144X.2021.1903902.

McGowan, Susannah, Peter Felten, Joshua Caulkins, and Isis Artze-Vega. "Fostering Evidence Informed Teaching in Crucial Classes: Faculty Development in Gateway Courses." *New Directions for Higher Education* 2017, no. 180 (2017): 53–62. https://doi.org/10.1002/he.20261.

Meehan, Catherine, and Kristy Howells. "In Search of the Feeling of 'Belonging' in Higher Education: Undergraduate Students Transition into Higher Education." *Journal of Further and Higher Education* 43, no. 10 (2019): 1376–1390. https://doi.org/10.1080/0309877X.2018.1490702.

Murphy, Colleen. "Academia Gives Me Hope: A Futurist Counternarrative from Bryan Alexander." *Culture Study* (newsletter), October 16, 2022..

Patton, Lori D, Ishwanzya D. Rivers, Raquel L. Farmer-Hinton, and Joi D. Lewis. *Reauthoring Savage Inequalities: Narratives of Community Cultural Wealth in Urban Educational Environments*. New York: SUNY Press, 2023.

Peseta, Tai, Jenny Pizzica, Ashley Beathe, Chinnu Jose, Racquel Lynch, Marisse Manthos, Kathy Nguyen, and Hassan Raza. "The Partnership Mindset." *The Power of Partnership*, edited by Lucy Mercer-Mapstone and Sophia Abbot. 2020. Elon, NC: Elon University. https://www.centerforengagedlearning.org/books/power-of-partnership/section-two/chapter-6.

Rattray, Julie. "Affective dimensions of liminality." In *Threshold Concepts in Practice*, 67–76. Rotterdam, Netherlands: Sense Publishers, 2016.

Ross, Howard J. *Reinventing Diversity: Transforming Organizational Community to Strengthen People, Purpose, and Performance*. Lanham, MD: Rowman & Littlefield, 2011.

Tippett, Krista. "Trabian Shorters: A Cognitive Skill to Magnify Humanity." *On Being with Krista Tippett*. Podcast, 11:44, February 3, 2022. https://onbeing.org/programs/trabian-shorters-a-cognitive-skill-to-magnify-humanity.

Solnit, Rebecca. *A Paradise Built in Hell: The Extraordinary Communities That Arise in Disaster*. New York: Penguin, 2010.

Woodson, Carter Godwin. *The Negro in our History*. Washington, DC: Associated Publishers, 1922.

chapter 12

Everything Is Different but Nothing Is New

The Missed Opportunity for Reform in the Wake of COVID-19

Kashema Hutchinson, Sujung Kim, Adashima Oyo, and Katina Rogers

The COVID-19 pandemic made visible inequalities that have long been present in graduate education. The rapid changes—in teaching modalities, research protocols, meeting structures, and more—also made clear how many seemingly unchangeable elements of universities can, in fact, be changed. With this increased visibility, along with the massive disruption that unfolded following March 2020, graduate programs had a unique opportunity to rebuild in a way that addressed longstanding issues of structural inequality. However, once people began returning to classrooms, it was unclear whether much structural change had occurred. In particular, graduate students and higher education workers who were already in positions of greatest precarity—for instance, international students, first-generation students, Black, Indigenous, and Person of Color (BIPOC) students and workers, and adjunct instructors—often saw even the supports that once existed fall away. If graduate education fails to change in the wake of this crisis, it is a lost opportunity. This is a moment to build something new, something grounded in hope and abundance, access, care, and joy.

Taking cues from Anna Lowenhaupt Tsing and Donna Haraway, we ask: What can we do in a context of ruin?[1] Rather than succumb to despair, we seek ways to thrive within this damaged reality. What can grow that might not have grown otherwise? Tsing describes how matsutake mushrooms grow precisely and only in landscapes of ruin: spaces of deforestation by logging, fire, or development that then see new species emerge. Without erasing that damage, the mushrooms suggest that beauty and sustenance are still possible. It is a different kind of sustenance.

If thriving can occur in a ruined forest, perhaps it is possible in a university. Higher education is a mess, with its own variants of racism, sexism, labor exploitation, and—insidiously—a capitalist and prestige-oriented mindset masquerading as the public good. That is our ruined forest. What might we see if we look down to the roots and soil under our feet?

Who We Are

The coauthors of this chapter share a connection through current and past work in the City University of New York (CUNY) system, where 2,800 adjuncts—many of them graduate students—were laid off in July 2020. These layoffs were devastating, particularly in a society where healthcare is tied to employment, and employment is controlled by immigration status. And yet, they track with a common pattern in which workers who are already in positions of greatest precarity see their meager supports fall away in a crisis.

Each of us brings a range of professional and personal perspectives to this piece. Our traditional bios are easily found elsewhere; here's what we think matters in the context of this chapter.

Kashema Hutchinson is an educator in and outside academia. She resists the notion that a "good education" can only be found within the ivory tower. As a pusher and preserver of Hip-Hop culture, Kashema employs Hip-Hop's fifth element, knowledge of self and community, while working in traditional and nontraditional educational spaces. Throughout her years in these spaces, she realized the significance of her identity and how important it is to see others. In addition to being a co-director of CUNY Peer Leaders Program, she is an editor of the digital project *Black Language Syllabus*; manager of the women's Hip-Hop initiative Fresh, Bold & So Def; and a CUNY adjunct professor.

Sujung Kim undertakes ethnographic research about doctoral students' experiences as graduate students and adjunct instructors. Concepts such as critical pedagogy in the humanities and reformative teaching and learning within higher education are essential to her work. She is originally from South Korea, where she earned her undergraduate degree; she also received a master's degree from the University of Hawaii at Manoa and a PhD in Educational Policy Studies from the University of Illinois at Urbana-Champaign. Based on her experience as well as on her research, she seeks to develop more inclusive, humanistic, and democratic teaching and learning communities within and beyond academia.

Adashima Oyo is a Black woman whose identity intersects many different roles in higher education. She is a researcher and adjunct instructor at a public and a private university in New York City and an administrator in higher education. Adashima holds a PhD from the Graduate Center, CUNY. She also holds two toddler sons under her care as she navigates different roles and spaces within and beyond higher education. Adashima will adamantly support her children in whatever career paths they choose, but they must obtain a college degree. Higher education is an investment beyond financial gain or job security. Adashima is a third-generation college student. #BlackScholarsMatter.

Katina Rogers worked at the Graduate Center, CUNY, from 2014 to 2021. She is among those who made radical career changes during the pandemic, opting to start her own educational consultancy to help universities build more supportive and sustainable graduate programs. She has two young kids, significant racial and class privilege, and a deep frustration with higher education that is inextricably bound up with hope. She holds a PhD in Comparative Literature from the University of Colorado, Boulder, and is the author of *Putting the Humanities PhD to Work: Thriving in and beyond the Classroom.*[2]

Case Studies: Intertwining Roots in Stories of Precarity, Learning, and Care

As coauthors, we want readers to hear our collective as well as individual voices. We offer a collection of vignettes that share a bit of each person's experience, research, and reflections on what higher education can still learn from the pandemic. Like fungi that flourish invisibly and sustain other beings in mycorrhizal networks before bursting through the soil after a rain, each of us works unnoticed at times, trusting that we are creating conditions that will one day bear fruit. We welcome this opportunity to let our experiences emerge in a visible and meaningful way.

In the case studies that follow, we offer a glimpse into some of the experiences we saw and lived from our various vantage points and positionalities. First, Sujung Kim considers the mixed experiences of isolation and belonging among international students. She notes that the valences of home and belonging may present in unexpected ways, leading some international students to feel a sense of reprieve during the isolation of the pandemic. Dr. Kim emphasizes the importance of fostering interpersonal connection so that students can find themselves within a web of support and engagement with others who are attuned to their circumstances. Furthermore, she proposes a more inclusive understanding of minority students that includes international students in order to underline an understanding of US graduate schools as cosmopolitan educational institutions beyond nationalistic institutional policies and practices.

Next, Adashima Oyo pulls back the curtain on her instructional methods to offer a sense of how classroom teachers might take steps toward broader change—and also where those possibilities for change may be limited by institutional resources and support. Dr. Oyo describes the ways she used the painful circumstances of the COVID-19 pandemic to draw students toward nuanced questions about inequity in public health and intersecting social services. And yet, the impact of an individual adjunct instructor is necessarily limited. Comparing her experiences as an adjunct in a highly resourced private university with a contrasting experience in CUNY, Dr. Oyo gestures toward both the power and the limits of individual actions in facing systemic challenges.

Finally, Kashema Hutchinson writes about her experiences as co-director of an undergraduate peer leadership program, and describes the kinds of solidarity and strength she cultivated in those environments. Through the examples she presents, Dr. Hutchinson ends this chapter on a note of hope and possibility, reminding us that students can thrive when they are given space to breathe combined with a sense that they matter.

Sharing these case studies is a way for us to give a prismatic view of the dynamics we see in universities today. What they collectively suggest is that there is no single approach that can revolutionize the university. Rather, the educational ecosystem we imagine will be a unique assemblage that is more than the sum of its parts. The successes and failures of university pandemic response have taught us that it will take the work of both individuals—in classrooms, in their research, and in meetings and committees and budget discussions—as well as strong leadership and institutional action to bring about a space that truly fosters growth and learning. The stories also remind us that these challenges extend far beyond the university, as students contend with the combined effects of racism, uneven access to resources, and many other inequities. Whether as students, faculty, or staff, we carry those experiences each time we walk into a classroom or other space of learning.

Many of the actions we describe as meaningful take place through individual interactions and efforts—but we underscore that those actions require resources, both material and emotional. Institutions must begin by supporting their communities so that people have the resources that they need. Students need teachers who have the bandwidth to offer extra help and connection when needed. They may also need food, or help with housing and social services. These are all part of learning conditions. Faculty and staff need adequate salaries and healthcare; they also need to know that the institution has their back. They need opportunities for growth and development, and they need social and intellectual connections among their peers.

Without adequate resourcing, too much burden falls on the shoulders of those who already carry heavy loads. But the good news is that these changes are possible—and now is the time to see them through. There is action to take at every level of the university. It is the moment to shift budget lines toward human support, to lobby legislators for state funding for higher ed, and to perhaps pause on pursuing new interventions in favor of supporting the humans who make the university possible. If graduate education fails to change in the wake of this crisis, it is a lost opportunity. This is not a time to return to the prestige economy of 2019 and prior, but to build something new, something grounded in hope, care, abundance, access, joy. What follows is our exploration of what that might look like.

Fostering Belonging by Listening to International Graduate Students, Contributed by Sujung Kim

"Thank you so much for today's conversation. For the first time in four years I have been listened to." Right after our interview, Mariana sent me this thank-you email.[3] But she was not the only one who was grateful; I was also so thankful to Mariana, who made my heart beat again. Our conversation was like a beautiful sprout that finally broke the frozen earth of the pandemic and stretched its stem toward me. As a former international graduate student and an Asian female researcher, I could read Mariana's frustrations and the desperation that she felt from being ignored. A sense of belonging is vital to student success; and yet, through Mariana's story and others, it is clear that international students often struggle to feel that they belong, even outside the alienation caused by the COVID-19 pandemic.

International Students, Not as Part of Minority Student Groups. This essay considers the experiences of three international graduate students who showed powerful critical perspectives and agency to advocate for their needs: Mariana, from South America; Farah, from the Middle East; and Jade, from Europe.

Although diversity and inclusion have become buzzwords in higher education, international students are typically not included in minority graduate student communities, something Mariana noted. Rather, she described international students as "machines." Surprisingly, this sentiment echoed one I had heard during my doctoral field research at a community college, where a Korean international student expressed the feeling that "we (Korean international students) are *'hyŏn'gŭ minch'ulgi* (ATMs)!'" Even though the graduate school that Mariana, Farah, and Jade attend is located in a diverse global city and publicly highlights its commitment to inclusion and social justice, their experiences were not very different from the Korean community college students in terms of being marginalized and overlooked by the institution. One key difference is that the Korean community college student had little opportunity to raise her voice. By contrast, Mariana actively participated in student committees at the departmental and institutional level, creating a sense of agency despite the alienation she felt.

Unexpected Refreshment during the Pandemic. Despite the difficulties of enduring the pandemic, these international doctoral students seemed surprisingly refreshed. During the pandemic, Mariana moved in with a friend in South America in order to save on expenses. Although this decision was primarily financial, Mariana looked rejuvenated as she was away from the fossilized relationships with US academics who knew little about her life experiences or future goals. About her future career path, she joked that she wanted to be a preschool teacher because at a preschool, teachers and children laugh, talk, smile to each other—in other words, everyone presents as human beings and interacts with one another as members of the community.

Farah, who is originally from a privileged family, had to start working since money transfer between the United States and her original country had been banned because of sensitive political issues. Farah was afraid of going outside before the pandemic because she faced explicit discrimination due to her nationality and ethnicity. So, ironically, she enjoyed staying home during the pandemic since she did not need to be exposed to public spaces in which she did not feel safe.

Listening, Connecting, and Supporting One Another. As a former international graduate student and an Asian American female researcher from a poor family in South Korea, I struggled during the pandemic as well. Although I had a full-time job, I also had a great deal of uncertainty. My role is grant-funded and has a set end date, and I am unsure of my further pathways after it ends. I also struggle with feeling unsafe in public spaces because of unpredictable Asian hate crimes.

However, I too experienced the hope and refreshment that the graduate students described. Together, we spoke not only about our experiences of alienation but also our efforts to make our own ways through more humanistic approaches as well as mutual support for each other. Like trees communicating and taking care of one another in the ecological forest, we were willing to connect with one another and exchange concern, hope, recognition, and encouragement. Although our conversations were also research interviews, it was precious for me, Mariana, Farah, and Jade to be empowered and to build solidarity. Just opening our hearts for listening to and sharing our life trajectories, dreams we had when we applied to graduate programs, struggles to manage our everyday life and study, uncertainties about our futures, and our refusal to abandon our hope for better societies opened up meaningful dynamics among us.

Mariana's words ask a fundamental question: without knowing graduate students' life trajectories, current living conditions, struggles and visions, how can faculty members guide them? Faculty members sometimes distance themselves in the interest of protecting students' privacy, and yet students so often want their professors to have a deeper understanding of their situations and to build supportive solidarity with them. Mariana, Farah, and Jade hoped the graduate school would become a humanistic and supportive community where administrators, faculty, and graduate students are curious about one another's stories, struggles, and passions. In such an environment, we can put down roots to support ourselves and one another, creating beautiful and thriving graduate school communities.

Toward that goal, critical self-reflection on existing practices both at the institutional and interpersonal levels are essential. Although graduate schools and institutional personnel often position themselves in opposition to US imperial and/or racist practices internally and abroad, the fact that international students experience alienation and degradation indicates a more complicated reality. It is essential to undertake critical examination not only on the official level, such as institutional official policies, but also the existence of a hidden curriculum that marginalizes international students in diverse practices. Most of all, it is urgent to include international students as a significant part of the minority student group, and their experiences must be reflected by creating more inclusive multicultural policies and practices at the institutional and interpersonal levels. Let us build a system where these deep, sustaining interconnections are part of the structure, not an exception to the rule. That furthermore asks us to imagine and reshape graduate schools as critical cosmopolitan institutions by overcoming nationalistic perspectives.

The Inadequacy of Individual Repair Work for Structural Problems, Contributed by Adashima Oyo

Throughout the pandemic, I frequently probed students with the question: what lessons is COVID-19 teaching us? This is a question I also asked myself as an adjunct instructor and graduate student. More than anything, COVID-19 highlighted and exacerbated issues of access and equity in the classroom. Educators and administrators must contend with these realities if higher education is to remain an essential pillar of opportunity and the public good.

Like many others, in spring 2020, I was forced to quickly pivot the courses I taught at CUNY and New York University (NYU) to virtual modalities. I teach classes that explore public health achievements, health care management, and health equity. I have been teaching these topics for years, but still the transition was challenging. Although it was easy to update a syllabus with a reduced workload for students, other decisions were more difficult. I pondered how to teach online when some students lack reliable internet connections. What about students who don't have a computer and must use their phone for a 90-minute lecture? It did not take long to realize that there were equity and access issues for many students that would impact learning outcomes.

Rather than carry on as normal, I tried to address these concerns with flexibility and creativity. For example, in place of traditional exams, I tasked students with keeping a COVID-19 journal. Students answered prompts about various topics related to COVID-19. The first prompt was always, "how is COVID-19 affecting your life?" As we delved into more specific prompts related to politics, mask mandates, vaccine hesitancy, or stimulus checks, I frequently reminded students that there were no wrong or right answers for their entries and to be respectful when commenting on another student's response.

The opportunity to use bidirectional learning and evaluation in the classroom was appealing to me. I relaxed traditional grading rubrics for final papers. I invited students to provide peer feedback and partial grading on assignments. I encouraged students to think about why and how COVID-19 was disproportionately burdening some communities in relation to the other topics we discussed. I included news articles and video clips that illustrated how the COVID-19 pandemic had not been an exception to the trend of health inequities; people of color experienced disproportionately higher rates of infection, hospitalizations, and death due to COVID-19.[4] I tried to make sense of statistics with my students as we discussed the impact of systemic inequities, racial inequalities and social determinants of health. Collectively, we reflected on what was surprising and not so surprising about the disproportionate burden of COVID-19 on some communities. I privately reflected about how COVID-19 impacted students differently based on socioeconomic status and other unseen variables.

On many occasions, upon hearing of struggles that my students were having related to employment, food insecurity, or family members dying from COVID-19, I was forced to play the role of counselor and social worker. Before diving into each lecture, I started doing simple 60-second check-ins with each student. I knew enough about social services and mental health support to know that I was not professionally trained in those domains. As a solution, I tried to outsource as much as possible. On the last page of the syllabus, I began to focus even more attention on resources for substance abuse, domestic violence, and mental health.

I realized some of my students were really struggling, just like some adjuncts were struggling. I pondered how COVID-19 impacted adjunct faculty versus tenure-track professors. At one school, instructors were instructed to make their lectures as "engaging as possible" and to provide voiceovers for the recorded PowerPoint lectures. Although that sounded like a great idea, I was already burned out, and I wouldn't be compensated for the extra labor. I wondered if the institution realized or cared that many adjuncts were wearing multiple hats during the pandemic and didn't have time for self-care because they were so severely overextended. Although many quit their positions during the pandemic,[5] this option was not on the table for many in precarious positions. For instance, adjuncts at CUNY relied on their positions for strong health insurance benefits—even more important than the meager salary, particularly during a public health crisis.

I also experienced the difference between teaching at two very different schools in New York City. CUNY is an underfunded public system and NYU is a well-endowed private school. The resources and support I received as an adjunct at each school neatly reflected the difference, even though NYU and CUNY students are both brilliant and qualified. During the beginning of the pandemic when New York City (NYC) was considered the epicenter, many of my NYU students left NYC and went back to their hometowns or vacation homes. Most CUNY students were not afforded that luxury and were forced to stay in NYC to try and learn despite unstable internet connections, having to read assignments and complete papers on their cell phone, or study with noisy family members in the background. Circumstances outside of the classroom always impact learning. I began to provide resources about free laptop loans for college students, discount codes for internet plans, virtual writing tutors, and so on, to level the playing field. But the actions of any one instructor will never be nearly enough to counter systemic inequalities.

Making Space to Breathe: Applying Mattering in Higher Education, Contributed by Kashema Hutchinson

As a recent PhD, co-director of the CUNY Peer Leaders (CPL) program, and an adjunct instructor, I have experienced firsthand the impact of COVID-19 on public higher education. What I have seen most of all is that students are rarely given space to breathe. And yet, my experience with CPL shows that a different model is possible.

CPL is a community-based program that supports City University of New York undergraduate students' scholarship.[6] Together with fellow co-directors Kaysi Holman, Lauren Melendez, and Stefanie Sertich, we worked hard to create a space that embodied the values of education we hoped for, rather than those we typically saw.

Whether we gather in person or virtually, CPL creates a rare space for students—the program's Peer Leaders—to breathe. During the pandemic's "lockdown," this space was essential. CPL has an embedded culture of care that centers the Leaders, allowing them to navigate their educational paths—which often includes figuring out how to overcome or manage hardships. There's no testing, there's no judgment. This allows Leaders to feel a sense of belonging and community. The space takes the Leaders out of their everyday rhythms and allows them to be, to understand, to work through, to interact and to find fellowship.

Conversations and Content. Our Friday evening meet-ups start with a check-in and heuristic: "How are you?" I learned this practice from Black feminist scholar and educator Dr. Carmen Kynard. If the responses are overwhelmingly negative, we as co-directors stop to address those feelings, because they matter. Letting them know they matter creates a space that allows the Leaders to respectfully create, question, and challenge, with the intention of surviving, healing, and growing despite the odds. According to Dr. Bettina Love, this is a form of abolitionist teaching.[7] CPL works with a community predominantly of color that centers mattering in order to counter injustice in schools and communities. The space is *their space*.

Even virtually, we are able to build community, to recognize and see each other. At the root of this is caring and mattering. Caring allows the group dynamics to flourish regardless of what's happening outside. If we were to take this and apply it to traditional academic spaces, it would mean acknowledging that students are human, that they have hardships, that you have hardships. We acknowledge and see that they may be going through things, even if they're not speaking up about it. If space and time is needed, we allow them to have it to talk about the things going on with them.

A big part of how we do this is through self-care. In particular, the co-directors and the Leaders practice a self-care of refusal: the refusal to be a cog in the capitalist machine. We acknowledge that we cannot destroy the machine, but we need to take breaks and take care of ourselves. It helps the Leaders recognize that while aspiring to be their greatest selves, they also need to pause, whether through yoga, a conversation with a friend, writing poetry, playing music, or taking a nap.

Creativity and Accountability. Self-care can also mean finding outlets for creativity and expression, and being socially and critically conscious. The CPL program uses blogging as a way to tap into this, and also to build community, because Leaders get to know each other by reading each other's blogs. The posts also help Leaders work toward their year-end project, in which they create something to share with the world. Regular blog posts hold them accountable and foster discussion with their peers.

The pandemic sharpened the focus on CPL and what we do. When times are at their worst, this community is a way of survival for some of our students. If we were to take some of these approaches into the classrooms, we would see the difference it makes in creating the classroom culture. I carry that lesson into each academic year. In my classrooms I ask, "how are you?"; my intent is to help students know that someone actually cares about their wellness because I know they have multiple courses, and what's going on in their life may be more important than what's happening in my classroom. By having grace with students, also have grace with me, too.[8] It is a small action that has an enormous impact.

The question is, can something like this be scalable—not just from a program to a classroom, but to an institution? The answer is yes, but perhaps not yet. Those within the institution need to have the compassion, bandwidth, and support to do so. Many institutions define success through numbers (enrollment, credits, and so on), rather than humans. The inability to sit back and reflect on what is happening and why things are the way they are was the missed opportunity.

Conclusion

As these case studies suggest, every person within the university has agency to support change. And, at the same time, we must push for something broader—for institutional and systemic change that *enables* students, faculty, and staff to take such actions more easily. The erosion of public funding for higher education that started in the 1970s continues unabated, and budgets are exceedingly tight. Students, faculty, and staff are constantly being asked to do more with less; this is not a road to sustainable change. It is not a moment to keep slicing the pie into ever-narrower slivers, but to fight together for a bigger pie.

We have seen exemplary programs and individual actions that support the mutual thriving of students, faculty, and staff. Many of these actions occur despite the prevailing atmosphere of scarcity and competition in the university. We imagine that diverting resources to areas of greatest need, supporting students and precarious workers both financially and socially, and advocating for increased public support of higher education could open the doors to building an educational environment that fosters not only learning, but flourishing.

Dr. Rogers wrote these words in another piece, much earlier in the pandemic:

> I think the first step may be to simply stop for a moment. There is power in collective action, in a protest, in a strike, in the act of saying, "No more." Before we can build new systems and structures and incentives and task forces, I think we need to pause and say no. No, some of this work does not matter, and we can let it drop. No, we will not continue to exploit adjunct labor. No, we will not ask the impossible of our underfunded institutions, constantly pressured to do more with less. For me,

there is hope in this refusal, because it says that a different way is possible.[9]

Now we ask: did we truly stop? Students, faculty, and staff are dealing with months and months of trauma and grief, and as is often the case, the effects weigh disproportionately on minoritized communities. In the midst of that trauma, the pressures of tenure and time-to-degree and the never-ending scramble for funding have continued. The reopening of universities feels like waking from a dream, shaking off the sleep of the past year and trying to get back in step with the way things were before. But why? It is so clear that the system was not working for many people, with gatekeeping occupying as much time and energy as generative scholarly work.

Higher education doesn't have to be the way that it is. It doesn't have to be an environment with higher-than-average depression and anxiety. It doesn't have to be a workplace replete with labor inequity or racial and gender bias. Instead, it could be a space of mutual support and care. We know this is possible; our experiences show this to be the case. Now, it is up to us to build it on a wider scale. COVID-19 has shown us that even a state of crisis is not enough to create lasting change. And yet, the system is built by a million decisions made by people. All of us who are a part of higher education, all of us who have a voice within the system—wherever we can fight for changes that support those whose voices may not be heard—it is time to take action.

Notes

1. Tsing, *Mushroom*; Haraway, *Staying with the Trouble.*
2. Rogers, *Putting the Humanities PhD to Work.*
3. Names have been changed to ensure confidentiality.
4. CDC, "Health Equity Considerations."
5. See for instance, Elfman, "Struggling for Stability."
6. CUNY Peer Leaders is a community-based program that supports CUNY undergraduate students' scholarship and creative work in the Humanities and supports them in developing leadership skills to implement within their communities and colleges. CUNY Peer Leaders participate in a variety of community building workshops and enrichment opportunities designed to explore concepts of voice,

respect, and presentation of self, which are essential to leadership; critical and creative thinking; sociopolitical issues and their impacts; various historical and cultural perspectives; aesthetic appreciation; and human connection. The CUNY Peer Leaders is a new iteration, supported by the Andrew W. Mellon Foundation, that combines elements of the CUNY Humanities Alliance LaGuardia Mellon Humanities Scholars program and the Futures Initiative Undergraduate Leadership and Democracy Fellows Program.

7. Love, *Pursuit of Eeducational Freedom.*

8. Ascencio et al. "Inclusion, Agency and Community."

9. Rogers, "COVID, Care, and Community."

Bibliography

Ascencio, Sam, Moses Matos, Ramesh Beharry, and Sheila Janeo. "Inclusion, Agency and Community in Higher Education: Making the Most of Student Life." Presentation at the Graduate Education at Work in the World Conference, CUNY Graduate Center, New York, February 19, 2021.

CDC (Centers for Disease Control). "Health Equity Considerations and Racial and Ethnic Minority Groups." April 30, 2020. https://www.cdc.gov/coronavirus/2019-ncov/community/health-equity/race-ethnicity.html.

Elfman, Lois. "Struggling for Stability: Some Adjuncts Are Leaving Higher Ed in Favor of Full-Time Employment." *Diverse: Issues In Higher Education*, October 2021. https://www.diverseeducation.com/faculty-staff/article/15280344/struggling-for-stability-some-adjuncts-are-leaving-higher-ed-in-favor-of-fulltime-employment.

Haraway, Donna Jeanne. *Staying with the Trouble: Making Kin in the Chthulucene.* Durham, NC: Duke University Press, 2016.

Love, Bettina. *We Want to Do More Than Survive: Abolitionist Teaching and the Pursuit of Educational Freedom.* Boston: Beacon Press, 2019.

Rogers, Katina. "COVID, Care, and Community." In *Digital Futures of Graduate Study in the Humanities*, edited by Simon Appleford, Gabriel Hankins, and Anouk Lang. Debates in Digital Humanities series. Minneapolis, MN: Minnesota University Press (forthcoming).

———. *Putting the Humanities PhD to Work: Thriving in and beyond the Classroom.* Durham, NC: Duke University Press, 2020.

Tsing, Anna Lowenhaupt. *The Mushroom at the End of the World: On the Possibility of Life in Capitalist Ruins.* Princeton, NJ: Princeton University Press, 2017.

chapter 13

In the Role of Learners

Nancy Chick

Of all the methods available for changing how we teach, putting ourselves in the role of learners has the greatest long-term effects.

—Stephen D. Brookfield

Stephen Brookfield's encouragement for all faculty to regularly experience being a student is a cornerstone of the process of (according to his title) *Becoming a Critically Reflective Teacher*. He had in mind faculty development programming, further graduate work, conference participation, learning new skills and hobbies, and other "opportunities for sustained autobiographical reflection on learning."[1] Nowhere on his list of empathy-building experiences was a global emergency that would require faculty to do several of these "opportunities" and more in a very short amount of time, but the COVID-19 pandemic pushed nearly all faculty—even seasoned online teachers—into the students' seat, a change that promises to transform how we teach.

In this chapter, I will look back on three phases of the pandemic in which faculty had no choice but to put themselves in the role as learners.

The Spring 2020 Pivot: Cramming *en Masse*

The now-infamous Spring 2020 Pivot, in which faculty had to move entire courses into remote environments in just a few days, was nothing short of a global cramming session. A survey of 641 institutions revealed that 97% of them used "faculty with no prior online teaching experience to quickly prepare themselves, their courses and their students" into online environments.[2] In addition to the ubiquity of the word "pivot," many were careful to describe what happened in March 2020 as "emergency remote teaching" to distinguish "existing well designed and planned online teaching programmes" from "having to teach online due to a crisis."[3] Even faculty on small liberal arts campuses that are philosophically opposed to online learning in favor of an intimate in-person experience were compelled to go virtual.

Suddenly, everyone from tech whizzes to Luddites had to digitize their course materials and upload them into a learning management system (LMS). They had to immediately translate their quizzes and exams into electronic and cheat-proof formats. They had to figure out how to facilitate labs, studios, rehearsals, and performances through cameras and screens. Some had to adapt to classrooms in which everyone was masked, stationary, and six feet apart, and some of these unlucky souls also had to struggle with dual-mode teaching with some of their students in the room and others present only through webcams. The truly unfortunate had to learn the Swiss Army knife of teaching situations called "HyFlex," reconfiguring their courses for online (LMS), virtual (web-conferencing), and in-person contexts and both synchronous and asynchronous delivery in order to offer students maximum flexibility.

In normal times, such shifts would take months and would be guided by an instructional designer, an educational technologist, and/or a faculty developer. In March of 2020, however, faculty had somewhere from a few days to a couple of weeks, and those traditional guides—on campuses that had them—did what they could while demand for their help exploded. Impromptu study groups in Twitter threads and Facebook groups buzzed with just-in-time idea exchanges and offers for immediate support across national borders, as well as—remarkably—those borders typically dividing K–12 and postsecondary teachers.

In their "need to 'just get it online,'" faculty became "instructional MacGyvers, having to improvise quick solutions in less-than-ideal circumstances."[4] Without the time to be thoughtful or planful, faculty had to hunker down, figure it out, and get it done—also known as cramming. And like cramming, they knew the resulting work wasn't their best. As one faculty member admitted, "We all dealt well with the disaster but it was still a disaster."[5] Ultimately, faculty acknowledged this imperfection but took heart in what they "got right," as documented in a study of faculty teaching 300 courses in March and April, 2020, summarized in *Inside Higher Education*:

> While 55 percent of respondents rated their students' learning experience as "lower quality" during the pandemic, more than 70 percent nevertheless felt that they had fulfilled their teaching objectives. Class cancellations proved relatively rare, affecting only about 40 percent of courses and usually involving just two or three classes. Assignment deadlines, word lengths and format requirements were relaxed in over 60 percent of courses, but without sacrificing fairness or transparency.[6]

This kind of "good enough" assessment—a kind of pass/fail approach that mirrored the grading system offered to many students during this time—is captured in one faculty member's lament, "we have to try, and it will not be perfect."[7]

Summer and Fall 2020: The Big Test

But that was just the spring. The pandemic persisted, of course, so faculty used much of the summer of 2020 and beyond for intentional study. As much as they needed a break, they knew the 2020–2021 academic year would be the big test. The stakes were high, as all eyes were upon higher education to demonstrate its relevance and adaptability. On two days alone in early summer, headlines proclaimed "Universities Will Never Be the Same after the Coronavirus Crisis" and "It's Now or Never," and the next day brought advice on "How Your College Can Survive the Pandemic" although another was less certain, asking "Can Higher Ed Survive the Pandemic?"[8] Faculty everywhere, but especially on smaller campuses, were keenly aware that they were being put to the test to see if their campuses and their profession would weather the global crisis.

Facing a sharp learning curve, faculty turned to each other and other colleagues for help. Many began—even if by necessity—working with others to aid in deeper learning beyond the spring's cram session. Even faculty who'd never before sought out faculty development suddenly reached out to these colleagues (now recognized as something akin to study partners) in teaching and learning centers in what seemed like record numbers. One study of this period is entitled "Learning Together in a Global Pandemic," alluding to the frequency with which survey respondents and interviewed faculty described the people they "always" or "often drew on," such as other faculty on their campuses, learning designers, information technologists, librarians, student services staff, and faculty teaching elsewhere.[9] (Chapter 2 in this book aptly reframes teaching during this time as a "team sport.") Many reached out to these colleagues to learn new-to-them teaching methods (e.g., flipping their classrooms, scaffolding assignments, and facilitating small group discussions) and to craft policies they'd never imagined, such as whether to require cameras on, or to maintain firm deadlines, or to give up grading altogether. They had used Zoom, Webex, Teams, and Google Hangouts to just get by in the spring, but now tech-savvy colleagues helped them learn to use these web-conferencing tools to more skillfully support their teaching by design. As one survey report noted, teaching in the pandemic "has been disruptive, forcing a sea change in behaviors and practices in academia."[10] And, while reaching out to peers like life preservers, faculty struggled to stay afloat.

Beyond 2020: Early Predictions

As part of the big test, everyone has been interested in what learning would stick, what new practices and skills would persist when teaching was "normal" again. While the headlines about K–12 education focused on students' "learning losses" and the profession's loss of teachers, conversations about higher education have swirled around the question of "What Will Remain?"[11] Campuses, higher ed researchers, and edtech companies have surveyed faculty about what changes in their teaching they would hold onto. For instance, a March 2021 press release featured the following highlight from a survey of 967 institutions:

> Faculty have radically changed teaching techniques since the pandemic, and don't expect to revert back: 71 percent of faculty said their teaching in Fall 2020 was either "very different" from pre-pandemic methods or included a "number of changes," and only 8 percent expect to revert back to pre-pandemic practices. Nearly half (47 percent) expect post-pandemic teaching will have a number of changes or look very different than how they taught pre-pandemic.[12]

Many of the changes reported in this survey (and many others) had a sharp focus on technology-based practices: "Digital materials use has soared," "Online homework and courseware systems use more than doubled," and "The majority of faculty are more positive about digital learning materials and online learning." Another study presents 19 case studies that illustrate how faculty "have learnt new practices, developed greater digital confidence, and shifted perspectives regarding the role of technology in enabling interaction with and between students."[13]

Although most reports of the pandemic's "enduring understandings"[14] feature technology, a promising lesson—but typically a buried lede—reported by many faculty follows a kind of grateful awakening about the kinds of assignments they can develop, and the kinds of thinking students show as a result. Admittedly, this epiphany is often described as simply "adopting new approaches to assessment," which is of course accurate but doesn't capture the learning experienced by these faculty. See, for example, the list of one faculty member's "Gains" in one study of teaching in the pandemic:[15]

- Forced stripping back of content and organization of key material, for practicals in particular, so it is more relevant to students.
- Many students demonstrated a deeper understanding of theoretical knowledge underpinning practical classes compared with normal on-campus classes.
- Finally achieving agreement from course lecturers to run an open-book exam with only short-answer questions (no multiple choice

questions) and the opportunity to educate receptive lecturers on how to write exam questions that extend students beyond fact recall, memory, and basic understanding.

This list, like many reports of what we've learned from the pandemic, captures promising teaching strategies that imply moving from a "coverage" to an "uncoverage"[16] approach: revisiting and cutting content, and replacing multiple-choice, recall-oriented exams toward constructed-response, open-book assessments that allow students to demonstrate conceptual knowledge. Others claim that "Moving online has made us have to focus on what we are trying to assess," so they are able to create "the authentic assessment we always wanted to have."[17] Again, these are promising, but we don't know if the adoption of uncoverage and authentic assessments is widespread or intentional in a way that will make these changes stick.

Intentions Matter

In many ways, the above are changes in teaching practices, techniques, and tools—all parts of the relatively superficial choreography of teaching. These visible aspects of teaching are important, of course, but if we view them through the lens of what we know about learning, they—like lessons learned from cramming—have questionable impact and durability for the learners (i.e., the faculty). This question of what will remain after the pandemic is ultimately a matter of transfer, so consider what the research tells us about what inhibits it. First, faculty may resort to "*overspecificity* or *context dependence*," associating what they learned "too closely with the context in which they originally learned it and thus not think to apply it—or how to apply it—outside that context."[18] In this case, faculty may feel like authentic assessments, flexible deadlines, trimming content, and other innovations are pandemic necessities and thus short-term adaptations, rather than effective pedagogies for all contexts.

Another reason why learners fail to carry forward new knowledge or practices is "if they do not have a robust understanding of the underlying principles and deep structure—in other words, if they understand what to do but not why."[19] In this case, the absence of a metacognitive intentionality relegates what they've learned to a kind of going through the motions, giving them no compelling reason to continue after the pressure is gone.

This latter explanation featuring the significance of understanding underlying principles, deep structures, and why to do or know something is related to another body of research that will help us speculate on how the pandemic might transform teaching and teachers in the long term. A series of studies by Keith Trigwell and Michael Prosser, with colleagues[20] demonstrated that students exhibited deeper learning when their professors thought of teaching as more complex, less transactional, and focused on students. The critical piece in this research is that it's the not the teaching practices or strategies (e.g., flipped classroom, interrupted lecture, group work) that correlate with deeper student learning; instead, it's the teacher's "approach to" teaching—how they *conceive of* teaching and learning, and the resulting *intentions* for the teacher personally as well as for the students—that have a direct relationship with the quality of student learning. An illustration of this unsettling conclusion is useful: if a teacher who sees the work as "teacher focused" and aimed at "information transfer" adopts the active learning technique of integrating buzz groups (i.e., small group discussion) into lecture, it's "likely" to be used "as a strategy to keep students from becoming bored with the lecture, rather than as a method to help the teacher find out about students' prior knowledge, or for students to become aware of the variation of the conceptions among their peers, or as a ways of developing discussion among students."[21] We can imagine the instructions given to students in the buzz groups guided by these different intentions.

Although Trigwell, Prosser, and colleagues are careful in their publications to present "just the facts" of each study, if we look at their collected body of research, the findings from this series of studies inductively build a theory of teaching and learning: the quality of student learning is associated less with the practices, techniques, and tools of teaching and more with *how the teacher thinks about teaching and learning.*

"Being the Human"

With this theory in mind as we make the slow transition from teaching in a global pandemic to whatever comes after, we should look beyond how this moment has affected the actions of teaching to how it has affected the approaches to teaching. We don't know what will happen with the "innovations" getting all the press, but few would dispute undergoing a fundamental reconceptualization of the humanity at the core of teaching and learning, which has affected how faculty think about their students, themselves, and each other.

Plenty of surveys, opinion pieces, and social media posts echo the findings from the faculty interviews described in "What Will Remain?": "While adoption of technology naturally played an important role, we found even more striking a fundamental shift in the faculty's attitude toward students and teaching."[22] Many students brought their home lives into the virtual classroom, and in-class check-ins and virtual office hours vividly exposed circumstances we'd previously known only in the abstract. We can't unsee homes where the traditional expectation of two hours of studying for every one hour in class is impossible. The vast majority of this recognition of "the whole student"[23] has centered on unprecedented attention to their mental health (i.e., how much it's suffering, what's needed, how to teach in ways that support well-being). Mays Imad's ubiquitous writings and webinars on trauma-informed teaching have helped faculty understand the effects of extreme stress on students' brains.[24] This increase in awareness of, sensitivity to, and strategies for supporting students' mental health is in itself significant, but there was also something more at play, something closer to how faculty relate to students. *Relationship-Rich Education: How Human Connections Drive Success in College* by Peter Felten and Leo M. Lambert—written before the pandemic but published in November 2020—became arguably the most important book in higher education during the pandemic, capturing what faculty leaned into as they connected with students.[25] Faculty describe missing "'the human connection' in teaching" and feeling a sense of grief over "the enormous loss in contact" with their students.[26] They also report a "heightened . . .

caring for" students and being "very touched by" the more personalized interactions with students afforded by virtual office hours and after class chats in the privacy of a Zoom room.[27] None of this should imply that faculty didn't care about students before, but instead that they felt deeply the students' absence and gained greater insight into students' full selves.

Faculty also experienced a sea change in their conceptions of themselves as teachers. As Felten and Lambert note in a brief postscript they were able to write in April 2020, "'being the human' has been a rallying cry for faculty and staff trying to interact meaningfully with students during remote learning."[28] In truth, faculty had little choice but to fulfill this call to "be the human" and to—as Parker Palmer proposed in the last century—bring their "inner [lives]" and "undivided [selves]" into the classroom, with a reality check that "teaching is a daily exercise in vulnerability."[29]

Indeed, they were regularly reminded that their expertise gets them only so far. Even the best teachers and the most experienced online instructors looked in the mirror of the Zoom self-view and found themselves coming up short. From the lack of necessary technical skills to the deadening effect of teaching to gray squares rather than students, the daily confrontation with the feeling of not teaching very well took a toll, fueling a "pervasive sense of 'I don't know what I'm doing.'"[30] Indeed, Imad's work on trauma-informed teaching didn't focus solely on students' trauma: in "Dear Faculty: 'Keep Walking,'" she acknowledges the "profound emotional crisis" made visible during this time.[31] On a far deeper level, exacerbated by this sense of inadequacy, faculty experienced "a mental exhaustion"[32] in ways that couldn't be contained outside the classroom. And so, many quit trying to hide their emotions and their full humanness from their students. Joshua Eyler's March 13, 2020, Tweet broadcasted—from nearly the first day of the Spring 2020 Pivot—what it would feel like to teach for a while: "Higher Ed folks: Deep breath. It's okay: you don't have to have all the answers. You can be honest w/ students & tell them that you're just as sad/confused/upset as they are but—step by step—you will get through this together. They will always remember your honesty & humanity."[33]

This Tweet also foretold the teaching community that emerged among "Higher Ed folks." In the "Learning Together in a Global Pandemic" report, there's a section called "Human Resources . . . Supporting the Move to Online Education," a heading that hardly captures what the highlighted faculty member expresses about her colleagues:

> The (two) colleagues planning and teaching the same course. One academic developer (at the Centre for Teaching and Learning), who has introduced us to all this in a very good way. The first time we met with her we had great fun, so it was a good experience. And my closest colleague—we help each other with different educational technologies, like Canvas and Zoom. I help her with one thing, and she helps me with another.[34]

And later in the report, another faculty member recalls that his course team "just pulled each other along and when someone was flagging someone else jumped in."[35] A more recent survey notes that "many faculty interacted meaningfully with the other educators on campus who could help them connect with assessment resources" but focuses on the pragmatic benefits of such campus partnerships, and nothing more.[36] Like Eyler's Tweet, there is an affective dimension in these utterances, well beyond the transactional nature of these peer interactions.

In the wake of the initial outreach to educational developers, instructional technologists, and other professionals to survive the Spring 2020 Pivot, the dynamics among these peers have been changing in ways that resonate with the title of Felten and Lambert's *Relationship-Rich Education: How Human Connections Drive Success in College*, even though their book focuses on what "drives success" for students. Faculty meetings, conference sessions, and other public spaces have been sites for radical conversations among faculty, rotating around nodes of identity that reach beyond their "faculty-ness" to caring for their children or elderly parents, living alone, or losing loved ones.

Described by Roxanne Atterholt and Laura Cruz as "academic witnessing," or "connecting with each other as human beings,"[37] faculty have begun talking with each other about their lived experiences tied to these identities, not just their common ground of devoting 110% to teaching and supporting students, sacrificing (often not by choice) research time, and being exhausted by having to spend even more time on Zoom for service obligations. The intimacy ranges from professional vulnerability ("For the first time, I find no joy in my work") to personal ("I haven't been touched by another human being in over a year"). Beyond the widespread idea exchange and pedagogical support, which by itself is remarkable, the pandemic deepened faculty members' relationships with others, bringing about an unexpected response to Lee Shulman's 1993 call to open our classroom doors and "put an end to pedagogical solitude."[38]

At some point in the wake of this difficult series of lessons, it will be time to return to Brookfield's call for "sustained . . . reflection on" what we've learned.[39] Some have probably been doing so, but others may feel it's too soon to relive the trauma, at least on their own. Imad would assure us that this is to be expected, and no one should be doing this necessary work alone. Our institutions—or, more precisely, the people within these institutions—can support this healing and meaning-making. Faculty developers, for instance, have undoubtedly been working overtime (still) to bring faculty together to reflect in book groups, learning communities, and even explicit programming about teaching in the pandemic.

But this phase requires the whole campus community. Mental health professionals on campus have rallied around students, as they should, but it's far too rare that faculty get the same proactive attention to mental well-being. These professionals can help faculty work on some of the trauma from the pandemic through individualized counseling as well as faculty support groups. As some of the most enduring campus citizens, they earn this support in normal times, so in the wake of the pandemic, it should be a given. Human Resources can also help faculty through employee resource groups and affinity groups, such as parents of young children, caring for elderly parents, and the like. In these groups, faculty can reflect on these specific experiences together. Presidents, provosts, and deans can extend meaningful gestures of gratitude like offering free lunches in campus dining halls to encourage faculty to come back together outside of meetings. These informal gatherings not driven by a task can become a space for the interpersonal (re)connection that has suffered in the pandemic.

This institution-wide support for faculty is especially needed on campuses where leadership has adopted either a sense of nostalgia for a past that we can't get back (or never existed in the first place) or the amnesia of moving forward without fully acknowledging the experiences of the past few years, much less provided a space and time and structure for the sustained reflection central to healing. Ultimately, the entire institution should collectively acknowledge the very specific experiences of the last few years, broadly support communities of healing and meaning-making, and answer the rallying cry of "being the human" by remembering that everyone has been in the role of learners during this time.

Conclusion

If we're looking for the long-term effects of the global pandemic on teaching and learning in higher education, the most honest answer is "We don't yet know." We do know that this experience overlapped with other unprecedented events like the cultural response to the murder of George Floyd and the political animosity culminating in the 2021 insurrection at the US Capitol Building, both of which left many Americans unmoored, but neither have been studied as dramatically effecting higher education. So the quest for the pandemic's long-term impact on teaching will always be messy. But we do know that faculty worldwide were suddenly recast as learners facing high stakes evaluations, an experience that laid bare the human connections at the core of teaching and learning. What will last? Only time will tell.

Notes

1. Brookfield, 51.
2. Cengage Blog. "Digital Learning Pulse Survey."
3. Matthews et al., *Online in Uncertain Times*, 3.
4. Hodges et al., "Difference Between Emergency."
5. Matthews et al., *Online in Uncertain Times*, 56.

6. Ross, "In Early Days."

7. Matthews et al., *Online in Uncertain Times*, 32.

8. Witze, "Universities Will Never Be the Same"; Latham and Braun, "Now or Never"; Baer, "Can Higher Ed Survive"; Miyares and Catalano, "How Your College Can Survive."

9. Matthews et al., *Online in Uncertain Times*, 7.

10. Matthews et al., *Online in Uncertain Times*, 50.

11. Dickler, "Learning Loss, Study Finds"; International Bank for Reconstruction and Development, "A Path to Recovery"; Gecker, "COVID-19 Creates Dire"; Miyagawa and Perdue, "What Will Remain?"

12. Cengage Group, "Materials in Place Post-Pandemic."

13. Matthews et al., *Online in Uncertain Times*, 3.

14. Wiggins and McTighe, *Understanding by Design*, 10.

15. Matthews et al., *Online in Uncertain Times*, 13.

16. Wiggins and McTighe, *Understanding by Design* 98.

17. Matthews et al., *Online in Uncertain Times*, 51.

18. Ambrose et al., *How Learning Works*, 108.

19. Ambrose, et al., 109.

20. See, for example, Trigwell et al., "Relations between Teachers' Approaches," 57–70; Trigwell and Prosser, "Relational Perspective"; Trigwell, "Evidence of the Impact," 95–105; Trigwell and Prosser, *Learning: Experience and Context*.

21. Trigwell and Prosser, "Congruence between Intention," 85.

22. Miyagawa and Perdue, "What Will Remain?"

23. Miyagawa and Perdue.

24. See, for example, her articles in *Inside Higher Ed* archived at "Mays Imad" and in the *Chronicle of Higher Education* at "Mays Imad."

25. Felten and Lambert, *Relationship-Rich Education*.

26. *Chronicle of Higher Education*, "On the Verge of Burnout"; Matthews et al., *Online in Uncertain Times*, 9.

27. Matthews et al., *Online in Uncertain Times*, 3, 54.

28. Felten and Lambert, 164.

29. Palmer, *Courage to Teach*, 3, 15, 17.

30. Lederman, "Shift to Remote Learning."

31. Imad, "Dear Faculty." Perhaps the extreme consequence of this emotional crisis is that some faculty have "checked out emotionally and mentally for their jobs" in what the *Chronicle* called "The Great Faculty Disengagement." McClure and Fryar; *Chronicle of Higher Education*. "I Cycle."

32. *Chronicle of Higher Education*, "On the Verge of Burnout," 10.

33. Eyler (@joshua_r_eyler), "Higher Ed folks."

34. Matthews et al., *Online in Uncertain Times*, 35.

35. Matthews et al., *Online in Uncertain Times*, 50.

36. Carrasco, "Assessing Pandemic Learning"; Jankowski and Bheda, "Equity, and Student Success."

37. Atterholt and Cruz, "Shock Waves."
38. Shulman, "End to Pedagogical Solitude."
39. Brookfield, "Becoming a Critically Reflective Teacher."

Bibliography

Ambrose, Susan A., Michael W. Bridges, Michele DiPietro, Marsha C. Lovett, and Marie K. Norman. *How Learning Works: 7 Research-Based Principles for Smart Teaching.* San Francisco: Jossey-Bass, 2010.

Atterholt, Roxanne, and Laura Cruz. "Shock Waves: Academic Witnessing as Resiliency Practice." Workshop at SoTL Commons Conference, Savannah, GA, February 24, 2022.

Baer, Daniel. "Can Higher Ed Survive the Pandemic?" *Democracy: A Journal of Ideas.* (June 2, 2020). https://democracyjournal.org/magazine/can-higher-ed-survive-the-pandemic/.

Brookfield, Stephen D., *Becoming a Critically Reflective Teacher*. San Francisco: Jossey-Bass, 1995.

Carrasco, Maria. "Assessing Pandemic Learning," *Inside Higher Ed* (blog), March 23, 2022. https://www.insidehighered.com/news/2022/03/23/survey-views-pandemic-learning-overwhelmingly-negative.

Cengage Blog. "Digital Learning Pulse Survey: Immediate Priorities—a Snapshot of Higher Ed's Response to the COVID-19 Pandemic [INFOGRAPHIC]," *Cengage* (blog), August 28, 2020. https://blog.cengage.com/digital-learning-pulse-survey-immediate-priorities-a-snapshot-of-higher-eds-response-to-covid-19.

Chronicle of Higher Education. "'I Cycle Between Nihilism and Rage,'" January 28, 2022. https://www.chronicle.com/article/i-cycle-between-nihilism-and-rage.

———. "Mays Imad." Accessed May 10, 2023. https://www.chronicle.com/author/mays-imad.

———. "Research Brief: On the Verge of Burnout." 2020. https://connect.chronicle.com/rs/931-EKA-218/images/Covid%26FacultyCareerPaths_Fidelity_ResearchBrief_v3%20%281%29.pdf.

Dickler, Jessica. "Virtual School Resulted in 'Significant' Academic Learning Loss, Study Finds." *CNBC*, March 30, 2021. https://www.cnbc.com/2021/03/30/learning-loss-from-virtual-school-due-to-covid-is-significant-.html.

Eyler, Joshua (@joshua_r_eyler). "Higher Ed folks: Deep breath. It's Okay: You Don't Have to Have All the Answers." Twitter. March 13, 2020. https://twitter.com/joshua_r_eyler/status/1238667740568788993?lang=en.

Felten, Peter, and Leo M. Lambert. *Relationship-Rich Education: How Human Connections Drive Success in College.* Baltimore: Johns Hopkins University Press, 2020.

Gecker, Jocelyn. "COVID-19 Creates Dire US Shortage of Teachers, School Staff." *AP News*, September 22, 2021. https://apnews.com/article/business-science-health-education-california-b6c495eab9a2a8f1a3ca068582c9d3c7.

Hodges, Charles, Stephanie Moore, Barb Lockee, Torrey Trust, and Aaron Bond. "The Difference Between Emergency Remote Teaching and Online Learning." *EDUCAUSE* (blog), March 27, 2020. https://er.educause.edu/articles/2020/3/the-difference-between-emergency-remote-teaching-and-online-learning.

Imad, Mays. "Dear Faculty: 'Keep Walking.'" *Inside Higher Education* (blog), November 24, 2020. https://www.insidehighered.com/advice/2020/11/24/advice-how-faculty-can-keep-going-and-find-clarity-and-resolve-during-challenging.

International Bank for Reconstruction and Development. "The State of the Global Education Crisis: A Path to Recovery." World Bank, UNESCO, and UNICEF, 2021. https://www.unicef.org/reports/state-global-education-crisis.

Jankowski, N. A., and D. Bheda. "Pandemic Insights to Shape a Better Future: Assessment for Teaching, Learning, Equity, and Student Success." *ExamSoft*, March 22, 2022. https://examsoft.com/es/download-assessment-insights.

Latham, Scott, and Michael Braun. "It's Now or Never." *Inside Higher Education* (blog), June 1, 2020. https://www.insidehighered.com/views/2020/06/01/survive-post-pandemic-world-colleges-must-rethink-their-value-proposition-now.

Lederman, Doug. "How Teaching Changed in the (Forced) Shift to Remote Learning." *Inside Higher Education* (blog), April 22, 2020. https://www.insidehighered.com/digital-learning/article/2020/04/22/how-professors-changed-their-teaching-springs-shift-remote.

Matthews, Kelly E., Gwendolyn Lawrie, Katarina Mårtensson, Torgny Roxå, Catherine Bovill, and Celeste McLaughlin. *Learning Together in a Global Pandemic: Practices and Principles for Teaching and Assessing Online in Uncertain Times.* Brisbane, Australia: University of Queensland, 2021. https://espace.library.uq.edu.au/view/UQ:d9d30c5.

"Mays Imad." *Inside Higher Ed* (blog). Accessed May 10, 2023. https://www.insidehighered.com/node/5284.

Miyagawa, Shigeru, and Meghan Perdue. "What Will Remain?" *Inside Higher Ed* (blog), June 9, 2021. https://www.insidehighered.com/advice/2021/06/09/survey-faculty-way-pandemic-has-permanently-transformed-teaching-opinion.

Miyares, Javier, and Darren Catalano. "How Your College Can Survive the Pandemic." *Chronicle of Higher Education*, June 2, 2020. https://www.chronicle.com/article/how-your-college-can-survive-the-pandemic.

Palmer, Parker. *The Courage to Teach: Exploring the Inner Landscape of a Teacher's Life.* San Francisco: Jossey-Bass, 1998.

Ross, John. "In Early Days of Pandemic, Teaching Suffered." *Inside Higher Ed* (blog), September 17, 2021. https://www.insidehighered.com/news/2021/09/17/survey-teaching-suffered-early-days-pandemic.

Shulman, Lee S. "Teaching as Community Property: Putting an End to Pedagogical Solitude." *Change* 25, no. 6 (1993): 6–7.

Cengage Group. "Survey: About Half of Faculty Are More Positive About Online Learning Today Than Pre-Pandemic, And Expect to Keep New Teaching Techniques and Digital Materials in Place Post-Pandemic." March 24, 2021. https://

www.cengagegroup.com/news/press-releases/2021/survey-about-half-of-faculty-are-more-positive-about-online-learning-today-than-pre-pandemic-and-expect-to-keep-new-teaching-techniques-and-digital-materials-in-place-post-pandemic.

Trigwell, Keith, "Evidence of the Impact of Scholarship of Teaching and Learning Purposes," *Teaching & Learning Inquiry* 1, no. 1 (2013): 95–105. https://doi.org/10.20343/teachlearninqu.1.1.95.

Trigwell, Keith, and Michael Prosser. "Changing Approaches to Teaching: A Relational Perspective," *Studies in Higher Education* 21, no. 3, (1996): 275–284, https://doi.org/10.1080/03075079612331381211.

———. "Congruence between Intention and Strategy in University Science Teachers' Approaches to Teaching." *Higher Education* 32, no. 1 (July 1996): 77–87.

———. *Exploring University Teaching and Learning: Experience and Context*. New York: Palgrave/Macmmillan, 2020. https://doi.org/10.1007/978-3-030-50830-2.

Trigwell, Keith, Michael Prosser, and Fiona Waterhouse. "Relations between Teachers' Approaches to Teaching and Students' Approaches to Learning." *Higher Education* 37, no. 1 (1999): 57–70. https://doi.org/10.1023/A:1003548313194.

Wiggins, Grant, and Jay McTighe. *Understanding by Design.* Alexandria, VA: Association for Supervision and Curriculum Development.

Witze, Alexandra. "Universities Will Never Be the Same after the Coronavirus Crisis." *Nature* 582, no. 7811 (June 1, 2020): 162–164. https://doi.org/10.1038/d41586-020-01518-y.

Part III

Toward Greater Access, Equity, and Inclusion

chapter 14

Beyond "Zoom University"

A Heuristic for Advancing Inclusive Digital and Online Pedagogy

Jenae Cohn

The global experience of remote learning during the COVID-19 pandemic exposed a lasting need for educators in colleges and universities to assess the use of digital and online technologies in their teaching practice. In the immediate wake of the pandemic, these assessments were superficial: is remote learning "good" or "bad?" Does online learning "help" or "hinder" student learning?[1] These kinds of assessments are impossible to conduct meaningfully because they ignore the intertwined relationship between learning environment and learner identities.

Asking whether remote learning is "good" or "bad" is a lot like asking whether it's better to sit or stand when working at a desk: the context fundamentally changes the answer. What kind of body is sitting or standing? For how long? With what other ergonomic equipment? The same logic applies to our assessment of higher education learning environments and, importantly, technologies, moving forward. What kinds of students are taking the courses? What are their prior learning experiences? What are their expectations and needs? What impacts do learning technologies have within the learning environments? Responses to these kinds of questions can and should be part of our collective decision-making for advancing inclusive digital and online pedagogy moving forward.

Recentering learning in higher education requires a radical rethinking of the learning environment and space. The brick-and-mortar classroom can be a valuable place for learning experiences to occur, but it is one among a diversity of spaces that may provide valuable experiences for students. Learning, working, and living in communities at home or abroad are all rich spaces for learning when distance learning environments are better integrated into the college experience. These learning environment choices are not fully interchangeable, however; part of the challenge and opportunity ahead is in recognizing the benefits, limitations, and values that digital and online spaces may confer for different students at different moments in their academic journeys.

Common online pedagogical advice often speaks to ways in which online environments can replicate brick-and-mortar classroom experiences. This advice, although well-intentioned, has the unfortunate effect of making a class's success seem dependent entirely on "translating" one particular tool or set of features for another. This act of "translation," can make learning tools, like the learning management system or a video conference tool, appear "neutral" or "culturally value-free," even though online spaces, like any on-campus classroom space, are not neutral.[2] When we treat online learning environments as mere substitutes or supplements for classroom spaces, we overlook the critical strategies we'll need to promote equitable teaching with technology.

For over a decade, education scholars and researchers have known that success in online classes depends largely on institutional contexts and who the students are.[3] A robust literature from instructional design and educational research has consistently demonstrated through quantitative and qualitative methods that there are clear correlations between frequent social interaction, student satisfaction, and the achievement of engaged student learning.[4] Participation, collaboration, and engagement are at the cornerstones of what Michelle Pacansky-Brock, Michael Smedshammer, and Kim Vincent-Layton refer to as "humanized online instruction."[5]

A future for developing inclusive digital and online pedagogy must focus on how to foster instructional interactions within a blend of learning environments that move fluidly between online and brick-and-mortar spaces. This chapter will first explore some contexts and frameworks for why a future for recentering learning in higher education must engage with an aligned understanding of technology and pedagogy. This chapter then offers a heuristic for assessing the incorporation of technologies into inclusive digital and online pedagogies. This inclusive digital and online learning heuristic can be used by instructors, academic administrators, and other academic stakeholders to help them in recentering the impact of learning technologies on learning experiences and interactions.

All Learning Is Online Learning: Moving beyond Modality in Articulating Inclusive Digital Pedagogy

It's not a question of whether instructors can or should use online learning technologies to teach the diverse students in their classes. Most already are, and were prior to the COVID-19 pandemic, even if they're convening with students in brick-and-mortar classrooms. As Joshua Kim and Edward Maloney explain, "arguably the greatest impact on learning in the past twenty-five years has been the ubiquity of digital and online technologies."[6] Distinguishing between "online" and "brick-and-mortar" classes, therefore, should be challenging for higher education administrators and faculty to articulate insofar as online infrastructures shape where, how, and when students receive course content and information no matter where their bodies wind up on a given day.

If, as educators, we can shift our thinking from "where" learning is happening to "how" learning is happening and with "whom" learning is happening, we can ask better questions about how technologies inform relationships and interactions between students and between students and instructors. Educators can, in the words of Derek Bruff, "be intentional in how we use technology, looking for ways the technology can support student learning."[7] We can't start with technology and then align the pedagogy as an afterthought, nor can we start with the pedagogy and align the technology afterward. Rather, we must holistically assess the intertwined relationship between technology and pedagogy.

The key is to approach decision-making about teaching with technology in an iterative, rather than a linear, way.

Educators must also articulate a vision for inclusive digital pedagogy that goes "beyond the limited notion of access and include the rules of engagement and the process of identification in learning contexts."[8] Online learning technologies don't just grant students access to course material; they fundamentally shape the students' lived experiences.

Assessing how and with whom inclusive digital pedagogy is happening means understanding the social, cultural, and political orientations of the classroom, and how technology exacerbates or ameliorates potential sociocultural and political tensions therein. As Maura Smale and Mariana Regaldo argue, "many of the structures of higher education replicate systemic inequalities of our broader society, and while the use of digital technology by college and university students may ideally be intended to resist and dismantle these inequalities, it may reinforce them instead."[9] We saw the systemic reinforcement of inequalities bear out in a number of ways during the emergency remote instruction experienced during the COVID-19 pandemic. The increased usage of automated remote proctoring tools to surveil student behavior[10] and forced "camera-on" policies during video conference calls,[11] among other trends, privileged instructor surveillance and control over student autonomy and trust.

To resist technologies with a known track record of discriminating against students with disabilities and/or students of color, educators need clearer and better critical heuristics for assessing and implementing learning technologies.

Two Core Frameworks: Technology, Pedagogy, and Content Knowledge and Community of Inquiry

Two existing frameworks inform this chapter's inclusive digital and online pedagogy heuristic. First, Matthew Koehler's and Punya Mishra's technology, pedagogy, and content knowledge (TPACK) framework builds off of Lee Shulman's descriptions of how teachers must align content knowledge with pedagogical knowledge.[12] Koehler and Mishra make the case that teaching effectively with technology requires

> an understanding of the representation of concepts using technologies; pedagogical techniques that use technologies in constructive ways to teach content; knowledge of what makes concepts difficult or easy to learn and how technology can help redress some of the problems that students face; knowledge of students' prior knowledge and theories of epistemology; and knowledge of how technologies can be used to build on existing knowledge to develop new epistemologies or strengthen old ones.[13]

In explaining the numerous ways that content knowledge, pedagogy, and technology all mutually inform each other, Koehler and Mishra demonstrate that the environments for learning experiences cannot be treated as isolated entities that could be plucked apart or rearranged without impact. The TPACK framework allows educators to "move beyond oversimplified approaches that treat technology as an 'add-on' [and] instead to focus . . . in a more ecological way, upon the connections among technology, content, and pedagogy as they play out in classroom contexts."[14] As such, the TPACK framework is vital to moving beyond instrumentalist heuristics of technology. Many instructor assessments of learning technologies are focused solely on what the tools could do. However, applying the TPACK framework to an inclusive digital pedagogy heuristic allows instructors to think instead about who is impacted by the technology and how the technology will be used in a digital pedagogy context.

A second core framework that informs this chapter's inclusive digital and online pedagogy heuristic is the revised community of inquiry (COI) framework from Marti Cleveland-Innes and Prisca Campbell, derived from D. Randy Garrison, Terry Anderson, and Walter Archer's online community of inquiry framework.[15] The COI framework suggests that effective online learning is advanced by the relationship between three elements: social presence, teaching presence, and cognitive presence. Cleveland-Innes and Campbell propose the addition of another element into the COI framework: emotional presence.[16] Social presence, teaching presence, cognitive presence, and emotional presence are four elements that instructors can use to determine whether a community can be successfully fostered among students and their instructor.

By combining the TPACK framework and the four elements of the COI framework, an inclusive digital and online pedagogy heuristic supports instructors in considering how they might make choices about online tools with an aligned understanding of the learners and the learning environment.

Recentering Learners: A Heuristic for Inclusive Digital and Online Pedagogy

A heuristic for inclusive digital and online pedagogy can guide higher education instructors to go beyond thinking of digital and online pedagogy as "Zoom University," and instead, to assess their teaching needs holistically. This heuristic is intended to disrupt the oversimplified stories that many educators and administrators have come to rely upon in the wake of the COVID-19 pandemic: that digital and online learning is primarily about Zoom lectures, breakout rooms, mishaps with being "on mute," and juggling multiple screens and share settings.

Although this one narrative may capture a sliver of experiences, focusing on these single sets of experiences ultimately will do higher education pedagogues a disservice: we become less resilient to encounter diverse experiences with new and evolving technologies and student situations.[17] Understanding the diversity of what's possible within our learning environments will also help us understand the diversity of ways to reach and engage with students equitably.

Inclusive Digital and Online Pedagogy Heuristic at a Glance

This inclusive digital and online pedagogy heuristic at-a-glance offers five core factors (figure 14.1) for assessing a digital learning experience with three sets of questions to consider in alignment with each factor (table 14.1). In the next section, these core factors and questions will be contextualized and explored in greater depth.

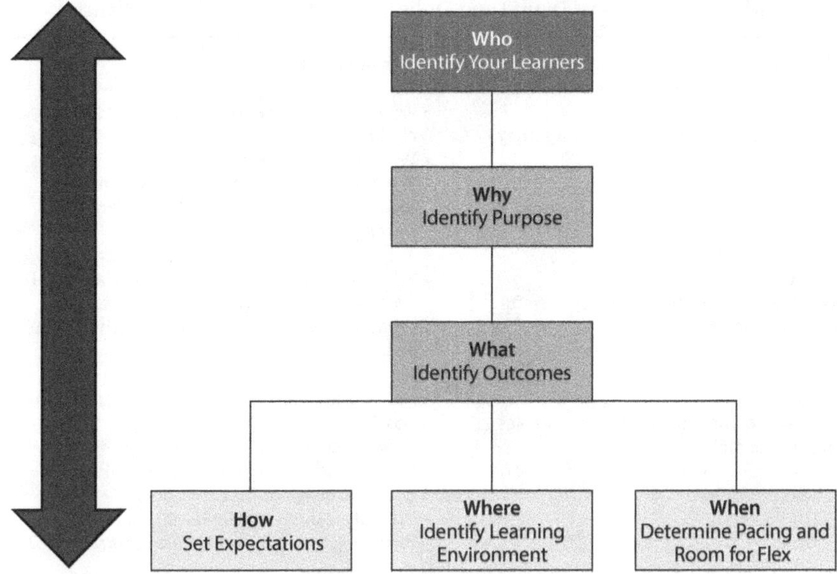

Figure 14.1. Inclusive digital and online pedagogy heuristic visualized.

Digital and Online Pedagogy Heuristic in Depth

Who *and* **Why**: *Who are your students?* Student-centered learning is not a new concept in the scholarship of teaching and learning, but an inclusive vision for digital and online pedagogy requires a willingness to either understand or, at the very least, anticipate who the students are at any given campus and in any given class environment. There are a few approaches instructors can use to understand who their students are. Ideally, an instructor can survey their students at the start of a course to learn about their needs, motivations, concerns, and anticipated frustrations with the course even before it begins. That way, decisions about technology integration and adoption can be well-aligned to the students who are in the class.

That said, there may be learning design decisions with online technologies that must be decided well before a class begins. In that case, an instructor may want to anticipate who their learners are. An exercise that can help is constructing an imagined student persona or an imagined set of student personas. Persona creation is a common design

Table 14.1. Inclusive Digital and Online Pedagogy Heuristic at a Glance

Core Heuristic Factors	Heuristic Questions
Who and **Why** Who are your learners and why are they in your class?	• What do you know about the learners in your class? • What are their needs? Motivations? Concerns? • What are their prior experiences with technologies for learning? With different learning environments?
What What do learners need to be successful in your course?	• What do learners need to do to be successful? • What support systems do learners need? • What resources (technological or otherwise) do learners need?
How How will learners understand their roles in your course?	• How will learners be asked to contribute to the class? • How will course activities and the uses of technologies be aligned with students' understandings of their roles? • How will learners' activities and uses of technologies help them achieve course goals?
Where Where will learning experiences take place?	• Where will formal learning experiences happen? • Where will knowledge be shared? • Where will conversation occur?
When When will learning experiences take place?	• Beyond scheduled "class time" or "seat hours," when do you anticipate learning will happen? • When will learners have time to process challenging ideas? • When will learners be given some degree of flexibility for demonstrating evidence of learning (e.g., in the form of assignments, exams, and other assessments)?

approach in the field of user experience (UX) research to anticipate an end user's experiences. When you construct a persona in the context of building a class, the goal is to keep the student's primary needs at the forefront. It's an exercise in empathy, ultimately, and remembering what it's like to be a student.

You might anticipate, for example, the following characteristics of students:

- **Prior learning experiences:** What are a student's prior learning experiences like? How do these prior learning experiences shape how they'll experience your course?

- **Future learning aspirations:** What does this student want to learn more about?
- **Motivations:** Why is this student in your class? Why do they want to be in college and graduate? How does their motivation to this class influence the ways that they might behave or respond?
- **Problems (or concerns, frustrations, etc.):** What concerns or frustrations does this student have with their learning? With the content/subject matter in your particular course?

It's worth noting that building an imagined persona carries several risks. It can be easy to reproduce stereotypes, for example, or to let imagined student's motivations or frustrations be guided too heavily by one demographic characteristic over another. Keep intersectionality in mind, understanding that no one's orientation to an experience is shaped solely by isolated factors related to, for example, age, gender, race, or ethnicity. It remains important to approach our own understanding of who our students are as students ourselves: we need to seek feedback constantly from students in current and future courses to gain ever-changing exposure to student needs.

What: *What do students need to be successful in your course?* In designing a course, most instructors think about students' success in terms of understanding or developing a certain amount of content knowledge or competency in the discipline. However, in the spirit of the TPACK framework, the second step in our inclusive digital pedagogy heuristic involves broadening a notion of student success to consider the support, interactions, and resources that students may need to be successful. The saying "Maslow before Bloom" is popular in educational development circles to underscore that students need to have basic needs met before they can engage with their learning.[18] As such, a heuristic for inclusive digital pedagogy can and should consider how the material realities of students' lived experiences may impact their abilities to engage with learning technologies.

Instructors may start by making a list of the materials that students need to be successful in their course. This may include access to course materials, such as textbooks or problem sets, but may also include access to student technologies for learning: a computer, a calculator, a pencil, a notebook. After examining that list, consider which of these materials have some specific requirements (e.g. a certain kind of calculator, a particular textbook) and which of these materials may be accessed in multiple ways. In the spirit of considering students' basic needs, consider the cost of these materials and options for finding these materials at reduced or zero cost. If students require specialized materials to be successful in your course, where do they find these specialized materials? Being explicit about where, when, and how students engage with technologies of all kinds in your class will allow them to have the basic material understanding of what they need to have to be successful.

Materials for learning may also involve software applications, and these applications may also have needs that should be explicitly articulated to help students to be successful. Consider the following:

1. Where does the software application work? On a Mac, PC, or Linux laptop? On a Chromebook (i.e., a laptop that can only use the Google Chrome browser)? On a tablet (e.g., an iPad)?
2. Can this software application be used on a mobile phone, particularly for students who don't have access to or can't access a computer consistently?
3. Can components of this software be used with assistive or adaptive technology, like speech-to-text tools or screen readers?

Instructors might not have all of the answers to these questions. Working through what students need to be successful in a given course may involve necessary partnerships between campus staff who would have a clearer sense of student infrastructure needs from staff in IT to the library to the campus bookstore and student advising. Anticipating where, as an instructor, you need to partner with the campus infrastructure community may also help deepen an understanding of students' material needs to be successful.

How: *How will students understand their roles in your course?* Students and instructors alike will make assumptions about what it means to be in a class together. Students and instructors will make additional assumptions about what it means to use digital and online technologies in a class context. Assumptions about technologies may sometimes overlap between students and instructors and other times they will differ. Although obvious, it's worth noting given the continued prevalence of the myth that students are "digital natives" or "natural" users of technologies. Learning authentically about who the students in a given class context are will continue to dispel this myth, given that facility with technology is more dependent on students' prior experiences and, more often, on socioeconomic status rather than on age.

The third component of an inclusive digital and online pedagogy heuristic, then, involves unpacking the "how" of using digital technologies with your students. Some of this unpacking may involve instructor direction up front about how instructors will ask students to contribute to the class environment using the chosen digital and online technologies. But there may also be more collaborative conversations between students and instructors about how the usage of technologies in the class environment may help students succeed in the course. Students may also want to offer input on how the technologies in a class may impact their experiences of interacting with the class community. Keeping the COI framework in mind, making space for students to discuss their feelings toward using particular technologies will build a stronger sense of class community.

As a first step, instructors may want to use a tool like the Transparency in Learning and Teaching (TILT) in Higher Education transparent assignment template.[19] These templates make space for instructors to articulate clear tasks for students so that students know exactly how to approach the work they're being asked to complete. A modified version of one of these transparent assignment templates may also make explicit how students will use technologies to engage in the required tasks. Instructors may even consider making a list of the technologies students will need to complete the tasks and links to resources where students can seek help on using the technologies if they're struggling to complete the tasks in the form of a digital toolkit.[20]

Where: *Where will learning experiences take place?* On the surface, determining "where" learning experiences should take place may seem obviously focused on seat time within an assigned brick-and-mortar classroom space. Online, perhaps the default is to imagine that learning will happen in a "Zoom room" as a replication of a brick-and-mortar classroom space. However, a heuristic for inclusive digital and online pedagogy should involve some deeper thinking about learning environments and spaces that takes into account the spaces where individual learning or informal group and peer learning may occur outside of formal or prescribed class time.

The first fact to acknowledge when considering where learning experiences will take place is that instructors have limited control over where and how students will ultimately learn. Although instructors may hope that students are actively learning when engaged in a formal experience, it is an impossible expectation for all students to be equally and fully engaged in formal learning experiences. As such, technologies that promise to focus student attention or control where students may find information for your course context should be treated with some suspicion. It is an overreach for an instructor to assume that they can control a student's full attentional environment even in a brick-and-mortar classroom environment.

Instructors may want to inventory the spaces that they are asking students to gather in, virtual and, as applicable, on a campus or in a classroom. Once this inventory is made, consider the following:

1. What kind of embodied action is possible in this space?
2. What kinds of accommodations are necessary for all bodies to feel included and present in this space?
3. What kinds of interactions are available in this space?
4. What tools are needed to make the interactions possible in this space? (e.g., a whiteboard? Sticky notes? A digital polling tool? A place where students can complete collaborative documents?)

These are questions that, again, instructors may need to take to other campus experts in the disability services office, IT department, and library.

When: *When will learning experiences take place?* It may seem easy and simple to assume that the "when" of an inclusive digital and online learning experience is simply the allocated class time in the schedule. But a truly inclusive digital and online pedagogical approach involves considering the pacing and rhythm of when students encounter new ideas in the course. Time to process challenging ideas, either individually or in groups, and time to complete independent assignments or activities are important parts of aligning technology with pedagogical and content-based knowledge for your course planning.

Instructors may try the activity of building a course map that imagines how students will get from the start to the end of the course. This is the last step in the heuristic of building an inclusive digital and online pedagogy insofar as determining "when" learning will happen, and it should be built upon the other factors considered previously: who the learners are, what they need to succeed, how they will interact, and where they will interact. Too often, the scheduling and logistics for a course come first in the course design process. But if you've built a clear understanding of who your learners are, what they need to succeed, and how and where learning will occur, you might find yourself surprised that the pacing required to support student success in the course may not be so dependent upon the allocated seat hours.

Conclusion

This chapter's digital and online learning heuristic may help instructors and other academic stakeholders make decisions that allow them to open up to more complex possibilities for digital and online learning moving forward. In developing digital and online pedagogies moving forward, we need more of what Sibylle Gruber calls "multiple stories" about online education.[21] Gruber makes the case that in narratives about online learning, there are clear, linear stories we often tell about successes: if we simply follow a few simple steps, like writing clear discussion prompts or encouraging instructors to create "welcome videos," we'll have created a learner-centered environment.[22] Gruber makes the case that this kind of pedagogical advice, however, flattens out the many complexities involved. She notes specifically how online learning environments may not always provide clear pathways for instructors to acknowledge student feelings of discrimination or discuss moments where students may have written something or said something sexist, racist, or homophobic in the digital class context. "Single stories" of online learning not only limit access to the full range of possibilities and complexities available when teaching with technologies, but they also erase important narratives about promoting equity and inclusion in the classroom.

To cultivate an environment where instructors and administrators can approach online and digital learning with this deserved complexity, the work of teaching and learning must be approached with a spirit of authentic collaboration across the university. It's past time to dismantle the myth that teaching is an individualistic enterprise. Leadership in teaching and learning centers, libraries, IT divisions, offices of equity and inclusion, and student advising must be in closer conversation to develop joint programming to expose the shared knowledge-building necessary to continue recentering learners across a variety of digital and online learning experiences.

A significant barrier in advancing an inclusive future of online learning is a common institutional tendency to organize faculty and staff work in siloes. For online and digital learning experiences to be developed more holistically, leaders advancing teaching and learning in different units across campus need to collaborate more closely. For example, if colleges and universities want faculty to have a clearer understanding of "where" student learning experiences can occur, programming about designing for hybrid and online experiences should be developed in partnership with classroom technologists and librarians because the classroom space and the library are core places on campus where learning happens. Even if that "where" of the student learning experience is happening fully online, both technologists and librarians have equally robust understandings of how the campus technologies, databases, and tools shape the experiences that students have accessing their services even when away from a brick-and-mortar campus.

A culture of elitism about who does the work of teaching and learning must also be remedied. Just as we must broaden, expand, and diversify our understanding of who we support as learners, we must similarly broaden, expand, and diversify our understanding of who's teaching students and who's supporting students. That means planning faculty development programming in ways that are fully inclusive of non-tenure-track faculty, academic staff, librarians, academic advisors, and other stakeholders on campus who impact the student learning experience. Acknowledging the common ground for educators working across different roles and ranks in the university and embracing the potential to form partnerships across faculty and staff lines with a spirit of generosity will improve the ability to implement a heuristic for digital and online learning effectively.

Looking beyond "Zoom University" is not about looking to "technological innovation"; it's about adopting a model of thinking about technology that's aligned with lived experiences. The heuristic developed in this chapter is simply a starting point to aligning technological and pedagogical decisions along with lived teaching experiences. A future for inclusive digital and online pedagogy is about seeing how we can leverage the presence of learning technologies in the service of (re)centering learners.

Notes

1. Bessette et al., "5 Myths"; Ralph, "COVID-19, and the Future."
2. Öztok, *The Hidden Curriculum*, 5.
3. Means et al., *Evaluation of Evidence-Based Practices.*
4. Bernard et al., "Treatments in Distance Education"; Martin and Bolliger, "Engagement Matters: Student Perceptions"; Lave and Wenger, *Legitimate Peripheral Participation.*
5. Pacansky-Brock et al., "Humanizing Online Teaching."
6. Kim and Maloney, *Learning Innovation*, 31.
7. Bruff, *Intentional Tech*, 2.
8. Öztok, *The Hidden Curriculum*, 7.
9. Smale and Regaldo, *Barrier to Higher Education*, 7.
10. Kelley, "Long Overdue Reckoning"; Swauger, "Our Bodies Encoded"; Young, "Pushback Is Growing."
11. Costa, "Cameras Be Damned"; Kizilcec et al., "Scaling up Behavioral Science."
12. Koehler and Mishra, "What Is Technological"; Shulman, "Knowledge and Teaching"; Shulman, "Those Who Understand."
13. Koehler and Mishra, "What Is Technological," 66.

14. Koehler and Mishra, "What Is Technological," 67.

15. Cleveland-Innes and Campbell, "Emotional Presence"; Garrison et al, "Conferencing in Higher Education."

16. Cleveland-Innes and Campbell, "Emotional Presence."

17. Quintana et al., "Extensibility, Flexibility, and Redundancy."

18. Mutch, "Caring Pedagogy during Covid-19"; Doucet et al., "School Closures, Version 2.0"; Lasic, "Maslow before Bloom."

19. Winkelmes, "Transparency in Teaching."

20. Cohn, "Building Online Toolkits."

21. Gruber, "Need for Multiple Stories."

22. Gruber, "Need for Multiple Stories," 42.

Bibliography

Bernard, Robert M., Philip C. Abrami, Eugene Borokhovski, C. Anne Wade, Rana M. Tamim, Michael A. Surkes, and Edward Clement Bethel. "A Meta-analysis of Three Types of Interaction Treatments in Distance Education." *Review of Educational Research* 79, no. 3 (September 2009): 1243–1289. https://doi.org/10.3102/0034654309333844.

Bessette, Lee Skallerup, Nancy Chick, and Jennifer C. Friberg. "5 Myths about Remote Teaching in the Covid-19 Crisis." *Chronicle of Higher Education*. May 1, 2020. https://www.chronicle.com/article/5-myths-about-remote-teaching-in-the-covid-19-crisis.

Bruff, Derek. *Intentional Tech: Principles to Guide the Use of Educational Technology in College Teaching*. Morgantown, WV: West Virginia University Press, 2019.

Cleveland-Innes, Marti, and Prisca Campbell. "Emotional Presence, Learning, and the Online Learning Environment." *International Review of Research in Open and Distributed Learning* 13, no. 4 (2012): 269–292. https://doi.org/10.19173/irrodl.v13i4.1234.

Cohn, Jenae. "Building Online Toolkits to Support the Development of Academic Skills and Digital Literacies." In *Resilient Pedagogy: Practical Teaching Strategies to Overcome Distance, Disruption, and Distraction*, edited by Travis N. Thurston, Kacey Lundstrom, and Christopher González, 187–201. Logan, UT: Utah State University, 2021. https://doi.org/10.26079/a516-fb24.

Costa, Karen. "Cameras Be Damned." *LinkedIn Blog* (blog). May 27, 2020. https://www.linkedin.com/pulse/cameras-damned-karen-costa/.

Doucet, Armand, Deborah Netolicky, Koen Timmers, and Francis Jim Tuscano. "Thinking about Pedagogy in an Unfolding Pandemic: An Independent Report on Approaches to Distance Learning During COVID 19 School Closures, Version 2.0." Education International and UNESCO, 2020. Retrieved April 6, 2024 from https://learningportal.iiep.unesco.org/en/library/thinking-about-pedagogy-in-an-unfolding-pandemic-an-independent-report-on-approaches-to.

Garrison, D. Randy, Terry Anderson, and Walter Archer. "Critical Inquiry in a Text-Based Environment: Computer Conferencing in Higher Education." *Internet and Higher Education* 2, no. 2–3 (1999): 87–105.

Gruber, Sibylle. "Ideologies in Online Learning Environments: The Need for Multiple Stories." *Journal of Interactive Online Learning* 13, no. 4 (2015): 39–53.

Kelley, Jason. "A Long Overdue Reckoning For Online Proctoring Companies May Finally Be Here." Electronic Frontier Foundation, June 22, 2021. https://www.eff.org/deeplinks/2021/06/long-overdue-reckoning-online-proctoring-companies-may-finally-be-here.

Kim, Joshua, and Edward Maloney. *Learning Innovation and the Future of Higher Education.* Tech.Edu: A Hopkins Series on Education and Technology. Baltimore: Johns Hopkins University Press, 2020.

Kizilcec, René F., Justin Reich, Michael Yeomans, Christoph Dann, Emma Brunskill, Glenn Lopez, Selen Turkay, Joseph Jay Williams, and Dustin Tingley. "Scaling up Behavioral Science Interventions in Online Education." *Proceedings of the National Academy of Sciences* 117, no. 26 (June 30, 2020): 14900–14905. https://doi.org/10.1073/pnas.1921417117.

Koehler, Matthew, and Punya Mishra. "What Is Technological Pedagogical Content Knowledge?" Edited by Judi Harris and Matt Koehler. *Contemporary Issues in Technology and Teacher Education* 9 (January 1, 2009): 60–70.

Lasic, Tomaz. "Maslow before Bloom." *Human.* November 8, 2009. https://human.edublogs.org/2009/08/11/maslow-before-bloom.

Lave, Jean, and Etienne Wenger. *Situated Learning: Legitimate Peripheral Participation.* New York: Cambridge University Press, 1991.

Martin, Florence, and Doris U. Bolliger. "Engagement Matters: Student Perceptions on the Importance of Engagement Strategies in the Online Learning Environment." *Online Learning* 22, no. 1 (March 1, 2018). https://doi.org/10.24059/olj.v22i1.1092.

Means, Barbara, Yukie Toyama, Robert Murphy, Marianne Bakia, and Karla Jones. *Evaluation of Evidence-Based Practices in Online Learning a Meta-Analysis and Review of Online Learning Studies*. Washington, DC: US Dept. of Education, Office of Planning, Evaluation and Policy Development, Policy and Program Studies Service, 2009.

Mutch, Carol. "'Maslow before Bloom': Implementing a Caring Pedagogy during Covid-19." *Teachers' Work* 18, no. 2 (December 10, 2021): 69–90. https://doi.org/10.24135/teacherswork.v18i2.334.

Öztok, Murat. *The Hidden Curriculum of Online Learning: Understanding Social Justice through Critical Pedagogy*. Milton Keynes, UK: Taylor & Francis, 2019.

Pacansky-Brock, Michelle, Michael Smedshammer, and Kim Vincent-Layton. "Humanizing Online Teaching to Equitize Higher Education." *Current Issues in Education* 21, no. 2 (Special Issue) (June 18, 2020). https://cie.asu.edu/ojs/index.php/cieatasu/article/view/1905.

Quintana, Rebecca M., Jacob Fortman, and James DeVaney. "Advancing an Approach for Resilient Design for Learning by Designing for Extensibility, Flexibility, and Redundancy." In *Resilient Pedagogy: Practical Teaching Strategies to Overcome Distance, Disruption, and Distraction*, edited by Travis N. Thurston, Kacey Lundstrom, and Christopher González, Logan, UT: Utah State University, 2021: 77–92. https://doi.org/10.26079/a516-fb24.

Ralph, Nate. "Research Article: Perspectives: COVID-19, and the Future of Higher Education. Bay View Analytics." Oakland, CA: Bay View Analytics, 2020. https://www.bayviewanalytics.com/covid-19_and_the_future_of_higher_education.html.

Shulman, Lee. "Knowledge and Teaching: Foundations of the New Reform." *Harvard Educational Review* 57, no. 1 (1987): 1–23.

———. "Those Who Understand: Knowledge Growth in Teaching." *Educational Researcher* 15, no. 2 (1986): 4–14.

Smale, Maura A., and Mariana Regaldo. *Digital Technology as Affordance and Barrier to Higher Education.* New York: Palgrave Macmillan, 2017.

Swauger, Shea. "Our Bodies Encoded: Algorithmic Test Proctoring in Higher Education." *Hybrid Pedagogy*. April 2, 2020. https://hybridpedagogy.org/our-bodies-encoded-algorithmic-test-proctoring-in-higher-education/.

Winkelmes, Mary-Ann. "Transparency in Teaching: Faculty Share Data and Improve Students' Learning." *Liberal Education* 99, no. 2 (2013).

Young, Jeffrey R. "Pushback Is Growing Against Automated Proctoring Services. But So Is Their Use - EdSurge News." *EdSurge*. November 13, 2020. https://www.edsurge.com/news/2020-11-13-pushback-is-growing-against-automated-proctoring-services-but-so-is-their-use.

chapter 15

Pandemic Fever Pitch Terms That Defined a Moment in Higher Education

Lorna S. Gonzalez, Megan Eberhardt-Alstot, and Jill Leafstedt

One way that historical moments are memorialized is through the cultural artifacts they produce. Some of these artifacts are iconic and visual, like the fall of the Berlin Wall, the Twin Towers of 9/11, or the peace sign of the 1960s American anti-war sentiment. The 2020–2021+ coronavirus pandemic period may be reflected by images of surgical and N95 face masks, of black box Zoom screens, or of public social distancing signs, for example.

In addition to the visual images that capture meaning, the terms that reached a fever pitch in public discourse can also become an artifact of the moment. Such terms encapsulate the social anxieties and dominant narratives of that particular period. They emerge, in part, out of an attempt to articulate a shared understanding of the world, especially as the world changes.

With this case study, we examine terms that emerged as artifacts of discourse in higher education during the COVID-19 pandemic. We focus primarily on terms related to teaching and learning, although we acknowledge that there are several others that also permeated discourses within and beyond higher education (e.g., antiracism, misinformation, essential services). We call these *fever pitch terms*; but, drawing from Donella Meadows's systems thinking framework, we approach these terms with each as a case of consequential, reinforcing feedback loops in and around a crisis period in higher education and in society writ large.[1] In addition to defining these terms, we treat them as artifacts of the moment, unpacking some of the contextual factors that produced the fever pitch, and considering how these artifacts help us explore the following inquiry questions:

1. During periods of change, how do rhetorical artifacts reify societal values and anxieties?
2. How can artifacts, such as fever pitch terms, function as vehicles for innovation?

To aid our analyses, we consulted Google Trends, a tool for analyzing terms or groupings of terms as they are entered into Google Search engines. These queries will yield results that show a term's popularity relative to itself over time. Users can adjust certain metrics, such as time range, category, and general geographic region, to review results within selected constraints. For the present inquiry, we examined two terms, *virtual learning* and *learning loss*, for their popularity in the United States and in the Education category during the five-year period of 2017–2021.

We also acknowledge our own positionality in the authorship of this piece. At the time of this publication, all three authors work within the same Teaching and Learning Innovations unit at a public four-year institution that is part of a larger university system in the United States. Our sense for the higher education discourse comes, in part, from our combined 50+ years in higher education, as well as our representation through professional and scholarly contributions to networks, such as the Online Learning Consortium (OLC), EDUCAUSE, American Association of Colleges and Universities (AAC&U), Professional Organizational Development (POD) Network, and several others. We were "on the ground," as the expression goes, teaching and supporting our campus through the emergency transition to remote and then virtual learning to maintain academic continuity, from an institutional perspective. We were also following and participating in the larger discourse community as a cultural consensus was forming around some of these terms. *Virtual learning* and *learning loss* invite us to recenter learning by taking a reflective-analytical stance on their rhetorical functions during a period of multidimensional crisis.

Case Study: Virtual Learning

The term *virtual learning* is not new to higher education, first appearing in the literature in the early 2000s.[2] However, a Google Trends graph illustrates a sudden interest in this term peaking in August 2020, just as higher education, like other educational sectors, began the 2020–2021 academic year remotely (figure 15.1). Furthermore, in comparison with the terms *online learning* and *remote learning*, *virtual learning* surpassed both (figure 15.2). We are left asking, Why did *virtual learning* peak and *online learning* and *remote learning* recede in August 2020, with the terms *online learning* and *virtual learning* equalizing in August 2021? After all, the term *online learning* was not only commonplace in the academy when speaking about learning at a distance prior to the pandemic but was clearly defined by approximately two decades of scholarly literature.

Curiosity in *virtual learning* might be attributable to the US Department of Education's use of the term when defining Family Educational Rights and Privacy Act (FERPA) policy for both kindergarten to grade 12 (K–12) and post-secondary Institutions. But perhaps more compelling than *virtual learning*'s sudden surge is the fact that these three terms, *online learning*, *remote learning*, and *virtual learning*, appear to be

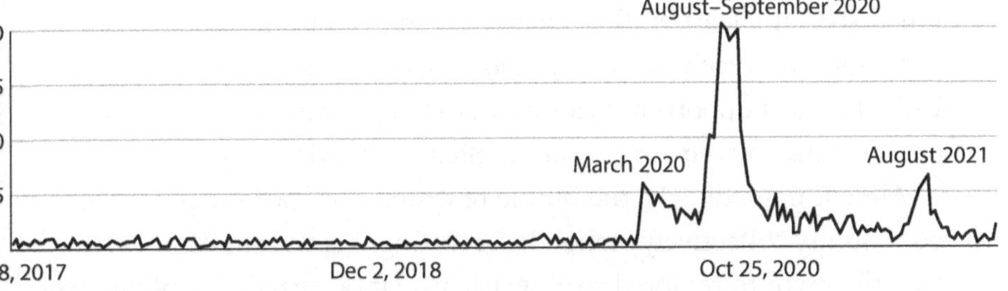

Figure 15.1. Google Trends search result for the term *virtual learning* during the five-year period from January 2017 through October 2021. The graph shows three peaks: March 2020, August 2020, and August 2021, with August 2020 showing the highest relative search.

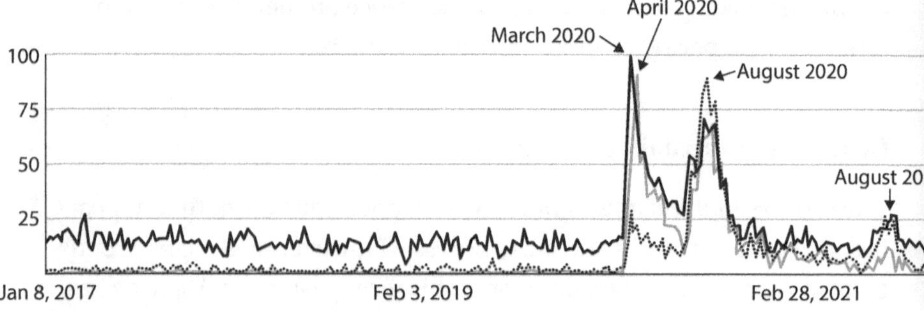

Figure 15.2. Google Trends search result for comparison of the terms *virtual learning* (*black line*), *online learning* (*dotted line*), and *remote learning* (*gray line*) during the five-year period from January 2017 through October 2021. The graph shows three peaks: March 2020, August 2020, and August 2021.

of equal interest following August 2020. When compared with the narrative taking place across vehicles of higher education discourse, including professional literature, blogs, podcasts, and university websites, the trajectory of these terms from March 2020 through August 2021 illustrates an attempt by some to use the forced pivot to remote instruction to fuel societal anxiety about the efficacy of *online learning*.

As early as March 10, 2020, when instruction moved out of the physical classroom during the pandemic, the *Chronicle of Higher Education* ran a provocative article entitled, "Coronavirus and the Great Online-Learning Experiment: Let's Determine What Our Students Actually Learn Online," in which the author, a highly esteemed history scholar with no background in online teaching and learning, posited the forced pivot to online learning presented the opportunity "to measure how much students learn in that medium compared to the face-to-face instruction they received earlier," and concluding that "refusing to do so isn't just a lost opportunity; it's a violation of our most sacred trust. We are scholars, and our job is to know. Shame on us if we fall down on it."[3]

Almost immediately, the online teaching and learning professional community collectively responded, refuting this and similar assertions that the pivot to remote learning, because it occurred via online technologies, was synonymous with what pre-pandemic was accepted as online learning, and a legitimate scenario by which to determine once and for all if online was truly as good as face-to-face.

Days following the March 10th piece, the terms "emergency remote instruction" and "remote instruction" resounded across professional higher education outlets. During March 2020, the *Chronicle of Higher Education* ran an article with a section titled, "What Most Colleges Are Doing Right Now is Not Online Education,"[4] and *EDUCAUSE Review* published "The Difference between Emergency Remote Teaching and Online Learning."[5] In April 2020, *EdSurge* contributed, "What Students Are Doing is Remote Learning, Not Online Learning. There's a Difference,"[6] and Drexel University posted, "Online vs. Remote Learning: What's the Difference?"[7] As of May 2020, most institutions were preparing for a fully remote 2020–2021 academic year, also documented in titles like *EdTech Magazine*'s "From Emergency Remote Teaching to Rigorous Online Learning,"[8] *Inside Higher Ed*'s "Turning Remote Education into Online Education this Fall,"[9] and Florida International University's "Remote vs. Online Learning: It Makes a Difference."[10]

Additionally, other professional outlets, such as University of Central Florida (UCF)'s *TOPcast*, took steps to reframe instruction as "emergency remote." The podcast, hosted by UCF's vice provost for digital learning, Tom Cavanagh, and executive director, Kelvin Thompson, added a "Field Report" series, described on the show's website as "offering collegial advice in getting through the current era of 'remote teaching' necessitated by COVID-19."[11] During the April 6 episode, "Making #Remote Teaching Happen," Cavanagh and Thompson articulated just how much of a disconnect existed between public perception and the scholarly field of online learning: "don't expect the public or senior institutional leaders or government officials to get it. As we've talked about in past episodes, here, . . . we have to speak plainly about the differences between robust online teaching and learning and our current emergency practices."[12] Their discussions made intentional efforts to disassociate *online learning* from *remote instruction.*

Case Study: Learning Loss

The term *learning loss* was already circulating in and out of public consciousness in the years preceding the coronavirus pandemic. It largely resided in the K–12 public school context, amid concerns that sustained breaks in an academic calendar (e.g., those that took a two-month summer break between academic years) resulted in a loss of academic content learning. This phenomenon has also been called "the summer slide."[13] During the coronavirus pandemic, families with socioeconomic means addressed fears of learning loss with learning pods, cohorts of school-aged children whose families agreed upon a common set of safety precautions and academic curriculum, and then hired a teacher to carry out instruction for these small groups.[14] *Learning loss*, then, would presume to explain effects of emergency remote and virtual instruction on students from low socioeconomic or lower-resourced (e.g., rural) contexts.

A Google Trends graph for "learning loss" (figure 15.3) reinforces the anecdotal perception that between 2017 and 2021, this was a term that meandered in and out of public interest in the "jobs and education" category, tending to spike in June (summer), November, and December (fall and winter term breaks). It peaked in May 2020, at the end or near-end of most academic calendars for the first year of the coronavirus pandemic, and made its way into higher education discourse. Another large spike occurred in March 2021, roughly around the one-year mark since college campuses had turned to emergency remote, and then virtual instruction. Also part of the Google Trends results are topics and queries related to the initial search term, meaning that users who searched for "learning loss" tended also to search for these

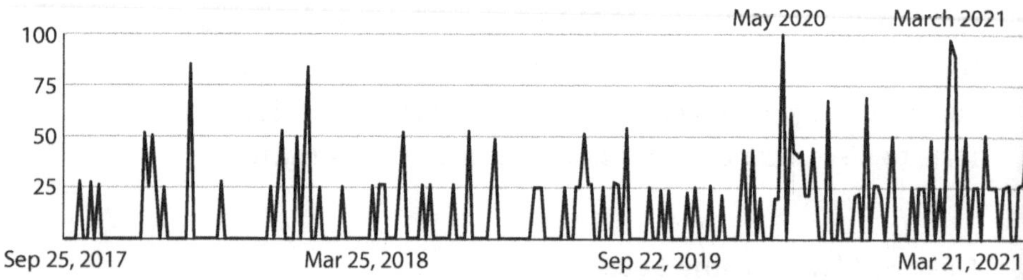

Figure 15.3. Google Trends search result for the term *learning loss* during the five-year period from September 2017 through July 2021. The graph shows two peaks following many midway points: May 2020 and March 2021.

related terms and topics: *coronavirus*, *summer school*, *learning disability*, *income*, and *active learning*.

The concept of *learning loss* is a social construction that assumes a linear learning timeline marked by academic achievement benchmarks, such as course completions and exam scores. It is a problematic narrative because it places the weight of inequitable outcomes—gaps between hegemonic expectations and actual performance—implicitly on the individual student. In *Whistling Vivaldi*, Claude Steele explained the problem inherent in this positioning of explanations for achievement gaps: "Almost invariably, they take an observer's perspective, and they are trying to explain poor performance, not success. Under these constraints, student deficiencies make sense as causes of those troubles."[15] In other words, the deficit is based on an assumed inadequacy of the learner, even if due to their circumstances. During the coronavirus pandemic, *learning loss* joined a collection of problematic narratives about today's underrepresented college students, such as their "lack of preparation," failure to achieve "college readiness," or the label of "left" or "fallen behind."

In a blog post written for higher education faculty, Betsy Barre, executive director at Wake Forest University's Center for the Advancement of Teaching, called attention to the deficit perspective of a learning loss narrative. Referring to the term as representative of a moral panic, she explained that "students are only 'behind' if we decide to hold them to the same standards as those who have not experienced such disruption."[16] She also articulated how this deficit narrative happens: "[Educators] have made certain assumptions about what our students know. If the students who walk into our classrooms are different from the students we expect, our carefully designed courses may fall flat. If we want to create meaningful learning experiences for our students, we must understand how the pandemic has changed our students and in what ways."[17] Barre's post was consistent with other advice in higher education outlets. For example, *EdSurge* touted titles, such as "Let's Not Think in Terms of Learning Loss—Let's Focus on Where Students Have Gained" and "Acceleration Is Better Than Focusing on Learning Loss. This Unique Summer School Shows Why."[18] In higher education, professional writings about learning loss seemed to plea for a rejection of its construct.

Additionally, some organizations did seek to gauge the college student perspective. In a podcast episode of *Inside Higher Ed*'s "The Key," Natasha Jankowski, former executive director of the National Institute for Learning Outcomes Assessment (NILOA), shared results from the College Pulse survey, which found that half of respondents self-reported that they learned less and felt unprepared for college during the pandemic.[19] Anxieties like these fueled the learning loss narrative as students shared their own concerns.

That it permeated and peaked in higher education discourse during the height of the coronavirus pandemic did result in institutional efforts to correct course. For example, the California Department of Education named its local funding allocations "Learning Loss Mitigation Funding (LLMF)," with an expressed purpose to "support pupil academic achievement and mitigate learning loss related to COVID-19 school closures."[20] Learning Management System representatives drew connections between their assessment technologies and the promises of measuring and addressing learning loss.[21] The Rand Corporation lauded corequisite remediation as an effective support for COVID-19 learning loss, citing success in multiple research studies.[22] Many colleges and universities waived certain admissions requirements, such as requisite grade point averages or standardized tests.

Whiplash and Whack-a-Mole: How Fever Pitch Terms Reify Societal Values and Anxieties

In higher education, March 2020 was breathtaking. To anyone trying to lead through the change or keep up with the pace of it, the issues that became crises during the pandemic generated feelings of whiplash and whack-a-mole, as one after the other required attention and intervention at a pace that many institutions were not fully equipped with an infrastructure to do on such a large scale. Online learning experts created a wealth of content to help their colleagues quickly change teaching plans necessitated by the pandemic. Between digital materials, learning management system course designs, and synchronous video class sessions, it may have been logical for many new to teaching this way to call it "online" because all of those elements occurred via internet connection and from a social distance.

This period of chaotic disruption produced productive narratives and reductive narratives with practical implications for higher education. *Virtual learning* was a productive narrative that helped us articulate pandemic teaching and learning by what it was not: It was not intentionally designed, pedagogically sound *online* learning.[23] The term itself was broad enough to encompass an array of alternatives to fully face-to-face teaching—asynchronous, synchronous, bichronous, hyflex, blendflex, well-facilitated, poorly facilitated—and flatten that cacophony into one note. Our hypothesis and lived experience is that *virtual learning* (and similar terms for remote instruction) came to the forefront by educators and online learning experts in an attempt to protect *online learning* from further harm to its reputation. By distinguishing teaching through an online platform during the COVID-19 pandemic from *online teaching and learning* prior to spring 2020, there would be space to reinforce what has been proven to be effective approaches for teaching and learning online from the perceived chaos taking place during the rapid move to instruction during the pandemic.

The coronavirus pandemic was a public health crisis, but it also magnified societal crises with consequences for learning: death and illness in families and communities; sustained fear and uncertainty as the disruption to familiar rituals of daily life stretched on; food and housing insecurity; unemployment and low-wage work; child and elder care; access to basic technologies like reliable internet and internet-connected devices; and psychological effects, such as loneliness and anxiety, resulting from sustained disruptions to social rituals and routines. These are complicated, systemic problems, but they were collapsed into a reductive narrative with the term *learning loss* to describe consequences of the pandemic on student learning. It became a fever pitch term in May 2020 and March 2021, conveying concerns about what had resulted from disruption to the status quo as well as anxieties about what to expect as new academic terms approached. Then, when fall 2021 played out and face-to-face instruction resumed (even if people were masked and met partially online in some instances), failures of the academic term were blamed on learning loss from the previous year, confirming what had been the fear. This confirmation bias became broad, social consensus as time went on.

Both terms revealed the fragility of ontological beliefs about *learning*—in particular, its susceptibility to confirmation bias, even in the common field of higher education. Describing why she had co-authored a response to an op-ed about virtual learning that was published in *Inside Higher Ed*,[24] instructional design and technology expert Stephanie Moore stated, "we felt it was important to get research into the dialogue."[25] This research disrupted the narrative that modality mattered and protected an entire field of study in online learning from reductive or anecdotal comparisons. In other words, promoting use of a term like *virtual learning* was a rhetorical act that reified the value of empirically proven, effective approaches to teaching and learning *online*. On the other hand, the term *learning loss* summarized concerning academic performance, a rhetorical act which reified social anxieties about the crises amplified by the pandemic and the perceived consequences on mainstream educational progress. That the terms have been described here as productive narratives and reductive narratives is not meant to be virtue-signaling that the terms are right/wrong or good/bad; rather, they represent an expansion of meaning or a reduction of complexity, both in the interest of sense-making during a period of rapid crisis, disruption, and ambiguity.

Fever Pitch Terms as Rhetorical Vehicles for Innovation

The pandemic produced a rapid response to cultural change in contexts where change is typically incremental. Narratives about learning, such as *virtual learning* and *learning loss*, may have accumulated strong connotative meaning in their uses during the coronavirus pandemic, but they also functioned as vehicles for innovation in higher education. For example, one societal answer to *learning loss* was the academic continuity enabled by *virtual learning*. In other words, physical campuses did close with statewide shutdowns and mandatory social distancing, but relationships, instruction, and learning continued within a new, mediated context. Familiar learning rituals were disrupted, making space for creative alternatives using video conferencing, digital materials, and learning technologies. Learning professionals were recognized for their expertise in learning design and technology, evidenced in part by the rapid increases in new postings for these jobs.[26] As another example, California Assembly Bill No. 128 allocated millions of dollars in one-time funding to provide instructional development for culturally competent, technology-enhanced teaching. Other regions adopted similar initiatives, and several institutions placed new focus on their digital and online learning program organizational strategies[27] to attract, retain, and graduate students.

Patterns across both fever pitch terms in this chapter point to the necessity of learning innovation to function as a professional field and as a scholarly discipline, as suggested by Joshua Kim and Edward Maloney in their pre-pandemic work, *Learning Innovation and the Future of Higher Education*. This case study traced two feedback loops as they were reinforced and disrupted in higher education during the coronavirus pandemic. Perhaps, one practical implication of this case is how necessary it is for scholars and practitioners of learning innovation to position themselves as change agents for the field. We can leverage this understanding as part of a framework for organization and action:

- Participate. Participating scholars and practitioners in learning innovation contribute to higher education discourse. When problematic feedback loops develop, these are recognized early on.
- Investigate. Scholars and practitioners in learning innovation will know where to locate reliable sources of data, information, and expertise. Peer review and scholarly publishing are part of a disciplinary tradition.[28]
- Evaluate. Using the ways of thinking and doing in the discipline, scholars and practitioners can work from an informed perspective to determine the extent to which narratives and feedback loops are reductive or productive, with what consequences, and for whom.[29]

- Communicate. In her book, *Thinking in Systems: A Primer*, Donella Meadows advocates "speaking and acting, loudly and with assurance" to deter reinforcing feedback loops that threaten to upend a new paradigm and strengthen an old one (e.g., online education does not work). She also suggests ignoring reactionaries; and to, instead, acknowledge anomalies and failures in the old.[30]
- Collaborate. Develop strategic partnerships between cross-disciplinary experts (e.g., professors and learning designers) to document cases where learning innovation is achieved when education is approached as what Joshua Kim describes as a "team sport."[31] Change agent scholars and practitioners can lead in moments of disruption.
- Innovate. If fever pitch terms can function as vehicles for innovation, then learning innovation scholars and practitioners have a responsibility for disrupting problematic feedback loops and leveraging tools of the discipline to drive change. This can include: scaling proven, working models; breaking through bottlenecks or barriers; or disrupting the status quo, for example.

Conclusion

In this essay, we have examined fever pitch terms as cultural artifacts from a remarkable historical moment. *Virtual learning* functioned to value the situated context where learning occurs, effectively preserving *online learning* from reductive value judgments. In the short term, this proved important, as political leaders resisted or banned remote instruction even as cases of infections from COVID-19 variants surged.[32] *Learning loss* reified social anxieties about academic performance and achievement impacted by the pandemic. There were many other narratives constructed during this period; and in this essay, we did not discuss the immediacy of information and misinformation or the networks through which information travels.[33]

We also sought to understand how these terms functioned as vehicles for innovation. The terms we use carry evocative power, and the narratives we construct influence action.[34] Although we named these narratives "fever pitch terms," we applied Meadows's feedback loop theory,[35] in proposing a practical framework for scholars and practitioners in the field of learning innovation, both to advance the field and the discipline and also to actively participate in consequential dialogue.

Notes

1. Meadows, *Thinking in Systems*.

2. See Dillenbourg et al., "Virtual Learning Environments"; Anohina, "Field of Virtual Learning."

3. Zimmerman, "Students Actually Learn Online."

4. Gardner, "Covid-19 Has Forced Higher Ed."

5. Hodges et al. "Remote Teaching and Online Learning."

6. Craig, "What Students are Doing is Remote Learning."

7. Willkomm, "Online vs. Remote Learning."

8. Manfuso, "From Emergency Remote Teaching."

9. Johnson, "Turning Remote Education."

10. Martin, "Remote vs. Online Learning."

11. Thompson and Cavanagh, "Making #RemoteTeaching Happen."

12. Thompson and Cavanagh, 15:24.

13. Quinn and Polikoff, "Summer Learning Loss."

14. See, for example, Widdicombe, "Why Learning Pods."

15. Steele, *Whistling Vivaldi*, 45.

16. Barre, "The Workload Dilemma," para. 4.

17. Barre, "The Workload Dilemma," para. 5.

18. Slade, "Let's Not Think"; LeBlanc, "Acceleration Is Better."

19. Lederman, "The Key Podcast."

20. California Department of Education, "Learning Loss Mitigation Funding."

21. Instructure, "Addressing Learning Loss."

22. Daugherty and Miller, "Next Year's Freshman."

23. Hodges et al., "Remote Teaching and Online Learning."

24. See Moore and Hill, "Planning for Resilience"; Laporte and Cassuto, "How to Responsibly Reopen."

25. Moore, "Ubiquitously Blended World."

26. See, for example, Garrett et al. "Tracking Online Learning.".

27. See, for example, Gallagher and Palmer, "Pandemic Pushed Universities Online."

28. Bazerman, "Powerful Words."

29. Wenger and Wenger-Trayner, "Introduction to Communities."

30. Meadows, *Thinking in Systems*, 164.

31. Kim, "Designers As Librarians."

32. Kosta, "But Let's Keep Dancing."

33. For an informative study on how people satisfy their information needs, see Lu and Yuan, "Shall I Google It."

34. For case studies, see Kania et al., "Water Systems of Change."
35. Meadows, *Thinking in Systems.*

Bibliography

Anohina, Alla. "Analysis of the Terminology Used in the Field of Virtual Learning." *Educational Technology & Society* 8, no. 3 (2005): 91–102.

Barre, Betsy. "Preparing to Teach after 16 Months of Disruption." Wake Forest University Center for the Advancement of Teaching. Last modified August 20, 2021. https://cat.wfu.edu/2021/08/learningloss.

Bazerman, Charles. "From Cultural Criticism to Disciplinary Participation: Living with Powerful Words." In *Writing, Teaching, and Learning in the Disciplines*, edited by A. Herrington and C. Moran. New York: Modern Language Association of America, 1992.

California Department of Education. "Learning Loss Mitigation Funding." Last modified November 3, 2021. https://www.cde.ca.gov/fg/cr/learningloss.asp.

California Legislative Information. "Assembly Bill No. 128." Last modified June 29, 2021. https://leginfo.legislature.ca.gov/faces/billNavClient.xhtml?bill_id=202120220AB128.

Craig, Ryan. "What Students are Doing is Remote Learning, Not Online Learning. There's a Difference." *EdSurge.* Last modified April 2, 2020. https://www.edsurge.com/news/2020-04-02-what-students-are-doing-is-remote-learning-not-online-learning-there-s-a-difference.

Daugherty, Lindsay, and Trey Miller. "Next Year's Freshman: How Corequisites Might Help Address COVID-19 Learning Loss." *RAND Blog*, July 13, 2021. https://www.rand.org/blog/2021/07/next-years-freshman-how-corequisites-might-help-address.html.

Dillenbourg, Pierre, Daniel Schneider, and Paraskevi Synteta. "Virtual Learning Environments." *Proceedings of the 3rd Hellenic Conference Information & Communication Technologies in Education,* (2002): 3–18. Rhodes, Greece: Kastanoitis Editions.

Gallagher, Sean and Jason Palmer. "The Pandemic Pushed Universities Online. The Change Was Long Overdue." *Harvard Business Review*, September 2020. https://hbr.org/2020/09/the-pandemic-pushed-universities-online-the-change-was-long-overdue.

Gardner, Lee. "Covid-19 Has Forced Higher Ed to Pivot to Online Learning. Here Are 7 Takeaways So Far." *Chronicle of Higher Education.* Last modified March 20, 2020. https://www.chronicle.com/article/covid-19-has-forced-higher-ed-to-pivot-to-online-learning-here-are-7-takeaways-so-far.

Garrett, R., B. Simunich, R. Legon, and E. E. Fredericksen. *CHLOE 7: Tracking Online Learning from Mainstream Acceptance to Universal Adoption, The Changing Landscape of Online Education*, 2022. https://www.qualitymatters.org/qa-resources/resource-center/articles-resources/CHLOE-7-report-2022.

Google Trends. (Search Engine). https://trends.google.com/trends.

Hodges, Charles, Stephanie Moore, Barb Lockee, Torrey Trust, and Aaron Bond. "The Difference Between Emergency Remote Teaching and Online Learning." *EDUCAUSE Review*. Last modified March 27, 2020. https://er.educause.edu/articles/2020/3/the-difference-between-emergency-remote-teaching-and-online-learning.

Instructure. "Addressing Learning Loss: Using Connected Assessments and LMS." *The Study Hall* (blog). Accessed August 28, 2021. https://www.instructure.com/canvas/resources/on-demand-webinars/addressing-learning-loss.

Johnson, Elizabeth. "Turning Remote Education into Online Education this Fall." *Inside Higher Ed*. Last modified May 20, 2020. https://www.insidehighered.com/advice/2020/05/20/how-turn-springs-remote-courses-high-quality-online-courses-fall-opinion.

Kania, John, Mark Kramer, and Peter Senge. "The Water Systems of Change." *Reimagining Social Change*, June 2018. https://www.fsg.org/publications/water_of_systems_change.

Kim, Joshua. "As Many Instructional Designers as Librarians." *Inside Higher Education* (blog), March 25, 2019. https://www.insidehighered.com/blogs/technology-and-learning/many-instructional-designers-librarians.

Kim, Joshua, and Edward Maloney. *Learning Innovation and the Future of Higher Education*. Baltimore: Johns Hopkins University Press, 2020.

Kosta, Karen. "The Anti-Online Rhetoric is Back. But Let's Keep Dancing." *Medium* (blog). Last modified January 3, 2022. https://karenraycosta.medium.com/the-anti-online-rhetoric-is-back-but-lets-keep-dancing-7f4a493c83c6.

Laporte, Claire, and Leonard Cassuto. "How to Responsibly Reopen Colleges in the Fall." *Inside Higher Ed*. Last modified April 16, 2020. https://www.insidehighered.com/views/2020/04/16/practical-advice-how-colleges-can-responsibly-reopen-fall-opinion.

LeBlanc, Elizabeth. "Acceleration is Better Than Focusing on Learning Loss. This Unique Summer School Shows Why." *EdSurge*. Last modified August 10, 2021. https://www.edsurge.com/news/2021-08-10-acceleration-is-better-than-focusing-on-learning-loss-this-unique-summer-school-shows-why.

Lederman, Doug. "Dealing with Students' Learning Loss: The Key Podcast." *Inside Higher Ed*. Last modified October 7, 2021. https://www.insidehighered.com/news/2021/10/07/dealing-college-students%E2%80%99-learning-loss-key-podcast.

Lu, Li, and Y. Connie Yuan. "Shall I Google It or Ask the Competent Villain Down the Hall? The Moderating Role of Information Need in Information Source Selection." *Journal of the American Society for Information Science and Technology* 62, no. 1 (2011): 133–145.

Manfuso, Lauren Glenn. "From Emergency Remote Teaching to Rigorous Online Learning." *EdTech Magazine*. Last modified May 7, 2020. https://edtechmagazine.com/higher/article/2020/05/emergency-remote-teaching-rigorous-online-learning-perfcon.

Martin, Michael. "Remote vs. Online Learning: It Makes a Difference." *FIU Online Insider*. Last modified May 4, 2020. https://insider.fiu.edu/remote-learning-vs-online.

Meadows, Donella H. *Thinking in Systems: A Primer*. White River Junction, VT: Chelsea Green Publishing, 2008.

Moore, Stephanie. "Active Learning in a Ubiquitously Blended World." Presentation, *Empirical Educator Project Summit*, online, October 20, 2021.

Moore, Stephanie and Phil Hill. "Planning for Resilience, Not Resistance." *PhilonEdTech* (blog). Last modified April 28, 2020. https://philonedtech.com/planning-for-resilience-not-resistance.

Quinn, David, and Morgan Polikoff. "Summer Learning Loss: What Is It, and What Can We Do about It?" *Brookings Institution* (blog), September 14, 2017. https://www.brookings.edu/research/summer-learning-loss-what-is-it-and-what-can-we-do-about-it.

Slade, Sean. "Let's Not Think in Terms of Learning Loss—Let's Focus on Where Students Have Gained." *EdSurge*. Last modified August 19, 2021. https://www.edsurge.com/news/2021-08-19-let-s-not-think-in-terms-of-learning-loss-let-s-focus-on-where-students-have-gained.

Soika, Brian. "How Should Schools Address Learning Loss?" *USC Rossier School of Education* (blog). Last modified August 2, 2021. https://rossier.usc.edu/how-should-schools-address-learning-loss.

Steele, Claude. *Whistling Vivaldi: How Stereotypes Affect Us and What We Can Do*. New York: W. W. Norton, 2011.

Thompson, Kelvin and Thomas Cavanagh. "63: Field Report #1: Making #Remote-Teaching Happen." April 6, 2020. In *TOPCast*. Produced by CDL Media. Podcast, 32:50. https://cdl.ucf.edu/topcast-s05e63.

Trust, Torrey, and Robert Maloy. "The Real Solution to Learning Loss: Valuing Teachers and The Teaching Profession." *EdSurge*. Last modified April 27, 2021. https://www.edsurge.com/news/2021-04-27-the-real-solution-to-learning-loss-valuing-teachers-and-the-teaching-profession.

US Department of Education. "COVID-19 and Virtual Learning Resources." *Protecting Student Privacy*. Accessed November 18, 2021. https://studentprivacy.ed.gov/covid-19.

Wenger, E., and Wenger-Traynor, B. "Introduction to Communities of Practice: A Brief Overview of the Concept and its Uses." Accessed October 7, 2022. https://www.wenger-trayner.com/introduction-to-communities-of-practice.

Widdicombe, Lizzie. "Why Learning Pods Might Outlast the Pandemic." *New Yorker*. March 14, 2021. https://www.newyorker.com/news/annals-of-education/why-learning-pods-might-outlast-the-pandemic.

Willkomm, Ann Converse. "Online vs. Remote Learning: What's the Difference?" *Goodwin College of Professional Studies* (blog). Last modified April 22, 2020. https://drexel.edu/goodwin/professional-studies-blog/overview/2020/April/online-vs-remote-learning.

Zimmerman, Jonathan. "Coronavirus and The Great Online-Learning Experiment: Let's Determine What Our Students Actually Learn Online." *Chronicle of Higher Education*. Last modified March 10, 2020. https://www.chronicle.com/article/coronavirus-and-the-great-online-learning-experiment.

chapter 16

Institutional and Instructional Humility for Equity-Forward Teaching and Learning

Amy M. Johnson, Jonathan Iuzzini, Peter Felten, and Tazin Daniels

The intersection of inequity, trauma, and teaching in higher education came into sharp focus in 2020. COVID-19's radical disruption exposed socioeconomic fault lines that have long existed in US higher education, the murder of George Floyd magnified long-standing pressures on colleges and universities to re-examine their curricula, policies, and public positions, and the chaos and crises surrounding the 2020 US presidential election added urgency to questions about the purposes and practices of the academy. However, none of this was new.[1] Indeed, the fact that it took a global pandemic, worldwide Black Lives Matter protests, and a violent insurrection in Washington, DC, to spark rapid evolutionary change in teaching and learning illustrates the persistent failure of many educators and institutions—particularly faculty and administrators at predominantly white institutions (PWIs)—to take seriously the ways structural and individual inequities and traumas influence learning, teaching, and student success.

In this chapter, we examine the concepts of institutional and instructional humility. Drawing on the concept of "cultural humility,"[2] institutional and instructional humility require critically examining structures, practices, and assumptions of teaching and learning to equitably center students in every aspect of our work. The three components of cultural humility provide a useful frame for this analysis: (1) ongoing learning and critical self-reflection; (2) challenging power imbalances; and (3) institutional and individual accountability. We offer two narrative vignettes to illustrate paths forward centering institutions of higher learning designed specifically to support students from marginalized and historically excluded populations.

Of course, some faculty and departments within PWIs have been working for years to close equity gaps and cultivate student learning, belonging, and success in their courses. This work has been powerful, even transformational, in many classrooms, for untold numbers of students, and at some institutions.

Too often, however, the pedagogical and curricular efforts of individuals or small groups of faculty have pushed against—or directly conflicted with—the assumptions, policies, and systems of both the particular institution where they are happening and the dominant culture of US higher education.[3] In many higher education circles—and at too many institutions—serious work on teaching, learning, and equity is not deeply valued in the faculty reward structures or in the myriad ways prestige—and budgets—are distributed.[4] This pervasive culture exists in no small part because most US colleges and universities were designed and built to support a particular type of student—white, wealthy, able-bodied, male—only to be retrofitted through recruitment initiatives and student success efforts in the name of increasing student diversity.[5] Yet, as research shows, many of the programs developed to enhance inclusion actually benefit and continue to center affluent, white, normative male students at the expense of the wellness and success of the very students these programs claim to serve.[6]

Given that the root cause of teaching and learning inequity is systemic, individual change alone is not sufficient. Institutions, and academic units within them, need to commit to deep cultural and policy change to redress inequities.[7]

Fortunately, US higher education is so diverse that it includes whole categories of institutions that exist to center students from communities that historically have been excluded, to cultivate the capacities of students who too often are seen as having only deficits, and to contribute to social, economic, and personal change. These institutions—community colleges, Historically Black Colleges and Universities (HBCUs), Tribal Colleges and Universities (TCUs), and Hispanic-Serving Institutions (HSIs)—have long operated near the bottom of the prestige (and financial) hierarchy of American higher education.

We call for institutional and instructional humility in our shared work toward more equitable teaching and learning in higher education. The vignettes below illustrate some of the possibilities for teaching and learning when we look for exemplars in places too often ignored in "elite" higher education circles. Although the historical foundations of PWIs cannot be changed to mirror an HBCU or community college, administrators and faculty at PWIs can—and should—look to institutions created specifically for historically marginalized and excluded learners to better cultivate their own equity-forward student-centered systems and orientations for teaching and learning. This will require institutional and instructional humility because US higher education too often equates excellence with the size of an institution's endowment and the percentage of applicants it rejects.[8]

As the vignettes illustrate, we also must move beyond a focus on teaching practices (even effective, equitable practices) to recognize how much we have to gain by paying less attention to entrenched notions of prestige and more attention to excellence that is built on an equitable foundation. We conclude this chapter with critical analysis, a call for action, and a set of prompts to guide your reflection and action toward more equity-forward teaching and learning informed by institutional and instructional humility.

Institutional Humility: Community Colleges as Student-Centered Institutions

Community colleges first developed in the United States in the early 1900s as an extension of high school, but over the last 100 years have evolved into multifaceted institutions with a mission to create greater opportunity for the people who live and work in close proximity to the college. By design, community colleges should be student-centered institutions, meeting students where they are and supporting their learning as they create new possibilities for increased social and economic mobility. These institutions provide a range of educational pathways, including dual-enrollment (i.e., students co-enroll in high school and college-level courses simultaneously); academic programs leading to transfer to baccalaureate-granting institutions; and certificate training programs that frequently prepare students for employment in high-need industries in their community.[9]

As engines of social and economic mobility in their local communities, these colleges often seize the opportunity to more deeply understand who their students are (i.e., learning about their assets and identifying the supports that will facilitate their success) and to rethink policies and practices that may serve as barriers to success.

One compelling example of this effort in practice comes from Amarillo College, a public two-year community college that serves over 10,000 undergraduate students in the Texas panhandle. Several years ago, a team of the college's senior leaders, faculty, and administrators examined their student success data and identified a troubling pattern of equity gaps in student learning, such that white students were succeeding at significantly higher levels in gateway courses relative to students from racially minoritized backgrounds and poverty-affected students.

This realization—that the college needed to develop a new strategy if it was truly going to fulfill its mission—led to the development of their *culture of caring*. This approach shows up across the college's student services departments and academic programs, as every employee works to "address student-defined needs, eliminate barriers, and love our students to success." The college's president, Dr. Russell Lowery-Hart, often reminds colleagues that the use of the word "love" is intentional: "Love is personal. And when we talk about systemic support, or holistic support, those things are important but they depersonalize it. It means that I can do it without heart. And the students that we have today need our heart more than they need anything else."[10]

The college's process of developing its culture of caring has focused on better understanding who its students are, the assets they bring, and the life challenges they're experiencing—and to design learning experiences with this understanding of students at the center. Amarillo is now widely seen as a national leader in supporting students' basic needs so that they can be successful in the classroom (e.g., food pantry, emergency financial aid).

Many higher education institutions limit their efforts to support students to resources and services that are situated outside of the classroom, focusing aid on students in immediate crisis. But colleges that truly embrace the challenge to be student-centered understand that they must strengthen teaching and learning, too.[11] At Amarillo, this has meant redesigning much of their curriculum to shift from 16-week to eight-week terms in which students take fewer courses at a time, with each course moving at a more rapid pace. Faculty have the support of the college's Center for Teaching and Learning as they take up these redesign efforts, identifying pedagogical approaches to maximize the learning opportunities that come with a shortened term structure. This support component is critical because it models the kinds of sustained peer-to-peer learning and exchange that research demonstrated can make a real difference in student learning as well.

The three components of cultural humility provide a useful frame for us to understand how community colleges like Amarillo navigated their journey to being student-centered institutions. The institution's educators and leaders must engage in *ongoing learning and critical self-reflection*. This cannot be a choice made by a few faculty or staff members who feel a special connection to their students' experiences. Rather, the college must engage in deep change by reforming its policies and practices and by investing in support for both full-time and part-time educators to continue learning and reinventing their teaching craft.

To be truly student-centered is to *challenge power imbalances*, understanding that traditional higher education status hierarchies will not facilitate—and may actually serve as a barrier to—the closing of equity gaps in student success. Finally, exemplar colleges like Amarillo develop practices, often in the form of annual faculty reflection and self-assessment, that reinforce the importance of *institutional and individual accountability*. Just as student-centered colleges call on our educators to be accountable for evolving their practice to facilitate their students' success, we must also seek accountability at the institutional level.

Instructional Humility: Orienting toward Teaching and Learning

As a graduate student at a top-tier research institution in the early 2000s, there were unspoken assumptions about where I (Amy Johnson) would teach and who I would be teaching. Like many in my cohort, I envisioned working at a research university with traditionally aged, full-time students whose primary focus would be their academic classes.

The prevailing narrative of who attends institutions of higher education and the role faculty can or should play at colleges and universities is both problematic and pervasive. Despite my own experience as a low-income, first-generation Black woman at a PWI in the 1990s, I gave little thought to teaching students who, like me, did not conform to the dominant image of the university student.

Faculty training in pedagogies of inclusive teaching have been the primary strategy at PWIs to prepare instructors to teach a diverse student body. Unfortunately, these pedagogies often center white, male, able-bodied students in their efforts to teach the "other." And at many institutions, the primacy and optional nature of this pedagogical training would have continued as the default strategy if not for the global pandemic. The disruptions caused by the COVID-19 virus required faculty at PWIs to grapple with questions of rigor, accommodate students with divided attention, and support those with financial instability in unprecedented ways. Consequently, inclusive pedagogies, largely seen as strategies to support "diverse students," took on new importance and urgency as white, affluent, and able-bodied students—those for whom PWIs were designed—suddenly began to encounter barriers that had historically been perceived as obstacles largely affecting racialized and marginalized others.

Many of the issues faculty at PWIs began noticing, some for the first time, were well-known to faculty at institutions explicitly chartered to educate historically marginalized and excluded students. Despite the achievements of faculty at HBCUs, HSIs, and TCUs and community colleges at supporting student success, scholars of teaching and learning have not paid adequate attention to their person-centered practices. Instead, centers for teaching and learning at PWIs often attempt to retrofit pedagogical development by inserting "inclusive pedagogical practices" into structures and systems designed to *not* be inclusive.

It was in the context of the global pandemic that I reflected on my pedagogical journey for the first time juxtaposing my preparation for classroom instruction at Saint Augustine's University (SAU), a small, private, historically Black university in North Carolina and at Elon University, a PWI, also in North Carolina.

In 2008, I accepted a position as an assistant professor of history at Saint Augustine's University. Although I had never attended a predominantly Black institution, I understood the benefits of teaching and learning in just such an environment. I was inspired by the university's mission to give every student the opportunity to earn a college education and to connect to a long history of Black excellence.

My queries about teaching and my role as a faculty member did not land me in a center for teaching, as one might expect. Although there was a teaching center at the institution, it was new, small, and underfunded. Instead, established colleagues took responsibility for orienting new faculty to teaching at Saint Augustine's.

Our discussions did not focus initially on *how* to teach, instead the emphasis was on *who* we were teaching.[12] Established faculty members centered (1) the history and mission of HBCUs, and (2) student demographics. My colleagues emphasized that pedagogical expertise disconnected from a deep understanding of those enrolled in our classes was ineffective. In this context, it was clear that students who we taught, not just what we taught, mattered deeply.

Most SAU students were Black-identified and worked full time in addition to being full time students. In addition, a significant portion of them were primary care providers. My colleagues made it clear that undergraduate studies were important to our students, but also stressed that there were competing interests for their emotional and intellectual attention, time, and money.

As part of the mentoring process, colleagues explicitly pointed out the need to be attuned to the costs of books and other materials students would require for my class. I was encouraged to think creatively to incorporate free resources as primary or supplementary course material. They showed me how to design classroom activities that supported resource sharing for those who could not purchase course material and to create lectures that introduced concepts covered in the reading material for those who did not have access to texts while deepening ideas for those who did. Next, my colleagues noted the varying levels of preparation for post-secondary education, particularly related to reading fluency and comprehension, and to writing proficiency and confidence—sharing strategies to help all students succeed. And finally, they spoke honestly about the amount of time I should expect students to work on my course outside of class time. I was advised to think strategically about what tasks I assigned outside of class. How did the homework allow students to develop proficiency or prepare for the next class meeting? Did work have to be done outside of class or could I organize our time together to accomplish the same goals? In this context, rigor was not measured in the *quantity* of work assigned outside of class, rather holding students to high standards and having them demonstrate progress toward mastery of the material.

In 2010, I transitioned to Elon University. Although both SAU and Elon are student focused, the preparation for teaching at Elon was remarkably different. Discussions of teaching began from the perspective of teaching as a discipline. Elon's Center for the Advancement of Teaching and Learning (CATL) was established in 2005 to serve two main purposes: promote teaching and learning at the institution and the scholarship of teaching and learning.

There is significant support for teaching faculty at Elon. CATL offers programs related to backward design and syllabus design to help faculty develop courses; workshops on effective lectures, group work, and flipped classrooms to prepare faculty for in-class activities; and assessment strategies to help faculty discern student learning and make necessary course adjustments. Likewise, there are resources to support faculty development as learners and practitioners. This includes funding to attend conferences and support teaching innovation; CATL-sponsored peer groups; and mid-semester course reviews. In all, there were robust opportunities to advance as a teacher at the institution.

Despite the laser focus on best practices, there was little explicit discussion of who was in our classrooms. Instead, there were oblique references to racial and economic diversity, ableism, equity, and inclusion. Discussions about the appropriate length of readings or providing effective feedback were situated in scholarship about students' attention spans and how they learn, not their backgrounds and lived experiences. Universal design techniques were encouraged to support *all learners*. Although preferable to pedagogies of difference—techniques to support non-white, non-normative students—universal design also makes it unnecessary to grapple with the systems and structures that promote and sustain educational inequities.

Until faced with teaching challenges stemming from the global pandemic, it was relatively easy to underappreciate, if not outright ignore, that not every Elon student was traditionally aged, well-resourced, or well-supported. The global pandemic made it clear that underpreparation, educational trauma, and competing priorities did not just affect low-income, first-generation, or students of color, but also those for whom the institution had been built.

Instructional humility practiced by faculty and teaching and learning scholars provides a useful frame for understanding the role of faculty in teaching and learning. Instructors must be knowledgeable about the students in our classroom—their needs, experiences, and abilities. They must also be aware of structures, systems, and pedagogies that replicate inequities, as well as develop teaching responses rooted in literature and best practices. Instructors and scholars of teaching and learning should look to institutions like HBCUs, TCUs, HSIs, and community colleges to better understand how inclusive teaching can be built into the fabric and culture of a classroom experience—and the faculty development program. The shortcomings of inclusive pedagogy at some PWIs is increasingly evident (1) when compared with teaching practices at institutions specifically designed for historically marginalized and excluded students, and (2) in the context of educational disruption.

Toward Institutional and Instructional Humility

A few years before the pandemic began, higher education scholar Alexander Astin argued that "The education of the underprepared student is the most important issue in American higher education. Providing more effective education for such students would not only further the cause of educational equity but also help alleviate some of our most serious social and economic problems."[13] The two vignettes provided in the preceding section offered concrete examples of what is possible when educators and the institutions they serve adopt a truly equity-forward, student-centered orientation to teaching and learning. They emphasize how we must move beyond traditional diversity, equity, and inclusion (DEI) practices and adopt a mindset of institutional humility and instructional humility that recognizes how much we have to gain by paying less attention to entrenched notions of prestige and more attention to excellence that is built on an equitable foundation.

Drawing on the concept of cultural humility, institutional and instructional humility require critically examining structures, practices, and assumptions of teaching and learning to equitably center students in every aspect of our work, including broad cultural change. After exploring the components of humility, we conclude with a call for action and guidance on how you can reflect and engage with colleagues from diverse institutions of learning, as described in the following subsections.

Ongoing Learning and Critical Self-Reflection

Both vignettes revealed a commitment to ongoing learning and critical self-reflection about students and teaching; at Saint Augustine's, for instance, senior faculty took responsibility for orienting their new colleagues toward the mission of the institution and the needs of their students. At many elite institutions, reflection on teaching usually occurs at predictable intervals through traditional mechanisms like accreditation or end-of-term student evaluations. Although these tools offer some insight into how educators are performing against some predetermined metrics, they typically offer little insight into how students—particularly minoritized students—are experiencing that campus or classroom, and they rarely require faculty to work together to address systemic issues.

For institutions, ongoing learning and critical reflection could involve conducting regular climate surveys coupled with qualitative methods like interviews and focus groups with minoritized and marginalized students. These will generate evidence of what is working well, what needs to change, and what opportunities might be overlooked. Normalizing these practices and addressing the difficult realities they reveal are essential steps to better serving students from all backgrounds. Consulting with colleagues from institutions where minoritized students excel, such as HBCUs that produce many Black students who go on to earn advanced degrees in medicine and STEM, also can spark critical reflection on institutional assumptions, structures, and practices that contribute to so many racially minoritized students abandoning STEM fields at PWIs.[14]

At the pedagogical level, self-reflection starts with learning about yourself and the institutional histories in which you are embedded. Identity work is central to the success of all DEI efforts. For educators who hold privileged identities, without understanding how you contribute to and benefit from systems like racism, sexism, classism, and ableism, it is hard to know how to effectively disrupt them. This also requires you to identify your own implicit biases and how they impact your teaching and administrative practices. For educators who hold minoritized identities, this means understanding how to advocate for yourself so you have the resources you need to support students while also receiving recognition for the invisible labor you often get saddled with. This kind of reflection and learning can occur individually or in affinity groups where persons who share identities can learn from one another and support each other in their growth. The vignettes above demonstrate the power of faculty and staff talking with peers about these issues, and research has revealed that cross-institutional faculty conversations can spark significant changes in teaching practices and broad institutional change.[15] As you begin to apply instructional humility and institutional humility lenses to your work as an educator, ask yourself and your colleagues: *How do we—and our institutions—engage in ongoing learning and critical reflection? What institutions do our administrators and faculty look to for benchmarking and modeling? Why those institutions? What would a list of more equity-centered institutions look like?*

Challenging Power Imbalances

Power imbalances within colleges and universities exist across social identities, between academic units, and among professional roles/titles. As a result, decisions that impact disempowered groups are often made without their input. Challenging these long-standing hierarchies is possibly one of the hardest things to do on the journey toward institutional change because they operate on oppressive assumptions that some voices are inherently more correct or valuable than others. Moreover, the very DEI efforts aimed at exposing these hierarchies are often regarded as secondary to other kinds of "legitimate" academic work (e.g., research, publication) and can be emotionally taxing, especially for minoritized members of a campus community. Correcting these systems and practices requires an admission of how stratified our institutions are, and how those strata are shaped by systems of power and oppression like racism, sexism, and ableism. Moreover, it requires a paradigm shift in how we understand and ascribe expertise and ability across institutional roles.

Institutions must have structures in place that aim to empower students, faculty, and staff who hold minoritized identities and also those who have developed expertise in DEI knowledge and skills. They can do this by adopting a student-centered approach, which means not only doing things to serve students, but collaborating with students to solve problems that they did not create.[16] Mechanisms like student advisory boards where students work collectively with faculty and staff to provide feedback on existing programs, or to help identify opportunities for new services, can be particularly powerful. For instance, North Carolina A&T State University, a large and research-intensive HBCU, compensates and trains a group of undergraduates to help administrators make sense of institutional survey data through analysis and student-facilitated focus groups.[17] But without the critical first step of self-reflection, these spaces can also be plagued by implicit biases about who holds relevant expertise or should be in charge of decision-making. As a result, minoritized members also experience a disproportionate amount of risk if they challenge the status quo, which is why accountability is a crucial piece of this work for institutional and faculty leaders.

On a pedagogical level, power dynamics play a major role in the relationships between students and instructors, and as a result, have a real impact on learning. Disciplines like social justice education promote relationships that situate instructors as co-learners in the classroom and facilitators of learning, rather than a traditional "sage on stage" model where instructors are the end-all-be-all expert in the room. Such an approach echoes indigenous pedagogies that challenge dominant narratives of who holds power and whose knowledge is deemed legitimate.[18] Students are encouraged to bring their full selves into the classroom, and assessment practices create opportunities for learning rather than simply evaluation. Individual educators and college leaders can take their work to a new level by applying an institutional humility lens and reflecting on these questions: *How do we engage students as partners, particularly minoritized students, in institutional and curricular decision making? How do we embed power sharing pedagogies in diverse fields of study? How do we reward and support students/staff/faculty for participation in partnership and DEI work?*

Institutional and Individual Accountability

Although the vignettes provide some general strategies for achieving a student-centered campus and classroom, palpable and sustainable change cannot occur without equity-oriented accountability measures.

The success of DEI initiatives are often measured in quantitative terms, like how many programs were implemented or how many people participated. At PWIs, these forms of measurement enact systems of white supremacy by "whitewashing" the experience of minoritized students as outliers in an otherwise inviting campus community. Instead, a first step to being accountable is taking a hard look at the disaggregated quantitative and qualitative metrics of student experience and achievement, and to do so in alignment with equity means to center those students who are usually left at the margins. Moreover, those programs or individuals that fail to actively promote equity and improve student experience and outcomes should face consequences for those failures in terms most PWIs understand: funding and promotion.

If an institution wants to create an equity-forward culture of teaching and learning, DEI knowledge and skills must be prioritized in hiring and promotion of faculty and other campus leaders. At minimum, this includes asking job candidates for diversity statements and teaching philosophies that speak to equitable teaching and requiring hiring committees to receive implicit bias training to signal institutional values and goals.[19] Not only should predominantly white institutions reward DEI knowledge and skills, it should be a requirement for retention and promotion, especially in teaching and leadership positions. Colleges and universities can demonstrate their commitment to this approach by supporting faculty, staff, and administrators with professional learning that guides ongoing growth and development around these skills. If you have explicit responsibility for this work on your campus, please take time to reflect on these questions as you apply an institutional humility lens to your work: *How do we gather, analyze, and use data about climate and student experience across our campus and within our courses/programs? Do our practices make visible the voices and experiences of students (and faculty and staff) from marginalized groups? What institutional and individual accountability measures and systems do we have in place to promote diversity, equity, and inclusion?*

Even without institutional pressure, individual educators can hold themselves accountable by looking outside themselves and their institutions. This includes attending professional learning programs and working with others to continue their identity work, and also partnering with colleagues from Minority Serving Institutions and community colleges to learn how they center students in their day to day work. As faculty we should take time to reflect on opportunities to bring greater instructional humility to our work. Consider questions like these, and find opportunities to engage around these themes with colleagues from colleges and universities that serve students different from our own: *What values do I promote in my teaching? How do I communicate and demonstrate these values to my students? How do I learn about my students' strengths and needs, and cultivate their sense of belonging? How do I support students in crisis? How do I handle mistakes in the classroom? How does my pedagogical approach engage students as partners in learning and teaching?*

Centers for Teaching and Learning (and other professional learning units) can play an important role by facilitating cross-institutional connections and providing professional development opportunities that challenge inequitable practices, assumptions, and systems. An important component of this includes formative classroom observations and helping faculty make sense of student feedback on how different students are experiencing classroom climate. To be equity-centered in this work, many educational developers will also benefit from professional learning and to hold themselves accountable through similar strategies. Regardless of our roles on campus, we encourage all of our readers to identify as educators and to reflect on these questions: *How do I hold myself accountable for my own ongoing learning? Who do I learn from about teaching and students? How would an instructional humility lens shape the people and places I look to for guidance on issues of teaching and learning?*

Next Steps toward Institutional and Instructional Humility

One of the challenges of looking beyond our own institutions and classrooms is resisting the urge to simply borrow the best ideas from our colleagues who have successfully centered student learning, wellbeing, and success. We cannot simply transplant a program and assume the rest of the institutional culture is built to sustain it. We need to first critically examine systems and assumptions that cause these inequities in the first place; otherwise, inclusive practices are band-aid solutions that are likely to fail—and ultimately may cause more harm than good. Accordingly, we encourage you to focus more on the values and processes (rather than specific programs and practices) that minority-serving educators and institutions rely on when identifying and addressing challenges. As we add institutional and instructional humility lenses to our work and our engagement with colleagues across the diverse range of higher education institutions, we can (re)build a truly learner-centered educational system.

Notes

1. Hurtado et al., "Enhancing Campus Climates"; Goldrick-Rab et al., *Still Hungry and Homeless.*
2. Fisher-Borne, "From Mastery to Accountability"; Murray-Garcia, "Rethinking Intercultural Competence."
3. McNair et al., *Becoming a Student-Ready College.*
4. Davidson, *World in Flux*; Bok, *Higher Education in America.*
5. Wilder, *Ebony & Ivy*; Malcom-Piqueux, "Implications for Racial Equity."
6. Harris, Barone, and Davis, "Who Benefits," 38.
7. Bensimon, "Higher Education's Racial Debt."
8. Astin, *Are You Smart Enough?*
9. Beach, *Gateway to Opportunity.*
10. "Culture of Caring Poverty Summit Handbook."
11. Eynon and Iuzzini, *ATD Teaching and Learning.*
12. My experience echoes this research: Williams et al., "Meeting at the Margins."
13. Astin. *Are You Smart Enough?*, 62.
14. Beasley and Fischer, "Why They Leave"; Ponjuán and Hernández, "Different Yet Similar."
15. O'Keeffe et al., "Conversations about Teaching and Learning."
16. De Bie et al., *Justice through Pedagogical Partnership.*
17. Cook-Sather et al., *Engaging Students as Partners.*
18. Pidgeon, More than a Checklist"; Stein, "Settler Colonial Contexts."
19. Booker et al., "Effects of Diversity Training"; House et al., "Faculty Mentors' Awareness and Behavior"; Chang et al., "Does Diversity Training Work."

Bibliography

Astin, Alexander W. *Are You Smart Enough? How Colleges' Obsession with Smartness Shortchanges Students.* Sterling, VA: Stylus, 2016.

Beach, Josh M. *Gateway to Opportunity? A History of the Community College in the United States*. Sterling, VA: Stylus, 2012.

Beasley, Maya A., and Mary J. Fischer. "Why They Leave: The Impact of Stereotype Threat on the Attrition of Women and Minorities from Science, Math and Engineering Majors." *Social Psychology of Education* 15, no. 4 (2012): 427–448.

Bensimon, Estela Mara. "The Case for an Anti-Racist Stance Toward Paying Off Higher Education's Racial Debt." *Change* 52, no. 2 (2020): 7–11. https://doi.org/10.1080/00091383.2020.1732752.

Bok, Derek. *Higher Education in America*. Rev. ed. Princeton, NJ: Princeton University Press, 2013.

Booker, Keonya C., Lisa Merriweather, and Gloria Campbell-Whatley. "The Effects of Diversity Training on Faculty and Students' Classroom Experiences." *International Journal for the Scholarship of Teaching and Learning* 10, no. 1 (2016): 1–7.

Chang, Edward, Katherine L. Milkman, Laura J. Zarrow, Kasandra Brabaw, Dena M. Gromet, Reb Rebele, Cade Massey, Angela L. Duckworth, and Adam Grant. "Does Diversity Training Work the Way It's Supposed To?" *Harvard Business Review*, July 9, 2019. https://hbr.org/2019/07/does-diversity-training-work-the-way-its-supposed-to.

Cook-Sather, Alison, Catherine Bovill, and Peter Felten. *Engaging Students as Partners in Learning and Teaching: A Guide for Faculty*. San Francisco: Jossey-Bass, 2014, 77–78.

"Culture of Caring Poverty Summit Handbook." Amarillo, TX: Amarillo College, 2018, https://www.actx.edu/president/filecabinet/222.

Davidson, Cathy N. *The New Education: How to Revolutionize the University to Prepare Students for a World in Flux*. New York: Basic Books, 2017.

De Bie, Alise, Elizabeth Marquis, Alison Cook-Sather, and Leslie Luqueño. *Promoting Equity and Justice through Pedagogical Partnership*. Sterling, VA: Stylus, 2021.

Eynon, Bret, and Jonathan Iuzzini, *ATD Teaching and Learning Toolkit: A Research-Based Guide to Building a Culture of Teaching and Learning Excellence*. Silver Spring, MD: Achieving the Dream, 2020. https://achievingthedream.org/teaching-learning-toolkit.

Fisher-Borne, Marcie, Jessie Montana Cain, and Suzanne L. Martin. "From Mastery to Accountability: Cultural Humility as an Alternative to Cultural Competence." *Social Work Education* 34, no. 2 (2015): 165–181.

Goldrick-Rab, Sara, Jed Richardson, Joel Schneider, Anthony Hernandez, and Clare Cady. *Still Hungry and Homeless in College*. Madison, WI: Wisconsin Hope Lab, 2018. https://hope4college.com/wp-content/uploads/2018/09/Wisconsin-HOPE-Lab-Still-Hungry-and-Homeless.pdf.

Harris, Jessica C., Ryan P. Barone, and Lori Patton Davis. "Who Benefits? A Critical Race Analysis of the (D)Evolving Language of Inclusion in Higher Education." *Thought & Action* 21 (2015): 38.

House, Stephanie C., Kimberly C. Spencer, and Christine Pfund, "Understanding How Diversity Training Impacts Faculty Mentors' Awareness and Behavior."

International Journal of Mentoring and Coaching in Education 7, no. 1 (2018): 72–86. https://doi.org/10.1108/IJMCE-03-2017-0020.
Hurtado, Sylvia, Alma R. Clayton-Pedersen, Walter Recharde Allen, and Jeffrey F. Milem. "Enhancing Campus Climates for Racial/Ethnic Diversity: Educational Policy and Practice." *Review of Higher Education* 21, no. 3 (1998): 279–302. http://dx.doi.org/10.1353/rhe.1998.0003.
Kezar, Adrianna. *How Colleges Change: Understanding, Leading, and Enacting Change.* 2nd ed. New York: Routledge, 2018.
Malcom-Piqueux, Lindsey. "Transformation in the U.S. Higher Education System: Implications for Racial Equity." Symposium on Imagining the Future of Undergraduate STEM Education. Washington, DC: Board on Science Education, National Academy of Sciences, Engineering, and Medicine, 2020. http://openwater-public.s3.amazonaws.com/sonar-uploads%2FjQKYVAAzRXG14hfPwtSY_NASEM_Malcom Piqueux_FINAL%20(2).pdf.
McNair, Tia Brown, Susan L. Albertine, Michelle Asha Cooper, Nicole L. McDonald, and Thomas Major. *Becoming a Student-Ready College: A New Culture of Leadership for Student Success.* San Francisco: Jossey-Bass, 2016.
Murray-Garcia, Jann, and Melanie Tervalon. "Rethinking Intercultural Competence: Cultural Humility in Internationalising Higher Education." In *Intercultural Competence in Higher Education: International Approaches, Assessment and Application*, edited by Darla K. Deardorff and Lily A. Arasaratnam-Smith. New York: Routledge, 2017, 19–31.
O'Keeffe, Muireann, Martina Crehan, Morag Munro, Anna Logan, Ann Marie Farrell, Eric Clarke, Michelle Flood, Monica Ward, Tatiana Andreeva, Chris Van Egeraat, et al. "Exploring the Role of Peer Observation of Teaching in Facilitating Cross-Institutional Professional Conversations about Teaching and Learning." *International Journal for Academic Development* 26, no. 3 (2021): 266–278. https://doi.org/10.1080/1360144X.2021.1954524.
Pidgeon, Michelle. "More than a Checklist: Meaningful Indigenous Inclusion in Higher Education." *Social Inclusion* 4, no. 1 (2016): 77–91. http://dx.doi.org/10.17645/si.v4i1.436.
Ponjuán, Luis, and Susana Hernández. "Different Yet Similar: The Educational Experiences of Latinx Male Students at Texas PWI, HSI, and HBCU Institutions." *Journal of Hispanic Higher Education* 20 no. 4 (2020): 453–465. https://doi.org/10.1177/1538192719896330.
Stein, Sharon. "'Truth Before Reconciliation': The Difficulties of Transforming Higher Education in Settler Colonial Contexts." *Higher Education Research & Development* 39, no. 1 (2020): 156–170. https://doi.org/10.1080/07294360.2019.1666255.
Wilder, Craig Steven. *Ebony & Ivy: Race, Slavery, and the Troubled History of America's Universities.* New York: Bloomsbury, 2014.
Williams, Krystal L., Steve D. Mobley, Erica Campbell, and Richard Jowers. "Meeting at the Margins: Culturally Affirming Practices at HBCUs for Underserved Populations." *Higher Education* 84 (2022): 1067–1087.

chapter 17

Ableism and Conflicts of Care in the Post-Pandemic University

Libbie Rifkin

It was September 24, 2020, and my Gender and Care in Modern US Poetry class had just had a tough conversation. For the first three weeks of the semester, the students had been remarkably engaged. But something shifted as we moved into week five. My carefully conceived arc from eugenic modernism to the "crip" poetics of Gertrude Stein's "Tender Buttons" fell flat. I stopped class and asked what was going on. After a quiet minute, students started to talk about exhaustion, fear, and a shared sense that school didn't matter at all. I listened, thanked them, and told them I would figure out how to make a change. That weekend, I revised the syllabus to focus immediately on the politics of self-care in Audre Lorde's "A Burst of Light" and the literature of HIV/AIDS. Student engagement shot back up. Students thought hard about how literary texts can be sites of care—and began to experience them that way when it really mattered.

The above is a true story, and it was an experience that enabled me to practice what I will broadly call a pedagogy of care in a more authentic way than I ever have.[1] Revising my course mid-semester helped me loosen my death-grip on the sanctity of my own preparation and think more openly about incorporating feedback and iterative design into my courses. Listening to my students and reconceiving my course in response to their needs required me to admit to them that my initial design might have worked well in 2019, but was inadequate to the realities of 2020. My vulnerability elicited their own caring responses, and this appeared to increase their sense of engagement with the course and each other, an association corroborated by research on transformational and dialogic learning.[2] Without intending to, I'd heeded Cathy Davidson's viral May 11, 2020, call to "*be human first, professor second*," to "design our courses with the awareness of pain, dislocation, uncertainty, and trauma now central to all our lives. And . . . to design with the antidotes to these central to the educational experience: pleasure, community, agency, and care."[3]

But this isn't the whole story. Here, I think more fully and skeptically about the role played by pedagogies of care in academic institutions where disabled, femme, and multiply-marginalized students and a teaching class that disproportionately shares those identities exist in a relationship of interlocking precarity. As a veteran full-time non-tenure-track (FTNTT) faculty member, recently appointed advisor on disability to the vice president of diversity, equity, and inclusion (DEI), mother of an intellectually disabled teenaged son, and person who manages depression and chronic illness, this is the space in which I live and work. I suggest that the COVID-19 pandemic both exacerbated this conjoined harm and created the conditions for beginning to repair it, including not only the expanded adoption of Universal Design for Learning (UDL) strategies in the classroom but new alliances between disabled and multiply-marginalized students and contingent teaching faculty. In tracing these connections within the University, I draw on the lessons learned by disability rights activists and advocates for care workers outside it. I argue that these issues need to be addressed at an institutional rather than just an individual level and must involve the re-allocation of resources and the redistribution of labor. Even more foundationally, they demand a care-web conception of access that draws in the whole University, rather than just an infusion of accessible or caring pedagogy into course design.

Disabled students represent the largest minority in higher education—19% of undergraduates report having a disability.[4] And yet their progress toward meaningful inclusion is clearly limited. Among other salient indicators, 25% of first-time students with disabilities drop out by the end of their first year and 35% by the end of their second.[5] The fates of these students are tied to those of members of what Karen M. Cardozo calls the "casualized and predominantly female teaching class," whose low pay and heavy service load "follows longstanding patterns of devaluing socially reproductive work under capitalism."[6]

How did we get here? The backstory could begin in many different places. I'll start with a brief sketch of the history of "academic ableism" that Jay Dolmage develops in his important recent book by that title. Dolmage argues that "disability has always been constructed as the inverse or opposite of higher education."[7] Using the metaphor of "steep steps" to indicate the structural role of inaccessibility and exclusivity in the architecture of the University, he traces the relationship between the rise of eugenics and the growth of the University in the twentieth century and shows how the contemporary University builds on this history through the promotion of academic disciplines that "sort[s] the population by a medicalized and legal definition of 'ability.'" University curricula help sustain the neo-eugenic tendencies of industries like healthcare and education. As Dolmage puts it, "universities create doctors and special educators and therapists who learn how to rehabilitate or cure disability."[8] Seeing disability as "fixable" undermines the capacity to understand disability identity and meaningfully include people who hold it.

Ableism, which disability justice scholar-activist T. L. Lewis defines as "a system of assigning value to people's bodies and minds based on societally constructed ideas of normalcy, productivity, desirability, intelligence, excellence, and fitness . . . [that] are deeply rooted in eugenics, anti-Blackness, misogyny, colonialism, imperialism, and capitalism,"[9] intersects with the other dimensions of the University's caste system, and the fortunes of disabled community members converge with the "casualized and predominantly female teaching class." Cardozo suggests that "the emergence of a two-tier faculty system can be reframed as one between faculty positions that retain the cultural, economic and social capital of 'productive' activities and those devoted primarily to caring labor."[10] At my R1 institution, Georgetown, more than 60% of courses are taught by non-tenure-track (NTT) and adjunct faculty members. Nationally, 53.9% of NTT faculty are women. More than 73% of faculty positions held by underrepresented racial and ethnic minorities are off the tenure track.[11] In other words, mostly women and disproportionately Person of Color (POC) NTT faculty perform the reproductive labors of teaching, student support, and service, creating the conditions for tenure-track (TT) faculty to secure grant funding, conduct research, and publish—to produce. Teaching is identifiable as a form of care work, "not only because it develops human capabilities or because faculty may develop emotional attachments to their students, but also because the creation of a devalued teaching class is consistent with the social construction of caring labor historically."[12]

Disability studies scholars argue that the devaluation of care work is bound to its association with dependency, which is itself enmeshed in the negative meanings of disability. Care workers and the people they serve are locked in a destructive dynamic of "courtesy stigma," foundationally defined by Erving Goffman as the phenomenon wherein "the problems faced by stigmatized persons spread out in waves of diminishing intensity among those they come in contact with."[13] The negative meanings travel the other direction as well. As historian Evelyn Nakano Glenn has shown, women of color's longtime conscription into both domestic and institutional care work brought the association of their socially degraded identities to these tasks, which was cemented by dramatically lower wages and less support for their own family care needs.[14] With much of the care labor covered by women of color, white women had the privilege to seek "independence" through "productive" educational and professional opportunities, reinscribing ableist ideals and hardening the divides within feminism along racial lines.

There are crucial differences in degree between the low pay and exploitation of NTT professors and that of home health aides and other domestic workers. And the disparity in social stigma and cultural capital is even more pronounced. But recognizing contingent teaching faculty as care workers is critical for understanding the ineffable combination of economic coercion, ethical commitment, and affective drive that keeps us in our jobs. Although the Great Resignation is hitting academia hard, and colleagues in student services are leaving for careers in industry sometimes at up to triple the salaries, the implications for faculty aren't yet clear.[15] Tenured professors may be "disengaging," an option obviously unavailable to contingent faculty. I don't have space or access to the current federal turnover data to develop this point, but I predict that when the dust settles, the teaching class will bear the burden of the pandemic economy's changes in higher education, taking up an even greater proportion of care for our increasingly high-risk students. Recognizing our place in the "social construction of caring labor historically" helps explain why, as a group, TT faculty don't stand with us in the fight for more equitable working conditions.

Since the 1970s, disabled people and care providers have competed for scarce resources. While disability rights organizations have long understood that higher wages for care workers yield higher quality care, private caregiving agencies and fiscally conservative lawmakers have controlled the purse strings and the terms of the policy discussions. The pandemic appears to be shifting the ground. Thanks to the vigorous collaborative lobbying of organizations like The Arc and the National Domestic Workers Alliance, the initially proposed and nearly passed Build Back Better legislation represented an historic investment in both the care infrastructure and self-determination for people with disabilities. The fact that these provisions didn't make it into the Inflation Reduction Act suggests the shape of the fight ahead.

Within higher education, the formation of analogous partnerships represents a hopeful, if also not fully realized prospect. In 2020 and 2021, the Accessible Campus Action Alliance (ACAA), a group of disabled faculty, allies of disabled university community members, and scholars of disability, health equity, institutional policy, and inclusion, released two statements that called for university re-opening policies that "prioritize relations of care," recognizing vulnerability as a universal condition and taking the burden off of "high risk" individuals to meet their access needs through the typical bureaucratic accommodation processes.

Importantly, even though the ACAA asserts that remote modes of instruction are "best practice in the context of the pandemic," it also argues for significant support to enable teaching faculty to redesign their courses in ways that meet their own access needs as well as those of their students. Among other institutional changes, the 2021 statement demands "designing accommodations policies that include household members' health and caregiving responsibilities as the basis for adaptations such as remote work" and "adjusting expectations for scholarship and service based on the disproportionate impacts of the pandemic according to gender, race, disability, class, family status, and other differences."[16] Together, the two statements recognize the outsized impacts of the pandemic on disabled and multiply-marginalized members of the University community—students, faculty, and staff—and argue for policies that embed accessible pedagogy in a more robust safety net for the obligations of care.

The ACAA statements represent a vision of a (post)-pandemic University that is attentive to the realities of the distribution of academic labor. Most of the coverage of the benefits of remote learning for disabled students doesn't take into account the access needs of the faculty and staff who serve them directly. Disabled students' stories need to be told. Neurodivergent students, along with students with mobility impairments, chronic illness flares, and learning and certain psychiatric disabilities, have long argued that remote learning options, including multi-modal delivery and asynchronous course content, are a necessary and "reasonable" accommodation. However, universities have often refused these accommodations on the premise that they would "fundamentally alter the nature of [their] service, program, or activity," or that they pose an "undue hardship" to administer.[17] The widespread adoption of online, hybrid, and hyflex modalities during the pandemic makes those refusals more difficult to sustain in legal, if not practical terms. Students are rightfully agitating to maintain the access victories for which they have fought.

UDL calls for providing learners with multiple means to encounter course content, become engaged, and demonstrate their learning. Effective UDL, by definition, demands a significant investment of time and resources, both in preparation for a course and during its teaching. Faculty need to anticipate students' access needs and build them into course design; they also need to create structures for students to provide feedback and iterate on that design. True UDL is a form of trying that is always in process, rather than a one-and-done checklist. As such, effective UDL-based pedagogy requires of instructors both the empathy to imagine the ways students learn and the capacity to create relationships with students in which both parties are comfortable enough to work together through the "access fails" that are an inevitable part of the quest for meaningful inclusion. Disability justice activist Mia Mingus has called this form of human connection "access intimacy," describing the participants in it as "people investing in remembering my access needs and checking in with me," and, most importantly, "listening to me and believing me."[18]

In Mingus's conception, access intimacy can be "elusive," even "magical" and can happen between "complete strangers," but more often it is "built over years." In other words, access intimacy takes *work*, and although Mingus is careful to stipulate that people who create access intimacy shouldn't expect payment in "emotional currency or ownership," it is crucial nonetheless to recognize the time and energy that it requires. Without structures of support and compensation, this way of being in relation can be exceedingly taxing. To ask it ethically of a person or of a particular group of people demands that resources be routed to them so that they can replenish their capacities and continue to practice care in a sustainable way. As I've demonstrated, this "care for the carer" has long been denied women and especially women of color, both outside of and within the academy, and this denial has destructive effects throughout the care ecosystem.

We can now return with a hopefully enriched perspective to Cathy Davidson's call to "*be human first, professor second*" and to the lessons my students and I learned from both the form and content of Gender and Care in Modern US Poetry. Of course, it is crucial that we draw from the collective pain of the pandemic in order to design our courses with empathy and love. But it is critical that we first make this apparently basic affective shift visible as *work*, rather than naturalizing it as humanity (or worse, femininity) and that we demand the compensation that this work requires. Both inside and outside the University, the people who perform this work and the people who rely on it most are intimately connected not just personally but structurally, through the ableist practices of the institutions within which we operate. Seeing those practices clearly, as "crip of color" scholar Jina B. Kim argues, requires that we listen to and learn from people in those populations who perform caring labor. Audre Lorde, whose transformative writing on her experience of living with cancer and fighting the racism of the healthcare system we studied in my Gender and Care in Modern US Poetry class, was one of those people. Lorde was denied a reduced teaching load and medical leave at Hunter College while she was going through and living with the aftermath of cancer treatment.[19] As Kim argues, this is disability history. It is also one of the many current realities faced by the "casualized and predominantly female teaching class" and student support staff that the University relies on to care for its students, through and beyond the pandemic.

Without institutional backing for what feminist care ethicist Eva Kittay calls "doulia," or "the public responsibility to provide support for the caregiver so that the caregiver can give care without depleting herself and her resources," the adoption of policies dictating multimodal and hybrid learning can open rifts between students and teaching faculty.[20] Putting accessible pedagogy into authentic practice requires universities invest not only in educational technology and related supports, but also in the mostly NTT teaching faculty's time and compensation. At the University and systems levels, this means creating programs that provide teaching faculty course release, funding, or both to redesign our courses and achieve greater ed tech literacy. It means granting NTT faculty equitable access to paid family leave and childcare and eldercare supports. It means fully funding classroom educational technology offices and fully outfitting classrooms to provide maximal support for effective multimodal course delivery.

There is some evidence that universities, at least wealthy ones, are beginning to meet these demands. At Georgetown over the last four years, NTT faculty members finally secured paid parental leave on par with TT faculty, and during the pandemic, dependent care and emergency relief grants were extended to all employees, regardless of rank or job status. But faculty can't operate alone; a care web approach also requires investments in student services, including substantial increases in funding for disability resource offices, whose median budget is less than $200,000, as well as for counseling and psychological services and student health more broadly.[21]

Beyond resource allocation, the change has to start deep within our conception of access itself: who needs it and who provides it. Higher education, like most industries, takes an accommodationist approach to access, maintaining a skeletal apparatus for student services and only retrofitting spaces and practices when required for compliance. In figuring disabled people as exceptional "misfits" in need of finite interventions, this approach to access ignores the ways in which our vulnerable body-minds move in and out of illness and wellness, debility and capacity. Fully reckoning with this reality means that, as Margaret Price put it, "we cannot rely on some individuals to articulate 'needs' and others to bestow 'accommodations,'" instead we need to create flexible structures that enable "collective accountability."[22] At a time of full employment, historic staffing shortages, and precipitously dropping enrollments, higher education investment in the broad infrastructure of care is a matter not just of ethics, but of economic exigency. In order to attract and retain students, universities will have to better support the labor that provides them with the "pleasure, community, agency, and care" that distinguishes high-tuition academic institutions from online alternatives and the world of work.

Notes

1. There is a lot of terminological slippage between several different student-centered and equity-focused approaches to teaching that account for the multiplicity of backgrounds and learning styles in the classroom: accessible pedagogy, inclusive pedagogy, UDL, and pedagogies of care. Broadly speaking, "accessible" and "inclusive" name the goal of these approaches, whereas UDL offers a template for practice: multiplying the means of representation, engagement, and expression in the classroom. "Inclusive" tends to focus on racial and socioeconomic difference among learners; "accessible" conceives its target student population in terms of body-mind variance or disability. UDL is more often associated with "accessible" pedagogy, but practitioners are increasingly recognizing that its iterative approach to course design

can help achieve higher education's broader equity goals. I am adding "pedagogies of care" to this list, and suggesting that it might encompass the others, but not uncritically. Pedagogies of care are rooted in Black feminist ethics. bell hooks' *Teaching to Transgress* is a foundational text here.

2. Walker-Gleaves, "Care in Higher Education."
3. Davidson, "Single Most Essential Requirement."
4. National Center for Education Statistics, "NCES Fast Facts."
5. Shaewitz and Crandall, "Higher Education's Challenge."
6. Cardozo, "Academic Labor: Who Cares."
7. Dolmage, *Academic Ableism*.
8. Dolmage, *Academic Ableism*, 20.
9. Lewis, "Working Definition of Ableism."
10. Cardozo, "Academic Labor: Who Cares," 408–409.
11. "Data Snapshot: Full-Time."
12. Cardozo, "Academic Labor: Who Cares," 407.
13. Goffman, *Stigma*.
14. Glenn, *Forced to Care*.
15. McClure and Fryar, "Great Faculty Disengagement."
16. Accessible Campus Action Alliance, "Beyond 'High-Risk.'"
17. Americans With Disabilities Act of 1990, Public Law 101–336.
18. Mingus, "Access Intimacy."
19. Kim, "Toward a Crip-of-Color Critique."
20. Kittay, "Loves Labor Revisited."
21. Scott, *AHEAD Biennial Survey*.
22. Price, "Precarity of Disability," 205.

Bibliography

Accessible Campus Action Alliance. "Beyond 'High-Risk': Statement on Disability and Campus Re-openings." 2020. https://bit.ly/accesscampusalliance.

Americans With Disabilities Act of 1990. Public Law 101–336. 108th Congress, 2nd session. (July 26, 1990).

Cardozo, Karen M. "Academic Labor: Who Cares?" *Critical Sociology*. vol. 43, no. 3 (2016): 405–428. https://doi.org/10.1177/0896920516641733.

"Data Snapshot: Full-Time Women Faculty and Faculty of Color." *AAUP*, December 9, 2020. https://www.aaup.org/news/data-snapshot-full-time-women-faculty-and-faculty-color.

Davidson, Cathy. "The Single Most Essential Requirement in Designing a Fall Online Course." *HASTAC*, May 11, 2020. https://www.hastac.org/blogs/cathy-davidson/2020/05/11/single-most-essential-requirement-designing-fall-online-course.

Dolmage, Jay. *Academic Ableism: Disability and Higher Education*. Ann Arbor, MI: University of Michigan Press, 2017.

Glenn, Evelyn Nakano. *Forced to Care: Coercion and Caregiving in America*. Cambridge, MA: Harvard University Press, 2012.

Goffman, Erving. *Stigma: Notes on the Management of Spoiled Identity*. Hoboken, NJ: Prentice Hall, 1963.

Hooks, Bell. *Teaching to Transgress: Education as the Practice of Freedom*. Oxfordshire, UK: Routledge, 1994.

Kim, Jina B. "Toward a Crip-of-Color Critique: Thinking with Minich's 'Enabling Whom?'" *Lateral*. July 10, 2021. https://csalateral.org/issue/6–1/forum-alt-humanities-critical-disability-studies-crip-of-color-critique-kim/#fn-1752–22.

Kittay, Eva. "Love's Labor Revisited." *Hypatia*, vol. 17, no. 3 (2002): 237–250. https://www.jstor.org/stable/3810805.

Lewis, Talila A. "Working Definition of Ableism: 2022 Update." *Talila Lewis* (blog), January 1, 2022, https://www.talilalewis.com/blog/working-definition-of-ableism-january-2022-update.

McClure, Kevin R., and Alisa Hicklin Fryar. "Opinion: The Great Faculty Disengagement." *Chronicle of Higher Education*. January 26, 2022. https://www.chronicle.com/article/the-great-faculty-disengagement.

Mingus, Mia. "Access Intimacy: The Missing Link." *Leaving Evidence*. August 15, 2017. https://leavingevidence.wordpress.com/2011/05/05/access-intimacy-the-missing-link.

National Center for Education Statistics. "NCES Fast Facts." 2023. https://nces.ed.gov/fastfacts/display.asp?id=60#:~:text=How%20many%20students%20in%20postsecondary,20%20percent%20for%20female%20students.

Price, Margaret. "The Precarity of Disability/Studies in Academe." In *Precarious Rhetorics*, 191–211, edited by Wendy Hesford, Adela Licona, and Christa Teston. Columbus, OH: Ohio State University Press, 2018.

Scott, Sally. *The AHEAD Biennial Survey of Disability Resource Office Structures and Programs*. Huntersville, NC: Association on Higher Education and Disability, 2019. https://www.ahead.org/professional-resources/information-services-portal/benchmark-data.

Shaewitz, Dahlia, and Jennifer R. Crandall. "Higher Education's Challenge: Disability Inclusion on Campus." *Higher Education Today*, ACE, October 19, 2020. https://www.higheredtoday.org/2020/10/19/higher-educations-challenge-disability-inclusion-campus.

Walker-Gleaves, Caroline. "Is Caring Pedagogy Really So Progressive? Exploring the Conceptual and Practical Impediments to Operationalizing Care in Higher Education." In *Higher Education and Hope*, edited by P. Gibbs and A. Peterson. London: Palgrave Macmillan, 2019.

chapter 18

Toxic to Transformational

Women and the Higher Ed Ecosystem Post-Pandemic

Patrice Torcivia Prusko

Much has been written about the issues women face in higher education, whether as staff, faculty, or student, and about the gaps that remain at every level, from undergraduate through PhD, at higher levels of leadership, and at the intersections. The pandemic further illuminated many of the systemic inequities that remain in place, the barriers women continue to face, the perceived ways women need to change, and what it means to be a woman in leadership. The trauma, pain, and suffering women have endured for years is in the spotlight, and we have felt sad, shocked, and grieved with them. It is going to take more than workshops and new diversity, equity, and inclusion (DEI) roles to heal their hearts and recenter learning. This is a pivotal moment to rethink our approach to leadership, our vision of equity, and the kind of culture our institutions truly aim to create. What are the leadership qualities needed to shift a culture that has kept women on the outside since as far back as the sixth century BCE at the time of Pythagoras?[1]

To recenter something means to move or put something at the center again.[2] In order for something to recenter, it must have at some point been at the center and shifted. The first question we must reflect on is what was at the center that shifted, and what exactly do we want to recenter? And how? In the *Dare to Lead* podcast,[3] Kevin Oakes uses an analogy to refurbishing an old house when discussing the idea of culture renovation. You first need to know both what parts to keep and why. What is foundational, and makes it what it is? When you peel away the paint, or pull up the rug, what do you find underneath? It might be beautiful hardwood floors or a rotting wall. What are the things that are unique to your universities that are traditions, celebrations, ways of teaching and learning, how things have always been done? When you look at those ways through a lens of Diversity, Equity, Belonging, Justice, and Access (DEBJA) what still holds up and what might need to be reimagined? What does your university currently privilege? Finances or student outcomes and student faculty and staff well-being? Keeping the faculty happy or doing what is best for the learners?

Universities are built on power differences and territory. How might we use critical self-reflection to help the administration see the value of shifting a new model of learning to the center, and to let go of some of their power and territory for the good of the learner? How do we create and nourish a culture of collaboration? To do this work, the university needs a vision that keeps the learner at the center, and transparent, open, honest discussion and feedback. They need to welcome diversity of thought. They need a feminist leadership model.

Historical Context

The history of women being both included and excluded from education is long. Education has both religious and class roots, with stories from as early as 64 BCE indicating that schools emerged based on statements in the Torah regarding the need to read, learn, teach, and write.[4] When the first universities were founded—in Bologna in 1190, Paris in 1200, and Oxford in 1210—the primary purpose was recruitment of male clergy in the church; women remained excluded.[5] In the seventeenth century, initial discussions of equality in education for women were halted by the churches and the current social order: "women have been more systematically excluded from doing serious science than from performing any other social activity except, perhaps, front-line warfare."[6]

In 1836, Wesleyan College was chartered as the first university created specifically for women, offering degrees in the liberal arts and emphasizing the sciences.[7] It opened in 1839, followed a few years later by Elmira College in 1855, the first college to grant degrees to women that were the equivalent to those granted to men.[8] It was only about 50 years ago that women reached parity in earning bachelor's degrees,[9] yet as recently as 10 years ago, only 22% of all college presidents were women.[10] And although Elizabeth Willard became the first female college president in 1871, it would take over 100 years for a woman to become president of a large research university, and until 1994 to have a female president of an Ivy League school.[11] From 1986 to 2016, the number of female university presidents increased from 10% to 30%.[12]

The first step into leadership for a woman at a co-ed university was as dean of women. This role, created in 1892 at the University of Chicago, was filled by Alice Freeman Palmer, previously president of Wellesley College. As colleges increasingly added this role to their administration, the Teacher's College of Columbia began a graduate program to train dean of women in 1916.[13] In the 1940s, this position transitioned to dean of students and became filled by men, with a woman reporting to the man and acting as liaison for women, thus removing the direct-to-president reporting structure.[14]

What Women Bring to Higher Ed

Before discussing the barriers women face in higher education and strategies for overcoming those barriers, it is paramount to discuss what women bring to higher education. Women bring different perspectives that are critical to conversations and that inform research. Women must be represented in research, in leadership, and in policy. Women tend to provide greater care and emotional support, higher levels of empathy, and greater teamwork skills.[15] This helps them build deeper relationships and greater levels of trust. Women tend to be much better listeners, are more likely to draw others into conversations, and less likely to dominate conversations with personal opinions. The collective intelligence of work teams rises when more female members are added.[16]

A recent study by the College and University Professional Association for Human Resources found that when an institution has a female president, women earn more and have a greater percentage of academic positions.[17] Teams with women on them perform better and have higher levels of innovation.[18] Different perspectives add value, allow for discussion, and enable people to see things from different viewpoints: "the sky is vaster than we know. . . . [W]e are always viewing only pieces of it. Which pieces get focused on are influenced by individual and social factors."[19]

There are countless examples showing that harm has resulted due to a lack of gender diversity on teams, resulting, for example, in crash-test dummies being designed around the average size of a man and the design of airbags causing harm to women;[20] differences in women's metabolic rate causing the average office temperatures to be too cold and uncomfortable; and differences in women's hormones and how they absorb medicine and chemicals resulting in medication designed for men and unsafe work environments for women.[21] According to the UNESCO report *Women in Higher Education: Has the Female Advantage Put an End to Gender Inequalities?*, only 30% of researchers across the globe are women.[22]

Although the number of women across all levels of higher education has increased, women continue to face barriers and a lack of support every step of the way. The patriarchal systemic structure of institutions was created for and designed by white, cisgender men. In 1950, women earned 31% of bachelor's degrees and 10% of PhDs.[23] It wasn't until 1980 that women and men were enrolled in the same numbers and 2004 for PhDs.[24] In 2012, 86% of all presidents, provosts, and chancellors were male, and 75% of full professors were also male.[25] Within universities, women continue to face a lack of support system, childcare issues, pay inequity, a toxic culture, gender discrimination, and take on greater amounts of service work.[26]

The pandemic,[27] budget cuts,[28] shifts in demographics,[29] issues women face,[30] and competition for labor[31] continue to present significant challenges for leaders in higher education. It is clear that in order for universities to survive, they must create a culture where all people, specifically women, within can thrive. A shift in what we expect from and need in leadership is warranted.

Leadership, at all levels, sets the climate and culture. We need a leadership type that is caring, collaborative, and relational. This type of leadership can lead to policies, support systems, and the systemic change needed to create an ecosystem that will enable women to be successful and to thrive in higher education. The critical challenges for attaining an ethic of care[32] are complex, human, and interdependent, and will require change and openness to new ways of being from all levels and roles in the university. This takes a leader who will do more than add programs and talk about equity. Leaders must be able to build coalitions and be seen as solution partners who can facilitate harmonious collaboration where people have mutual regard for one another.

Feminist Leadership

When people hear the term feminist, they frequently think of women, and some even think of extremism. Feminist leadership is not about gender identity, but identity as a leader. It is not only a privilege to lead a university, but this critical role impacts the ability of communities across the globe to thrive. A leader with a deeper understanding of the lived experiences of the learners, who exemplifies care, is self-aware, open to both sharing power and being transparent about power, and has courage will be able to influence the perseverance of women who are students, staff, and faculty. Feminist leadership could encourage meaningful, systemic change that would lead to gender equity in higher education institutions.

The quest toward an ecosystem where all women can feel safe, enjoy a sense of belonging, and be supported and cared for must begin with leaders who are focused on gender justice.[33] The shift to feminist leadership will require an understanding of what distinguishes it from other types of leadership, why we must now embrace it, and how it is independent of gender identity. Being focused on gender justice means reimagining structures and processes that are non-oppressive, in support of "a shared agenda of social, cultural, economic and political transformation for equality and human rights for all."[34] It will not be easy to empower people who have been previously oppressed, or to shift the mindset of current leaders to a model built around shared power, to being relational and transparent.

When we look at current leadership models and programs, we must reflect on who created them and how they reflect the patriarchy. We consistently read books, listen to podcasts, and attend leadership programs, but have you reflected on who wrote the frameworks these are based upon? A first step is to recognize that the frameworks we have traditionally followed and relied upon, written by and about cis white men,[35] may not be what is needed to effect real systemic change. We need a new conceptual framework. Similar to discussions about reviewing syllabi for diversity in authors, there is a need for diversity in leadership frameworks and theories. We can look to examples of the impact of feminist leadership styles, and the impact they have had on the people within an organization and society at large.

A study by Mohammed Shaed found that feminist leadership styles kept the human at the center, were more caring, and led with a participative, democratic model that resulted in greater transformation.[36] Several stories emerged during the pandemic around leaders who led with a feminist approach and the impact this had. A United Nations study found that the following attributes led to more successful leadership and crisis management: collaborative decision-making, balance between empathy and science, and socially inclusive policies.[37] This aligns with feminist values such as equity, human rights, right to basic needs being met, peace, a healthy planet, democracy, transparency, and shared power.[38] Srilatha Batliwala proposed a Feminst Leadership Diamond that would encompass the four qualities needed for social transformation: Power, Principles, Politics, and Practice (figure 18.1).[39]

How might we both bring in new leaders and enlighten current leaders with the importance of incorporating a feminist leadership model?

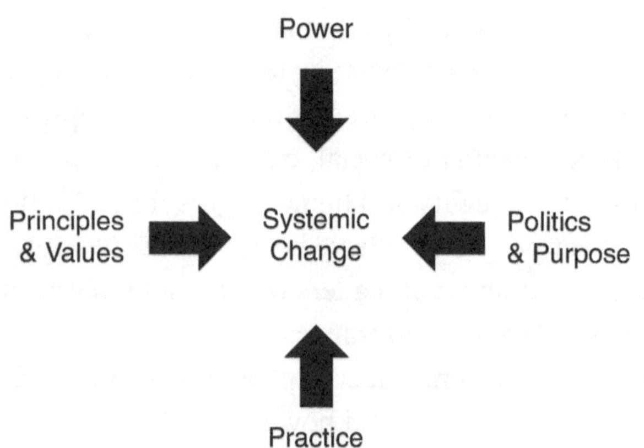

Figure 18.1. Feminist leadership diamond. Adapted from Batliwala, *Feminist Leadership for Social Transformation*

Specifically, we must make the argument that transformation and systemic change that recenters learning in ways that create a caring and supportive system, and pushes out those things that create a toxic environment, will not happen without incorporating the principles of feminist leadership. Leaders must be open to changing the ways they think about leadership and commit to more than funding for new roles and professional development. They must commit to changing their practice, sharing power, and to an introspection of their values and purpose. Leaders must explore what lived experiences they as individuals bring and how that has shaped them as leaders. This includes their social and cultural capital and the intersections of identity, personal attributes and abilities, and background.[40]

Conclusion

Lee Bolman and Terrence Deal developed a model with four constructs, Structural, Human Resource, Political, and Symbolic.[41] I would like to focus on two constructs, Human Resource and Political. Human Resource proposes that the organization should prioritize human needs and, importantly, align with the specific needs of those people within its structure. The Political construct proposes that power and influence impact the ways in which resources within an organization are administered.[42] Bolman and Deal use the metaphor of family for Human Resource and jungle for Political, with the main challenges being alignment of organizational goals with the needs of the people and issues around agenda and power.[43]

A shift to recentering learning would require those at all levels, including staff, educators, and those at the leadership levels, to both think of themselves as leaders and reimagine what it looks like to have learning at the center and to be a leader in higher education. The process would involve not only reviewing and reimagining mission, vision and values, but creating a plan for operationalizing the new values.[44] This work would then inform a redesign of faculty development, the curriculum, and student support services.[45] A feminist leadership model will enable universities to center diversity, equity, belonging, justice, and access in a truly transformational way that supports women at all levels of the university and intersections of identity.

In order to do this, leaders must practice critical self-reflection around their role in the systemic issues, the biases they bring with them, and how they can evolve, learn, and grow.[46] Steps each of us can take to shift the story and create more stories of thriving communities include three levels of reflection: reflection on self, reflection on self as part of the university system, and reflection on self in relation to those over which they hold power. I propose future research around a theory of action that examines what kind of change occurs when university leaders practice critical self-reflection through a lens of feminist framework, and its effect on women's ability to persevere within the higher education ecosystem as students, staff, and faculty.

Notes

1. Wertheim, *Pythagoras's Trousers*, 8.
2. Free Dictionary, "Recenter."
3. "Culture Renovation with Kevin Oates."
4. Compayré, *History of Pedagogy*.
5. Wertheim, *Pythagoras's Trousers*, 44.
6. Wertheim, *Pythagoras's Trousers*, 11.

7. Wesleyan College, "The History of Wesleyan College."

8. Elmira College, "Fast Facts."

9. Fry, "U.S. Women near Milestone."

10. Kim and Cook, "Diversity at the Top."

11. Pew Research Center, "The Data on Women Leaders."

12. "Quick Take: Women in Academia."

13. Schwartz, "How Deans of Women."

14. Parker, "Historical Role of Women."

15. Zenger and Folkman, "Research: Women Score Higher."

16. Woolley and Malone, "What Makes a Team."

17. Whitford, "Study: Women-Led Colleges."

18. Dezsö, and Ross, "Does Female Representation"; Hoogendoorn et al., "Impact of Gender Diversity"; Dai et al., "Teams on Innovation Performance"; McCausland, "Innovation Needs More Diversity."

19. Henrion, *Women in Mathematics*.

20. Criado-Perez, *Invisible Women*.

21. Criado-Perez, *Invisible Women*, part 4: Going to the Doctor; Criado-Perez, *Invisible Women*, part 2: The Workplace.

22. Vieira do Nascimento et al., *End to Gender Inequalities*.

23. Duffin, "Number of Bachelor's Degrees"; Duffin, "Number of Doctoral Degrees."

24. Duffin, "Number of Bachelor's Degrees"; Duffin, "Number of Doctoral Degrees."

25. AAUP, "Here's the News"; Parker, "Historical Role of Women."

26. Marken, "28% of Women."

27. Ramlo, "Address the Financial Impact"; Wolinsky, "Mobile Students, Remote Education."

28. PR Newswire, "New SHEEO Report."

29. Dennis, "Impact and Opportunities: COVID-19's."

30. Augustus, "Working in Higher Education"; Davis et al., "Pandemic-Related Barriers"; Porter et al., "Toward Understanding COVID-19's Economic."

31. Caterine, "Mass Exodus"; Decherney and Levander, "Hottest Job"; Novotney, "Leaving Academia."

32. "Carol Gilligan."

33. Batliwala, *Feminist Leadership for Social Transformation*.

34. Batliwala, *Feminist Leadership for Social Transformation*.

35. Ayman and Korabik, "Why Gender and Culture Matter"; Hartzell et al., "Just White Men."

36. Mohammed Shaed, "Participative Management Theory."

37. Piscopo and Och, "Effective, Decisive, and Inclusive."

38. Batliwala, *Feminist Leadership for Social Transformation*.

39. Batliwala, *Feminist Leadership for Social Transformation*.

40. Batliwala, *Feminist Leadership for Social Transformation*.

41. Bolman and Deal, *Artistry, Choice, and Leadership*, 50.
42. Bolman and Deal, *Artistry, Choice, and Leadership*, 185.
43. Bolman and Deal, *Artistry, Choice, and Leadership*, 115.
44. Brown, "Operationalizing Your Organization's Values."
45. Palestini, *Feminist Theory and Educational Leadership.*
46. Martinez, "Engaging Aspiring Educational Leaders."

Bibliography

American Association of University Professors (AAUP). "Here's the News: The Annual Report on the Economic Status of the Profession 2012–2013." AAUP. Accessed October 22, 2022. https://www.aaup.org/report/heres-news-annual-report-economic-status-profession-2012–13.

Anderson, Emily W., Catherine Vanner, Christine Min Wotipka, and Kristy Kelly. "'Participation Does Not Equal Voice': Gendered Experiences in an Academic and Professional Society." *Comparative Education Review* 65, no. 3 (August 1, 2021): 534–54. https://doi.org/10.1086/715115.

Ashencaen Crabtree, Sara, and Chris Shiel. "Loaded Dice: Games Playing and the Gendered Barriers of the Academy." *Gender and Education* 30, no. 7 (October 3, 2018): 899–916. https://doi.org/10.1080/09540253.2018.1447090.

Augustus, Jo. "The Impact of the COVID-19 Pandemic on Women Working in Higher Education." *Frontiers in Education* 6 (May 14, 2021): 648365. https://doi.org/10.3389/feduc.2021.648365.

Ayman, Roya, and Karen Korabik. "Leadership: Why Gender and Culture Matter." *American Psychologist* 65, no. 3 (2010): 157–170. https://doi.org/10.1037/a0018806.

Batliwala, Srilatha. *Feminist Leadership for Social Transformation: Clearing the Conceptual Cloud.* Creating Resources for Empowerment in Action, 2010. https://justassociates.org/wp-content/uploads/2022/02/feminist-leadership-clearing-conceptual-cloud-srilatha-batliwala.pdf.

Bolman, Lee G., and Terrence E. Deal. *Reframing Organizations: Artistry, Choice, and Leadership.* 3rd ed. San Francisco: Jossey-Bass, 2003.

Brown, Brené. "Culture Renovation with Kevin Oates." January 11, 2021, in *Dare to Lead with Brené Brown.* Podcast, 1:21:14. https://brenebrown.com/podcast/brene-with-kevin-oakes-on-cultural-renovation.

Brown, Brené. "Operationalizing Your Organization's Values." *Brené Brown* (blog). Accessed October 18, 2022. https://brenebrown.com/operationalizing-your-orgs-values.

Carlson Reis, Tania, and Marilyn L. Grady. "Women and the University Presidency: Increasing Equity in Leadership." *Journal of Research on the College President* 3, no. 1 (2019): 47–61. https://doi.org/https://doi.org/10.54119/ jrcp.2019.306.

"Carol Gilligan." *Ethics of Care* (blog), July 16, 2011. https://ethicsofcare.org/carol-gilligan/.

Caterine, Christopher L. "Mass Exodus." *Inside Higher Ed*, April 30, 2020. https://www.insidehighered.com/advice/2020/04/30/pandemic-threatens-force-more-phds-leave-academia-ever-and-they-will-need-career.

Compayré, Gabriel. *The History of Pedagogy*. Boston: D. C. Heath & Company, 1886. Translated by William Harold Payne. New York: Legare Street Press, 2022. https://books.google.com/books?vid=HARVARD:32044030440390&printsec=titlepage#v=onepage&q&f=false.

Criado-Perez, Caroline. *Invisible Women: Exposing Data Bias in a World Designed for Men*. London: Chatto & Windus, 2019.

Dai, Ye, Gukdo Byun, and Fangsheng Ding. "The Direct and Indirect Impact of Gender Diversity in New Venture Teams on Innovation Performance." *Entrepreneurship Theory and Practice* 43, no. 3 (2019): 505–28. https://doi.org/10.1177/1042258718807696.

Davis, Pamela B., Emma A. Meagher, Claire Pomeroy, William L. Lowe Jr., Arthur H Rubenstein, Joy Y. Wu, Anne B. Curtis, and Rebecca D. Jackson. "Pandemic-Related Barriers to the Success of Women in Research: a Framework for Action." *Nature Medicine* 28, no 3 (2022): 436–438. https://doi.org/10.1038/s41591-022-01692-8.

Decherney, Peter, and Caroline Levander. "The Hottest Job in Higher Education: Instructional Designer." *Inside Higher Ed*, April 24, 2020. https://www.insidehighered.com/digital-learning/blogs/education-time-corona/hottest-job-higher-education-instructional-designer.

Dennis, Marguerite J. "Impact and Opportunities: COVID-19's Effect on Higher Education." *College and University* 96, no 2 (2021): 31–38. https://www.proquest.com/openview/634b3af70e91f11ecb70f0c0855fb67f/1.pdf.

Dezsö, Cristian L, and David Gaddis Ross. "Does Female Representation in Top Management Improve Firm Performance? A Panel Data Investigation." *Strategic Management Journal* 33, no. 9 (2012): 1072–1089. https://doi.org/10.1002/smj.1955.

Duffin, Erin. "Number of Bachelor's Degrees Earned in the United States from 1949/50 to 2029/30, by Gender." Statista. Last modified March 24, 2022. https://www.statista.com/statistics/185157/number-of-bachelor-degrees-by-gender-since-1950.

Duffin, Erin. "Number of Doctoral Degrees Earned in the United States from 1949/50 to 2029/30, by gender." Statista. Last modified March 24, 2022. https://www.statista.com/statistics/185167/number-of-doctoral-degrees-by-gender-since-1950.

Elmira College. "Fast Facts." Accessed April 3, 2022. https://www.elmira.edu/about/Fast_Facts.html.

Free Dictionary. "Recenter." Accessed October 18, 2022. https://www.thefreedictionary.com/Recenter.

Fry, Richard. "U.S. Women near Milestone in the College-Educated Labor Force." *Pew Research Center* (blog), June 20, 2019. https://www.pewresearch.org/short-reads/2019/06/20/u-s-women-near-milestone-in-the-college-educated-labor-force.

Hartzell, Joshua D., Jessica T. Servey, Guen Hunt, Melanie Wiseman, and Kim Gibson. "Teaching Leadership . . . More Than Just White Men." *American Journal of Medicine* 135, no. 8 (2022): 929–930. https://doi.org/10.1016/j.amjmed.2022.02.033.

Henrion, Claudia. *Women in Mathematics: The Addition of Difference*. Bloomington: Indiana University Press, 1997.

Hoogendoorn, Sander, Hessel Oosterbeek, and Mirjam van Praag. "The Impact of Gender Diversity on the Performance of Business Teams: Evidence from a Field Experiment." *Management Science* 59, no. 7 (2013): 1514–1528. https://doi.org/10.1287/mnsc.1120.1674.

Kim, Young M., and Bryan J. Cook. "Diversity at the Top: The American College President 2012." *On Campus with Women* 41, no. 1 (2012). Gale Academic OneFile. https://link.gale.com/apps/doc/A298503871/AONE?u=mlin_oweb&sid=googleScholar&xid=f3dd66d0.

Marken, Stephanie. "28% of Women in Academia Say Gender Limits Their Advancement." *Gallup Blog*, March 29, 2022. https://news.gallup.com/opinion/gallup/391226/women-academia-say-gender-limits-advancement.aspx.

Martinez, Melissa A. "Engaging Aspiring Educational Leaders in Self-Reflection Regarding Race and Privilege." *Reflective Practice* 16, no. 6 (2015): 765–776. https://doi.org/10.1080/14623943.2015.1095727.

McCausland, Tammy. "Why Innovation Needs More Diversity." *Research Technology Management* 64, no. 2 (2021): 59–63. https://doi.org/10.1080/08956308.2021.1868003.

Mohammed Shaed, Maslina. "Participative Management Theory and Feminist Leadership Styles." *Geografia: Malaysian Journal of Society and Space* 14, no. 4 (2018): 332–345. https://doi.org/10.17576/geo-2018-1404-27.

Novotney, Amy. "Leaving Academia." *Monitor on Psychology* 53, no. 2 (March 10, 2022). https://www.apa.org/monitor/2022/03/career-leaving-academia.

Palestini, Robert H. *Feminist Theory and Educational Leadership*. New York: Rowman & Littlefield Education, 2013.

Parker, Patsy. "The Historical Role of Women in Higher Education." *Administrative Issues Journal: Connecting Education, Practice, and Research* 5, no. 1 (2015): 3–14. https://doi.org/10.5929/2015.5.1.1.

Pew Research Center. "The Data on Women Leaders." September 13, 2018. https://www.pewresearch.org/social-trends/fact-sheet/the-data-on-women-leaders.

Piscopo, Jennifer M., and Malliga Och. "Effective, Decisive, and Inclusive: Women's Leadership in Covid-19 Response and Recovery." UN Women, September 2021. https://www.unwomen.org/sites/default/files/Headquarters/Attachments/Sections/Library/Publications/2021/Effective-decisive-and-inclusive-Womens-leadership-in-COVID-19-response-and-recovery-en.pdf.

Porter, Christa J., LaWanda Ward, and Lori D. Patton. "Toward Understanding COVID-19's Economic Impact on Black Women in U.S. Higher Education." *Journal of Student Affairs Research and Practice* 60, no. 1 (2023): 66–80. https://doi.org/10.1080/19496591.2021.2006678.

PR Newswire. "New SHEEO Report Finds State Funding Remains Below Historic Levels as Public Colleges Brace for a Recession and Expected Budget Cuts." May 5, 2020. https://sheeo.org/new-sheeo-report-finds-state-funding-remains

-below-historic-levels-as-public-colleges-brace-for-a-recession-and-expected-budget-cuts.

"Quick Take: Women in Academia." *Catalyst*, January 23, 2020. https://www.catalyst.org/research/women-in-academia.

Ramlo, Susan E. "Universities and the COVID-19 Pandemic: Comparing Views about How to Address the Financial Impact." *Innovative Higher Education* 46, no. 6 (2021): 777–793. https://doi.org/10.1007/s10755-021-09561-x.

Ropers-Huilman, Becky. *Gendered Futures in Higher Education: Critical Perspectives for Change.* Albany: State University of New York Press, 2003.

Schwartz, Robert Arthur. "How Deans of Women Became Men." *Review of Higher Education* 20, no. 4 (1997): 419–436. https://doi.org/10.1353/rhe.1997.0011.

Silbert, Andrea, Magdalena Punty, and Elizabeth Brodbine Ghoniem. "The Women's Power Gap at Elite Universities: Scaling the Ivory Tower." Eos Foundation, 2022. https://www.womenspowergap.org/wp-content/uploads/2022/01/WPG-Power-Gap-at-Elite-Universities-v17.pdf.

Vieira do Nascimento, Daniele, Jaime Roser-Chinchilla, Jaime, Takudzwa Mutize, *Women in Higher Education: Has the Female Advantage Put an End to Gender Inequalities?* UNESCO, March 8, 2021. https://unesdoc.unesco.org/ark:/48223/pf0000377182

Wertheim, Margaret. *Pythagoras's Trousers: God, Physics and the Gender War.* New York: W. W. Norton & Company, 1997.

Wesleyan College. "The History of Wesleyan College." Accessed April 3, 2022. https://www.wesleyancollege.edu/about/history/wesleyan-college-history.cfm.

Whitford, Emma. "Study: Women-Led Colleges Hire More Women and Pay Them Better." *Inside Higher Ed*, January 26, 2022. https://www.insidehighered.com/news/2022/01/26/study-women-led-colleges-hire-more-women-and-pay-them-better.

Wolinsky, Howard. "Mobile Students, Remote Education, Free-Fall Economics: Campus Life in 2020: The Pandemic-Triggered Economic Crisis Will Have an Unprecedented Impact on Higher Education Globally." *EMBO Reports* 21, no. 9 (2020): 1–5. https://doi.org/10.15252/embr.202051430.

Woolley, Anita, and Thomas W. Malone. "What Makes a Team Smarter? More Women." *Harvard Business Review*, June 2011. https://hbr.org/2011/06/defend-your-research-what-makes-a-team-smarter-more-women.

Zenger, Jack, and Joseph Folkman. "Research: Women Score Higher Than Men in Most Leadership Skills." *Harvard Business Review*, June 25, 2019. https://hbr.org/2019/06/research-women-score-higher-than-men-in-most-leadership-skills.

chapter 19

Access ≠ Equity

A Primer on Reconsidering Edtech in Higher Education

Rolin Moe

It's a metaphor in a picture: two panels show the same three children past the outfield of a sporting event, standing behind a fence and looking toward the game (figure 19.1). The children are of different heights, and in the first panel, each child is standing on a box beside the fence. This panel, titled "Equality," provides the middle child with enough of a boost to see over the fence, but the shortest child is still left unable to see the game, while the tallest child is standing on a box he did not need to view the game. This is rectified in the second panel, titled "Equity," where the shortest child now has two boxes to stand on, the tallest child has none, and all three children can see the baseball game at the same level from behind the fence.

Between 2012 and 2016, this particular image was a viral sensation across social and other digital media outlets. Born from a 2012 political argument on social media,[1] the image has been adapted dozens of times in different settings and languages. One common contextualization of the graphic is education,[2] leading institutions, governments, and other constituents to design derivative cartoons to point out the need for changes to financial allocation models to fix the disparity in student performance across socioeconomic levels, known as the achievement gap. A popular example, from promotional materials for the Association of American Colleges and Universities,[3] replaces the baseball game

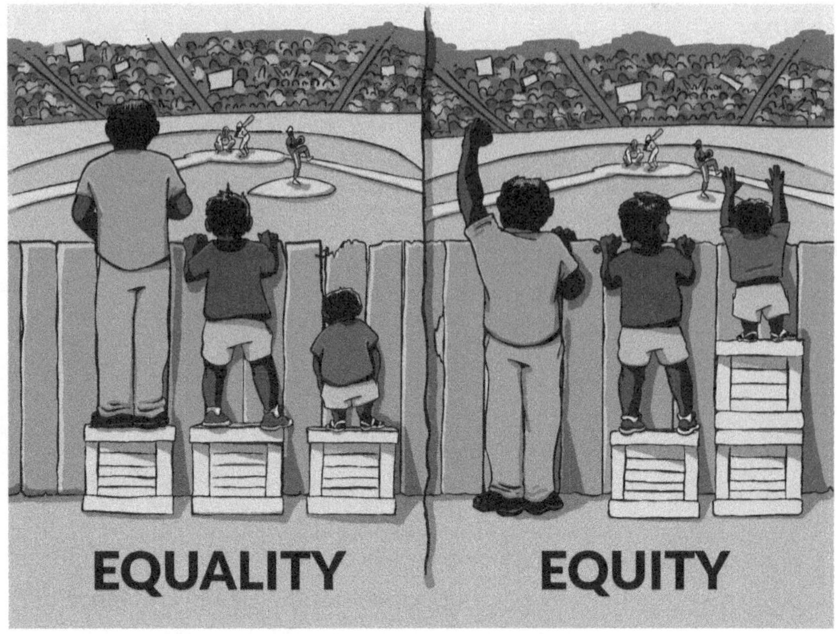

Figure 19.1. Equality versus equity. Source: Interaction Institute for Social Change; Artist: Angus Maguire; Creative Commons Attribution-ShareAlike 4.0 International. CC BY-SA 4.0. https://creativecommons.org/licenses/by-sa/4.0/

with bells hanging from the ceiling, keeping the original cartoon sentiment that access is the lynchpin for solving the achievement gap. A reconsidering and reordering of the distribution of resources, similar to the rearrangement of boxes in the equality versus equity cartoon, is cast as the intervention needed to move from the problematic to a positivist reality.

The achievement gap was first addressed on a national level in 1966 as part of the Equality of Educational Opportunity Commission, colloquially known as the Coleman Report based on the commission's lead investigator, James Coleman. The Coleman Report was a requirement of the Civil Rights Act, which mandated an assessment of educational institutions' affordance to provide equal educational opportunities to all children in the United States. Coleman's findings were controversial at the time and remain so today: the inputs of an education (school buildings, dollars spent per student, teacher experience) were not as significant of student success as the inputs external to the school (e.g., parental education level, family income). Coleman's report did not negate the importance of resource allocation, but focused its intervention on outputs, or efforts to measure student success through standardized assessments.[4]

Criticism of Coleman's report and findings was immediate, questioning not only his findings but his methodology too.[5] Further studies of input-driven interventions have provided more research and evidence showing links between input inequality and the achievement gap.[6] At the 50-year mark of the Coleman Report, a number of research studies emerged to see how the policy decisions post-Coleman had affected the achievement gap. Researchers who had historically focused on output-driven measures found there was no statistical change between the achievement gap of 1966 and that of 2016,[7] whereas researchers who had historically focused on input-driven measures found the achievement gap had grown considerably, in some cases by nearly 40%.[8] Any agreement within the ideological debates of educational policy and sociology is centered around the evidence that the achievement gap remains as sizeable an obstacle for US youth as it has ever been.

This achievement gap stagnation exists despite two considerably significant educational phenomena of the twenty-first century: the rise of educational technology (edtech) and the growth of equity-minded research and policy through the development of diversity, equity, and inclusion (DEI) offices. Both edtech and DEI have been promoted by its practitioners as well as media and politicians as the key missing pieces of the education puzzle, elements to insert into an equation to solve the consistent problems of educational inequality such as the achievement gap.

Both have seen considerable adoption this century, with technology-infused online and in-person educational environments the expected standard for any institution, as well as offices dedicated to DEI established at the majority of institutions across the United States. Cottage industries for edtech and DEI are seeing remarkably success as well, with special research periodicals, mass media authoring, boutique conferences, workshops, seminars, trainings, and more dedicated to these distinct spaces of study and production. As education's local and national leaders forecast the most important factors in the future of higher education, the key elements novel to a post-Coleman world are edtech and DEI.[9]

Despite the parallel growth patterns and historical timelines of edtech and DEI, the integration of one into the other's ecosystem has not been ubiquitous. And even though both fields have seen considerable popular attention and practice-based adoption in recent years due to the COVID-19 pandemic and the societal movement of antiracism as catalyzed by the death of George Floyd, the relationship of edtech and equity is at best seen as one where technological inputs or outputs will be utilized to provide the opportunities identified by DEI as lacking for historically marginalized populations. Such an arrangement has so far failed to provide the promised gains, and if the parallels of the Coleman Report continue, will at best keep the gap stagnant and at worst feed an accelerating divide.

This chapter identifies the obstacles facing edtech in its recognition of and ability to support the DEI missions not only of local institutions but the higher education landscape in general. As a trained scholar in the field of educational technology, my foundation is one based in edtech and so my introduction of the topic will come from the edtech trajectory and its intersection with the DEI trajectory. I will then analyze the primary mechanism by which edtech engages with DEI: technological accessibility. From there, I will identify two key obstacles an access-to-equity approach faces in results-based implementation: structuralism and solutionism. I will then call on education to rethink the access-to-equity approach and adopt a developmental working model and provide examples of grassroots efforts to rethink edtech and DEI.

Within traditional volumes similar to the stated goals of *Recentering Learning*, a chapter such as this normally aligns with a section dedicated to equity, but it is vital to recognize the inherent obstacle of taxonomizing a chapter that challenges the de facto relationship of equity and access within the equity space. If the rapid evolutionary change at the foundation of this volume is now recognized as the standard operating procedure for higher education institutions, a more robust understanding of equity at core levels is a necessity for our future. If education is a human right and a tool for mobility and opportunity, wrestling with structural and transactional visages of equity must happen across not only the silos of our institutions but also the silos built to organize our research volumes. It is from this perspective that this chapter wrestles with the themes inherent in *Recentering Learning*, understanding that equity is currently a hot topic of interest but also a fundamental element of how systems and structures manifest.

The choice of which shorthand to use when referring to both educational technology and diversity/equity/inclusion is important because each field wrestles with the weight of what letters to include or not include and the meaning of capitalization in different places within the shorthand.[10] Both phenomena are evolving at a rapid rate but are still considered by style manuals to be field-specific jargon and therefore have not been defined by MLA, AP, APA, *Chicago Manual*, and other authorities on usage. Because this chapter seeks to pinpoint a particular moment of this history for congruent analysis prior to the terms entering mainstream adoption, the decision on which acronym to use incorporates mass media attitudes in addition to the particulars within each discipline.

"Educational technology" has seen a multitude of shorthand derivations over the last 20 years: ed-tech, edtech, EdTech, EduTech, and ed tech being some of the most commonly used. In this chapter, I will use edtech because it serves the largest audience for this particular portmanteau and has been identified as the sociocultural representative for the phrase.[11] The other options are regularly used in literature as of this writing and would serve well in this space too—in particular EdTech, which alludes to the corporate power of this particular movement by separating the Education and the Technology, and e-learning, which was the original phrase for the phenomenon of learning with computers. The most common shorthand is edtech, and here references the field of scholars, practitioners, and companies seeking to identify and leverage contemporary technologies for the purposes of educational achievement.

“Diversity, equity, and inclusion” has an even greater debate around its acronym for several key reasons: the order of recitation can signify the order of operation,[12] and there is rampant debate as of this writing about whether other elements, such as justice (e.g., JEDI) or belonging (e.g., DIB) should be included or replace existing elements. As of this writing, a growing number of educational institutions are opening or reorienting their missions to include justice, leading to DEIJ or JEDI as the acronym of choice. However, in mainstream media, DEI remains the primary reference to the equity conversation in higher education today, and with the focus of this chapter on identifying the phenomenon at this cultural point, DEI remains the acronym used to identify education's engagement with the equity phenomenon of the twenty-first century.

Access to Technology as an Equity Plan

The concept of educational access is a foundational part of US culture and has been for nearly 200 years since Horace Mann took Enlightenment-era philosophy on the nature of man and developed local policy and action to ensure all citizens had the ability to attend school at no out-of-pocket cost.[13] It must be noted that the early nineteenth-century definition of citizen in the United States was remarkably exclusionary and, to this day, continues to evolve to be more inclusive or accessible. Innovations in the delivery of education in the time since Mann, from correspondence institutions to the growth of land-grant colleges, from the GI Bill to radio and television instruction in the twentieth century, were presented in no small part as further opportunities for education to reach all citizens no matter the circumstances obstructing their progress: geography at first, but later religion, gender, race, sexual orientation, and persons with a disability. At each moment, the number of higher education institutions grew (land grant, then state legislature and community colleges), and the ability for educational content to be shared across distance expanded (first by post, then by radio, television, and now Internet), and popular media framed the growth as indicative of a national agreement of the value of education.[14]

That agreement may have been aspirational rather than foundational. Despite being the founding point for much of the technological innovation around distance education between 1850 and 1990, acceptance of these educational models in the United States was much less successful than in European countries. Private companies innovating in boutique markets, such as the Phonographic Institute developing a course in Pitman Shorthand in the 1850s, found success in the United States and later the world; however, it was German and British higher education institutions that translated correspondence courses to formal education because in the United States efforts such as Cornell's Correspondence University were massive failures.[15]

Another example was the growth of radio and television studios across American colleges and universities in the twentieth century. At one time, 10% of radio call stations were controlled by education institutions, as well as the mid-twentieth-century efforts to establish broadcast television institutions such as the University of Mid-America,[16] enrollments were never strong enough to support the initiatives and they were largely abandoned.[17] Despite significant modality innovations for the dissemination of education and the heralding of educational access, the US education system did not accept these accessible modalities.[18]

This creates a problematic contradiction: US society celebrates the opportunity to provide accessible education but does not support it as a certificated or credentialed form of learning. Arguments of rigor are not novel to the United States, but institutions such as the Open University (United Kingdom), Athabasca University (Canada) and the National University of Distance Education (Spain) have provided accredited university-level curricula and degrees for more than 50 years each without sacrificing rigor. Instead, prior to online education, US learners wishing to access remote learning were largely relegated to specific trades or for-profit institutions.[19]

The rise of computers in education in the last decades of the twentieth century was not originally referred to as edtech but rather e-learning. The particulars of this are important to distinguish because at the end of the twentieth and beginning of the twenty-first centuries, researchers of the third generation of technology (telecommunications and computers) recognized access was only one element of the potential educational revolution.[20] Unlike correspondence, radio, and television, e-learning saw a direct relationship between new tools and new pedagogies, and efforts to build within the ecosystem were designed to engage learners in modalities and methodologies meeting their life experiences.[21] Because the computer itself was a mechanism of creation, learning required an element of building, which led in no small part to the practical establishment of constructionism and constructivism as accepted learning methodologies.[22]

As the computer became ubiquitous in global society, its means as a tool of creation was more and more usurped by the opportunity to push it as a mechanism of consumption. The connection of technological and pedagogical innovation in distance education was relegated to a background player as corporations and businesses emerged as key constituents in the education and technology sector. Much of this was due to the promise of scalability in the general technology sector, which stood in stark contrast to the lack of scalability of the pedagogically rich digital initiatives of the first decade of the twenty-first century. Historically this aligns with private industry as the most successful space for educational modality access in US distance education, able to engage the market and receive buy-in before educational institutions reach consensus. The result was a shift between the first and second decades of the twenty-first century from e-learning as a new way of learning in a new modality to edtech as a new modality providing educational access across the globe.[23]

With distance education receiving societal approval in part due to its foisted requirement as part of the COVID-19 pandemic response, technology gaps have received increased public attention alongside achievement gaps. Initiatives to provide learners an array of inputs such as broadband access and computing devices are presented as equity interventions that will result in beneficial outputs showcasing student success.[24] Those outputs, historically based on standardized assessment scores, are now engaging a multitude of data points based on any information that can be gathered from a computer: "demographic, behavioural and digital trace data."[25] This element of the learner analytics field identifies a substantial need for this information because it is integral to data-informed decision-making that directly relates to equity practices.[26] Learners are provided with inputs, and then equity-based objectives are measured and decisions are made based on the outputs that come from their engagement with and consumption of curricular materials.

Structuralism and Equity: A Slanted Foundation

Data-informed decision-making has become an operational buzz phrase over the last decade, in that it purports utilizing agreed-upon tools to influence important choices. However, the explosion of the attention economy over the last decade has led to technological developers to build products and engagements focused on creating a desired outcome rather than impartially observing the agency of the user.[27] As education and technology researcher Neil Selwyn has noted, "most often [learning analytics] are used to direct (if not determine) human decision-making. These systems separate teaching and learning processes into different components to model past behaviours with a view to recommending future actions. As such, learning analytics systems arguably run the risk of diminishing the ability of students and teachers to exercise judgment and expertise in the overall process."[28] Freedom of choice is often problematized for this very reason; the systems and structures supporting the perceived choice are rarely neutral, so to then pull information from that system to inform future supports leads to the perpetuation of the status quo.

This example makes structuralism an apt term for the initial problematization of edtech and DEI. Without context, structuralism can read as basic as "referring to structures," of which we can discuss educational institutions, public policy, technology corporations, and more. But within social science, structuralism is a concept wherein society and meaning are based on relationships developed through the sharing of signs consisting of concepts (the signified) and the sound image associated with the concept (the signifier). In his work on kinship,

Claude Levi-Strauss recognized that freedom of choice was problematic because it is impossible to extract the actions of humans from the social structures and systems set up around them, not only dictating actions but superimposing meaning.[29] By this definition, structures cannot exist neutrally; they are elements of their society, and the reflexivity between the abstract notion and the audio/visual cipher establishing the symbol determine the meaning. From this vantage, any software must recognize not only in development but also in use the uniqueness of its signs and symbols and how those will address and be addressed by users/learners.

Within DEI, the structuralist status quo is problematic, and too often, the foundational products and processes made available for innovation or change are feeding the system the intervention is designed to upend. Examples such as proctoring systems point out not only the inherent biases of the status quo but also fail to recognize the societal obstacles facing the populations the software is designed to support. Proctoring software is presented as an opportunity for access, allowing students to engage in assessment from anywhere they have an Internet connection while ensuring the integrity of the assessment exchange, a presentation squarely aligned with research showing that students of color disproportionately utilize online learning and thus proctoring software.[30] Facial recognition algorithms at the core of proctoring software have failed to properly identify people of color at significantly high percentages,[31] yet the software remains in operation and is required utilization for hundreds of thousands of students. Beyond the failures of these algorithms, the methods of online test proctoring cause disproportionate harm to historically marginalized populations, ranging from the abdication of user agency to doxxing of private information in a public forum.[32]

Learning analytics as an example field shares with the broader education sector idealistic intentions for their contribution to the education ecosystem, seeing opportunities to utilize newfound sources of information to better understand learners and enact mechanisms to provide change. A structuralist critique would recognize that the system is not producing objective, unbiased data independent of not only its social contexts but its development cycle from ideation to programming and distribution. This in itself is a problem, as the seeming benevolence of the field can result in errors of omission to a degree that the oversight is not isolated but rather foundational to the work of the field, which only further reinforces the inequities of the system.[33]

Solutionism and Equity: One-Way Communication

Everett Rogers's seminal work, *Diffusion of Innovations*, is a collection of failed initiatives and post-mortem analyses of why the policies and practices within its chapters failed to gain adoption. Throughout the book, Rogers identifies dozens of examples of social innovations across sociological, anthropological and psychological studies, identifying obstacles, interventions, implementations, and iterations presented to create the change needed and objective sought. The innovations presented are largely the result of scientific discovery and hard process, adaptations of existing tools and norms rather than the presentation of modern novelties. When these processes do not work out, Rogers identifies the spaces and places where policy, practice or messaging was unable to bridge the gap between historic and intended behavior change, the recognition being that the difficult part of innovation is not the intervention but the follow-through.

In 1999, Sugata Mitra began a research experiment in an impoverished area of New Delhi, India. His team carved a hole out of a wall of their headquarters and placed an English language computer terminal in the space. They then left it there, with no instructions and no expectations on how it could or should be used. The belief was that having a computer available for the curious and the inspired would lead to acts of creation and intelligence, considered in the scholarship to be an act of minimally invasive education.[34] Mitra reported considerable success in the area, as children flocked to the terminal and utilized it despite most having no knowledge of the English language. The results are legendary: Mitra's organization continued to place dozens of terminals in nearby areas, which was partly the inspiration for the book *Q&A*, which was the inspiration for the Academy Award winning movie

Slumdog Millionaire, which happened a few years before Mitra became a fixture in educational media and won the 2013 TED Prize and $1 million for his talk about his research, "Build a School in the Cloud."

The impact of Mitra's research in the following decade was practically non-existent. There were technical problems (electricity, vandalism, Internet connectivity), logistical problems (larger children crowding the devices), and pedagogical problems (the devices being used for gaming). Mass media during the year of Mitra's TED Prize largely reported on the reported successes of the project, but later media noted the obstacles of implementation and sustainability.[35] In 2013, Mitra announced internal restructuring of the research center that would spark a massive extension of the Hole-in-the-Wall Education Project (HiWEP), but there is no evidence of the continuation of HiWEP anywhere.[36] Neither the HiWEP nor the website for the restructured research center discuss HiWEP beyond 2013, and HiWEP has not been updated since 2014. In the place of celebrations of new HiWEP stations, the literature is dotted with images of empty or shuttered holes,[37] blogs and media pieces about the devices crowded by older kids to play games, and references to Mitra as a snake-oil salesman.[38]

Solutionism is a term coined by technology author Evgeny Morozov to identify the belief that problems largely have basic and objective solutions involving the introduction of technology.[39] Morzov argues that when popular opinion believes a problem can be solved with a simple introduction of technology, the focus and resources of society transition from addressing the difficulties associated with massive change and foundational realignment and instead seeks to find more examples of technologies that can be plugged into societal obstacles. In the case of HiWEP, the solution was emblematic of solutionism because the intervention required nothing more than the input. Whether HiWEP had potential or promise is immaterial because the focus of the innovation and the society celebrating it was in the moment of the solution launch, not the widespread successful adoption of the project.

Initiatives such as the 1619 Project have identified foundational obstacles people of color have found in achieving equity and justice in US society, recognizing a culture of signs and symbols developed by a group of people who actively disvalued another group. For technological innovations to be a part of a comprehensive DEI strategy, the focus of the innovation would need to be on rooting the intervention in systems and processes within our institutions and the longitudinal effort necessary for embedding. Technology may be a part of that process, but solutionism that negates the complexity of the problem or the effort required between implementation and social outcome will only exacerbate the problem.

A Future for Edtech and DEI: Constructionism and Constructivism

This chapter has taken a critical historical look at the integration of DEI within the field of edtech, problematizing general trends and highlighting examples where intentions were not aligned with objectives or cognizant of their impact. This is not uncommon in burgeoning fields; as a discipline establishes itself, it must identify its boundaries and its language of signs and symbols, signifiers and signifieds, a process that is not without obstacles. At the first symposium of cultural studies, Stuart Hall brought the conference together to discuss the growth of a discipline rooted in equity and justice, with the intention to build a foundation of scholarship for future constituents.[40] During the initial question-and-answer period, bell hooks spoke up about the placement of the microphones in the ballroom and how this seemingly benign action had in fact perpetuated a status quo of privileging ableism and dominant cultures. I mention this because it is important to recognize that although intent does not negate the impact of an action, it does provide insight into the beliefs and values of its participants. Despite the impacts of examples provided in this chapter, the intent of the vast majority of actors was and remains to improve the educational experience of learners in society.

Higher education, from its institutions and its academic guilds to its corporate partners and its public policy practitioners, has taken considerable steps to address the lack of DEI expertise within its organizations, and edtech has followed suit with staffing and mission development. At the same time, the problem of focusing entirely on inputs and outputs manifests in organizational culture contexts; woke-washing is a phenomenon where institutions embark on DEI hiring but do so without institutional engagements, proper staffing, or proper financial support.[41] Conferences and symposia act in similar manners, providing space for DEI conversation but largely without greater context or embedding within historical practices. Providing space for a conversation or a department without grounding that conversation or department in the fabric of the systems and processes can exacerbate inequalities because it fails to adjust resources or map progress.[42]

The Society of Learning Analytics Research (SoLAR) provides an example of how such a conversation can begin. Within their discipline journal, they dedicated an installment to problematize their burgeoning field, inviting noted technology critic Neil Selwyn to provide an assessment of the field as well as members of the community to think critically about the group actions in an effort to reorient potential problems before they calcified within the culture. Selwyn noted more than a dozen obstacles or areas for consideration and growth, and those elements have continued to be addressed as the society and the greater learning analytics research field grows.[43] Such proceedings are not rare in higher education, and edtech and its subgenres could benefit from dedicating journal issues, conferences and proceedings to DEI through a guided assessment process.

Part of the problem with woke-washing, however, is that without adequate mission alignment and staffing, the observations and suggestions from DEI experts lack adequate opportunity for success. The burgeoning DEI consulting industry exists to intervene when organizations recognize their DEI inefficiencies, but long-term results of such interventions are at best questionable, in no small part due to the gap between intervention and follow-through.[44] Successfully including DEI expertise within edtech would need to mirror the successful establishment of collaborative equity partners in business and general higher education, embedding the work as foundational in the same way accessibility and instructional design are considered in many institutions.[45]

One particular opportunity for institutions is to utilize their newfound offices and centers of diversity/equity/inclusion to support the construction of equity expertise within their campus climates and cultures. Unlike partners in industry and elsewhere, the ability for our institutions to build knowledge and understanding is at the core of our work. A shift of framing equity as an issue of access that is built upon compliance to an issue of culture that is built upon collaboration and communication would support administrations and governing boards to shift financial and staffing resources to the production of equity-base artifacts for the development of equity-minded environments.

Colleges such as those within the San Mateo County Community College District in California have leveraged the development of equity organizational units to develop equity expertise among its faculty and staff so they can create and perpetuate equity-minded instructional practice and academic programming. Not only has the district seen gains in retention and student success since developing programs such as the Equity Training Series,[46] but a newfound Equity Institute has been established to link the internal production of equity knowledge with external support of equity practice in local communities. Rather than finding third-party individuals outside of the ecosystem to provide training, this approach centralizes the importance of equity in the context of a knowledge-building institution.

Beyond our campuses, edtech research and organizations have grown considerably in the twenty-first century, and its discipline-related offshoots are wide and varied, in part due to the ubiquitous nature of technology in society and its impact on education. Fields such as learning analytics, as well as open education resources and educational multimedia, have grown from subcultures of existing conferences and movements into their own fully fledged fields, with their own offshoots and growth trajectories. If edtech were to invite education DEI experts into their spaces and provide time and opportunity to assess climate, suggest interventions, develop programming, and iterate on the outcomes, it could lead to the development of a new edtech subculture. Similar to the approach of building institutional knowledge with existing practitioners, if these groups were to create scaffolding and structure to support the development of equity conference tracks, journal special issues, and even addendum conferences, the opportunity for equity to more clearly be established as foundational to the mission work of these bodies could yield immediate results.

It is also incumbent upon DEI scholars and practitioners to recognize technology as more than the establishment of inputs designed to secure particular outputs. The mainstream connection of technology with solutionism permeates the manner in which edtech scholars and practitioners can engage outside their ecosystems, creating more obstacles for synergy between edtech and DEI. Here, we could benefit from the aspirational technology viewpoint of the late twentieth century as shared by G. Garrison, where tools are a conduit to connecting and creating, and human behaviors must be recognized and accounted for when designing not only the technology but the environments of its use.[47]

Conclusion

In the same way bell hooks questioned the placement of microphones in the conference hall as part of the first cultural studies symposium, we must question structural and foundational assumptions in our approach to considering the field of higher education in the wake of unprecedented change both in strategy and speed. This collection is dedicated to the *recentering* of learning, a title that presumes a time in which learning was centered positively. By utilizing this title, the editors of this collection have determined that the stated goal of this work is more aligned with a return to a past rather than a *reclaiming*, *revolutionizing*, *refreshing*, or *redistributing* of learning. If equity/access/justice is one of the key elements of this collection, then within it we must recognize two difficult facts: the structure of our institutions has not been created to foster equity, and the centered learning we again seek is at best a simulacrum or at worst a reinvention of disproportionate outcomes and opportunities but in the guise of solutionism. In terms of equity, a title such as *Reconciling Learning* would more aptly problematize the foundational assumptions of our systems with which this collection is designated to address.

Equity in higher education is inextricably linked to the COVID-19 pandemic. Within edtech, this is often seen as a matter of access; the affordances of higher education were laid bare in a global pivot to online emergency education, and the peripherals necessary for many to participate were found to be lacking. However, just several months after the near-global lockdown caused by COVID-19, the United States and much of the Western world publicly reckoned with racial injustice in the wake of numerous events and protests around the globe. The cultural catalyzing point on this phenomenon was the disparity between the death of George Floyd as presented through mass media by the Minneapolis Police Department versus bystander footage of the incident shared later through social media. When addressing phenomenological attitudes of society at the height of the pandemic, the lockdown cannot readily be abstracted from racial reckoning as seen in protests such as Black Lives Matter.

Recentering Learning has brought together some of the world's most erudite, passionate, critical, and caring scholars and practitioners in the field of educational innovation for a compendium of knowledge designed to support the field of higher education as it adjusts to more changes at greater speed than at any point in its history. Our challenge as posed by our editors was to provide our research and study to the group while also identifying the themes from their contributions, weaving the unfolding dynamic into our artifacts in real-time. From the perspective of edtech, this asynchronous collaboration proved remarkably fruitful in aligning trends and themes between individual scholarship and the broader public.

This synergy was not as successful when considering a conversation about equity, likely due to the discrepancy at the core of this chapter: a focus on access not only misses the key obstacles of equity in higher education but perpetuates a solutionistic framework for recommendations and further exploration. This is endemic in siloed research, and by identifying equity as a key component of the future of learning the objective is to engage with this courageous conversation; however, we must recognize that intention is not synonymous with outcomes, and thus this volume is a starting point that should both be celebrated for its engagement of the topic while also criticized for the engagement as listed here.

As a white, cis-normal, male edtech scholar and practitioner, my understanding of the field of diversity, equity and inclusion is limited by my prior experiences, the scholarship of my field to this point, and my unconscious biases. Although I have engaged in recognizing these obstacles, I have presented this chapter from the perspective of edtech and its intersection with DEI. There will be gaps in my analysis and understanding of the edtech and DEI relationship, and it is my intention for this chapter to help establish the connection between these two disciplines so that future chapters can more readily analyze these species and their overlap.

Notes

1. Froehle, "Accidental Meme."
2. Kuttner, "Equality Graphic You're Using."
3. Froehle, "Accidental Meme."
4. Coleman, "Educational Opportunity Study."
5. Jencks, *Inequality: a Reassessment.*
6. Bourdieu, "Cultural Reproduction."
7. E.g., Hanushek and Petersen, "Haves and Have-Nots."
8. E.g., Reardon, "Evidence and Possible Explanations."
9. Grajek, "DEI and 21st-Century"; Marcus, "How Technology Is Changing."
10. Martinez and Truong, "DEI to JEDI."
11. Veletsianos and Moe, "Sociocultural and Ideological Phenomenon."
12. Hammond et al., "Why the Term JEDI."
13. Messerli, "Horace Mann's Childhood."
14. Sleator, "Background, Blends and Blackboard."
15. Gerrity, "College-sponsored Correspondence Instruction."
16. Smith, "Television Is Not Educating."
17. Levin and Hines, "Educational Television, Fred Rogers."
18. Twigg, "Academic Productivity."
19. Cottom, *Lower Ed.*
20. Garrison, "Conferencing in Higher Education."
21. Weller, *25 Years of Edtech.*
22. Ackermann, "Piaget's Constructivism."

23. Moe, "Brief & Expansive History."
24. Wood, "Bridging the Digital Divide."
25. Francis et al., "Equity of Attainment."
26. Zalaznick, "4 Ways Learning Analytics."
27. Ferguson, "Challenges for Learning Analytics."
28. Selwyn, "Problem with Learning Analytics."
29. Levi-Strauss, "Structural Study of Myth."
30. Smith and Reeves, "SAT Math Scores."
31. Feathers, "Proctorio."
32. Barrett, "Rejecting Test Surveillance in Higher Education."
33. Williamson and Kizilcec, "Learning Analytics Dashboard Research."
34. Wilby, "Head in the Cloud."
35. Wilby, "Head in the Cloud."
36. Hole-in-the-Wall, "About HiWEP."
37. Clark, "Sugata Mitra: Slum Chic?"
38. Dellar, "Takeover in Sheep's Clothing."
39. Morozov, *To Save Everything*.
40. Hall, "Forward at Cultural Studies."
41. Dowell and Jackson, "Woke-Washing."
42. Dowell and Jackson, "Woke-Washing."
43. Selwyn, "Problem with Learning Analytics."
44. Friedersdorf, "The DEI Industry."
45. Nunes, "New Directions for Diversity."
46. Payares-Montoya, "Improving Online Courses."
47. Garrison, "Innovation in Distance Education."

Bibliography

Ackermann, Edith. "Piaget's Constructivism, Papert's Constructionism: What's the Difference?" *Future of Learning Group Publication* 5, no. 3 (January 1, 2001): 438.

Barrett, Lindsey. "Rejecting Test Surveillance in Higher Education." SSRN Scholarly Paper, February 1, 2023. https://doi.org/10.2139/ssrn.3871423.

Bourdieu, Pierre. "Cultural Reproduction and Social Reproduction." In *Power and Ideology in Education*, edited by Jerome Karabel and A. H. Halsey, 487–511. New York: Oxford University Press, 1977.

Clark, D. "Sugata Mitra: Slum Chic? 7 Reasons for Doubt." *Plan B* (blog), March 4, 2013. https://donaldclarkplanb.blogspot.com/2013/03/sugata-mitra-slum-chic-7-reasons-for.html.

Coleman, James S. "Equality of Educational Opportunity Study." Washington, DC: Inter-university Consortium for Political and Social Research, 1966. https://doi.org/10.3886/ICPSR06389.V3.

Cottom, Tressie McMillan. *Lower Ed: The Troubling Rise of for-Profit Colleges in the New Economy*. New York: The New Press, 2017.

Dellar, Hugh. "Why We Should Be Afraid of the Big Bad Wolf: Sugata Mitra and the Neoliberal Takeover in Sheep's Clothing." *Learn Jam* (blog), April 9, 2014. https://learnjam.com/why-we-should-be-afraid-of-the-big-bad-wolf-sugata-mitra-and-the-neoliberal-takeover-in-sheeps-clothing/.

Dowell, Erin, and Marlette Jackson. "'Woke-Washing' Your Company Won't Cut It." *Harvard Business Review*, July 27, 2020. https://hbr.org/2020/07/woke-washing-your-company-wont-cut-it.

Feathers, Todd. "Proctorio Is Using Racist Algorithms to Detect Faces." *Vice* (blog), April 8, 2021. https://www.vice.com/en/article/g5gxg3/proctorio-is-using-racist-algorithms-to-detect-faces.

Ferguson, Rebecca. "Ethical Challenges for Learning Analytics." *Journal of Learning Analytics* 6, no. 3 (December 13, 2019): 25–30. https://doi.org/10.18608/jla.2019.63.5.

Francis, Peter, Christine Broughan, Carly Foster, and Caroline Wilson. "Thinking Critically about Learning Analytics, Student Outcomes, and Equity of Attainment." *Assessment & Evaluation in Higher Education* 45, no. 6 (August 17, 2020): 811–821. https://doi.org/10.1080/02602938.2019.1691975.

Friedersdorf, Conor. "The DEI Industry Needs to Check Its Privilege." *The Atlantic*, May 31, 202. https://www.theatlantic.com/ideas/archive/2023/05/dei-training-initiatives-consultants-companies-skepticism/674237.

Froehle, Craig. "The Evolution of an Accidental Meme." *Medium* (blog), April 14, 2016. https://medium.com/@CRA1G/the-evolution-of-an-accidental-meme-ddc4e139e0e4.

Garrison, G. "Three Generations of Technological Innovation in Distance Education." *Distance Education* 6, no. 2 (1985): 235–241.

Gerrity, Thomas W. "College-Sponsored Correspondence Instruction in the United States: A Comparative History of Its Origin and Its Recent Development." Doctoral Dissertation, Teacher's College, Columbia University, 1976. http://pocketknowledge.tc.columbia.edu/home.php/viewfile/download/18777.

Grajek, Susan. "DEI and 21st-Century Business Strategies." *Educause Review* (blog), April 29, 2019. https://er.educause.edu/blogs/2019/4/dei-and-21st-century-business-strategies.

Hammond, J., Sara E. Brownell, Nita A. Kedharnath, Susan J. Cheng, and W. Carson Byrd. "Why the Term JEDI Is Problematic for Describing Programs That Promote Justice, Equity, Diversity and Inclusion." *Scientific American* (blog), September 23, 2021. https://www.scientificamerican.com/article/why-the-term-jedi-is-problematic-for-describing-programs-that-promote-justice-equity-diversity-and-inclusion/.

Hanushek, Eric A., Paul E. Peterson, Laura M. Talpey, and Ludger Woessmann. "The Achievement Gap Fails to Close: Half Century of Testing Shows Persistent Divide Between Haves and Have-Nots." *Education Next* 19, no. 3 (2019): 8–17.

Hall, Stuart. "Race, Culture, and Communications: Looking Backward and Forward at Cultural Studies." *Rethinking Marxism* 5, no. 1 (March 1992): 10–18. https://doi.org/10.1080/08935699208657998.

Hole-in-the-Wall. "About HIWEP." https://www.hole-in-the-wall.com/abouthiwel.html.

Jencks, Christopher. *Inequality: a Reassessment of the Effect of Family and Schooling in America.* New York: Basic Books, 1972.

Kuttner, Paul. "The Problem with That Equity vs. Equality Graphic You're Using." *Cultural Organizing* (blog), November 1, 2016. http://www.socialventurepartners.org/wp-content/uploads/2018/01/Problem-with-Equity-vs-Equality-Graphic.pdf.

Levi-Strauss, Claude. "The Structural Study of Myth." *Journal of American Folklore* 68, no. 270 (October 1955): 428–444. https://doi.org/10.2307/536768.

Levin, Robert A., and Laurie Moses Hines. "Educational Television, Fred Rogers, and the History of Education." *History of Education Quarterly* 43, no. 2 (2003): 262–275. https://doi.org/10.1111/j.1748-5959.2003.tb00123.x.

Marcus, Jon. "How Technology Is Changing the Future of Higher Education." *New York Times*, February 20, 2020. https://www.nytimes.com/2020/02/20/education/learning/education-technology.html.

Martinez, Kay, and Kimberly A. Truong. "From DEI to JEDI." *Diverse: Issues In Higher Education* (blog), April 9, 2021. https://www.diverseeducation.com/opinion/article/15109001/from-dei-to-jedi.

Messerli, Jonathan C. "Horace Mann's Childhood: Myth and Reality." *Educational Forum* 30, no. 2 (January 1966): 159–168. https://doi.org/10.1080/00131726609339664.

Moe, Rolin. "The Brief & Expansive History (and Future) of the MOOC: Why Two Divergent Models Share the Same Name." *Current Issues in Emerging Elearning* 2, no. 1 (2015):11–27.

Morozov, Evgeny. *To Save Everything, Click Here: The Folly of Technological Solutionism.* New York: Public Affairs, 2013.

Nunes, Ludmila. "New Directions for Diversity, Equity, and Inclusion in Higher Education." *Association for Psychological Science* 34 (January 6, 2021). https://www.psychologicalscience.org/observer/words-to-action.

Payares-Montoya, Daniel. "After COVID, Community Colleges Must Focus on Improving Online Courses." *Public Policy Institute of California* (blog), August 17, 2022. https://www.ppic.org/blog/after-covid-community-colleges-must-focus-on-improving-online-courses/.

Reardon, Sean. "The Widening Academic Achievement Gap between the Rich and the Poor: New Evidence and Possible Explanations." In *Whither Opportunity? Rising Inequality, Schools, and Children's Life Chances*, edited by Greg J. Duncan and Richard J. Murnane, 91–115. New York: Russell Sage Foundation, 2011.

Rogers, Everett. *Diffusion of innovations.* New York: Free Press, 1995.

Selwyn, Neil. "What's the Problem with Learning Analytics?" *Journal of Learning Analytics* 6, no. 3 (December 13, 2019): 11–19. https://doi.org/10.18608/jla.2019.63.3.

Sleator, Roy D. "The Evolution of Elearning Background, Blends and Blackboard . . ." *Science Progress* 93, no. 3 (August 2010): 319–334. https://doi.org/10.3184/003685010X12710124862922.

Smith, Ember, and Richard V. Reeves. "SAT Math Scores Mirror and Maintain Racial Inequity." *Brookings Institute* (blog), December 1, 2020. https://www.brookings.edu/blog/up-front/2020/12/01/sat-math-scores-mirror-and-maintain-racial-inequity/.

Smith, Richard W. "Media: Educational Television Is Not Educating." *Change: The Magazine of Higher Learning* 10, no. 11 (December 1978): 62–78. https://doi.org/10.1080/00091383.1978.10569565.

Twigg, Carol. "Academic Productivity: The Case for Instructional Software." Report for the Broadmoor Roundtable. Colorado Springs, CO: Educom, January 1, 1996. https://net.educause.edu/ir/library/html/nli0002.html.

Veletsianos, George, and Rolin Moe. "The Rise of Educational Technology as a Sociocultural and Ideological Phenomenon." *Educause Review*, April 10, 2017. https://er.educause.edu/articles/2017/4/the-rise-of-educational-technology-as-a-sociocultural-and-ideological-phenomenon.

Weller, Martin. *25 Years of Edtech*. Athabasca, AB, Canada: Athabasca University Press, 2020.

Wilby, Peter. "Sugata Mitra—the Professor with His Head in the Cloud." *The Guardian*, June 7, 2016. https://www.theguardian.com/education/2016/jun/07/sugata-mitra-professor-school-in-cloud.

Williamson, K., and R. Kizilcec. "Learning Analytics Dashboard Research Has Neglected Diversity, Equity and Inclusion." In *Proceedings of the Eighth ACM Conference on Learning @ Scale*, 287–290. London: Association for Computing Machinery, 2021.

Wood, Sarah. "How Colleges Are Bridging the Digital Divide." *U.S. News and World Report*, November 10, 2021. https://www.usnews.com/education/best-colleges/articles/how-colleges-are-bridging-the-digital-divide.

Zalaznick, Matt. "4 Ways Learning Analytics Lead to Equity in Higher Ed." *University Business* (blog), September 9, 2020. https://universitybusiness.com/equity-learning-analytics-college-access-outcomes.

Part IV

The Post-Pandemic University

chapter 20

The Post-Pandemic University

Critical Questions for Infrastructure, Practice, and Culture

Kathryn E. Linder, Constancio Nakuma, and Monique L. Snowden

For all industries, the COVID-19 pandemic and its resulting aftermath represented what Rita McGrath refers to as an "inflection point" or "a single moment in time when everything changes irrevocably."[1] McGrath offers a framework for how to see inflection points coming within and across various industries so that one can prepare for the pivots that they will require—and leverage the change to strengthen business foundations. Written prior to the pandemic, McGrath's framework still holds true. Unfortunately, although higher education futurists have for years forecasted the rise of online education, the need for more flexible alternative credentials, and the importance of creating equity-focused strategies and practices that support all learners, many of us were not prepared for the inflection point that the pandemic created.

There are many lessons that we can learn from our recent experiences during the pandemic and in response to many challenging national and global events. Flexible. Hybrid. Inclusive. Resilient. All of these words have been used to describe the future of higher education following the difficult events of the early 2020s. But, for some institutions, shaping this vision is easier said than done. To help higher education leaders meet this challenge, this chapter will utilize a case study of one institution's conversations about leading change to provide an opportunity for reflection and application.

Case Study

In this section, we offer a case study of how leaders at the University of Colorado Denver are engaging in conversations around infrastructure, practice, and culture in light of recent national and global events. The different sections of our case study include a series of reflective questions and recommended resources that might help you to apply what you are learning from this edited collection to your own unique institutional context. We aim for this chapter to serve as a starting point for higher education administrators, leaders, and other institutional populations in need of practical guidance for where and how to begin institutional transformations caused by irrevocable change.

Understanding and Enacting Change

When we consider the current state of higher education, we often explore what is working well for our learner populations and what is creating barriers to teaching and learning. We seek to identify areas where we can take immediate action to create positive change. However, before diving into these questions, it is important to unpack how change has previously happened at your institution. By understanding your institution's previous motivation for change, what worked well, and what caused the most challenges, you can design change initiatives that will be effective for your goals. Here are some guiding questions to consider:

- What has previously motivated change at your institution?
- What has allowed change to be successful?
- What has impeded change at your institution?
- Who is included in institutional change initiatives?
- Who has led or guided the institution's change initiatives?
- What kinds of resources have you needed to create successful change?
- What has facilitated sustainable change at your institution?

In his book *Change Leadership in Higher Education*, Jeffrey Buller notes that "while members of all organizations tend to resist change because it promises uncertainty and discomfort (at least temporarily), members of distributed organizations tend to resist change most strongly because they view what's being discarded as a part of themselves. It's no wonder that so many faculty members take proposals for change personally. They view the status quo as a key ingredient in their own identities in a way that people who 'just work here' never do."[2] Indeed, change in higher education is often seen as a form of loss. This loss may be tied to identity, traditions, or ways of being that impact operations, practices, and cultures within our institutions. Moreover, this sense of loss in higher education may be more present and debilitating than in other industries because of long-standing immutable structures in the academy that can tend to constrain change and innovation.

Buller recommends that "the key to effective change is not, for the most part, engaging in quick and resolute decision making. It derives more gradually from awareness—awareness of our own values, of what's going on all around us, of the needs of others, and of the effect our choices have on the larger world."[3] In other words, change is a constant. It is always around us, impacting our choices, values, and our positioning as institutions of higher education, but change can look different based on our unique institutional contexts, constraints, and strengths. As Monique Snowden argues, "it is neither necessary nor obligatory for higher education leaders to subjugate their institutional missions to the market," but also asks, "are and should those missions be immutable?"[4] Asking these larger questions are at the heart of understanding your institution's approach to changing societal and market forces.[5]

Infrastructural Transformations

For many higher education institutions, their infrastructures often present the most challenges to initiating, creating, and implementing change. Old technology, staffing structures, and facilities can impede efforts to be cutting edge, responsive, and nimble. Some institutions, such as our own at the University of Colorado Denver, have created change management offices, staffed with credentialed professionals who can help institutional stakeholders tackle change at scale through proven facilitation methods, best-practice research, and project management skills. As you explore what changes you might want to make at your institution to position it for the future, consider the following guiding questions:

- What feels the most behind-the-times at your institution? Where are you falling behind other institutions of higher education?
- What areas are you most afraid to change?
- What areas of your institution will not survive without changes?
- What roles might you no longer need at your institution?
- What roles do you need to fill at your institution?
- What is most important to keep in terms of your infrastructure? What's working well?
- What areas of your institution need to be completely rethought, overhauled, or revised?
- How clearly has your organization articulated its values, and how aligned is your institutional infrastructure with the organizational values?

Infrastructure changes and decisions can be driven by an institution's values. At the University of Colorado Denver, our recent (2020–2030) strategic planning initiative and its subsequent resourcing resulted in several conversations about how our infrastructure must align with our vision to be an equity-serving institution. This ongoing community discussion is impacting decisions related to our organizational design more broadly, including new leadership roles, staffing changes, and additional resources allocated to diversity, equity, and inclusion efforts occurring across our university.

Through identifying your institution's most pressing infrastructure roadblocks, you may be able to see where an infrastructural change could have broader positive impacts on practice and culture. The changes that are most needed at your institution might also highlight alignment (or misalignment) with your organizational values, mission, and vision.[6]

Promising Practices

Positioning our learners as the focal point of our institutional practices can ensure a learning-centered approach that prioritizes students. Following this, we must also begin to know our faculty and staff. If the drivers of institutional change genuinely invest in understanding the unique needs and contributions of all community members, the institutional practices to support learners and create an inclusive, welcoming college or university environment will follow that lead. As you think about your own learner populations, faculty, and staff, consider the following guiding questions:

- How would you describe your current learner population(s)?
- What characteristics do your learners have?
- What are the most pressing needs of your current learners?
- What are the most pressing needs of your future learners?
- What environments best serve your learners?
- What institutional characteristics can you foster to best serve your learners?
- How would you describe your faculty and staff populations?
- What draws people to work at your institution?
- What shared values do your employees have with your institution?
- What are the most pressing needs of your faculty and staff?
- How does your institution serve all members of your community through its practices?
- What is the alignment between your institutional practices and your institutional values?

At the University of Colorado Denver, we continue to work toward a better understanding of our learner populations. Located in the heart of downtown Denver, we serve a wide range of learners who each have a different definition of what success looks like for them. The majority of our students commute to campus for in-person classes. Over half of our students are the first generation to attend college, one-quarter are adult learners (over the age of 25), and over 40% of our students identify as persons of color. The University of Colorado Denver is an emerging Hispanic-Serving Institution (HSI), and we also identify as an Asian American and Native American Pacific Islander–Serving (AANAPISI) Institution.

Whether your institution engages in high-impact practices, universal design for learning practices, equity-serving practices, or other paradigms, it is important to place these practices in the context of your institutional values and mission. How do these practices contribute to the success of your students, faculty, and staff? What practices are holding your community members back from achieving their educational and professional goals? In our recent strategic planning process, we identified goals to become an equity-serving institution and a "best place to work" for our faculty and staff. These goals have energized our leadership and community members to comprehensively review our practices, policies, brand, and administrative procedures to (re)align them with our institutional mission and values moving forward.[7]

Cultural Shifts

As we mentioned above, at the University of Colorado Denver, we are an emerging HSI. This identity, which supports our vision to be an equity-serving institution for all learners, has spurred ongoing conversations within our community about what it means to be an HSI. How will this new status shape the institution's culture going forward? How will this new status encourage additional changes in our institution's culture moving forward? Gina Ann Garcia describes HSIs as "culturally enhancing spaces" and suggests that "providing an experience that is racially and culturally enhancing for minoritized students is a form of serving them."[8] Garcia encourages HSIs to center the experiences of racially minoritized people, while also working toward "decolonizing" our individual mindsets as well as our institutional practices and paradigms.[9]

The cultural shift toward becoming an equity-serving institution has impacted our institution's infrastructure, budget decisions, hiring plans, curricular priorities, and student services. It has caused changes that have touched every aspect of our institution. As you explore your own institutional culture, consider the following guiding questions:

- What aspects of the institutional culture are rooted in tradition?
- What aspects of the institutional culture are relatively new in forming?
- What parts of your institutional culture are overt? What parts are more tacit?
- What parts of your institutional culture need to be preserved? What parts need to be changed?
- Who decides the characteristics of your institutional culture?
- How does your institutional culture impact actions or decisions at your institution?

We have intentionally placed this discussion of cultural shifts after our discussions of infrastructure and practices because culture blends with and is experienced through these practical elements of our institution. It must be intentionally designed to achieve alignment with institutional values, but it must also be prioritized in such a way that it sets down roots that seep into all aspects of the institution. As Jeffrey Buller notes, "if you want to improve an outcome, don't spend your time thinking about the outcome itself. Spend your time improving the culture that produces the outcome."[10] We would also argue that culture grows from a constellation of outcomes that are impacted by each individual serving within an institution and each learner who is served.[11]

Planning for the Future

If anything is clear in this volume, it is that change will be constant as we look to the future. Even as our unique institutional contexts ensure that change will look different for our faculty, staff, and learners, there are several guiding questions that we can explore to prepare ourselves for what is around the corner:

- What is your long-term vision for your institution?
- What changes do you need to make now to accomplish your long-term vision?
- What do you envision your institution to look like in 10, 20, or 50 years?
- Who will be attending your institution then?

- What changes are your learners experiencing in their lives and careers now?
- What changes are your employees facing in their lives and careers now?
- What will those changes look like in the future?
- What national or global trends do you project will impact your institutional decision-making?

In *The 100-Year Life*, Lynda Gratton and Andrew Scott describe how children being born right now have a 50% or higher chance of living to be 105 years old.[12] For these children, higher education will look significantly different. They will presumably be preparing for a work life of, at minimum, 60–65 years, with retirement occurring after the age of 80. The reskilling and upskilling required for this population of learners to remain relevant will mean significant shifts, pivots, and refreshes of higher education curricula in the decades to come.

At the University of Colorado Denver, we have articulated a goal to be a "university for life" that endeavors to make higher education work for all, over the course of our students' lifetimes. This will mean creating integrated student support structures that effectively serve each of our unique populations across all digital and physical spaces. We will also need to utilize strategic program design to increase retention, shorten time to degree, and reduce student debt load. With over 50% of our undergraduate population identifying as transfer students, we continue to work toward designing clearer mechanisms for learners to "earn as they learn" through stackable credential models. Our program development pipelines prioritize relevant content, focused skill development, and impactful experiential learning that provide career-enhancing educational experiences. We are also exploring ways to acknowledge, evaluate, and award credit for students' prior learning. Importantly, we do all these things through the lens of being an equity-serving institution.[13]

Taking Action

As you have explored each of these areas, you may have a better understanding of where your institution is now and the directions where you would like it to go. You may have located infrastructural, practice-based, or cultural changes that you think are necessary to create a learner-centered, future-oriented institution of higher education. As you review your responses to previous questions, begin to consider where you most want to take action. Here are some guiding questions to consider:

- What have you learned about the changes that are needed at your institution through reading this volume?
- What areas of change or transformation do you still have questions about?
- What are your current institutional strengths that will assist you in making needed changes?
- What are your current institutional challenges that might impede your change efforts?
- Choosing one initiative area where you want to take action, what would be a helpful starting point to initiate that change conversation at your institution?
- Who is most important to involve in conversations about the changes that you want to make?
- Who are your best change initiators and leaders?
- What is one step that you can take today to launch action?

In *Theorizing the Resilience of American Higher Education*, Geoffrey Mark Cox states that "higher education must change if it is to continue to be relevant to society."[14] To be effective change agents, we must remain open to questioning our assumptions, reframing our traditional paradigms, and connecting what our institutions can offer with the goals and needs of our current and prospective learners.[15]

Conclusion

The recent experience of the pandemic as well as other national and global events in the early 2020s have tested our ability to transition into a new reality. As we have been confronted with new paradigms of adaptability, flexibility, and hybridity that are ostensibly more necessary now than ever before, we find ourselves at a point worthy of reflection. What are the assumptions that we have made about infrastructure, practice, and culture that may need to be revisited? What conventions might we need to reconsider as we move forward? What changes will best serve our learner populations now and into the future?

These questions, as well as all the reflective prompts included in this chapter, can be asked and answered by a range of participant groups within our institutions. Given the complexities of the problems that we face, leaders cannot undertake this journey alone. In addition to university leaders, we might also ask for the perspectives of academic departments, staff units such as facilities and technology support, teaching centers, learner support offices, graduate instructors, and our diverse learner populations. With such complicated questions, university leaders—operating at every level—have a clear opportunity to inclusively tackle and respond to institutional constraints and opportunities, and to bring the advancement of student learning to the core of university operations and culture.

Notes

1. McGrath, *Seeing around Corners*, 1.
2. Buller, *Guide to Academic Transformation*, 19.
3. Buller, *Guide to Academic Transformation*, 94.
4. Snowden, "Leading Through Fragmentation."
5. If you need additional resources to better understand change within the higher education environment, we recommend: Buller, *Guide to Academic Transformation*, 19; Gibbons, *Science of Organizational Change*; *Change Management*, vol. 1; *Change Management*, vol. 2.
6. If you need additional resources to better understand organizational-level transformation within the higher education environment, we recommend: Kesler and Kates, "Leading Organization Design"; Senge, *The Fifth Discipline*.
7. If you need additional resources to better understand how to learn about your student populations, we recommend: Bonner et al., *Square Pegs and Round Holes*; Gardner et al., *Equitable and Successful Postsecondary System*; McNair et al., *Becoming a Student-Ready College*; Torres et al., *Understanding the Latinx Experience*.
8. Garcia, *Becoming Hispanic-Serving Institutions*, 49.
9. Garcia, *Becoming Hispanic-Serving Institutions*, 137.
10. Buller, *Guide to Academic Transformation*, 217.

11. If you need additional resources for supporting cultural shifts, we recommend: Coyle, *Culture Code*; McHale, *Insider's Guide to Culture Change.*

12. Gratton and Scott, *100-Year Life.*

13. If you need additional resources for planning for the future, we recommend: Alexander, *Academia Next*; Davidson, *World in Flux*; Dede, *60-Year Curriculum*; Weise, *Long-Life Learning.*

14. Cox, *Changing Social and Economic Conditions*, 8.

15. If you need additional resources for supporting actions toward change, we recommend these: Hultman, *Making Change Irresistible*; Johnson, "Build an A-Team"; and W. Johnson, *Disrupt Yourself.*

Bibliography

Alexander, Bryan. *Academia Next: The Futures of Higher Education*. Baltimore: Johns Hopkins University Press, 2020.

Bonner, Fred A., Rosa M. Banda, Stella Luciana Smith, Aretha Faye Marbley, Jamie Washington, and Amelia R. Parnell. *Square Pegs and Round Holes: Alternative Approaches to Diverse College Student Development Theory*, edited by Fred A. Bonner, Rosa M. Banda, Stella Luciana Smith, and Aretha Faye Marbley. Sterling, VA: Stylus Publishing, 2021.

Buller, Jeffrey L. *Change Leadership in Higher Education A Practical Guide to Academic Transformation*. Hoboken, NJ: Wiley, 2014.

Cox, Geoffrey Mark. *Theorizing the Resilience of American Higher Education: How Colleges and Universities Adapt to Changing Social and Economic Conditions*. New York: Routledge, 2019.

Coyle, Daniel. *The Culture Code: The Secrets of Highly Successful Groups*. New York: Bantam Books, 2018.

Davidson, Cathy N. *The New Education: How to Revolutionize the University to Prepare Students for a World in Flux*. New York: Basic Books, 2017.

Dede, Christopher, and John Richards, eds. *The 60-Year Curriculum: New Models for Lifelong Learning in the Digital Economy*. New York: Routledge, 2020.

Garcia, Gina Ann. *Becoming Hispanic-Serving Institutions: Opportunities for Colleges and Universities*. Baltimore: Johns Hopkins University Press, 2019.

Gardner, John N., John. Hitt, Michael J. Rosenberg, Andrew K. Koch, and Sanford Shugart. *The Transfer Experience: A Handbook for Creating a More Equitable and Successful Postsecondary System*. Bloomfield, IN: Stylus Publishing, 2021.

Gibbons, Paul. *The Science of Organizational Change: How Leaders Set Strategy, Change Behavior, and Create an Agile Culture*. Fort Collins, CO: Phronesis Media, 2019.

Gratton, Lynda, and Andrew Scott. *The 100-Year Life: Living and Working in an Age of Longevity*. London: Bloomsbury, 2016.

HBR's 10 Must Reads on Change Management. Boston: Harvard Business Review Press, 2011.

HBR's 10 Must Reads on Change Management, vol. 2. Boston: Harvard Business Review Press, 2021.

Hultman, Ken. *Making Change Irresistible: Overcoming Resistance to Change in Your Organization*. Palo Alto, CA: Davies-Black, 1998.

Johnson, Whitney. "Build an A-Team." *Harvard Business Review*, December 14, 2018. https://hbr.org/webinar/2018/12/https-hbrwebinars-wins-net-hbr121418mweb.

Johnson, W. *Disrupt Yourself*. Boston: Harvard Business Review Press, 2020.

Kesler, Gregory, and Amy Kates. *Leading Organization Design: How to Make Organization Design Decisions to Drive the Results You Want*. Hoboken, NJ: John Wiley & Sons, 2010.

McGrath, Rita Gunther. *Seeing around Corners: How to Spot Inflection Points in Business before They Happen*. Boston: Houghton Mifflin Harcourt, 2019.

McHale, Siobhan. *The Insider's Guide to Culture Change: Creating a Workplace That Delivers, Grows, and Adapts*. New York: HarperCollins Leadership, 2020.

McNair, Tia Brown, Susan L. Albertine, Michelle Asha Cooper, Nicole L. McDonald, and Thomas Major. *Becoming a Student-Ready College: A New Culture of Leadership for Student Success*. San Francisco: Jossey-Bass, 2016.

Senge, Peter M. *The Fifth Discipline: The Art and Practice of the Learning Organization*. Rev. and updated ed. New York: Doubleday/Currency, 2006.

Snowden, Monique. "Leading through Fragmentation: Kaleidoscope Thinking and Shaking Up Patterns to Innovate." *The EvoLLLution: A Modern Campus Illumination* (blog), February 23, 2021. https://evolllution.com/revenue-streams/market_opportunities/leading-through-fragmentation-kaleidoscope-thinking-and-shaking-up-patterns-to-innovate.

Torres, Vasti, Ebelia Hernández, Sylvia Martínez, Sarita Brown, and Deborah Santiago. *Understanding the Latinx Experience: Developmental and Contextual Influences*. Sterling, VA: Stylus Publishing, 2019.

Weise, Michelle R. *Long-Life Learning: Preparing for Jobs That Don't Even Exist Yet*. Hoboken, NJ: John Wiley & Sons, 2020.

chapter 21

From COVID-19 to Climate Change

Parallels, Parables, and Possibilities for the Future of Higher Education

Bryan Alexander

I am advancing the hypothesis, as have many others, that the health crisis prepares, induces, incites us to prepare for climate change. This hypothesis still needs to be tested.

—Bruno Latour[1]

When SARS-CoV-2 spread rapidly around the world in early 2020, it collided with the enormous challenge of climate change. For some, it offered a dress rehearsal for how civilization could respond to a complex and global crisis. For others, the pandemic drew precious attention away from a building climate action consensus, one crisis eclipsing the other, in David Wallace-Wells's words: "a white-noise machine, drowning out what would be, in any other year, the unmistakable signal of a climate emergency."[2] For many, COVID-19 was a terrible blow, a powerful drain that exhausted human capacity, perhaps reducing our ability to take challenging steps concerning global warming. It is my contention that the pandemic experience gives us insights into how higher education might grapple with the unfolding climate crisis.

Connecting and comparing these two global crises can be daunting, even risky. Each event was and is both extensive and deep, structured and contoured by technical and cultural complexity. Both events are also sources of psychological dread and trauma, due to the real damage done to humanity from sickness and death to displacement and immiseration. In connecting the two analytically, I want to make clear that I am fully mindful of the terrible costs to human bodies. We should not lose sight of human realities when thinking at the macro level.

We can begin that analytical exploration by discussing the question of causal linkages between global warming and pandemics. We know that climate change can drive the spread of diseases into new domains by rearranging parts of the ecosystem. For example, rising temperatures change animals' migratory habits, then yield secondary effects. The latest Intergovernmental Panel on Climate Change (IPCC) report summarizes the latest research: "In all regions increases in extreme heat events have resulted in human mortality and morbidity (*very high confidence*). The occurrence of climate-related food-borne and water-borne diseases (*very high confidence*) and the incidence of vector-borne diseases (*high confidence*) have increased."[3]

This pandemic–climate connection does *not*, however, directly function for SARS-CoV-2 because there does not seem to be a direct causal arrow between climate change and COVID-19. According to the World Health Organization (WHO), "There is no evidence of a direct connection between climate change and the emergence or transmission of COVID-19 disease."[4] That said, the WHO adds that climate change can make COVID worse: "climate change may indirectly affect the COVID-19 response, as it undermines environmental determinants of health, and places additional stress on health systems." This is an important point, identifying a second form of pandemic–climate interactions beyond directly spreading disease. Global warming can reduce public health and medical care responses to current and emerging diseases. Further, the unequal and unjust ways the climate crisis impacts different members of humanity can further accentuate inequities in pandemic response. These three forms by which climate can worsen public health emergencies bear strongly on institutions of higher education, as they suggest our population's increased vulnerability to pandemics, as well as increasing challenges in trying to care for academics and in doing so justly.

A second close connection between climate and COVID-19 appeared in early 2020 when many economic systems drastically cut back operations. The macroeconomic impacts were immediately expressed in the form of recession and short-lived depression, of course, but I raise the point here to identify another impact: the sudden reduction of carbon dioxide emissions as industry and transportation slowed.[5] Famously, skies above smog-swaddled cities like Beijing and Los Angeles cleared, and humanity in developed nations received an extraordinary glimpse of pre-industrial environments. For the first time absent war or economic collapse, we deliberately paused transmitting CO_2 into the atmosphere. It was proof of concept for a key argument within the climate movement that we could choose to reduce emissions. It was not done for climate reasons, of course, but the capacity was revealed.

That capacity momentarily opened the way for further potential transformations. As Li Edelkoort observed at the time: "The virus will slow down everything. . . . We will see an arrest in the making of consumer goods. That is terrible and wonderful because we need to stop producing at such a pace. We need to change our behavior to save the environment. It's almost as if the virus is an amazing grace for the planet."[6] One might observe that this forecast proved wrong because neoliberal economies resumed operation. Indeed, I argue that the resumption of pre-COVID-19 economic activities even in the midst of the pandemic demonstrated the extent to which neoliberalism necropolitically accepts certain levels of death in order to proceed. I will return to this point below. For now, I want to emphasize this brief moment of revealed possibility, when the pandemic demonstrated our ability to suspend CO_2 emissions if we chose to. That may afford a glimpse of potential changes, when we might voluntarily adjust industrial output. Edelkoort's insight adds the possibility of further economic transformations in the future.

Higher education has a particularly fraught connection to one aspect of that emissions pause. Air travel contributes more than its share of CO_2, and the early 2020 lockdowns greatly reduced jet aircraft activity. As with the rest of the industrial economy, air travel resumed, but the pause offered an instance of civilization voluntarily flying less.

Academics depend on jet-powered flight for a range of activities, such as travel to conferences, research sites, job interviews, campus visits, sports events, and meetings. The pandemic demonstrated that we could shift some, even many of those functions online, especially through live video. Looking ahead, we have the option of conducting such a digital migration again, but for climate crisis reasons. Several academic conferences have already made efforts in this direction by shunting paper presentations online and making in-person events local, which required less travel.

This may be a difficult shift for academics to make. We often see air travel as vital to our work. It helps us maintain and deepen professional social networks, especially for people new to their careers. Some research requires onsite presence if the materials (archives, environmental sites) have not been digitized. There are other advantages to academic travel, such as the emotional rewards of reconnecting with peers and friends, not to mention getting away from one's institution for a break. Some perceive other disadvantages to digital travel substitutes, including difficulties in making those emotional connections or serendipitous conversations in bars or elevators. Speaking from experience, I have heard many faculty and staff passionately defend their air travel practices for these reasons. Looking ahead, we may anticipate institutional struggles over jet flights as we weigh the preceding benefits and problems against the climate crisis.

A third direct COVID-19–climate connection appears in terms of campus emergency planning and operations. The pandemic placed many institutions on an emergency footing, involving contingency plans, pandemic committees, negotiations around faculty governance, and rebudgeting. Community–campus relations also adjusted as infections crossed local borders, and relationships were renegotiated. Generally, we all worked and lived through a crisis, learning coping skills and habits. If we respect and retain them, those skills and habits may prove useful in the decades to come as global warming drives a variety of emergencies into academic precincts. Disaster planning, a capacity exercised unevenly during the COVID-19 experience, may become a higher institutional priority. Sadly, the experience of disaster can better prepare survivors for the next stressor, as some nations who experienced SARS were to an extent well suited to react to COVID-19.[7]

We can now shift from direct COVID-19–climate connections to ways by which experiencing one augurs ways we may respond to the other. One such parallel involves a sociological response to disaster in diachronic time. The accumulation of witnessed pain and suffering can gradually shift our understanding of what counts as noteworthy outrage and what we deem to be the ordinary friction of daily life. Literary accounts of historical plagues demonstrate this, as people become inured to illness, injury, and death as weeks, then months, pass. More recent accounts describe that social process in terms of shifting baselines. In George Loewenstein's words: "There is a tremendous amount of research showing that we tend to adapt to circumstances if they are constant over time, even if they are gradually worsening. . . . Fear tends to diminish over time when a risk remains constant. . . . You can only respond for so long. After a while, it recedes to the background, seemingly no matter how bad it is."[8]

In the first two years of COVID-19, US journalists noted death toll milestones of 100,000, then 200,000. Yet crossing the 1.1 million threshold received no such commemoration. This behavioral shift seems likely to occur with climate devastation, as damages incrementally rise over time. Each story of a flooded city or continental fire can become a media spectacle, in the situationist sense, only to be succeeded by unrelated events. Such shifting baselines, such acculturation of damage, may reduce human willingness to take climate action. Put another way, if we see something as extraordinary, we might respond with extraordinary measures; ordinary challenges will only merit ordinary responses. College and university leaders and academic communities may similarly deem climate action a low priority if we become inured to the accumulation of disasters.

A related point to the preceding is the potential for politicizing climate science. The first three years of COVID-19 offered many examples of different actors urgently casting medical science and public health in various political terms. National leaders, social media influencers, political factions, religious representatives, captains of industry joined medical professionals in arguing for political interpretations of pandemic data and policy. This sometimes happened with blurry inconsistency or ambiguity, as opinion leaders reversed course or redefined positions into new frameworks, sometimes in response to changes in pandemic reality. We also witnessed the reverse, whereby political actors used their programs and ideology to define health policy. Depending on one's political stance, different public data streams became unreliable. Further, resentment of scholarly elites has grown, with a disturbing number of people denying the relevance of academic research.

Clearly, it requires no forecasting ability to see potential politicization of climate science, because that is already occurring. Climate-denying politicians across the global right have used all kinds of ideological arguments to oppose climate action. In their views, climate mitigation is anti-business, limits personal freedom, shuts down technological progress, or is a ploy by presumably undeserving nations for more funds. Some reactionaries link even climate adaptation with racist views, although the nature of that linkage can vary.[9] Progressives have to some extent already welded climate action in various forms to their political platforms. As the climate crisis unfolds over the next decades, it seems prudent to expect our understanding of it, and our reactions to it, will occur across very political terrain.

This presents a series of challenges to academics. To begin with, there is the likelihood of political threats to faculty, as well as staff and students, who work on climate issues. We have recent historical evidence in the example of ClimateGate (2009), when hacked emails between global warming scientists appeared in time to discredit a major conference. We also have examples of local governments trying to control researchers' speech about the climate crisis. Any academic planning to work in this field will run some risk of being targeted politically, which poses choices for individuals and institutions in terms of security and support.

Furthermore, to the extent that climate pseudo-science and misinformation spreads through media, some academics may feel compelled to oppose it through public scholarship. Moreover, the perception that global warming is a deeply politicized topic may reduce other academics' desire to engage, at least publicly. This can, in turn, yield academic institutions where arguments over climate science and its implications become part of campus political struggles.

Those politics may tend to the national and local if the pandemic experience can continue to serve as a precedent. Although we saw some excellent examples of international collaboration around the world, and the WHO sought to organize global intelligence and action, we also experienced national governments acting in isolation from each other. Political leaders who denied COVID-19 was a serious disease, such as Brazil's Jair Bolsonaro, withdrew their countries from international public health work. Other nations celebrated and promulgated their own vaccines, including Russia, China, Britain, and the United States. The United States saw its national pandemic strategy struggle under the presidential administration of Donald Trump, with most effective action taking place at state, county, and city levels. Bruno Latour criticized this approach early in the pandemic:

> What is more worrying is that we do not see how that state would prepare the move from the one crisis to the next. In the health crisis, the administration has the very classic educational role and its authority coincides perfectly with the old national borders—the archaism of the sudden return to European borders is painful proof of this. In the case of ecological change, the relationship is reversed: it is the administration that must learn from a multiform people, on multiple scales, what will be the territories upon which people are trying to survive in many new ways as they seek to escape from globalized production. The present state would be completely incapable of dictating measures from above. If in the health crisis, it is the brave people who must relearn to wash their hands and cough into their elbows as they did in primary school, in the case of the ecological mutation, it is the state that finds itself in a learning situation.[10]

We have seen similar signs of how humanity might grapple with the climate crisis. Although the problem is self-evidently global, based on Earth systems without respect to national boundaries, most decisions are made at the national level. Each Congress of the Parties (COP) gathering has sought to redefine commitments and policies from individual nations, one after the other. The United Nations is not a major climate player. No supranational entity has surfaced so far. There is no equivalent binding agreement along the lines of the Montreal Protocol, which famously addressed ozone-layer depletion. Looking ahead, Geoff Mann and Joel Wainwright offer several potential scenarios for international work. In one of them, climate-denying states refuse to act, although they do so informally. In another scenario, neoliberal states organize to some extent. In a third, the Chinese government leads allied states in a kind of neo-Maoist and green One Belt, One Road.[11] Each of these scenarios presents challenges for academics. What governmental policies and inducements should we anticipate, especially when it comes to supporting research and teaching?

I would like to conclude by making several further observations and arguments. This parallel we have explored between two great world crises can be overstated. It falls apart on sufficient contact with reality, as do all analogies. To return to Latour, my source for this comparison:

> [I]n the health crisis, it may be true that humans as a whole are "fighting" against viruses—even if they have no interest in us and go their way from throat to throat killing us without meaning to. The situation is tragically reversed in ecological change: this time, the pathogen whose terrible virulence has changed the living conditions of all the inhabitants of the planet is not the virus at all, it is humanity![12]

I think each situation is more complicated than that, as during the height of the pandemic we struggled both with an alien life form (the virus) as well as the behaviors of others (masking, vaccine "hesitancy," and so on). Meanwhile, while humanity caused and continues to cause the climate crisis, we must grapple with its many nonhuman elements, from meteorological systems to changing animal behavior. Yet Latour's point, if considered as one of emphasis, does show the parallel's limits.

As a futurist, I am trained in seeing the full range of potential futures, from the very negative to the very positive, depending on a given situation. Some lessons drawn from COVID-19 appear optimistic, or at least point in the direction of hope. At several points, the pandemic represented a conceptual break in daily life and neoliberalism. The suspension of carbon emissions was one such radical moment. The desire to address racial inequalities offered a similar shift. Arundhati Roy best captured this potential, I think, in an essay that concludes with these exhilarating lines:

> Historically, pandemics have forced humans to break with the past and imagine their world anew. This one is no different. It is a portal, a gateway between one world and the next.
>
> We can choose to walk through it, dragging the carcasses of our prejudice and hatred, our avarice, our data banks and dead ideas, our dead rivers and smoky skies behind us. Or we can walk through lightly, with little luggage, ready to imagine another world. And ready to fight for it.[13]

I argue that the climate crisis presents a similar portal to possibilities. Already, there is a body of literature and a growing politics around how to rethink human civilization in light of how we have heated the planet. In economics, for example, we now see schools of thought which vie with received market economies. No-growth economics urges us to suspend the practice of ever-rising gross domestic product, while degrowth calls on us to shrink not only our carbon, but our economic footprint upon the Earth. In political economy and political science, there are new critiques of liberalism and individualism, with both placed in the dock as responsible for the growing crisis. Religion and indigenous studies offer ways to rethink humanity as supreme ruler of the Earth system, a rethinking perhaps accentuated by the bitter lessons a virus just taught.

I have described these in academic terms, because the academy is where they are rooted, and universities may become the world's great source of innovation as this century progresses. Across the disciplines we teach, research, and develop knowledge and practice for the Anthropocene. We may apply those ideas to our own practices, rethinking and redesigning everything from academic travel to assessment, campus energy to computation, our roles as public intellectuals and community partners. Through such praxis, colleges and universities may nurture the ideas which enable humanity to survive, or even thrive through the next generations of climate crisis.

But we must bear in mind alternative futures. I have noted our apparent willingness to accept a certain amount of COVID-19-caused human suffering and death in order for ordinary life to continue functioning (minus some participants). We may experience—and enable—a similar attitude as the climate crisis gradually worsens. As Britt Wray wonders, we may become even more callous about human suffering as global warming sets in:

> It was deeply frustrating to watch the world acknowledge the Grim Reaper when he arrived in viral form but completely ignore his presence in the changing physics all around us. The message the coronavirus pandemic seemed to be sending was: We'll only deal with the climate crisis when it starts killing the people we love, but even then, we still won't agree about the legitimacy of the threat, and we'll be ready to sacrifice a lot - old people, poor people, racial minorities. Our leaders will say we're all in this together when they know that's really a lie.[14]

How much of this necropolitics will we agree to uphold, either actively or passively? My negative forecast is that we will be able to move the goalposts, especially if disasters are sufficiently mediated to remove active personal connection, as noted earlier. Like the famous boiled frog parable, we have the capacity to think ourselves into inaction, and to rationalize the mounting dangers.

My hope and final argument is that the global academic community has an alternative capacity. We have enormous intellectual strengths and the unusual social situation to both build on and transmit them. We have demonstrated immense creativity. Perhaps the COVID-19 experience cracked open the present world a little, letting some light in, as Leonard Cohen wrote.[15] The climate crisis gives us the opportunity for far more illumination.

Notes

1. Latour, "Is This a Dress Rehearsal?"
2. Wallace-Wells, "What Climate Alarm"; Mealy, "To Halt Climate Change."
3. IPCC, "Synthesis Report."

4. World Health Organization, "Coronavirus Disease "(COVID-19)"; Harvard T.H. Chan School of Public Health, "Coronavirus, Climate Change"
5. Le Quéré et al., "Temporary Reduction."
6. Quito, "Design Trends Forecaster."
7. Sharma, "Disaster Preparedness."
8. Roberts, "Scariest Thing."
9. Malm, *White Skin, Black Fuel.*
10. Latour, "Is This a Dress Rehearsal?"
11. Wainwright and Mann, *Climate Leviathan.*
12. Latour, "Is This a Dress Rehearsal?"
13. Roy, "Arundhati Roy: 'The Pandemic.'"
14. Wray, *Generation Dread*, 68.
15. Cohen, "Anthem."

Bibliography

Cohen, Leonard. "Anthem." New York: Columbia Records, 1982.

Harvard T.H. Chan School of Public Health. "Coronavirus, Climate Change, and the Environment. A Conversation on COVID-19 with Dr. Aaron Bernstein, Director of Harvard Chan C-CHANGE," May 19, 2020. https://www.hsph.harvard.edu/c-change/subtopics/coronavirus-and-climate-change.

Intergovernmental Panel on Climate Change (IPCC). "Synthesis Report of the IPCC Sixth Assessment Report (AR6)." Summary for Policymakers, March 2023. https://report.ipcc.ch/ar6syr/pdf/IPCC_AR6_SYR_SPM.pdf.

Latour, Bruno. "Is This a Dress Rehearsal?" *Critical Inquiry* (blog), March 26, 2020. https://critinq.wordpress.com/2020/03/26/is-this-a-dress-rehearsal.

Le Quéré, Corinne, Robert B. Jackson, Matthew W. Jones, Adam J. P. Smith, Sam Abernethy, Robbie M. Andrew, Anthony J. De-Gol, et al. "Temporary Reduction in Daily Global CO_2 Emissions during the COVID-19 Forced Confinement." *Nature Climate Change* 10, no. 7 (July 2020): 647–653. https://doi.org/10.1038/s41558-020-0797-x.

Malm, Andreas. *White Skin, Black Fuel: On the Danger of Fossil Fascism*. London: Verso, 2021.

Mealy, Dominic. "To Halt Climate Change, We Need an Ecological Leninism." *Jacobin*, June 15, 2020. https://jacobin.com/2020/06/andreas-malm-coronavirus-covid-climate-change.

Quito, Anne. "A Design Trends Forecaster Calls the Coronavirus 'an Amazing Grace for the Planet.'" Quartz, March 5, 2020. https://qz.com/1812670/a-design-trends-forecaster-calls-the-coronavirus-an-amazing-grace-for-the-planet.

Roberts, David. "The Scariest Thing about Global Warming (and Covid-19)." *Vox*, July 7, 2020. https://www.vox.com/energy-and-environment/2020/7/7/21311027/covid-19-climate-change-global-warming-shifting-baselines.

Roy, Arundhati. "Arundhati Roy: 'The Pandemic Is a Portal.'" *Financial Times*, April 3, 2020. https://www.ft.com/content/10d8f5e8-74eb-11ea-95fe-fcd274e920ca.

Sharma, Yojana. "Disaster Preparedness Would Improve HE Pandemic Response." *University World News*, July 18, 2020. https://www.universityworldnews.com/post.php?story=20200715113545432.

Wainwright, Joel, and Geoff Mann. *Climate Leviathan: A Political Theory of Our Planetary Future*. London: Verso, 2018.

Wallace-Wells, David. "What Climate Alarm Has Already Achieved." *New York Intelligencer*, August 14, 2020. https://nymag.com/intelligencer/2020/08/what-climate-alarm-has-already-achieved.html.

World Health Organization. "Coronavirus Disease (COVID-19): Climate Change." World Health Organization, April 22, 2020. https://www.who.int/news-room/questions-and-answers/item/coronavirus-disease-covid-19-climate-change.

Wray, Britt. *Generation Dread: Finding Purpose in an Age of Climate Crisis*. Toronto: Alfred A. Knopf Canada, 2022.

chapter 22

The New Experimental College

Elliott Visconsi

All their minds transfigured so together,
More witnesseth than fancy's images
And grows to something of great constancy

—Hippolyta, describing the young lovers,
A Midsummer Night's Dream, 5.1.25–27

The art of democracy is the art of thinking independently together.

—Alexander Meiklejohn,
Teachers and Controversial Questions (1938).

Act 1. Our Experimental Winter

A Midsummer Night's Dream begins by launching an education. Young Hermia, frustrated in her desire to marry boyfriend Lysander (who favors this plan), is taught to obey or face punishment. None other than the speaking law himself—Duke Theseus of Athens—compels her obedience to her father's will and more broadly requires her and Lysander to align their behaviors with the epistemic authority of the City and its traditions. The unbending command to the curious young lovers prompts them to flee that night into the nearby forest where hijinks ensue, inversions and subversions unfold, experiments are made and unmade, and illuminations disorder their understanding and turn their worlds upside down. Freed from the staid constraints of obedience, in the moonlit forest, the young lovers are imbued with greater knowledge, deeper illumination, richer curiosity, and matured desire—having grown and stretched their minds through the experience. This newly acquired knowledge is given purpose by their regenerative return to the city and to ordered social life, a return solemnized and celebrated through marriage. In *Dream*, as in other Shakespearean comedies, the mulish misjudgments of parental authority create obstacles from which the younger generation flee, entering an alternative summer world of chaotic discovery, subversion, and illumination that prompts their growth and from which they return to be fully integrated into social life, often with their autonomy vindicated and the parents/authorities corrected. The young lovers' marriage celebrates their reintegration into existing social life and the triumph of desire, but also signals broad optimism about the future by gesturing toward posterity.

At first glance, seeing the underlying archetypal structure of Shakespearean comedy as a fable of education might seem strained. But the structure of comedy provides a useful overlay for imagining educational reform that is subversive without being iconoclastic, audaciously experimental without promoting a scorched-earth rebellion. Existential threats to democracy, knowledge institutions, and even human thriving are real and not diminishing. Our Athenian citadels of authority and expertise need the exuberant individual agency of daring, uncertain experimentation in the forest; we also need to welcome that imaginative energy back into our institutions for renewal that looks optimistically toward the future.

US higher education is in the icy grip of an "experimental winter." Our citadels of epistemic authority are, in the main, undersupplied with the subversive energies and integrative turbulence of audacious experimentation. Put another way, our colleges and universities could use the illumination and regeneration that follows from the productive energies and creative inversions of a summer night's flight into the forest (and back). The reasons for the persistence of our collective "experimental winter" have been thoroughly served by commentators expanding on the value proposition of higher education (degree attainment leads to economic opportunity), the contributions of the modern multiversity to regional economic prosperity, the transformational breakthroughs of science in technology now in everyday use, the university's opportunity to drive inclusion, pluralism, and racial justice, the enduring value of liberal education, or the imperative to increase access and reduce costs to students and their families while supporting a vast and costly array of increasingly complex core functions. With such multifarious aims—not to mention the political revivification of an anti-intellectual tradition that sees knowledge institutions and their professional practitioners as inherently suspicious—it is no surprise that our collective appetite for educational experimentation has diminished. What scope remains for trials that might fail? Or for experiments that might not make the cut when the value engineers dig in?

Alternative futures for higher education abound. Reformist impulses are many; the path of reform usually leads through undergraduate education.[1] If higher education is to survive the coming artificial-intelligence/Web3/robot apocalypse, for Northeastern President Joseph Aoun, a redesign of undergraduate education is urgent: The new model ought to "nurture our species' unique traits of creativity and flexibility . . . [preparing] students to compete in a labor market in which brilliant machines work alongside human professionals." Aoun mints the neologism "humanics" to describe his preferred blend of literacies (e.g., skills for navigating technology, data, and sociocultural contexts, and interpreting complex systems) and cognitive capacities (e.g., mindsets for creative problem-solving including systems thinking and cultural agility).[2] The dismal neoliberalism of this vision (prepare to outcompete cheap robot labor!) hides a timely rearticulation of undergraduate priorities.

In *What Universities Owe Democracy*, Johns Hopkins University's president Ronald Daniels outlines a bundle of reformist imperatives for higher education directly aligned with the stewardship of liberal democracy.[3] Liberal democracy hopes to mediate among irreconcilable conceptions of the good and proposes to "care for individual autonomy and dignity" through practices of deliberation and self-governance, tolerance, and freedom, and "the free flow of information and ideas."[4] For Daniels, the university is critical to securing democracy under threat and is deeply shaped by many of these core commitments—"the fates of liberal democracy and higher education," he writes, "are deeply, inexorably intertwined."[5] The obligations of universities to democracy can be partially fulfilled through structural reforms that model purposive pluralism, promote true equity of access, educate for democratic citizenship, and check power with new knowledge.

Aoun and Daniels urge us to avoid the brittleness and inertia that leads to institutional drift and the abdication of our obligations to students, faculty, staff, and the public good. Taken together, their reforms might provide a blueprint for optimism—a stronger institutional obligation to democratic norms and practices, skills, and capacities more aligned with the needs of the present than of the past, and more generosity of institutional design. However, both Aoun and Daniels limit their implementation plans to institutional fine-tuning. Put another way, they are insufficiently audacious, insufficiently experimental, and perhaps overly directive. This essay journeys into the subversive forest of educational experimentation, through an historical illustration that sets up a series of actionable proposals aligned with the opportunities and limitations of the digital age. In the process, I hope to discover some potential experiments that might nurture democratic pluralism and individual dignity and cultivate the creation, stewardship, and sharing of knowledge for our common thriving and perhaps our survival.

Act 2. A Noteworthy Triumph of the Academic Mind over Academic Machinery

What might it look like in the digital age to channel and update the experimental energies of the progressive era? In this earlier winter of discontent, college and university life was, for reform-minded critics, overly focused on social life and athletics in undergraduate education, notable for poor teaching via tedious lectures and the quasi-Fordist insertion of practical skills into students. It was hamstrung by overmighty trustees, and dominated by class privilege and extensive exclusion on the basis of race, gender, and class. Educational experiments abounded in the 1920s, some fueled by a then-radical reorientation of the purpose and experience of learning as directed toward cultivating individual agency, freedom of inquiry, and an appeal to the common good. Not coincidentally, these years also witness the rapid rise of industrial mass media and the manipulation of public opinion through propaganda and advertising, the legal entrenchment of capacious corporate authority, the development of modern counter-majoritarian free speech doctrine in the United States, and the growth of fascist and totalitarian political movements.

I'd like to consider the Experimental College offered at the University of Wisconsin between 1927 and 1931 and designed by the great First Amendment scholar and progressive educator Alexander Meiklejohn as a prompt to help illustrate principles and approaches and questions worth considering as higher education steers towards an uncertain future.[6] Meiklejohn ran his experimental venture during an historical moment that features crude parallels to the 2020s—the hegemony of mass media, the flourishing of nativist fascism, thriving anti-intellectualism, and in some quarters, a loss of confidence in the capacity of the people to withstand concentrated power sufficiently in order to participate in democratic self-government.[7]

Sweeping progressive reform of undergraduate education is a theme Alexander Meiklejohn first sounded at Amherst College, where his presidency led to soaring gains in intellectual engagement and also heavy resistance from entrenched interests in the faculty, trustees, and alumni. As elaborated in his 1923 book *Freedom and the College*, Meiklejohn proposed scholarly disinterestedness and objective expertise fused with institutional independence as the *sine qua non* of the liberal college. It is a place, he writes, "in which the human mind is seeking deliverance from its bonds—the bonds of partial knowledge and self-interest."[8] Freedom of the college could be achieved through disentanglement from special pleading, through cultivated impartiality on matters of controversy, and by refusing obeisance to the will of external interests and motivated benefactors with unexalted intentions.[9]

No dogmas or doctrines would be free from critique under Meiklejohn's regime; even when a college maintained a "partial interest" such as special pleading for the teachings of its religious confession, it must encounter all ideas and doctrines with generosity.[10] Such essential independence is for Meiklejohn motivated by the institution's obligations to the public:

> Unless a people find, in colleges or elsewhere, some place of criticism, some place where truth is sought, where thought is free, there is no hope for freedom of the people. . . . How shall we let them know that we are building knowledge for their use, that we are serving their every interest that they have . . . that we will listen to every thought they bring and yet will weigh and value them with thoughts of other men in mind?[11]

Building knowledge for public use is accompanied in Meiklejohn's theory by an expansive vision of who might be suited to a liberal education. There is not much merit in polishing the well-cultivated and privileged. Rejecting the "aristocratic division of people into two classes," Meiklejohn welcomed "the general run of students" into a liberal education. "Our primary task," he wrote, "is taking all types of young people and discovering their powers."[12] Such an expansive vision of human potential—of confidence in the intellectual capacities of all learners—is later expressed in Meiklejohn's adult and workers' education programs in San Francisco.[13] More immediately, Meiklejohn's theories of integrated liberal education in the service of individual freedom and democratic flourishing would be planted in the fertile soil of Madison, Wisconsin.

"What we must do is give the students a chance to learn for themselves," Meiklejohn remarked within his implementation plans for his new Midwestern venture.[14] To achieve this end, Meiklejohn and his many progressive admirers had persuaded the University of Wisconsin (UW) to welcome an Experimental College to open on campus in the fall of 1927. As he wrote in the *New York Times*, the enthusiastic support of the Madison faculty "represents the triumph of the academic mind over academic machinery. It makes possible a free experiment—that is to say, a real experiment. It authorizes a group of teachers to proceed without hindrance to see what they can do 'to formulate and to test under experimental conditions suggestions for the improvement of methods of teaching, the content of study, and the determining conditions of undergraduate liberal education.'"[15] The principle of discovery through experimentation is tied to the humility of the venture. Meiklejohn and his fellow travelers sought to test a curriculum they believed would model liberal education; it could only be an honest attempt to develop intelligence and nurture freedom when everyone recognized the uncertainty of the outcomes, developed the experiment with feedback and collaboration, and undertook to report on progress in disinterested fashion. The experimental thesis is fundamental to Meiklejohn's project; the College does not yet know the better way to learn and teach but wishes to see if it might be discovered through collective inquiry.

At the heart of Meiklejohn's plan for the Experimental College at Wisconsin lay the desire to cultivate the individual agency of students by providing them an integrative common curriculum pursued in partnership with their expert advisers (the faculty) and as part of a residential community on the Madison campus. Meiklejohn set out to test the assumption that his model of integrative study during the first and second years of college would empower liberal education and create the capacities necessary for democratic self-government and individual freedom in a milieu where such attributes were growing increasingly unwelcome. Such an experiment in collective inquiry must however have a common direction of travel—a "sameness of obligation . . . and a certain compelling, dominant, central motive, which every member of the community takes as his own."[16] The Experimental College, moreover, must be aligned with the challenges of the moment:

> The world into which young Americans are now entering will demand of them something far more important than the technical skill they so easily acquire. It will demand of cultivation of the powers of the mind; breadth and depth of acquaintance with available knowledge of the world; shrewdness of judgment and sensitiveness of appreciation of the values and meanings that human living is intended to serve; sympathetic understanding of other men, whatever their race, creed or social status.[17]

The sociopolitical occasion calls for an audacious experiment to better cultivate intellectual growth, individual agency, and collective responsibility. Developing general intelligence, individual initiative and freedom in students is far from idle academic navel-gazing. The Experimental College is "deliberately, persistently practical," for it pursues "a scheme of individual and group living, which will meet the human demands for beauty, strength, justice, generosity, and the like."[18] The time has been put out of joint by mass movements and mass persuasion that are, for Meiklejohn, increasing unfreedom—and underscoring the urgency of educational reform in the service of democracy. "The teachers of a democracy," he writes, "must be its critics, [and in] the training of its youth they must fight an unending battle against the blindly hostile forces of its popular drift."[19]

So much for the theory; what form did Meiklejohn's journey into the experimental forest of actually take? Some of the core features are by now routine—the Experimental College was a living-learning residential community ensconced in UW's Adams Hall (and as required by the University housing policy, it was male only—a fact Meiklejohn lamented). In place of faculty, the College featured "advisers," or professors with the breadth to teach across the curriculum, the appetite for integrative pursuit of freedom and intellect, and a hunger to cultivate learning through individual discussion and feedback for students of any background or capacity whatsoever.[20] The two-year common course of study was dominated by a humanistic curriculum—Meiklejohn's "guinea pigs" shared common texts, cadences, assignments, and vocabularies as they studied history, philosophy, literature, economic and social institutions, and (to a degree) physical sciences.

The collective imagination was trained on two representative civilizations—fifth century Athens and nineteenth century United States. The premise of this integrative cross-disciplinary study was to confront the large problems the civilization faced and to witness the collective "intelligence at work upon its situation."[21] Stacking two civilizations up was designed as a pedagogical catalyst of "minds stirred to action" rather than a presentation of specific facts, with the overall goal of preparing students to form a comprehensive "scheme of reference for . . . human living" in a democracy—that is, liberal intelligence.

The third civilization to be studied was closer to home—quite literally. A signature of the Experimental College was the Regional Study.

Inspired by the groundbreaking *Middletown*, Robert Lynd and Helen Merrell Lynd's 1929 study of a small midwestern city, Meiklejohn's students would apply their analytical frameworks to a local setting, ideally their "home village or town or city or county," which they would write of as an "episode in human civilization."[22] Stretching over eight months and requiring in-person fieldwork, the assignment was to subject a specific locality to a "detailed and systematic investigation" of the institutions, social habits, economic features, histories and cultural traditions (including those of indigenous precursors), natural geography and physical infrastructure, and its manners, customs, and beliefs.[23] The regional study, Meiklejohn wrote in retrospect, was of the highest educational value, for it combined the methods of integrative analysis developed earlier with personally engaging fieldwork as for example in the student's intentional conversations with "his parents, with the minister, the keeper of town or county records, the librarian and school principal, the antiquarian, the leading merchants, the teller of town stories."[24]

The Experimental College was organized around progressive pedagogy, with discussion given pride of place and conducted in small groups and within individual conferences between advisor and student. The overt goal of pedagogy was to inspire in "the student the sense of his primary responsibility for the making of his own education."[25] Intensive feedback (here called criticism) was incumbent upon the advisers, as was the need, in view of the heterodox design of the curriculum, to maintain high and consistent intellectual standards. That quest was not always successful, a fact that was recorded in the narrative evaluations that took the place of traditional grades. Bowing to pressure, the Experimental College issued a single leaving grade to certify progress and a degree of mastery achieved during their first two years at Madison.

Meiklejohn upheld his obligation to subject the Experimental College to disinterested analysis, and was candid about shortcomings, and transparent about significant changes made from year to year. The Athens-US curriculum grew and shifted to better deliver integrative learning; the pedagogical method worked well in facilitated discussions but small-group conversations remained hit or miss; the regional study, first an occasion of dread, became widely popular; the teaching of natural science was in the main a struggle; the intensive obligations and breadth of work laid upon the advisers were often hard to manage; administrative interference and faculty skepticism laid mines in the path of success.

The Experimental College was wildly risk-taking, subversive and occasionally chaotic; it was always and by design a work in progress that Meiklejohn argued should "lead on indefinitely along the road of experimental inquiry."[26] Although the Experimental College shut down in June of 1932 (a victim of Depression-era financial constraints, political skepticism, and its subjection to the unforgiving gears of academic machinery), it remains an unambiguously influential model for integrative liberal education that has much to teach us—like any good experiment—as we imagine the future of higher education.[27]

Act 3. The New Experimental College in the Digital Age

"Who needs democracy when you have data?" wondered the reporter Christina Larson in a searing article illustrating contemporary cultures of omnipresent governmental techno-surveillance. In this account, comprehensive data collection, analysis, and application becomes the primary method for centralized state governance.[28] Aggregated data can describe collective sentiments and behaviors as a surrogate for public opinion, and because data can be focused to the individual or small-group level, ubiquitous collection can also reveal individual sentiments and behaviors to the state. Most obviously, the felt experience of ubiquitous collection chills political freedom and incentivizes desirable obedience while automated behavioral nudges, recommendation engines, and engagement boosters all train users to comply with the will of the state.[29] Other concentrated interests (e.g., corporations) can use the same techniques to maximize their market performance and manipulate users into desired consumer behaviors.[30]

In the United States, the architecture and design features of social media platforms, including especially features like microtargeting and recommendation algorithms, have helped to accelerate an insidious drift away from a coherent conception of the public and toward an atomized dissensus of users inhabiting a common geolocation. To be sure, there are plenty of powerful critiques of the techno-surveillance state (and of the quasi-state-actors like Amazon) practicing data-driven governance to cultivate desirable behaviors and sentiments.[31]

The sketch above is meant to surface some of the prevailing conditions that we face in US higher education—many of which are more opaque than they should be. Can universities meet their obligations to democracy, deliver new skills and capacities to students, create and share new knowledge, *and* repair the atomic dissensus of social life? How can colleges and universities tap into the experimental tradition, learning from Meiklejohn's model (and others) while adjusting to the urgent needs of the future before us? To answer these questions, an experiment is in order—or a journey into the forest of subversion and illumination.

Let us begin with three concepts that might animate an educational experiment: **pluralism, democratic competence, and dignity**—principles critical to the exercise of independent intellectual life, political freedom, and common flourishing.

By *pluralism*, I mean a commitment within an intellectual community to cultivate multiple shared visions of identity and thriving, one in which multiple conceptions of the good coexist within a framework of productive difference. Knowledge-seeking institutions, like democracies, thrive when identities and perspectives and disciplines collide, intermingle, overlap, and enlarge each other. The healthy coexistence of multiple identities and conceptions of the good requires, as the liberal philosopher John Rawls has proposed, a shared commitment to widely accepted underlying principles that are latent and fundamental.[32] For Rawls, within pluralist liberalism, this underlying principle is captured in the ideas of "justice-as-fairness" (a fair system of social cooperation assuming equality and individual agency) and "free public reason" (the publicly recognized procedures, rules and guidelines for to be applied to social cooperation).

Colleges and universities are systems of free intellectual inquiry organized around common procedures, rules, and disciplinary norms necessary to the creation, stewardship, and transmission of knowledge. The existence of multiple overlapping identities, standpoints, and conceptions of the good within such intellectual communities enhances agency, promotes capacious imagination, and energizes the disciplines. Common rules and procedures to which all agree—and in which all have had a role in shaping—are an essential foundation for an intellectual community. Disciplinary norms and standards of inquiry are likewise necessary for epistemological coherence. Taken together, these underlying commitments to (1) pluralism as a desirable feature of an intellectually robust community, (2) participatory agreement to common rules and procedures, and (3) disciplinary norms that shape the creation and distribution of knowledge describe a model for inquiry anchored in seeking, recognition, and solidarity. Curricula, pedagogies, and organizational designs that reflect such a commitment to energetic, enlarging pluralism should be central to our experimental college.

The second concept is the disinterested scholarly expertise and independent professional judgment, which Robert Post sees as fundamental to *democratic competence*, defined as decision-making shaped by verifiable expert knowledge within public discourse (e.g., the political domain of free speech).[33] In this account, the First Amendment protects and nurtures the free exchange of opinion and ideas necessary to vibrant public discourse and legitimate self-government; within such public discourse, "there is no such thing as a false idea."[34] Such protected exchange of ideas and opinions develops in citizens the experience of participating in democratic processes of self-government—even if those opinions are not adopted by the majority, the opportunity to be heard and the opportunity to persuade others enforces the legitimacy of democratic procedures.

However, for Post, in universities and within scholarly disciplines, expertise consists in acts of epistemic judgment—of weighing truth claims, noting falsehoods, evaluating evidence, and accepting work products as knowledge. Professional expertise—the deployment of disciplinary norms to judge and authenticate what counts as knowledge—is a remedy for junk information in public discourse and a critical counterbalance to an unregulated marketplace of ideas in which the acceptance of false ideas and bad information is easily solicited by the speaker with the loudest megaphone and the most effective "reach." Democratic competence (decision-making based on facts rather than loud, popular opinions), for Post, thus requires that some "speech be subject to a disciplinary authority that distinguishes good ideas from bad ones."[35]

Under the First Amendment, there may be no such thing as a false idea, but within universities, disciplines, and professions, there absolutely is. Disinterestedness is moreover crucial to the development of public trust in the epistemic authority of the disciplines. If scholarship (and universities) are to serve the public interest, their methods of analysis and judgment, their principles of evidence and inquiry, and their sources of support should be independently motivated, transparent, and agreed to by all parties to the endeavor. If institutions, disciplines, or professions are captured by the state or heavily subservient to the goals of their funding source, by contrast, their claims of disinterestedness and intellectual freedom will be attenuated or insincere. Universities are those institutions specially dedicated to the creation, stewardship, and transmission of knowledge and are underwritten by the epistemic authority of the disciplines (including their historical accumulation of knowledge and their norms, standards of evidence, and rules of assessment). Democracies need expert-authenticated knowledge to make wise collective decisions that are influenced by trusted knowledge and high-quality information circulating freely.

A second characteristic of our experimental venture must therefore be the disciplined cultivation of reliable forms of knowledge that shape public opinion, enhance democratic decision-making, and increase public trust in the epistemic authority of their institutional incubators. Contributing thus to competent democratic decision-making also includes the obligation to communicate effectively with the public about the nature, purpose, and implications of the knowledge they create.

Our third concept to be expressed in the mission and implementation of our experimental venture is *dignity*. In human rights jurisprudence and fundamental law, dignity is a chameleonic but aspirational ideal—expressing inalienable moral qualities common to all persons but in practice difficult to define.[36] Thinking of dignity more narrowly as a status-concept or an attribute of all members of a college or university community provides us functional clarity. For our purposes, we might define dignity as (1) individual agency (choice, privacy, autonomy), (2) standing to be recognized and speak within a participatory and interactive community, and (3) freedom to inhabit a community on the basis of mutually inalienable respect.[37]

Understood this way, dignity has a liberty interest and a democratic purpose—that is, the individual is empowered to pursue personal curiosity and intellectual ambitions, valued and recognized within participatory governance even when roles or status are asymmetrical, and enabled to thrive by acknowledging the equal status of all members of the community and being acknowledged as possessing such status. Students, faculty, and staff possess equal dignity as members of a knowledge-seeking community even when their roles and expertise necessarily differ. Dignity is conceptually appealing because it acknowledges the standing and agency of all members and affirms their participatory contributions to the common endeavor while making room for necessary asymmetries within decision-making due to the requirements of disciplinary expertise or functional operations.

Colleges and universities make evaluative judgments all the time; disciplines reject some ideas as bad ones and embrace others as good; universities expand programs, shutter majors, invest in emerging areas, assert values through curricular requirements, issue grades and prizes, and a thousand other daily acts of credentialing and judgment. Such decisions, when procedures and norms are transparent and self-aware and followed faithfully, are not harms done to the dignity of a student, faculty, or staff member. Actions that seek intentionally to alienate dignity from a person or group (harassment, racist hate speech) are inimical to a thriving college or university. Centering dignity as a characteristic of an educational venture honors all members as agents who deserve recognition and a voice and who have the right to have their motives and curiosities and identities respected; it also models the practice (learned from and modeled for democracy) of acknowledging the moral standing of all while cultivating expertise to inform difficult decision-making.

Finally, let us propose that these three concepts (pluralism, democratic competence, dignity) should be *coeval and inseparable characteristics* of our experimental college. Put another way, an experimental venture in higher education should not only promote these principles but also instantiate them in its curriculum and pedagogy, its policies and governance practices, and its institutional self-concept or public service mission. If the venture succeeds, these principles might find their way into the institutional design and mission of more colleges and universities.

But what does our experimental college look like in practice? It adopts and updates some of the structural features of Meiklejohn's model at Wisconsin while embracing the mobility, connectivity, and learning affordances of technology. The principles of pluralism, democratic competence, and dignity are instantiated in the formal features, curricular designs, and structures of the offering—which should and must change as evidence of what works emerges.

Foundations. The model is directed at the undergraduate experience but could be applied to graduate or professional study in a more concentrated form. Any mid-sized college or university is capable of hosting this experimental model with existing personnel, facilities, and services; new faculty and staff do not need to be recruited, although complete reallocation of faculty and staff time is necessary to provide the necessary depth of focus. The institutional commitment to the experiment must be for at least eight years in order to collect and implement feedback for the purpose of improvement and to study the efficacy of the design for seven student cohorts—and there must be a recognition that the experimental college might be time-limited rather than perpetual in nature. [38] Participating instructors should be committed fully to the experiment for three years, with an initial year released from teaching for the purpose of planning, developing and preparing to teach the integrated curriculum.

Academic Characteristics of an Experimental College for the Digital Age. The experimental college will include approximately **22 months of carefully planned, mostly continuous, and cohort-centered study,** including two academic years (nine months each, with breaks) with a four-month required summer fieldwork/research/ experience (the updated regional study). After the 22 months of experimental college, students return to the general population to engage their major in depth (a pattern that will require a degree of flexibility from the receiving departments). The assumption is that any general-education or core curriculum requirements are completely satisfied by the time in the experimental college. Following Meiklejohn, the experimental college will consume the **first two years** of the undergraduate course of study with a dedicated cohort of students who live together on a residential campus, although they will conduct site-specific research and experiential learning as well as work collaboratively with students at other institutions, practitioners/professionals, and the public. The remaining years of study (currently usually two for most US undergraduates) will be devoted to the discipline-based major.

Because the students live together as a cohort, they develop common vocabularies and frameworks for analysis while working on their grand challenge or complex problem collaboratively. Traveling together on a common intellectual journey (including living in common) deepens the bonds between peers—as well as between students and faculty—that is so crucial to thriving. Equity of experience is crucial. Students must have equal access to computing technologies, residential settings, wraparound services, funding for their regional studies, and experiential learning. The experimental college includes compulsory principles and structures designed to cultivate a common experience, but does not include compulsory readings or the reception and maintenance of canonical doctrines.

At the heart of the experimental college will be **two integrated cross-disciplinary yearlong courses** that pursue a grand challenge theme or complex "civilizational" problem, align with the public purpose of the college, and require cross-disciplinary engagement in order to cultivate useful knowledge. Students take a single course per academic year, which makes up their full-time course of study. While the thematic focus/course topic will change regularly, the underlying integrative methods and alignment to the core principles of the college will remain constant.

How are the integrative course topics identified? Using the core principles of pluralism, democratic competence, and dignity as steering currents and common commitments, a given instructional team proposes and designs a year-long integrative course on a grand challenge topic or complex problem of public significance. These courses are designed collaboratively by the faculty team, each of whom contributes disciplinary knowledge to the design effort during the planning year and who teach as part of the team for at least two and no more than four years.

Because the teaching team and students are all committed fully to the experimental college without other teaching or study obligations, the usual obstacles to coordinated learning across disciplines evaporate. Designing and sequencing the different components of the integrated course is thus done on a blank canvas, allowing for faculty maximum creativity to build a coherent offering. Because the purpose of the integrated course is not to prepare students for the next course in a given discipline, but rather to equip students with the tools, habits, and knowledge to engage the complex problem or topic, the faculty can be efficient, including in the course only those topics, methods, readings, and activities that align with the challenge at hand.

In place of Meiklejohn's Athens-US set-texts curriculum (one year studying Athens, one year the nineteenth-century United States), this more flexible model is focused entirely on the ideas, methods, and experiences necessary to (1) develop meaningful integrative knowledge about a major problem, topic, or grand challenge, and (2) involve the public in the creation and communication of such knowledge. **Faculty expertise and disciplinary norms** are fundamental to this model, because a transcendent purpose is to model how disciplines harvest insights, curiosity, evidence, observation, and analysis to turn information into new knowledge. This work also requires intentional design and planning in advance for all the pieces to fit together coherently.

The experimental college's curriculum follows the expertise of the faculty teams closely and therefore changes as the faculty teams rotate back to their regular departmental service. The regular movement of faculty teams in and out of the experimental college refreshes the endeavor with new colleagues bringing new disciplinary insights, new questions, and mindsets to the endeavor, especially as the grand challenge problems are expected to change. The nature of the integrative course design requires the topics to be aligned with the moment as well as shaped by the deep expertise of their faculty leads.

The experimental college requires creative energy and abhors intellectual inertia. Cycling faculty through the experimental college increases the distribution of effort across departments and disciplines, enhances the creativity and integrative depth of the courses, and maintains a high level of collaborative energy. Because students will take only one comprehensive course per year, leadership (as informed by student voice) should be careful to combine course elements in a two-year sequence that provides breadth of focus. Pairing, for instance, a first-year course devoted to the integrative study of race in the United States with a second-year course on carbon and climate would provide complementary but not closely overlapping grand-challenge topics; almost any discipline represented in colleges and universities could contribute significantly to the integrative study of at least one of these courses.

Although an experimental college benefits from in-person living and learning, the affordances of **new technologies** also provide profound opportunities to involve others in the work of the integrated course. An online phase of the integrated course might include deep inter-institutional collaboration, for instance joint meetings and collaborative projects with students at another college or university. Ideally, experimental colleges at multiple institutions would be working from a common syllabus or tackling the same complex problems, meaning that online multi-campus learning can enhance the diversity and perspectival richness of a given course community. Such co-located learning can also easily engage remote experts, guest faculty, project sponsors, community partners, and the general public at large.

By removing the barriers to communication and interaction between students and the public, technology also removes the excuse for failing to communicate with and learn from the very public for whom knowledge is being created. In the new experimental college, meaningful public engagement (ideally from a posture of accompaniment and listening rather than "service learning") should be a required experience. Technology should be intentionally woven into the integrated course for three purposes: (1) increase co-located learning/expand the learning community, (2) involve expert partners and collaborating organizations, and (3) listening to and sharing work with members of the public. It should not be possible to complete an integrated course without meaningful activities that fulfill these goals..

Technology is also the tether that connects students to their cohort and their faculty during their required **summer study**, which is devoted to fieldwork, research, and experiential learning. Using the template of Meiklejohn's regional study, students build on their curiosity and deepen their independence of inquiry through cross-disciplinary research and engagement away from campus. Experiential learning broadly construed might include internship work, or interview, lab, or field research; most of all, it should be deeply aligned with the student's curiosity. Some students might choose to live at home whereas others would be living in the field close to their subject of study or research facility. While in the field, students will participate in an online course devoted to sharing work, providing feedback and updates, connecting with experts and faculty advisors, and participating in a lightweight transitional seminar with readings and activities that bridge year one and year two. The college will be responsible for facilitating and funding opportunities for each student to remove any barriers related to cultural or financial capital; skilled staff who can facilitate a funded placement preserves student time and effort at this early stage.

The experimental college draws plainly on the principles of progressive liberal education and the pedagogies of liberation. Justice-oriented pedagogies affirm and model the values of pluralism, democratic competence and dignity in part by recognizing and often centering the experiences and insights of minoritized voices.[39] Pedagogy in the experimental college is focused on active problem-solving, debate and discussion, simulation and case-method activities, cross-disciplinary contextual imagination and analysis, lab and field work, evidence-driven argument, depth of engagement, high academic expectations, and the persistent inclusion of student voice and the honoring of student curiosity. It cultivates optimism and perseverance and intellectual agility (skills often notably present in first-generation and low-income students). Proficiency-based learning (or "mastery-grading") is the norm; students are asked to achieve proficiency within a specific set of activities and provided opportunities to continue developing their skills until they can do so in place of traditional grades. Universal design for learning is a priority; faculty working to ensure that all students have their learning needs met equitably, and that coaching and feedback is the basis of the peer-to-peer and student-instructor relationship.

Listening to student feedback is critical, and shaping activities and materials in conversation with students improves the horizontality of the community. Students must be provided with meaningful access to governance and planning processes, and recognized as fundamental stakeholders who deserve recognition and voice. Learning goals, understood as a target set solely by the instructor and subject to external measurement, are abolished. Instead, students will demonstrate proficiency in the various skills, ideas, and attributes required by their integrative course; at the end of the two year cycle, students will share their experiences in a "viva" or public culmination that combines the submission and presentation of work products with a rigorous examination and discussion with a panel of external experts and members of the public. Integrated courses should weave into their practice not only modeling the creation of new knowledge but also the processes whereby such knowledge is solicited by, aligned with and ultimately communicated to the public for use in wise democratic decision-making. The experimental college may not train students as experts in a specific discipline; instead it models agile, curious, problem-solving habits of mind, and principles of common responsibility that are essential to liberal education in the digital age.

Although the experimental college uses technology as a force multiplier, tether, and enabler, the model builds on a foundation of in-person learning within a cohort and of study within a campus community where rich resources and support structures are available for undergraduates. Underlying the **wise use of the best learning technologies** and most effective pedagogies are intentional adoption decisions to ensure that technology tools and pedagogical strategies are motivated solely by their utility within the curriculum. Because technologies can reduce privacy, increase the feeling and fact of surveillance, and overquantify people and their cognitive processes, the experimental college prefers a lean data profile and comprehensive transparency around the entire "learning stack." Only data essential to learning should be collected; no data should be shared with or monetized by third-party providers; the production conditions and business models of hardware and software providers should be made visible; tools and systems should be selected when they meet strict standards of algorithmic fairness and privacy protection. The decision to integrate technology into a learning experience must be accompanied by ethical frameworks for adoption developed collaboratively by students, faculty, and staff in alignment with the principles of the experimental college but updated regularly as new cohorts and teaching teams move through.

Epilogue

Does this model of integrative, cohort-driven, situated learning enhance the success of students as thinkers and citizens? Does the model connect learning and knowledge with public purpose? Does the model instantiate the steering principles effectively and does it more effectively fulfill the obligations of colleges and universities to their publics? Too soon to tell. An experiment is in order—and such sustained experiments can be undertaken at colleges and universities with different characteristics and missions. Ideally an archipelago of experimental colleges would emerge together, enhancing inter-institutional collaboration and co-located learning.

The new experimental college described above is one possible response to the challenges facing higher education. It is meant to take risks, to embrace heterodoxy, to nurture blue-sky thinking and disciplinary precision. It is designed to explore structures and pedagogies that cultivate a shared intellectual journey and a deep sense of obligation to work in the service of common interests. It promotes creative problem-solving and capacious imagination through immersive, focused cross-disciplinary engagement with questions that matter. While the steering principles of pluralism, democratic competence, and dignity remain constant, the complex problems tackled in the curriculum are always changing. It uses technology to enable and connect but not as an end in itself. It seeks to cultivate democratic habits and ways of thinking not through doctrine but in the applied practice of learning, participatory governance, and the integrative creation and communication of new knowledge—in a virtuous cycle of communication and listening with the public whose interests are served.

Can new experimental colleges help higher education respond to the existential challenges to our common value proposition in an increasingly skeptical era? Perhaps. It's time to find out.

Notes

1. A partial list includes: Staley, *Alternative Universities*; Alexander, *Academia Next*; Fitzpatrick, *Generous Thinking*; Bowen, *Higher Education in the Digital Age*; Davidson, *New Education*; Crow and Dabars, *Fifth Wave*. See also the expansive vision outlined in Korstange et al., "A Theory of Public Higher Education."

2. Aoun, *Robot-Proof.*

3. Daniels et al., *What Universities Owe Democracy.*

4. Daniels et al., *What Universities Owe Democracy*, 9.

5. Daniels et al., *What Universities Owe Democracy*, 20.

6. The most substantial treatment of Meiklejohn's thought, life, and career is Nelson, *Education and Democracy*. See also Brennan, "The Making of the Liberal College," and Brown, "The Experimental College Revisited."

7. Hofstadter, *Anti-intellectualism.*

8. Meiklejohn, *Freedom and the College.*

9. The challenges particular to the contemporary college presidency are well captured in Rosenberg, "Should Universities Take Political Stands?"

10. Meiklejohn, *Freedom and the College.*

11. Meiklejohn, "The Liberal College," 96.

12. Meiklejohn, "Wisconsin's Experimental College," quoted in Brown, "The Experimental College Revisited," 94.

13. Nelson, in *Education and Democracy*, provides a detailed account of the San Francisco School of Social Studies, Meiklejohn's venture into adult and workers education, 199–232.

14. "Meiklejohn Heads New Test College."

15. Meiklejohn, "A New College with a New Idea," 2.

16. Meiklejohn, Speech to National Student Federation, quoted in Brown, "The Experimental College Revisited," 95.

17. Meiklejohn, "A New College with a New Idea," 2.

18. The detailed, mostly disinterested, and candid report to the University of Wisconsin was published as Meiklejohn, *The Experimental College*, see 17; xvii.

19. Meiklejohn, *The Experimental College*, 139.

20. The most thorough accounts of the inner workings and curricular arrangements are outlined in *The Experimental College* and elaborated upon in Nelson, *Education and Democracy*, 133–196, and Brown, "The Experimental College Revisited."

21. Meiklejohn, *The Experimental College*, 73. Meiklejohn was quite aware of the limitations of his model and noted the perhaps unsatisfactory ways in which his venture struggled with the teaching of natural sciences. See, for instance, discussion in *The Experimental College*, 10.

22. Lynd and Merrell Lynd, *Middletown: A Study of Contemporary American Culture*. Discussion in Meiklejohn, *The Experimental College*, 90.

23. Meiklejohn, "Wisconsin's Experimental College." The assignment prompt itself is in *The Experimental College*, 82–83.

24. Meiklejohn, *The Experimental College*, 92

25. Meiklejohn, *The Experimental College*, 144.

26. Meiklejohn, *The Experimental College*, 318. Although Meiklejohn wished ardently for the Experimental College to continue its work, the university's faculty and administration felt otherwise.

27. Brown, "The Experimental College Revisited," 104.

28. Larson, "Who Needs Democracy."

29. Fourcade and Gordon, "Learning Like a State; Noble, *Algorithms of Oppression*; Zuboff, *Age of Surveillance Capitalism*; Eubanks, *Automating Inequality*; Cohen, *Between Truth and Power*; Klonick, "The New Governors."

30. Martin, "Manipulation, Privacy, and Choice."

31. Morozov, "Digital Socialism?"

32. Rawls, "Overlapping Consensus."

33. Post, *Democracy, Expertise, & Academic Freedom*.

34. Gertz v. Robert Welch, Inc. 418 U.S. 323 (1974).

35. Post, *Democracy, Expertise, & Academic Freedom*, 34.

36. Whitman, "Two Western Cultures"; Daly, *Dignity Rights*.

37. "Dignity is the status of a person predicated on the fact that she is recognised as having the ability to control and regulate her actions in accordance with her own apprehension of norms and reasons that apply to her; it assumes she is capable of giving and entitled to give an account of herself (and of the way in which she is regulating her actions and organizing her life) an account that others are to pay attention to; and it means finally that she has the wherewithal to demand that her agency and her presence among us as a human being is to be taken seriously and accommodated in the lives of others, in others' attitudes and actions towards her, and in social life generally." Waldron, "How Law Protects Dignity," 202.

38. "Educational institutions are good at adding things but not good at subtraction. . . . Institutional rigidities are facts of life that in many, but not all, cases derive from the very nature of the academic enterprise. It is harder, however, to defend antiquated organizational structures such as "centers" of one kind or another, which are notoriously difficult to dismantle even when they have ceased serving their purpose. A good rule of the road is to use flexible structures such as workshops or experimental colleges that do not take on lives of their own." Bowen, *Higher Education in the Digital Age*, 11.

39. A partial list of sources includes Dewey, *Democracy and Education*; Friere, *Pedagogy of the Oppressed*; hooks, *Teaching to Transgress* and *Teaching Community*; Rendón *Sentipensante (Sensing/Thinking) Pedagogy*; Hogan and Sathy, *Inclusive Teaching Strategies*; Fink, *Designing Significant Learning Experiences*; Addy et al., *What Inclusive Instructors Do*; Gannon, *Radical Hope*.

Bibliography

Alexander, Bryan. *Academia Next: The Futures of Higher Education*. Baltimore: Johns Hopkins University Press, 2020.

Addy, Tracie Marcella, Derek Dube, and Khadijah Mitchell. *What Inclusive Instructors Do*. Sterling, VA: Stylus Press, 2021.

Aoun, Joseph. *Robot-Proof: Higher Education in the Age of Artificial Intelligence*. Boston: MIT Press, 2017.

Bowen, William. *Higher Education in the Digital Age*. Princeton, NJ: Princeton University Press, 2013.

Brennan, Robert Thomas. "The Making of the Liberal College: Alexander Meiklejohn at Amherst." *History of Education Quarterly* 28, no. 4 (Winter 1988): 569–597. https://doi.org/10.2307/368850.

Brown, Cynthia Stokes. "The Experimental College Revisited." *Wisconsin Magazine of History* 66, no. 2 (1982–1983).

Cohen, Julie. *Between Truth and Power: The Legal Constructions of Information Capitalism*. Oxford, UK: Oxford University Press, 2019.

Crow, Michael, and William Dabars. *The Fifth Wave: The Evolution of American Higher Education*. Baltimore: Johns Hopkins University Press, 2021.

Daly, Erin. *Dignity Rights: Courts, Constitutions, and the Worth of the Human Person*. Philadelphia: University of Pennsylvania Press, 2012.

Daniels, Ronald, Grant Shreve, and Philip Spector. *What Universities Owe Democracy*. Baltimore: Johns Hopkins University Press, 2021.

Davidson, Cathy. *The New Education*. 2nd ed. New York: Basic Books, 2022.

Dewey, John. *Democracy and Education*, edited by Nicholas Tampio. New York: Columbia University Press, 2024.

Eubanks, Virginia. *Automating Inequality: How High-Tech Tools Profile, Police, and Punish the Poor*. New York: St Martin's Press, 2018.

Fink, L. Dee. *Designing Significant Learning Experiences*. Rev. and updated ed. New York: Jossey-Bass, 2013.
Fitzpatrick, Kathleen. *Generous Thinking: A Radical Approach to Saving the University*. Baltimore: Johns Hopkins University Press, 2019.
Fourcade, Marion, and Jeffrey Gordon. "Learning Like a State: Statecraft in the Digital Age." *Journal of Law and Political Economy* 1, no. 1 (2020). https://doi.org/10.5070/LP61150258.
Friere, Paulo. *Pedagogy of the Oppressed*. 30th anniversary ed. New York: Continuum, 2022.
Gannon, Kevin. *Radical Hope: A Teaching Manifesto*. Morgantown: West Virginia University Press, 2020.
Gertz v. Robert Welch, Inc. 418 U.S. 323 (1974).
Hofstadter, Richard. *Anti-intellectualism in American Life*. New York: Vintage, 1964.
Hogan, Kelly, and Viji Sathy. *Inclusive Teaching Strategies for Promoting Equity in the College Classroom*. Morgantown: West Virginia Univsity Press, 2022.
hooks, bell. *Teaching Community: A Pedagogy of Hope*. New York: Routledge, 2003.
hooks, bell. *Teaching to Transgress: Education as the Practice of Freedom*. New York: Routledge, 1993.
Klonick, Kate. "The New Governors: The People, Rules, and Processes Governing Online Speech." *Harvard Law Review* 131 (2018). https://harvardlawreview.org/wp-content/uploads/2018/04/1598-1670_Online.pdf.
Korstange, Ryan, Susan Blum, Oscar Fernandez, Mays Imad, Thomas Nelson Laird, and Kate Pantelides. "A Theory of Public Higher Education." *Soundings: An Interdisciplinary Journal* 104, nos. 2–3 (2021): 141. http://dx.doi.org/10.5325/soundings.104.2-3.0141.
Larson, Christina. "Who Needs Democracy When You Have Data?" *Technology Review* 121, no. 5 (September/October 2018). https://www.technologyreview.com/2018/08/20/240293/who-needs-democracy-when-you-have-data.
Lynd, Robert, and Helen Merrell Lynd. *Middletown: A Study of Contemporary American Culture*. New York: Harper & Row, 1929.
Martin, Kirsten. "Manipulation, Privacy, and Choice." *North Carolina Journal of Law & Technology* 23, no. 3 (April 2022). https://scholarship.law.unc.edu/ncjolt/vol23/iss3/2.
Meiklejohn, Alexander. *The Experimental College*. New York: Harper & Bros, 1932.
Meiklejohn, Alexander. *Freedom and the College*. New York: Century, 1923.
Meiklejohn, Alexander. "A New College with a New Idea." *New York Times*, May 29, 1927.
Meiklejohn, Alexander. Speech to National Student Federation, Ann Arbor, MI (1926), in Brown, "The Experimental College Revisited."
Meiklejohn, Alexander. "Wisconsin's Experimental College." *Graphic Survey*, June 27, 1927.
Meiklejohn, Alexander. "Wisconsin's Experimental College." *Journal of Higher Education* 2 (December 1930).

"Meiklejohn Heads New Test College." *New York Times*, February 13, 1927.
Morozov, Evgeny. "Digital Socialism?" *New Left Review* 116/117 (May/June 2019). https://newleftreview.org/issues/ii116/articles/evgeny-morozov-digital-socialism.
Nelson, Adam. *Education and Democracy: The Meaning of Alexander Meiklejohn.* Madison: University of Wisconsin Press, 1992.
Noble, Safiya. *Algorithms of Oppression: How Search Engines Reinforce Racism.* New York: New York University Press, 2018.
Post, Robert. *Democracy, Expertise, and Academic Freedom: A First Amendment Jurisprudence for the Modern State.* New Haven, CT: Yale University Press, 2012.
Rawls, John. "The Idea of an Overlapping Consensus." *Oxford Journal of Legal Studies* 7, no. 1 (1986): 1–25. https://www.jstor.org/stable/764257.
Rendón, Laura. *Sentipensante (Sensing/Thinking) Pedagogy: Educating for Wholeness, Social Justice and Liberation.* Sterling, VA: Stylus, 2014.
Rosenberg, Brian. "Should Universities Take Political Stands?" *Chronicle of Higher Education* March 31, 2022. https://www.chronicle.com/article/should-universities-take-political-stands.
Staley, David. *Alternative Universities: Speculative Design for Innovation in Higher Education.* Baltimore: Johns Hopkins University Press, 2019.
Waldron, Jeremy. "How Law Protects Dignity." *Cambridge Law Journal* 71, no. 1 (March 2012): 200–222. https://doi.org/10.1017/S0008197312000256.
Whitman, James Q. "The Two Western Cultures of Privacy: Dignity Versus Liberty." *Yale Law Journal* 113, no. 6 (April 2004): 1151–1221. https://doi.org/10.2307/4135723.
Zuboff, Shoshanna. *The Age of Surveillance Capitalism: The Fight for a Human Future at the New Frontier of Power.* New York: Public Affairs, 2019.

chapter 23

Architecture of the Unexpected

Beyond the Learning Paradigm

Randy Bass

We can think of the pandemic as having arrived somewhere in the middle of a multi-decade arc of progress around what, nearly 30 years ago, Robert Barr and John Tagg named "the learning paradigm."[1] They argued that we were in a transition from an "instructional paradigm," where our designs were focused on the inputs of instruction, to the "learning paradigm," where we would prioritize environments that advanced student learning outcomes. In their essay, they illustrated the paradigmatic "shift from instruction to learning" by pairing a range of elements side by side in tables. Table 23.1 has a selection.

The shift in these values all feel pretty familiar, in that have increasingly become commonplace in higher education, if not yet fully realized. But then there are other features outlined in the paradigm shift that are perhaps not yet so widely distributed, including whether one thinks of overall curricular designs as atomistic versus holistic, or time versus learning as the constant.

Although we can find some of these elements present in the higher education sector, they are certainly not yet mainstream. Taking all 30-plus factors together, Barr and Tagg speculated that it would indeed take several decades for this shift in paradigms to be fully realized (table 23.2). Looking over the course of change since 1995, they certainly did not overestimate that.

Table 23.1. Side-by-Side Comparison of Educational Paradigms

Instruction Paradigm	Learning Paradigm
Provide/deliver instruction	Produce learning
Transfer knowledge from faculty to student	Elicit student discovery and construction of knowledge
Offer courses and programs	Create powerful learning environments
Achieve access for diverse students	Achieve success for diverse students
Quality of entering students	Quantity and quality of outcomes

Source: Adapted from Barr and Tagg, "From Teaching to Learning"

Table 23.2. Instructional Paradigm versus Learning Paradigm

Instruction Paradigm	Learning Paradigm
Atomistic, parts prior to whole	Holistic, whole prior to parts
Time held constant, learning varies	Learning held constant, time varies
Degree equals accumulated credit hours	Degree equals demonstrated knowledge and skills
"Live" teacher, "live" students required	"Active" learner required but not "live" teacher
Faculty are primarily lecturers	Faculty are primarily designers

Source: Adapted from Barr and Tagg, "From Teaching to Learning"

Yet, even if mixed and slow, progress toward the "learning paradigm" has been significant in that enormous changes have been taking place across higher education in pedagogy, instructional design, equity and inclusion, curricula, and assessment across the entire sector. These expansions have been rooted in two converging revolutions: digital and human. For higher education's survival of the pandemic disruption, the digital revolution provided the technological infrastructure, course management systems, widespread connectivity (albeit inequitably distributed) and at least minimal digital competence. The human revolution, connected to a global emphasis on human capacities, equipped the cultural and social infrastructure of institutions with an effective toolbox of evidence-based pedagogies and an expanding consciousness for well-being and a community of care in the context of the academic learning environments. As a result, the vast majority of colleges and universities stayed open, served their mission, and valued responding to diverse student needs.

In many ways, higher education had been preparing for the unexpected without entirely realizing it. I assert that it was primarily the progress of the learning paradigm—the growth of the multi-layered practices related to good pedagogy and educational caretaking—that provided the essence of higher education's capacity to survive the pandemic. All this progress was rooted in the knowledge and expertise of teaching professionals, and achieved through one form or another of communally-held professional practice. These human capacities, organized around principles of effective practice, made adaptation to the pandemic crisis possible.

I want to give this phenomenon a name. I'm calling it the *architecture of the unexpected*, and it is directly related to the progress made toward the learning paradigm. If valuing the capabilities of what we might think of as the new educational paradigm was a critical underpinning of higher education's adaptation to the crisis that began in 2020, then it is this *architecture of the unexpected* that we need to expand if we are to prepare for an uncertain future in which potentially calamitous disruptions lay ahead.

The Pandemic and the Learning Paradigm, 2020–2025

In using the term "architecture," I am not talking here about physical structures of campuses,[2] but the immaterial structures, processes, and ethos that set up institutions to adapt to disruptive change. This conceptual and organizational architecture includes institutional beliefs, processes, policies, and practices that enable the educational activities of an institution and the experience of students. Yet, in framing this architecture on *the unexpected*, I want to focus on how those same advances in evidence-based pedagogies and relational practices of care form a new set of core practices that can also be seen as institutional capacities for operating in conditions of uncertainty and complexity. There is an important alignment between institutional capacity to learn and adapt, and the capacities we seek to give our students to learn and adapt. That is, the values and frameworks that serve the readiness of *institutions* for an uncertain future are entirely aligned with—if not identical with—the conditions in which we might best educate all our graduates for navigating a complex and uncertain future. An architecture of the unexpected implies that there is a deep relationship between institutional capacities and human capacities for cultivating adaptiveness and agility, even humility, in encountering volatility and uncertainty.

Extrapolating from the pandemic experience, I'm proposing that the best path to growing such an architecture is to focus on the vectors already pointing toward the strengthening of teaching and learning environments based on evidence-based pedagogies, engaged learning, and a robust vision for a culturally responsive and equitable quality education.

To understand this better, we might turn to a simple but powerful tool for understanding long-term transformation, known as the "Three Horizons framework," presented in figure 23.1.

The Three Horizons framework is a way of looking at three dimensions of transformation that are all represented in the present. The first is the current state or dominant paradigm, known as H1. This is "business as usual." Because the Three Horizons framework is a tool for navigating transitions from one state to another, it is presumed that there

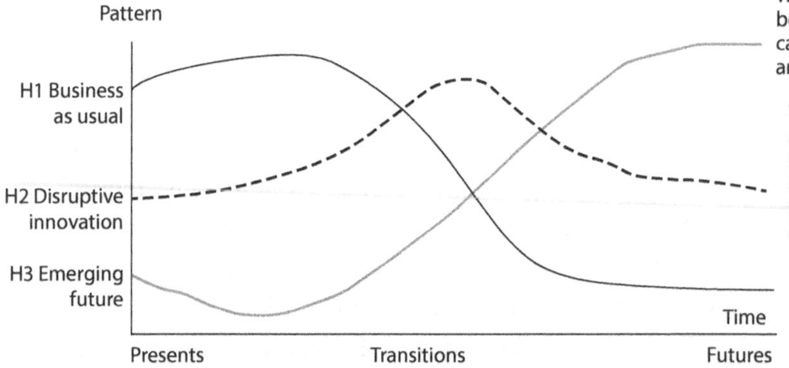

Figure 23.1. Three Horizons framework. Source: Three Horizons framework created by Bill Sharpe, Creative Commons Attribution-ShareAlike 4.0 International. CC BY-SA 4.0. https://creativecommons.org/licenses/by-sa/4.0/. This figure is an adaptation of the Three Horizons framework by principals at Solvable.ca: Adam Lerner, May Bartlett, and Charles Holmes, https://www.solvable.ca/three-horizons

are significant dimensions of the H1 paradigm that are no longer "fit for purpose" and have to go away. The next dimension to introduce is the emerging paradigm known as H3. This is the future you are hoping to bring into being that will replace H1. Between them is the horizon of disruptive innovation, known as H2, which gives rise to the "dynamics of transition." Disruptions along the H2 line (intentional or not) either have effect of sustaining H1, in which case the disruption can be thought of as H2–, or have the effect of helping H3 to come into existence, thought of as (H2+).

The Three Horizons framework is not predictive. It provides a way to look at the interaction of events and forces that have the potential to effect transitions from one paradigm to another. As the creators put it, like the "five lines of a musical stave," the Three Horizons framework "is a notation that enables us to express and share the infinite possibilities of transformative innovation."[3]

The Three Horizons framework is relevant to an architecture of the unexpected in many ways. Most fundamentally, it entails the very nature of making the future present: "exploring the third horizon is a skill in working creatively with the unknown, the partially known and the uncertain. It is a skill we all have, but have not fully developed as a collective capacity of transformation."[4]

The Three Horizons also provides a way to think about the role of the pandemic adaptation in Robert Barr and John Tagg's instructional to learning paradigm transition. Let's populate the framework in figure 23.2 using just the terms set out in Barr and Tagg's article from 1995.

In their language, the dominant paradigm, or "business as usual," would be the instructional paradigm H1, with the learning paradigm emerging H3. In this case, H1 "business as usual," labeled A in figure 23.2, would focus on the teacher as the primary actor ("transfer of knowledge," "deliver instruction," and "primarily lecturer"), a focus on inputs ("degree equals credits," student "access," and "time" as a constant) and not particularly integrated or coherent ("atomistic").

On the other hand, H3, the emerging future (labeled B in figure 23.2) focuses the teacher's role on creating "learning environments," whose purpose is to "produce learning" and lead to "student discovery," with

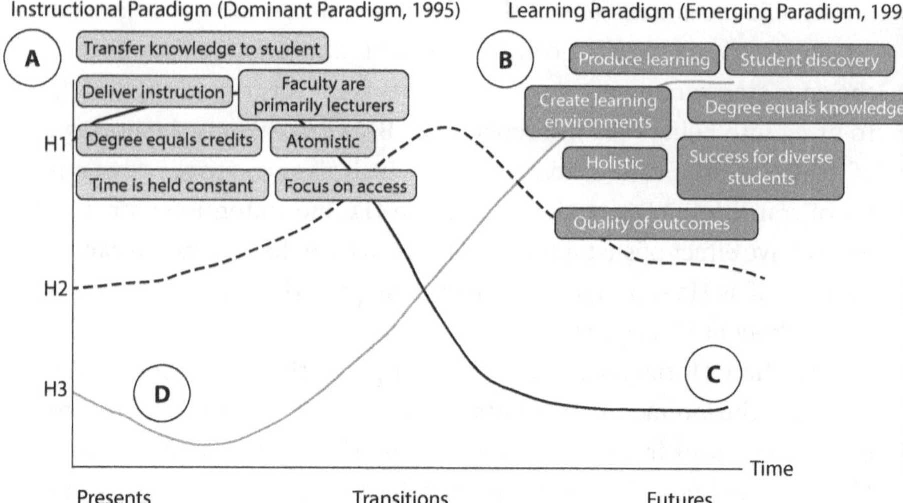

Figure 23.2. Three Horizons mapping with terms from Barr and Tagg's "From Teaching to Learning." Source: Bill Sharpe, Three Horizons framework. Creative Commons Attribution-ShareAlike 4.0 International. CC BY-SA 4.0. https://creativecommons.org/licenses/by-sa/4.0/

a focus on outcomes ("success," "quality of outcomes," and "degree equals knowledge") and an approach to curriculum that is "holistic." The populating of the framework could continue to name what of the dominant paradigm needs to go away (labeled C in figure 23.2) or where there are seeds of the emerging paradigm already in existence (labeled D in figure 23.2).

Even with this broad and basic mapping of the paradigms, we can use the framework to consider the role that the pandemic adaptation played as an H2 force. That is, if we consider COVID-19 as a "creative disruption," we can ask questions about whether the shift to remote learning is advancing (H3), that is, helping the learning paradigm to emerge and therefore is H2+, or sustaining H1, or delaying the decline and replacement of the "instructional" paradigm, or H2–.

How might we imagine the pandemic advancing or hindering the progress of the learning paradigm? In this context, the following widespread effects of the pandemic educational adaptation might be considered (H2+):

- Distributed faculty competence more widely with educational technologies.
- Advanced the awareness of evidence-based pedagogies and principles of engaged learning.
- Helped to decouple "contact time" from "time on task," as many faculty learned to mix synchronous and asynchronous instruction.
- Helped build an ethos of community and care, as the shift to remote instruction gradually led many faculty to realize that their online courses needed to be places of at least nominal community in the absence of other campus or institutional supports that in-person presence distributes in other ways.
- Fostered widespread attention to equity, as the shift to remote instruction made visible the differential contexts from which students come, and generated equity-minded responses, from bandwidth and home learning spaces, to grading practices and flexibility and leniency with deadlines.

These features would all be considered H2+ in that the pandemic disruption seems to have accelerated the decline of the dominant instructional paradigm and the rise of an emerging learning paradigm.

On the other hand, there are dimensions of the pandemic disruption that might well serve to prolong the H1 dominant instructional paradigm, and therefore be considered H2–. For example:

- The pandemic will certainty give online education a huge boost, which has the risk of privileging functionality over transformative education.
- It might mean the erosion of community and presence, and the slowing of an evolution toward a more relationship-rich education.
- It might mean further inequality of education as the pandemic will lead the more resource-rich institutions to value presence as part of their high-cost value proposition, but expand other kinds of education for ever larger numbers of people.
- It might create a situation where educational innovation is largely equated to opening new markets on the back of online education.
- The financial impacts of the pandemic and its aftermath could mean financial constraints that will restrict an emphasis on resource-

intensive high-impact practices in favor of scaling and automated instructional processes.

After the first couple semesters of remote instruction, many campuses were asking, "What will we want to remember and retain from this experience?" A different way to ask that question in the context I'm offering is "How will the experience of the pandemic adaptation help advance a learning paradigm?" Put in the context of Three Horizons, this new question recontextualizes "educational innovation" from something that merely reacts to the present (providing solutions to instructional problems) to something that is helping to usher in a desired and emerging future.

The Three Horizons framework does not necessarily lead to one future or another, but it allows a community of stakeholders to understand disruption and innovation in light of the paradigm being brought into existence, as opposed to solely being measured against the present paradigm and past practices. Mapping the pandemic as an H2 disruption provides a way for educators and institutional communities to discuss and speculate on the short- and long-term effects of the COVID-19 crisis on the progress on the many dimensions of the learning paradigm, including quality teaching and learning, student success, equity, and inclusion. Mapping the pandemic disruption in the context of a transition between paradigms also makes visible the fragile state of those progressive (H2+) forces and the need for an ongoing intentional response for the purposes of advancing the features of a desired emerging future.

Beyond the Learning Paradigm, 2025–2045

This way of mapping also raises the question of whether the emerging future we want or need is sufficiently captured by the defining features of the learning paradigm, as Barr and Tagg described them. In 1995, they asserted that the "instruction paradigm" no longer served the needs of higher education. It was, in a phrase, no longer "fit for purpose." I propose that this "post-pandemic" moment gives us an opportunity both to take the measure of the ways that the learning paradigm provided us an "architecture of the unexpected" for the pandemic response; it also allows us to pose questions about what kind of architecture higher education needs to keep preparing for an even more uncertain future.

In 2021, in a course I regularly co-teach called The University as a Design Problem, our students undertook a thought experiment, asking what it might look like to think beyond Barr and Tagg's learning paradigm. This impulse grew out of the students' observations about certain limitations of the "learning paradigm" as Barr and Tagg framed it, despite its positive values. For example, it is still very much tied to the learning of individuals, where the evidence of impact and outcomes resided with individual student success. The learning paradigm could be seen to overemphasize education as a solely private good, evidenced and evaluated only by those outcomes that are most easily quantifiable and contributing to concrete metrics of success.

These and other critiques raised questions about whether the learning paradigm was sufficient for education to meet the challenges of the rest of the twenty-first century. We wondered is there something beyond the learning paradigm that might shift the emphasis from student success to societal success, or what Gert Biesta would call a turn from "student-centered education" to "world-centered education"?[5] Acknowledging there is still plenty of work to do in the "learning paradigm"—to improve design learning environments and design more coherent curricula—we can also look beyond it, asking, What kind of paradigm is needed to reshape education in order to foster social transformation? Education theorist Zachary Stein argues that "*twenty-first century education is an unknown entity*. It is still a future unrealized." We need, he says, new "educational configurations in the twenty-first century" that "provide for the proliferation of different and better capabilities than we now possess, new and better identities than we now live with—nothing less than a new and better humanity is needed."[6] An education that is aimed at creating a "new and better humanity" needs an architecture that includes but also exceeds the learning paradigm.

This is why I argue for thinking of the architecture that prepared us for the pandemic as an *architecture of the unexpected*, because if "*twenty-first century education is an unknown entity*," then the project in front of us is more about discovery than implementation. In this sense, an architecture of the unexpected is not a blueprint but a conceptual space whose goal is to stretch institutions into an increasingly better position to realize their educational aims in the face of uncertainty. To focus on the unexpected is decidedly not to go about strategic planning as if it were a search for a new business model (e.g., expanding online education to each new markets). Nor is it about locking down an architecture of *the expected*, guaranteeing the relationship between learning designs and outcomes. Alternatively, an architecture of the unexpected supports the "adjacent possible" so that new possibilities might emerge.[7]

The architecture of the unexpected is aspirational, playful and speculative, but it is also pragmatic in the ways that the architect Bjarke Ingels describes "pragmatic utopia": "Architecture seems to be entrenched in two equally unfertile fronts: either naively utopian or petrifyingly pragmatic. We believe that there is a third way wedged in the no-mans-land between the diametrical opposites. Or in the small but very fertile overlap between the two. A pragmatic utopian architecture that takes on the creation of socially, economically and environmentally perfect places as a practical objective."[8]

In this spirit of pragmatic utopianism, an architecture of the unexpected follows the impulses of the writers like Stein calling for an entirely new way of thinking about education that reimagines its purposes and aims for a different kind of future. These educational thinkers are variously calling for a new *planetary paideia* (Stein), a new *Bildung for the twenty-first century* (Jonathan Rowson), a *new pedagogical dreamfield* (Laura Rendón), an *ecological university* (Ronald Barnett), a *Third University* (la paperson), or just simply a whole new paradigm that would finally be higher education's *Copernican moment* (David Scobey).[9]

The architecture of the unexpected is situated among these visions, building on—and beyond—the architecture that rode the vectors of the learning paradigm to the pandemic adaptation. It is my hope that building an architecture for the unexpected prioritizes a growth mindset model for institutions that can provide a framework for stretching beyond current practices, just as the various streams of "learning paradigm" activity over the last few decades stretched the teaching and learning mindset of higher education.

How might we start to map this new paradigm? We can use the Three Horizons framework to start (figure 23.3).

In this forward-looking view, let's redefine H1 as the current state of the learning paradigm, being a mixed combination of residual practices of the instruction paradigm co-existing with the emergent qualities of the learning paradigm. Here "business as usual" (labeled A in figure 23.3) is characterized by both lecturing and active learning, is both inequitable and equity-minded; the current state is still based on time and credits, but with increased attention to learning outcomes; and although there is interest in holistic approaches to education (both the coherence of curricula and attention to the whole person), there are also powerful tendencies toward what Biesta calls "learnification"

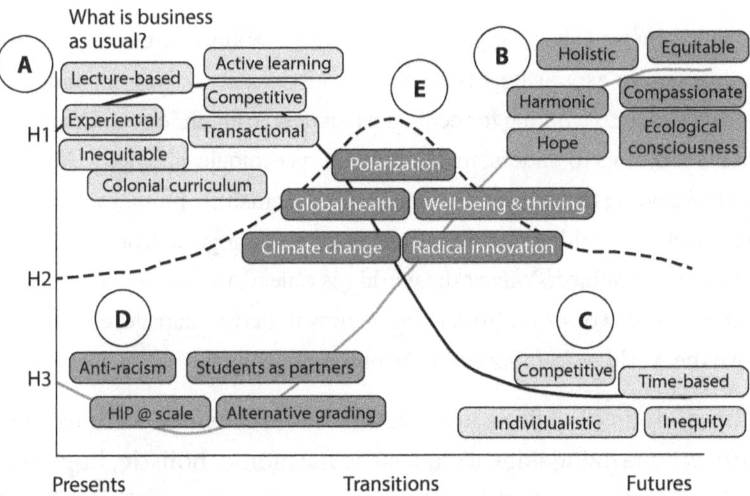

Figure 23.3. Mapping an emerging paradigm in the Three Horizons framework. HIP = high-impact practices. Source: Bill Sharpe, Three Horizons framework. Creative Commons Attribution-ShareAlike 4.0 International. CC BY-SA 4.0. https://creativecommons.org/licenses/by-sa/4.0/

that seeks to reduce the broad aims of education to increasingly narrow and measurable activities.

Out of this current state of things, there will be elements we want to keep and others that we want to shed (labeled C in figure 23.3). But in order to move toward an educational paradigm that could bring about a "new and better humanity," we will surely need to start naming what we want the emerging paradigm to be. With limited remaining space here, I'll turn to a couple of writers to give us some content for this vision. First, Laura Rendón: "I join the many existing voices of educational transformation to contribute to the generation of *a new tipping point*—a movement that wishes to create a new dream of education. The foundation of this dream is a more harmonic, holistic vision of education that honors the whole of who we are as intellectual, compassionate, authentic human beings who value love, peace, democracy, community, diversity, and hope for humanity."[10]

And then a second vision, from the Common Worlds Research Collective,[11] who declare that if we are to have a future, then "business as usual is no longer an option." They argue that the future of the planet depends on making "a fundamental break with humanist education":

> This is why we call for an inter-related series of shifts: from promoting humanism to exercising an ecological consciousness; from working for social justice to working for ecological justice; from understanding humans as social beings to understanding humans as ecological beings . . . from understanding teaching and learning as an exclusively human activity to approaching worldly relations as inherently pedagogical; from teaching students (as subjects) *about* the world (as object) to learning *with* others in our common worlds . . . from learning how to better manage, control or save the world to *learning how to become with the world.*

These kinds of visions are selectively represented here as the H3 future, emphasizing education that is harmonic, holistic, hopeful, focused on compassion and ecological consciousness (labeled B in figure 23.3). We can certainly find seeds of this emerging future (labeled D in figure 23.3) in any number of progressive educational practices, such as the spread of high-impact practices, students-as-partners movement and anti-racism. All of these could plausibly be seen as the continuity of the learning paradigm with whatever will unfold beyond it. The architecture of the unexpected comes into play with H2, the forces of change and disruption. Here (labeled E in figure 23.3), we can imagine disruptions that are external and beyond institutional control, such as the environmental crisis, future global health crises, and increasing polarization and widening inequality. However, H2 creative disruptions can also be intentional and serve to stimulate transformation, such as more radical educational innovations, or movements toward institutional values that if taken seriously would be radically reframing, such as "well-being."

The architecture we need to develop this vision will be built on a set of design principles that will allow for emergence and experimentation:

- It will be built on what we now know about learning, but it will also be animated by a belief in the "wicked" complexity of the problem of reshaping education for a better future.[12]
- The architecture that we need will reflect that higher education institutions are themselves complex adaptive systems mediating between the internal dynamics of diverse learning communities and the external forces that shape social formations around diversity, equity, and justice.[13]
- An architecture of the unexpected anticipates that a new educational paradigm must be centered on the inner transformation of learners, fostering those capacities that are most intrinsically human, and with a new consciousness that situates humanity fluidly and humbly among natural, social, and technological systems.
- An architecture of the unexpected will understand that institutional change is built to tolerate a limited amount of incremental reform, and will on its own resist more radical transformation. Therefore, it must be built for what Stewart Brand calls "pace layering," forming a diversified portfolio of innovation strategies, each with different rates of change and risk.[14]

An architecture of the unexpected assumes that the only way of pursuing these questions is to prepare our institutions and our students to take on a world of problems whose full scope and shape we do not yet know. We need such an architecture so that when we look back from 2045, we'll be reminded that educating the next generation for an uncertain and perilous future was the most present, profound and vexing problem of them all.

Notes

1. Barr and Tagg, "From Teaching to Learning."

2. This is not to suggest that a focus on physical architecture and adaptation to future climate impacts, for example, would not also be appropriate. For that, see for example, Alexander, *Universities on Fire.*

3. Sharpe, *Three Horizons*, 28.

4. Sharpe, *Three Horizons*, 28.

5. Biesta, *World-Centered Education.*

6. Stein, "Metacrisis," 2019.

7. The phrase "adjacent possible" comes from the biologist and author Stuart Kauffman, *At Home in the Universe.*

8. Ingels, *Yes Is More.*

9. Stein, "Education is the Metacrisis"; Rowson, "Bildung in the 21st Century"; Rendón, "Realizing a Transformed Pedagogical Dreamfield"; Barnett, *Ecological University*; la paperson, *Third University Is Possible*; Scobey, "A Copernican Moment" and "The Paradigm Project."

10. Rendón, "Realizing a Transformed Pedagogical Dreamfield."

11. Common Worlds Research Collective, "Learning to Become with the World."

12. For more on a "wicked problems mindset," see Bass, "Mindset for Educational Development"; Bass, "What's the Problem Now?" For more on "wicked problems," see Rittel and Webber, "General Theory of Planning"; Head and Alford, "Wicked and Less Wicked Problems."

13. See for example, Hurtado et. al., "Diverse Learning Environments."

14. Brand, *How Buildings Learn.* At Georgetown, we have created such an innovation context that distinguishes three levels of change and risk: venture research and development, applied innovation, and long-term institutional transformation. See Bass and Selingo, "Higher Education Needs an Innovation Strategy," 2022.

Bibliography

Alexander, Bryan. *Universities on Fire: Higher Education in the Climate Crisis.* Baltimore: Johns Hopkins University Press, 2023.

Barnett, Ronald. *The Ecological University: A Feasible Utopia.* New York: Routledge, 2017.

Barr, Robert B., and John Tagg. "From Teaching to Learning—a New Paradigm for Undergraduate Education." *Change (New Rochelle, NY)* 27, no. 6 (1995): 12–26. https://doi.org/10.1080/00091383.1995.10544672.
Bass, Randall. "Coda: A Wicked Problems Mindset for Educational Development." *To Improve the Academy* 41, no. 1 (April 26, 2022). https://doi.org/10.3998/tia.2373.
———. "What's the Problem Now?" *To Improve the Academy* 39, no. 1 (January 14, 2020). https://doi.org/10.3998/tia.17063888.0039.102.
Bass, Randall, and Jeff Selingo. "Higher Education Needs an Innovation Strategy." *Jeff Selingo Newsletter and Podcast*, September 3, 2022.
Biesta, Gert. *World-Centred Education: A View for the Present*. New York: Routledge, 2022.
Brand, Stewart. *How Buildings Learn: What Happens after They're Built*. New York: Viking, 1994.
Common Worlds Research Collective. "Learning to Become with the World: Education for Future Survival." Education Research and Foresight Working Papers, November 2020. Paris: UNESCO. https://unesdoc.unesco.org/ark:/48223/pf0000374032.
Head, Brian W., and John Alford. "Wicked and Less Wicked Problems: A Typology and a Contingency Framework." *Policy and Society* 36, no. 3 (2018): 397–413. http://dx.doi.org/10.1080/14494035.2017.1361634.
Hurtado, Sylvia, Cynthia L. Alvarez, Chelsea Guillermo-Wann, Marcela Cuellar, and Lucy Arellano. "A Model for Diverse Learning Environments: the Scholarship on Creating and Assessing Conditions for Student Success." In vol. 27 of *Higher Education: Handbook of Theory and Research*, edited by J. C. Smart and M. B. Paulsen, 41–122. New York: Springer.
Ingels, Bjarke. *Yes Is More: An Archicomic on Architectural Evolution*. Exhibition, Danish Architecture Center, Copenhagen, Denmark, February 21–May 31, 2009. Köln: Evergreen, 2009.
Kauffman, Stuart. *At Home in the Universe: The Search for the Laws of Self-Organization and Complexity*. Oxford: Oxford University Press, 1995.
la paperson. *A Third University Is Possible*. Minneapolis: University of Minnesota Press, 2017.
Rendón, Laura. "Realizing a Transformed Pedagogical Dreamfield: Recasting Agreements for Teaching and Learning." In *Sentipensante (Sensing/Thinking) Pedagogy: Educating for Wholeness, Social Justice and Liberation*. New York: Stylus Publishing, 2005.
Rittel, Horst W. J., and Melvin M. Webber. "Dilemmas in a General Theory of Planning." *Policy Sciences* 4, no. 2 (1973): 155–69. https://www.jstor.org/stable/453152.
Rowson, Jonathan. "Bildung in the 21st Century—Why Sustainable Prosperity Depends upon Reimagining Education." CUSP Essay Series on the Morality of Sustainable Prosperity, no. 9 (June 19, 2019). https://cusp.ac.uk/themes/m/essay-m1-9.

Scobey, David. "A Copernican Moment: On the Revolutions in Higher Education." In *Transforming Undergraduate Education: Theory That Compels and Practices That Succeed*, edited by Donald Harward, chap. 1. Lanham, MD: Rowan & Littlefield, 2011.

Scobey, David. "The Paradigm Project: A Call for Radical Renewal of Higher Education." *Change Magazine*, March–April 2023, 14–19.

Sharpe, Bill. *Three Horizons: A Patterning of Hope.* Dorset, UK: Triarchy Press, 2013

Stein, Zachary. "Education is the Metacrisis." *Perspectiva*, January 27, 2022. https://systems-souls-society.com/education-is-the-metacrisis.

ACKNOWLEDGMENTS

This book began with conversations with colleagues during the early days of the pandemic about how we could continue to teach and learn at a time when we couldn't enter our physical classrooms. Most of the contributors to this volume worked overtime during the emergency pivot to remote learning, which left little time for conversation. Nevertheless, we reached out to one another to find support and meaning during a difficult time. What started as frantic Zoom calls has turned into a book in which we try to make sense of what happened and prepare for the inevitable challenges to higher education on the horizon.

We are grateful for the intellectual support from not only the contributors to this volume but also from our amazing colleagues at Georgetown's Center for New Designs in Learning and Scholarship and Dartmouth College. Their commitment, as well as the dedicated work of faculty at our institutions to keep learning going, reminded us that teaching really is at the heart of what we do. We also want to thank Greg Britton and the team at Johns Hopkins University Press for their support and encouragement.

We want to thank in particular a group of exceptional graduate students who helped us pull this volume together: Sophie Grabiec, Noah Leiter, Joyce Zhao, and Racquel Nassor. In addition, we want to recognize the graduate students in Georgetown's Learning, Design, and Technology Program, who have been with us every step of the way as we asked questions about the future of higher education and what it means to put teaching and learning at the center.

Without these communities of educators, *Recentering Learning* would not have been possible.

CONTRIBUTORS

Bryan Alexander is a futurist and senior scholar with Georgetown University's Center for New Designs in Learning and Scholarship, where he teaches seminars in the Learning, Design, and Technology program. He curates the Future Trends Forum video discussion, and his latest book is *Universities on Fire: Higher Education in the Climate Crisis* (Johns Hopkins University Press).

Drew Allen is the associate provost for institutional research and analytics at Harvard University and a senior lecturer on education at Harvard's Graduate School of Education. He served previously as the associate vice president for institutional data analytics at Georgetown University.

Isis Artze-Vega, EdD, serves as the college provost and vice president for academic affairs at Valencia College in Central Florida, long regarded one of the nation's best community colleges. She is the lead author and editor of the *Norton Guide to Equity-Minded Teaching* and a coauthor of *Connections Are Everything: A College Student's Guide to Relationship-Rich Education* (Johns Hopkins University Press).

Betsy Barre serves as the executive director for the Center for the Advancement of Teaching at Wake Forest University. Previously, she was named a founding assistant director at Rice University's Center for Teaching Excellence in 2014 and has been teaching in philosophy and religious studies for 10 years.

Randy Bass is the vice president for strategic initiatives and a professor of English at Georgetown University, where he leads the Designing the Future(s) of the University initiative and the Red House incubator for curricular transformation. For 13 years, he was the founding executive director of Georgetown's Center for New Designs in Learning and Scholarship.

MJ Bishop is the vice president of learning design at the University of Maryland Global Campus, where she leads the evidence-based design and development of learning experiences across disciplines, delivery modalities, and global boundaries. She previously served as the inaugural director of the University System of Maryland's Kirwan Center for Academic Innovation.

Derek Bruff is an educator, author, and higher education consultant. He is a visiting associate director at the Center for Excellence in Teaching and Learning at the

University of Mississippi. Bruff is the author of *Intentional Teaching: Principles to Guide the Use of Educational Technology in College Teaching* (West Virginia University Press, 2019) and the producer of the *Intentional Teaching* podcast.

Molly Chehak is the director of digital learning at the Center for New Designs in Learning and Scholarship at Georgetown University and has been an instructor in the Writing Program since 2007. She has extensive experience in educational technology as well as faculty, program, and curriculum development.

Nancy Chick is the director for the Endeavor Center for Faculty Development at Rollins College and serves as copresident for the International Society for the Scholarship of Teaching and Learning. She's been teaching English since 1998 and working in faculty development since 2006.

Cynthia A. Cogswell works in higher education assessment as the director of strategic planning and assessment at Ohio University. Previously, she worked at Indiana University, Bloomington, for seven years, engaging with survey data and project assessment.

Jenae Cohn writes and speaks about teaching and learning in digital spaces and works as the executive director of the Center for Teaching and Learning at the University of California, Berkeley. She is the author of two books: *Skim, Dive, Surface: Teaching Digital Reading* (West Virginia University Press, 2021) and *Design for Learning: User Experience in Online Teaching and Learning* (Rosenfeld Press, 2023). She previously worked as the director of academic technology at California State University, Sacramento, and as an academic technology specialist in the Program in Writing and Rhetoric at Stanford University.

Tazin Daniels is an assistant director at the Center for Research on Learning and Teaching at the University of Michigan. She is an educational developer, consultant, and coach who has published on strategies for equitable online teaching and preparing the next generation of inclusive educators.

Maggie Debelius is the senior director of faculty initiatives at the Center for New Designs in Learning and Scholarship at Georgetown University, where she also serves as a professor of English and teaches in the Learning, Design, and Technology program.

David Ebenbach, the author of 10 books of nonfiction, fiction, and poetry, teaches creative writing and literature at the Center for Jewish Civilization at Georgetown University and promotes student-centered teaching as the assistant director for graduate student and faculty programs at the Center for New Designs in Learning and Scholarship.

Megan Eberhardt-Alstot is a lecturer in the School of Education at California State University, Channel Islands, a Google-certified educator, and an instructional designer supporting faculty at Fresno State and Channel Islands in the Cooperative Online Doctorate in Educational Leadership program.

Peter Felten is the executive director of the Center for Engaged Learning, a professor of history, and the assistant provost for teaching and learning at Elon University. He has published seven books about undergraduate education, including *Connections Are Everything: A College Student's Guide to Relationship-Rich Education* (Johns Hopkins University Press, 2023), coauthored with Isis Artze-Vega, Leo M. Lambert, and Oscar R. Miranda Tapia, with an open-access online version free to all readers.

Lorna S. Gonzalez is the director of digital learning at California State University, Channel Islands, where she oversees academic technology, learning design, academic media, and digital accessibility initiatives.

Michael Goudzwaard is the associate director of learning innovation in the Dartmouth Center for the Advancement of Learning. Currently, his areas of focus are classroom designs, universal design for learning to support wellness, and leading a teaching innovation grant program.

Sophie Grabiec works as a communications and events coordinator for the Center for New Designs in Learning and Scholarship at Georgetown University and teaches first-year writing in the English Department. At the time of writing the contribution in this volume, she was a graduate student at Georgetown, earning her master's degree in English and writing a thesis on design thinking in composition classrooms.

Sean Hobson, the inaugural chief design officer for EdPlus at Arizona State University, plays a pivotal role in transforming higher education by leading strategic design initiatives and promoting innovation through his expertise in communications and instructional design. Currently pursuing a PhD in higher education transformation from Dublin City University, Hobson advises educational institutions and tech companies worldwide, leveraging design and research-driven strategies to instigate significant and purposeful change.

Kashema Hutchinson is a PhD student in the Urban Education program at the Graduate Center at the City University of New York (CUNY). She is currently a communications and leadership fellow specialist in the Undergraduate Leadership Program and a doctoral fellow at the CUNY Graduate Center in the Futures Initiative.

Amanda Irvin is the senior director of faculty programs and services at Columbia University's Center for Teaching and Learning. Irvin develops and facilitates professional development programs for faculty, postdoctoral, adjunct, and other instructors at Columbia. Prior to joining the Center for Teaching and Learning, Irvin served as the assistant director of faculty development of the Koehler Center for Teaching Excellence at Texas Christian University. She teaches courses in American Literature, composition, and women's and girls' studies.

Jonathan Iuzzini is the director of teaching and learning at Achieving the Dream (ATD), where he is responsible for the strategic leadership and implementation of ATD's teaching and learning portfolio, including coaching services related to teaching, learning, and faculty/educational development. He is coauthor of the *ATD Teaching & Learning Toolkit: A Research-Based Guide to Building a Culture of Teaching and Learning Excellence.*

Amy M. Johnson is the assistant provost for experiential education and undergraduate affairs, a professor of the practice in the American Studies program, and the faculty head of Warren College at Vanderbilt University. Previously, she served as the executive director of the core curriculum and an associate professor of history at Elon University. She has provided strategic leadership in general education and curriculum development, assessment, first-year experiences, independent major and interdisciplinary studies, integrative core capstones, common reading programs, residential initiatives, and experiential education.

Briana Johnson is currently the vice president of LX design at iDesign. She has worked in higher education for 16 years. Her areas of focus are rapid-response instructional design at scale, strategic and effective leadership of diverse remote teams, and partnership relationship management.

Matthew Kaplan is the executive director of the University of Michigan's Center for Research on Learning and Teaching and has over 30 years of experience in the field of educational development. Coauthor of *Advancing the Culture of Teaching on Campus: How a Teaching Center Can Make a Difference,* he leads new initiatives on teaching and learning and runs professional development programs for University of Michigan department chairs and associate deans as well as international higher education leaders.

Whitney Kilgore is currently the cofounder and chief academic officer for iDesign, a partner to institutions of higher education to support strategic initiatives related to online and blended learning. She has an extensive background in educational leadership, educational technology, strategic planning, professional service delivery, and organizational change.

Joshua Kim is the assistant provost for online learning strategy at Dartmouth College and a senior scholar at Georgetown University. With Eddie Maloney, he wrote *Learning Innovation and the Future of Higher Education* and *The Low-Density University: 15 Scenarios for Higher Education.* He has written the *Learning Innovation* blog on InsideHigherEd.com since 2009. He earned his PhD in sociology and demography from Brown University.

Sujung Kim is a Mellon Humanities Alliance research fellow for the Futures Initiative at the Graduate Center, City University of New York. She is an interdisciplinary scholar whose scholarship addresses critical pedagogy in higher education for the public good and educating students as critical public intellectuals and reforming doctoral education. Her research and teaching interests are located at the intersection of class, race, citizenship, power, and subjectivity, and she studies how these intersecting conditions affect undergraduate and graduate students' sense of institutional and social belonging and their racial and class identities. She earned her PhD from the Department of Educational Policy Studies at the University of Illinois at Urbana-Champaign.

Suzanna Klaf is the associate director of faculty programs and services at Columbia University's Center for Teaching and Learning. Klaf facilitates professional development services and guides the reflective practice of faculty, postdoctoral, adjunct, and other instructors at Columbia through the design and implementation of pedagogical programs, consultations, and resources.

Martin Kurzweil is the vice president of educational transformation at Ithaka S+R, a non-profit research and consulting service, where he studies and supports the implementation of practices, policies, and innovations that improve student postsecondary access and success.

Natalie Landman is currently a clinical assistant professor in the Department of Physician Assistant Studies at Northern Arizona University, an instructor at the W. P. Carey School of Business at Arizona State University, and a consultant in the dean's office at EdPlus@ASU. Landman is also the founder and chief executive officer of Nvisio, LLC, a boutique business strategy consulting firm with a focus on higher education and health care.

Jill Leafstedt is currently serving as the director of teaching and learning innovations for California State University, Channel Islands, guiding faculty in exploring and developing innovative methods of improving student learning. She is also an associate professor in the School of Education.

Kathyrn E. Linder serves as the associate vice chancellor for academic innovation and strategy at the University of Colorado Denver. Previously, she served as the associate dean of Global Campus at Kansas State University and also directed the award-winning Ecampus Research Unit at Oregon State University. She is a certified coach, project manager, and change manager.

Sherry Lee Linkon is a professor of English and American studies at Georgetown University. Her research and teaching engage a range of fields, including American literature and culture, interdisciplinary teaching and learning, working-class studies, and writing studies.

Edward Maloney is the executive director of the Center for New Designs in Learning and Scholarship and a professor and founding director of the program in Learning, Design, and Technology. With over 30 years of experience in the teaching and innovation field, he works to help to define Georgetown's strategy to advance teaching and learning practices, including developing innovative approaches to technology-enhanced learning, learning analytics, and inclusive pedagogy. He is the author of two books (with Joshua Kim), *Learning Innovation and the Future of Higher Education* (Johns Hopkins University Press, 2020) and *The Low-Density University: 15 Scenarios for Higher Education* (Johns Hopkins University Press, 2020).

Susannah McGowan serves as the director of curriculum transformation initiatives at the Red House at Georgetown University. Previously, she cofounded King's Academy at King's College London. She is the associate editor for *Teaching and Learning Inquiry*, the official journal of the International Society for the Scholarship of Teaching and Learning.

Isabel McHenry is a senior undergraduate student at Georgetown University, pursuing a BA in Spanish with business coursework in management. She works as a program assistant at the Center for New Designs in Learning and Scholarship, where she supports digital learning strategies.

Lillian Nagengast is a doctoral student in American studies at the University of Texas at Austin. Her current research explores the histories of gender, sexuality, and feminism in the rural United States.

Constancio Nakuma is the provost and executive vice chancellor for academic and student affairs at the University of Colorado Denver. Previously, he had a 19-year tenure at Clemson University, where he served as the associate provost for academic affairs. In addition to his administrative role at Clemson, Nakuma was a professor of French and linguistics and served as a senior associate dean of academic affairs and a department chair.

Rolin Moe currently serves as Skyline College's dean of academic support and learning technologies as well as the San Mateo County Community College District's director for the distance education initiative.

Nancy O'Neill is currently the executive director of the William E. Kirwan Center for Academic Innovation of the University System of Maryland. Prior to joining the Kirwan Center in 2016, she served as the director of the Center for Excellence in Learning, Teaching, and Technology at the University of Baltimore.

Adashima Oyo is the director of the Futures Initiative and the director of programs and administration at the Humanities, Arts, Science, and Technology Alliance and Collaboratory (HASTAC). She is a former Futures Initiative fellow and HASTAC scholars director. She is finishing her PhD in the Social Welfare program at the Graduate Center, City University of New York. Prior to pursuing a PhD, she acquired more than 10 years of experience in several director-level positions at various non-profits and social service organizations in New York City.

Matthew Rascoff is the founding vice provost for digital education at Stanford University, where he has worked since 2021. He is also a lecturer at the Stanford Graduate School of Education and teaches in the undergraduate COLLEGE (Civic, Liberal, and Global Education) program for first-year students. Previously he was the associate vice provost for digital education and innovation at Duke University, where he established and led the Duke Learning Innovation team. Earlier in his career, he helped launch the strategy group at ITHAKA, an incubator of higher education technology ventures (now Ithaka S+R).

Libbie Rifkin is a teaching professor in the Department of English at Georgetown University and was the founding director of the Program in Disability Studies, in which she now serves as the associate director. In addition to her teaching and curricular innovation, Rifkin is special advisor to the vice president of diversity, equity, and inclusion for disability, a new role that expands Georgetown's commitment to valuing disability as an identity and dimension of diversity.

Katina Rogers is the author of *Putting the Humanities PhD to Work: Thriving in and beyond the Classroom* (Duke University Press, 2020) and *Presence of Absence: Meditations on the Unsayable in Writing* (Punctum Books, forthcoming 2024). With over a decade of experience as a researcher, administrator, and educator, she works with colleges and universities to design and implement creative, sustainable, and equitable structures for graduate education. Her work has been featured in the *New York Times*, *LA Review of Books*, *Chronicle of Higher Education*, and *Inside Higher Ed*. She is the founder of Inkcap Consulting and holds a PhD in comparative literature from the University of Colorado at Boulder.

Catherine Ross is the executive director of the Center for Teaching and Learning at Columbia University. She has worked in higher education for more than 25 years. Prior to coming to Columbia, Catherine served as the executive director of the Teaching and Learning Center at Wake Forest University, the associate director of the Institute for Teaching and Learning at the University of Connecticut, and the coordinator of the International TA Program in the Center for Teaching Excellence at the University of Texas at Austin.

Annie Sadler is the assistant director of project evaluation and research at Stanford Digital Education. She previously worked at the Center for Academic Innovation at the University of Michigan and at Davidson College. She is also an instructor for Outward Bound Schools.

Monique L. Snowden is the senior vice chancellor of strategic enrollment and student success at the University of Colorado Denver, where she also holds an appointment as a professor adjoint of communication. Snowden previously served as the provost and senior vice president at Fielding Graduate University in Santa Barbara, California. In June 2023, she completed a six-year commissioner appointment on the Senior

College and University Commission of the Western Association of Schools and Colleges.

Patrice Torcivia Prusko is the associate director of learning design in the office of Learning Initiatives and Teaching Support at the Harvard University Graduate School of Education.

Elliott Visconsi is the provost and dean of the College of the Holy Cross in Worcester, Massachusetts. Prior to this appointment, he taught at Notre Dame and Yale. He is a scholar of early modern English and American literature, history, and law and is currently working on freedom of speech in the digital age and the future of higher education. His contribution to the volume draws from a bigger project on the history, philosophy, and future of the experimental college.

Mary C. Wright is the associate provost for teaching and learning, executive director of the Sheridan Center for Teaching and Learning, and a professor (research) in the Department of Sociology at Brown University. She is also a former president (2017–2018) of the Professional and Organizational Development Network in Higher Education, the US professional association for educational development.

INDEX